Essential
FILM
A WORLD HISTORY

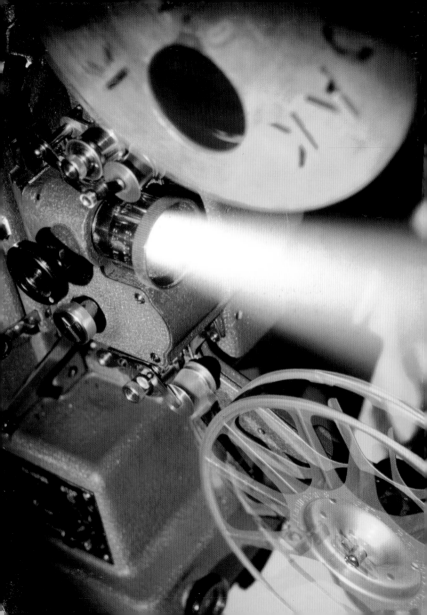

Essential
FILM
A WORLD HISTORY

Daniel Borden, Florian Duijsens,
Thomas Gilbert, and Adele Smith

HERBERT PRESS · LONDON
an imprint of A&C Black

Contents

Georges Méliès: A Trip to the Moon, page 24

Charlie Chaplin: The Great Dictator, page 59

Film: A World History

4

Victor Fleming: The Wizard of Oz, page 109

Billy Wilder: Some Like it Hot, page 169

Akira Kurosawa: Rashomon, page 218

Stanley Kubrick: A Clockwork Orange, page 247

Film: A World History

Michael Antonioni: Blowup, page 239

7

Contents

Miloš Forman: One Flew Over the Cuckoo's Nest, page 344

Pedro Almodóvar: Women on the Verge of a Nervous Breakdown, page 433

Quentin Tarantino: Kill Bill: Vol. 1 & 2, page 416

Origins of Film
1895–1919

"The whole world was its [film's] stage."

Buster Keaton: Sherlock Jr., 1924, USA, starring Buster
Keaton, Kathryn McGuire, and Joe Keaton
Quote: Buster Keaton from his autobiography, *My Wonderful
World of Slapstick*, 1960

Origins of Film

First Inventions and Innovations

Early filmmakers explore the new medium, often in surprising and delightful ways

1895   1900   1905

Artistic Films in America and Europe

As cinema is taken more seriously, directors create a visual language specifically for film

p. 25

1895–1919

Origins of Film

Technological Capability

Cinema was made possible thanks to optic science in the late 19th century, which allowed new physiological observations and technical advancements, as well as increased leisure time and wealth of the middle class. From magic lantern shows to peephole devices, optics proved a popular form of entertainment.

Scientists such as Edward Muybridge and Étienne-Jules Marey led the way with photographic studies of motion. Thomas Edison's Kinetoscope, a peep show–style viewing box, was a great success and, in 1895, the French Lumière brothers introduced the first practical camera and the concept of public screenings. Film continued to be a novelty well into the 1900s.

■ **Illustration of a Victorian peephole**
■ **Study of an Athlete Kicking a Rugby Ball**, ca. 1895

■ Edwin S. Porter: Life of an American Fireman, 1903

The First Stories

Taking their cue from vaudeville, the first programs offered a variety of entertainment. Early films rarely ran for more than one shot and when films were longer, the exhibitor would decide whether several shots should be shown alone or consecutively. These films ranged from reportage *actualités*, which showed everyday scenes, to re-enactments of current events, to simple fiction scenes.

While the Lumières focused on travelogues, early filmmakers like Georges Méliès and Edwin S. Porter experimented with storytelling. Méliès built a studio, from where he made advancements in film illusions and effects. Porter, who worked for Edison, pushed narrative boundaries with his *Life of an American Fireman*. It featured a relatively complicated sequence of shots, including one of a fireman "imagining" (in superimposition) a fire. He also introduced the use of intertitles—title cards—to American filmmaking.

The First Cinemas, Studios, and Stars

With the introduction of nickelodeons and other "legitimate" film theaters, cinema started to be seen as a more serious type of entertainment. Producers formed stock companies and audiences began to recognize the actors they watched on the screen. Florence Lawrence first worked as an actor and seamstress for Vitagraph, but it was when she starred in a string of hits at Biograph that admirers wrote in to ask her name. Worried that stardom—a long-established selling point on the stage—would cause their actors to demand more money, the studio only referred to her as the "Biograph Girl."

Lawrence's first director at Biograph was D. W. Griffith, who rapidly made a name for himself as the creator of "artistic" films. With the help of cameraman Gottfried Wilhelm "Billy" Bitzer and actors like Blanche Sweet and Lillian Gish, and the influence of European films, he popularized many new techniques.

■ **Florence Lawrence as the "Biograph Girl"**

■ **D. W. Griffith on location for *Way Down East*,** ca. 1919

■ **Paul Wegener:**
The Student of
Prague, 1913

■ **Louis Feuillade:**
Fantomas, 1913

Cinema as Culture

Before World War I, European film industries were on
an equal or superior level to the United States. Each
country came to be associated with a different style.
Italy made classical epics like *The Fall of Troy* (1910).
France created costume dramas such as *The Assassination of the Duke de Guise* (1908) and Max Linder's comedies. Denmark made tragedies like *Atlantis* (1913) and
Germany popularized prestigious *Autorenfilme*, written
by famous authors, such as *The Student of Prague*.

One of the most popular forms in the
1910s was the serial. Although each
episode was intended to stand on its own,
suspense was sustained for months by an
over-arching storyline. Louis Feuillade
made a number of crime serials in France,
starting with *Fantomas*, while Pearl White
became America's "serial queen" in the
adventure series *The Perils of Pauline* (1914).

Rules of the Game

As the conventions of film "language" were formalized with narrative tools, such as continuity editing and intercutting, and production techniques, such as the writing of a shooting script, distinct genres also developed. Tom Mix's rodeo tricks won a wide audience for westerns, although his athletic style was far removed from the emotive realism of his rival, the actor and filmmaker William S. Hart.

Slapstick comedies also drew in crowds with their antics and athletic tricks. When one of the genre's top stars, Roscoe "Fatty" Arbuckle, brought already brewing fears about the "loose morals" of stars and filmmakers to a head in 1921 with his trial for alleged rape and murder, the studios attempted to prevent a national clampdown. To stop the possible institution of censorship laws and to regain the approval of audiences, they brought in William H. Hays, a former Postmaster General, to "clean up the pictures."

■ Tom Mix in *Rough Riding Romance*, 1919

■ Charlie Chaplin, Mary Pickford, Douglas Fairbanks, and others at the signing of United Artists, 1919

■ **Roscoe Arbuckle: Coney Island**, 1917, starring Roscoe "Fatty" Arbuckle and Buster Keaton

■ **Irving Thalberg on the set of La Boheme**, 1926

The Studio System

In the early 1910s, key figures like Carl Laemmle (Universal) and Adolph Zukor (Paramount) moved to consolidate power in the American industry. To extend their control from filmmaking to film screening, they merged their production companies with distributors and theater chains, creating a vertically integrated system that bolstered the cinematic supremacy of the United States. The most prominent companies established themselves in vast complexes in Hollywood, California.

Studio bosses often exerted creative control. At Universal and MGM, the charismatic Irving Thalberg gained a reputation for choosing good stories, but not all producers were so popular. Frustrated by the restrictions they faced, four of the era's biggest stars—Mary Pickford, Charlie Chaplin, Douglas Fairbanks, and D. W. Griffith—formed United Artists together in an attempt to create a company that would allow them to produce and distribute their own films.

The Film Camera and Cinemas

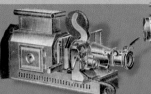

The invention of the film camera evolved concurrently in Europe and the United States. The photographer Edward Muybridge had no interest in moving pictures, but his photographic studies allowed Étienne-Jules Marey to combine an intermittent mechanism with flexible film. Louis Le Prince shot the first motion picture in 1888, but disappeared from a train (along with his camera) in 1890. From Marey's advancements, Thomas Edison and his assistant W. K. L. Dickson built the Kinetograph camera and the Kinetoscope viewer. But it was the Lumière brothers (p. 22) who finally constructed the Cinématographe, a camera and projector that was both functional and practical.

■ **Fred Ott's sneeze** in 1894 was captured with Dickson's "Kinetoscope Record." The film reveals early cinema's defining characteristic; movement itself was the primary focus, even in fiction films. The crashing surf in Birt Acres's *Rough Sea at Dover* (1895) was also very popular with audiences.

■ **Moving pictures** began as a novelty. Thomas Edison installed his Kinetoscopes in "parlors," where customers could peer into the machines. Later, the Lumière brothers' projected programs started a trend for communal viewing. Films were integrated into live shows in theaters and vaudeville houses until, in 1905, exhibitors began opening nickelodeons. These rudimentary cinemas ran programs all day long. Entrance only cost a nickel (hence the name) and the films changed several times a week. Cinema became a habit audiences would never break.

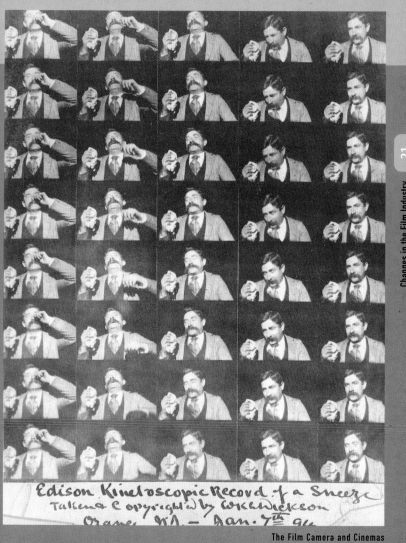

Edison Kinetoscopic Record of a Sneeze
Taken & Copyrighted by W.K.L Dickson
Orange N.J. — Jan. 7th 94

Auguste and Louis Lumière

1862, Besançon—1954, Lyon (Auguste)
1864, Besançon—1948, Bandol (Louis)

■ Fathers of cinema and inventors of the Cinématographe ■ Popularized motion pictures by displaying their invention and sending cameramen abroad ■ French ■ Documentary ■ Directed about 60 films

■ **1862** Auguste is born

1864 Louis is born

1894 Begin experimenting with moving pictures

1895 The brothers present 10 short films at the Grand Café in Paris

1900 Project film onto a large screen at the Paris Exposition, but later abandon cinema exhibition

1903 They produce Autochrome, the first commercially successful color photography process

1911 Lumière and Sons becomes the Industrial Photographic Union

1948 Louis dies

1954 Auguste dies

■ **Employees Leaving the Lumière Factory**, 1895

The earliest images filmed were simple *actualités*, or shots of everyday life. Here workers leave the Lumière factory at closing time. A single, minute-long stationary shot, the film premiered at the Grand Café screening. It ran at 16 frames a second, which became silent film's most common speed, and was the model for the Lumières' many films.

Origins of Film 1895–1919

The Lumière brothers ran a successful photographic business before they turned to moving images. By addressing the flaws in Edison's Kinetograph and Kinetoscope, they developed the Cinématographe, a small 35 mm film camera whose intermittent shutter mechanism was based on a sewing machine motor. This camera could also print positive copies and, when attached to a magic lantern, act as a projector. The Lumières introduced it to the general public in a screening at the Grand Café in Paris on December 28, 1895. The Cinématographe attracted large crowds and interest from prospective filmmakers including Georges Méliès (p. 24). The Lumières refused to sell copies of their invention, preferring to send their representatives out to exhibit it. In 1896 alone, Lumière programs were shown—and filmed—throughout Europe as well as in Russia, India, Brazil, Mexico, China, and Egypt.

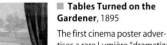

■ Tables Turned on the Gardener, 1895

The first cinema poster advertises a rare Lumière "dramatization." The film is considered to be the first slapstick comedy as well as narrative film. A gardener, unable to understand why his hose is not working, looks down its nozzle and is drenched by a burst of water because a boy who was stepping on the hose lifted his foot. The film was so popular the Lumières remade it in 1896, but they later went on to focus on *actualités* and travelogues.

■ Arrival of a Train at La Ciotat, 1895

This film inspired one of cinema's great anecdotes: At the first screening of *Arrival of a Train at La Ciotat* audiences are reported to have panicked when they saw the train seemingly moving toward them, and people sitting in the front rows fled or hid under their seats. Whether or not the story actually happened, it correctly evokes the amazed reactions of early cinemagoers to the power of the new medium.

Other Works
Baby's Dinner, 1895
The Sea, 1895
Panorama des Rives du Nil, 1897
Niagara Falls, 1897
Spanish Bullfight, 1900

Auguste and Louis Lumière

Georges Méliès

1861, Paris—1938, Paris

■ First to exploit cinema's magical potential and filmic fiction ■ Pioneered many key effects, including stop-motion photography, fades, dissolves, multiple exposures, split screens, and animation ■ Rediscovered by the Surrealists ■ French ■ Science Fiction, Fantasy ■ Made over 500 films

1861 Born in Paris
1895 Sees the Lumière Cinématographe
1896 Makes *Une Partie de Cartes*
1897 Starts Europe's first film studio
1913 Goes out of business and abandons film
1931 Receives medal of the French Legion of Honor
1938 Dies in Paris

An illusionist by trade, Georges Méliès revolutionized early cinema. Along with his famous special effects and story ideas, he initiated many practices, such as storyboards and multiple negatives for foreign distribution that became fundamental aspects of the filmmaking process. Despite his popularity, Méliès could not compete with the output of larger studios like Pathé and he spent his last years selling toys in a Paris train station, until the importance of his work was recognized shortly before his death in 1938.

The Conquest of the Pole, 1912

This quixotic race to the North Pole was Méliès's last significant work. It featured all the classic elements of his earlier films—pompous scientists, strange machines, and ingenious special effects—but by 1912 his style already looked dated. Méliès struggled in the increasingly commercial French film industry and his films were brutally edited by distributors indifferent to their artistic value.

A Trip to the Moon, 1902

Méliès wrote, directed and acted in nearly all of his films. In his Star studio, he combined ornate stage sets with in-camera effects, creating amazing and fantastic worlds. His most famous film, *A Trip to the Moon*, relates the cosmic adventures of a band of mad scientists. It was an international hit, but by the time he set up his New York office, pirated copies of the film had already been widely distributed in America (a common practice at the time).

Other Works
L'Affaire Dreyfus, 1899
The Music Lover 1903
The Devilish Tenant, 1909

An Impossible Voyage, 1904

Méliès again looked to the work of Jules Verne for inspiration; the intrepid travelers in *An Impossible Voyage* embark on an attempt to use every known (and imagined) form of transportation. A mix of live action and animation, the film was hand-painted in bright colors.

Georges Méliès

The First Divas

As cinema's popularity increased in the 1910s, a series of screen beauties captured the public imagination. Lifelike performances from Asta Nielsen and Francesca Bertini—particularly in *Assunta Spina* (1915)—redefined dramatic acting for the screen, but before the advent of sound, the right look was more important. Femme fatale Theda Bara, who was actually from Ohio, benefited from the inventiveness of her studio publicists, who claimed she was born in Egypt. Some new stars had significant acting credentials, such as Mary Pickford, a stage veteran who became the first truly powerful film star, while others, such as Marion Davies and Louise Brooks, had danced in sexy Broadway productions such as the Ziegfeld Follies.

■ **Theda Bara**—from *Carmen* (1915) to *Cleopatra* (1917, above) to *Salome* (1918), her exotic and usually scantily clad characters first popularized the concept of a "vamp"—though Musidora, star of Louis Feuillade's French crime serial *Les Vampires* (1915), may have initially provoked the use of the term.

■ **"Madcap" Mabel Normand** was the most successful comedienne of the silent era. In films such as *Tillie's Punctured Romance* (1914) and *He Did and He Didn't* (1916, left), she worked with—and helped launch the careers of—many of slapstick's funniest men. Charlie Chaplin, Harold Lloyd, and Roscoe "Fatty" Arbuckle all owe part of their popularity to her.

■ **Asta Nielsen's** naturalism and androgynous sexuality made her Europe's first film star and inspired a generation. After acting with Nielsen in *Joyless Street* (1925), Greta Garbo said "she taught me everything I know." The Danish actress and producer became the hub of the German film industry. Like stage actress Sarah Bernhardt before her, she refused to adhere to gender constraints—most notably in *Hamlet* (1920, above).

■ **Mary Pickford** was the queen of early Hollywood. She was very influential and possessed a sharp eye for business—something she masked well when she played children in films such as *Pollyanna* (1920).

The First Divas

Mack Sennett

1880, Richmond–1960, Los Angeles

■ "King of Comedy" ■ Founded Keystone Studios, the birthplace of slapstick
■ Launched the film careers of Charlie Chaplin, Mabel Normand, Marie Dressler,
Roscoe "Fatty" Arbuckle, Gloria Swanson, W. C. Fields, and Bing Crosby
■ Canadian ■ Comedy ■ Produced more than 1,000 films

Mack Sennett began his career with D. W. Griffith (p. 32), but the films he went on to make at Keystone Studios were the opposite of his mentor's carefully constructed melodramas. His chaotic shorts set the standard for slapstick comedies—it was in a Sennett film that Mabel Normand threw the first pie and his series *Keystone Cops* perfected the comedy chase scene. Sennett believed that spontaneity created the best humor and, because shooting scripts were rarely used in the 1910s, he relied entirely on improvisation. Sennett even allowed his stars to direct their own pictures as long as he had the final say over the finished product. He discovered some of early cinema's most famous comedians, yet rarely managed to keep them once they became famous because Keystone Studios never attempted to match the high salaries offered by other studios.

■ In the Clutches of the Gang, 1914

The inept Keystone Cops are Sennett's most enduring invention. Their surreal stunts became so strongly associated with slapstick humor that in 1955, decades after the last Cops film, Abbott and Costello paid them homage. The films were made with a constantly rotating team of actors hired primarily for their ability to "take a fall," but some, such as Roscoe "Fatty" Arbuckle (far right), became stars in their own right.

■ **Tillie's Punctured Romance**, 1914, starring Mabel Normand and Charlie Chaplin

Comedies were rarely longer than one or two reels (about 12 or 24 minutes) and screened before the main film. Sennett knew he was taking a risk by making *Tillie's Punctured Romance*, the first comedy feature film, so he cast popular and talented actors. The film was one of the era's most successful films.

Other Works
Mabel's Strange Predicament, 1914, starring Mabel Normand and Charlie Chaplin
He Did and He Didn't, 1916, starring Mabel Normand

■ **Ben Turpin with Sennett's Bathing Beauties**, ca. 1920

While male stars such as Ben Turpin—who eventually insured his crossed eyes for $25,000—and Roscoe "Fatty" Arbuckle played up their physical peculiarities for comic effect, the women at Keystone Studios were nearly always young and pretty. The ubiquitous "Sennett Bathing Beauties" delighted audiences with their charm and their short bathing dresses, launching the careers of some of Hollywood's early stars.

Monumental Films

■ Epic cinema ■ Present a great historical sweep, massive sets, impressive landscapes, large casts, and dramatic story lines ■ Many technical effects, including the tracking shot and the crane shot, were created in the making of monumental films

■ *left:* **Intolerance: Love's Struggle Throughout the Ages**, by D. W. Griffith, 1916

■ **1912** *Quo Vadis?* starts the trend for antiquity-themed "sword and sandal" epics

1916 *Intolerance: Love's Struggle Throughout the Ages* uses more than 3,000 extras

1953 *The Robe* is the first film to be shot in the wide-screen CinemaScope format

1963 *Cleopatra* is filmed with a monumental budget—$44 million

2000 *Gladiator* wins the Academy Award for Best Picture

■ **Fred Niblo: Ben-Hur: A Tale of the Christ**, 1925, starring Ramon Novarro

At $6 million, the film was the most expensive at the time. *Ben-Hur: A Tale of the Christ*'s most famous sequence is the chariot race, directed by second-unit director B. Reaves Eason. The scene combined long shots of action with evocative close-ups. It wasn't the only sequence filmed on a grand scale: Nearly 50 cameras were used for the single scene of a battle at sea.

Origins of Film 1895–1919

Film enabled directors to work on a scale previously undreamed of. Filmmakers could—and did—recreate any real or imagined moment in time. Many of these epics combined cinematic decadence with meticulous realism: The medieval castle in Douglas Fairbanks's *Robin Hood* (1922) is still the largest film set ever built in Hollywood. Other countries quickly put their own artistic stamp on the genre—Mauritz Stiller's *The Saga of Gosta Berling* (1924) is a stylish example of early Swedish cinema, while Fritz Lang's (p. 76) two-part legend *Siegfried's Death* (1924) mixed classical poetry with the contemporary style of German Expressionism, and in *Storm Over Asia* (1928), Vsevolod Pudovkin applied Soviet montage theory to Mongolian history.

GABRIELE D'ANNUNZIO

CABIRIA

■ Giovanni Pastrone: Cabiria, 1914

Giovanni Pastrone's *Cabiria* was the first blockbuster. In order to create smooth shots with a moving camera, Pastrone pioneered the dolly-track system, which places the camera on rails so that it can slide yet remain steady. This effect was popularly called a "*Cabiria* movement" by people in the

Other Works

Spartacus, by Stanley Kubrick, 1960, starring Kirk Douglas

Lawrence of Arabia, by David Lean, 1962, starring Peter O'Toole

Gladiator, by Ridley Scott, 2000, starring Russell Crowe

film industry. As well as inventive camera movements, *Cabiria* featured terrifying pirates, human sacrifice, and Hannibal's elephants.

■ Richard Attenborough: Gandhi, 1982, starring Ben Kingsley

Cecil B. DeMille's biblical interpretations kept the epic alive until the 1950s when producers, anxious to combat television, wanted ever bigger films. *The Ten Commandments* (1956) and *Ben-Hur* (1959) were remade. After *Gladiator*, monumental films saw another revival due to a technical revolution—crowds are now filled out with CGI instead of casts of thousands. Before this, the funeral scene in *Gandhi* used about 400,000 extras. The biopic has proved to be a perennially popular subgenre and *Gandhi* contains all the key elements: a compelling main character, stunning scenery, and a story based on actual events.

31

Film Genres

Monumental Films

D. W. Griffith

1875, Floydsfork—1948, Los Angeles

■ The first great American filmmaker ■ Made the most-viewed film of his era, *The Birth of a Nation* ■ Advanced many important techniques including intercutting, close-ups, rhythmic editing, complex narratives, and naturalistic acting ■ American ■ Drama, Historical Epic ■ Directed 33 features and 450 total films

Early Film in the United States

1875 Born David Llewelyn Wark Griffith in Kentucky

1908 Joins Biograph Studios and directs *The Adventures of Dollie*

1912 Lillian Gish makes her first Griffith film, *An Unseen Enemy*

1913 Leaves Biograph

1915 *The Birth of a Nation* is released to wide acclaim and considerable controversy

1919 Forms the production company United Artists with Mary Pickford, Douglas Fairbanks, and Charlie Chaplin

1948 Dies in Hollywood

D. W. Griffith dreamed of being a successful playwright, but failed. Instead, his quest for artistic legitimacy drove him to push cinema's stylistic boundaries further than most of his contemporaries had ever dreamed possible. At Biograph Studios he built up a stock cast of actors, whom he trained to convey emotion with subtlety rather than in crude pantomime, and filmed in close shots to capture every detail. This naturalistic manner of acting revolutionized cinema. With his long-term cameraman Billy Bitzer, he strove to expand the medium's rudimentary grammar by experimenting with new filming and editing techniques. A characteristic example of his innovative intercutting can be seen in *Intolerance: Love's Struggle Throughout the Ages* (1916), in which an image of Babylonian chariots cuts to a train—a direct edit between different time periods and narratives.

■ **The Musketeers of Pig Alley**, 1912, starring Lillian Gish

Griffith's many muses included Mary Pickford and Blanche Sweet, but Lillian Gish starred in his best work. This crime drama, described as the original gangster film, was co-written by Anita Loos, and shot on location in New York. *The Musketeers of Pig Alley* tells the story of an impoverished "little lady" and her musician husband. When a gangster robs them, the husband sets out to retrieve the money and a cinematically innovative chase scene follows.

Origins of Film 1895–1919

■ **Broken Blossoms**, 1919, starring Lillian Gish

Griffith followed two epics with a romance between an abused Cockney girl and a Chinese Buddhist who has recently moved to London. *Broken Blossoms* contains one of the best examples of Griffith's preferred method of naturalistic acting—as Lillian Gish tries to escape from her violent father, she screams so compellingly her terror is almost audible despite the film being silent.

■ **Orphans of the Storm**, 1921, starring Lillian Gish and Dorothy Gish

In his last successful film, Griffith brought the Gish sisters together to play a heroine (Lillian) and her blind sister (Dorothy) who get mixed up in the French Revolution. He chose the historical backdrop to add substance to a popular stage melodrama and, after the racial controversy over *The Birth of a Nation*, he was keen on distancing himself from any modern-day parallels—in this case with Communist Russia.

Other Works
The Birth of a Nation, see p. 34
Her Awakening, 1911, starring Mabel Normand
The New York Hat, 1912, starring Mary Pickford
Judith of Bethulia, 1913, starring Blanche Sweet
Intolerance: Love's Struggle Throughout the Ages, 1916

Early Film in the United States

D. W. Griffith

The Birth of a Nation

■ by D. W. Griffith, USA, 1915, Drama

D. W. Griffith (p. 32) applied his considerable skills—from complex intercutting to innovative lighting effects—to filming Thomas Dixon Jr.'s novel *The Clansman*. The film portrays, as the book did, a bigoted vision of the American Civil War, where corrupt and criminal African Americans are chased out of free society by the white supremacist Ku Klux Klan. Friends are forced to fight for opposite sides; historical events and dramatized stories unfold. Despite causing mass protests and race riots as well as being banned in several cities, *The Birth of a Nation* broke all box-office records. Along with its technical virtuosity, the film's length was a groundbreaking three hours and lent authority to its content. Because of the widespread popularity of the film, which had hooded clansmen at the premiere as a publicity stunt, the Ku Klux Klan unfortunately saw a rebirth in many Southern states.

■ **The Birth of a Nation**, 1915, starring Lillian Gish and Mae Marsh

In its presentation of the lynching of the would-be-rapist Gus, the film equates Klan violence with the restoration of peace in the South. On the set, this distorted view was accentuated by the fact that nearly all of the "black" characters who came in contact with white women were played by white actors wearing black face makeup.

The film presents the crude stereotype of sexually predatory African-American men as a reality. Black characters are repeatedly shown lusting after white women. *The Birth of a Nation*'s most extreme embodiment is the attempted rape of a young Southern belle named Flora (Mae Marsh, pictured) by the renegade soldier Gus (played by Walter Long, in blackface). Cornered at the edge of a cliff, she commits suicide to escape from him. In a direct allusion to this scene Oscar Micheaux reversed the situation in *Within Our Gates* (1920), intercutting scenes of a white man's assault on a black woman with images of her father's lynching.

Origins of Film 1895–1919

The Birth of a Nation

Cecil B. DeMille

1881, Ashfield—1959, Los Angeles

■ The "P. T. Barnum of the movies" ■ Created lavish spectacles ■ Was the first to publicize the names of stars ■ The risqué content of his epics caused controversy, but he satisfied censors by including strict moral lessons ■ American ■ Historical Drama, Comedy ■ Directed 80 films

1881 Born in Massachusetts to a playwright

1900 Acts on stage

1914 Directs his first film, *The Squaw Man*

1915 Begins "prestige" collaborations with stage star Geraldine Farrar

1927 *The King of Kings* opens, causing just as much controversy in its day as Mel Gibson's *The Passion of the Christ* (2004)

1940 Makes *Northwest Mounted Police* in Technicolor

1953 Wins an Academy Award for Best Picture for *The Greatest Show on Earth*

1956 Suffers a heart attack on the set of his remake of his own film *The Ten Commandments*, but returns to finish the film a week later

1959 Dies in California

Other Works

Joan the Woman, 1917, starring Geraldine Farrar

The King of Kings, 1927

Cleopatra, 1934, starring Claudette Colbert

Samson and Delilah, 1949

The Greatest Show on Earth, 1952

Cecil B. DeMille's former protégée Gloria Swanson mischievously described him as "Almighty God himself," he was the self-crowned king of Hollywood, and the man who inspired the stereotype of the autocratic silent-film director. DeMille worked in the theater before forming a film partnership with the producer Jesse Lasky. He involved himself in every aspect of production, from scriptwriting to publicizing his films, and strode around in jodhpurs scoffing at the weakness of actors—particularly the star of *Samson and Delilah*, who refused to wrestle a lion for a scene. DeMille's hardline policies paid off: He is quoted to have said that he received his award "at the box office."

■ **Male and Female**, 1919, starring Gloria Swanson

After five years of making everything from literary adaptations to social dramas, DeMille found a formula that worked: light but moralistic comedies about the battle of the sexes. Their sumptuous settings and stylish costumes were offset by his new discovery, Gloria Swanson. She became one of the era's biggest stars, but DeMille remained the only director able to convince her—as he did in *Male and Female*—to pose beneath a live lion.

■ The Sign of the Cross, 1932, starring Claudette Colbert

While DeMille was often praised for his cinematic innovations—for example, the inventive use of contrasting lighting in the racial drama *The Cheat* (1915)—he also developed a reputation for coaxing his female protagonists into sunken baths. DeMille titillated his audiences with scenes of glamorous debauchery, only to then remind them of the proper moral code in onscreen lectures by "good" characters and punishments for "bad" ones. The strict censors allowed the "bad" in with the "good" and audiences rarely complained, finding that a glimpse of Claudette Colbert reclining in gallons of donkey's milk, as she did in *The Sign of the Cross*, was worth the moralizing.

■ The Ten Commandments, 1923

The extended historical scenes DeMille included in his films evolved into a series of elaborate epics. *Joan the Woman* (1917), which starred the opera singer Geraldine Farrar, featured a remarkably realistic rendition of a burning at the stake. *The Ten Commandments* was even more ambitious: DeMille rebuilt the city of Pharaoh in a California desert, shipping out hundreds of extras (including 250 "Old World Israelites") and 3,000 animals to populate it. To save money, the vast set was buried in the sands, to be discovered 60 years later. The director remade the story in 1956, with Charlton Heston.

Westerns

■ Portraits of the lawless western frontier in 19th-century America ■ Morality and freedom play key roles ■ Landscape shaped the wide, empty shots that are often used to highlight humanity's insignificance and the immensity of nature ■ Made stars of John Wayne, Clint Eastwood, and many more
■ *left*: **The Great Train Robbery**, by Edwin S. Porter, 1903

1903 *The Great Train Robbery* introduces the western genre
1923 *The Covered Wagon* raises westerns' artistic profile
1939 With *Stagecoach*, John Ford establishes both John Wayne as a star and Monument Valley on the border of Arizona and Utah as the genre's setting
1964 Sergio Leone makes *A Fistful of Dollars*, the first spaghetti western
2005 *Brokeback Mountain* wins the Venice Film Festival's Golden Lion

The moment a bandit fired his gun straight at the camera in *The Great Train Robbery* (1903), westerns became a classic film genre. Their protagonists are typically forced to restore order in towns in the western United States that have been corrupted by violence and greed, but other stories—such as *Red River* (1948), in which a conflicted father-son relationship is set against a forced cattle drive—are not uncommon. The genre is not solely American in origin—Sergio Leone's (p. 264) spaghetti westerns drew inspiration from Akira Kurosawa's (p. 216) films set in feudal Japan. Later filmmakers focused more on presenting "real" life, but in films like *Butch Cassidy and the Sundance Kid* (1969) and *McCabe and Mrs. Miller* (1971), the moral questioning of earlier films continued.

■ **Anthony Mann: Winchester '73**, 1950, starring James Stewart

James Stewart, playing against his type, stars as a rough gunslinger. Like William S. Hart's good badman, he is redeemed at the end, but the film is much grittier than its predecessors.

Origins of Film 1895–1919

■ **Andrew V. McLaglen: Chisum**, 1970, starring John Wayne

In a career that spanned five decades, John Wayne brought a strong, rugged presence to his roles. The most fondly remembered western star, he shaped the world's image of cowboys.

■ Kevin Costner: Dances with Wolves, 1990, starring Kevin Costner

With glamorous shots of the Great Plains, Kevin Costner's film brought the genre back into fashion. Although it used a traditional western plot, many of the films that followed dealt with controversial issues. *Lone Star* (1996) and *The Three Burials of Melquiades Estrada* (2005) explored racism. *Brokeback Mountain* (2005) told of a love affair between two cowboys, while *The Proposition* (2005) proved that as long as there are gunfights and gore, westerns do not even need to be set in the West.

Other Works

Unforgiven, by Clint Eastwood, 1992, starring Clint Eastwood and Morgan Freeman

The Assassination of Jesse James by the Coward Robert Ford, by Andrew Dominik, 2007, starring Brad Pitt and Casey Affleck

▣ James Cruze: The Covered Wagon, 1923

The epic running times and sweeping panoramas of modern westerns owe their existence to *The Covered Wagon*. Although producers like Thomas H. Ince began shooting on location as early as 1912, films were made as cheaply and quickly as possible. Cruze changed all that with this monumental wagon journey, which broke box-office records and started the trend for more "prestigious" westerns.

Thomas H. Ince

1882, Newport—1924, Los Angeles

■ "Father of the western" ■ Rivaled D. W. Griffith as the most popular silent era producer-director ■ Standardized the mechanics of film production by pioneering crucial aids such as shooting scripts, schedules, and budgets ■ American ■ Western ■ Directed and produced more than 500 films

1882 Born in Rhode Island

1910 Producer Carl Laemmle hires Ince as a director

1914 Produces the first William S. Hart western, *The Bargain*

1915 Forms the Triangle Motion Picture Company with D. W. Griffith and Mack Sennett

1918 Buys out his partners and creates Thomas H. Ince Studios

1924 Ince dies and Cecil B. DeMille purchases his lot for DeMille Studios a year later

■ **The Gun Fighter** (supervisor), 1917, starring William S. Hart

William S. Hart started out as a Shakespearean actor, but once he switched to films he quickly became known as the rugged face of Ince's "western realism." He aimed for authenticity and, rather than imitating the black-and-white characterizations in earlier westerns, he almost always played a flawed hero, a good-badman reformed by the love of a good woman.

A savvy showman and inspired producer, Thomas H. Ince was more of an businessman than a director. Before he founded his first production company, Ince created a name for himself by filming dozens of westerns. Some critics dispute the legitimacy of Ince's directorial claims, but few doubt his eye for talent—he launched the career of William S. Hart, one of the first influential cowboy stars. After the partial failure of *Civilization*, which was meant to be an answer to D. W. Griffith's (p. 32) epic style of film-making, Ince focused on producing until his sudden death in 1924. The official cause was heart failure, but rumor has it that media magnate William Randolph Hearst shot Ince by mistake at a party on his yacht, then covered up the story.

■ Civilization, 1916

When a submarine commander dies in battle, Jesus Christ enters his body and orchestrates peace. Ince's spectacle was a hit until America entered WWI—his battle scenes were shot on a staggering scale, but once they became reality audiences stayed away.

THOS·H·INCE'S
MILLION DOLLAR SPECTACLE
CIVILIZATION
BY C. GARDNER SULLIVAN
THE GREATEST PRODUCTION
OF MODERN TIMES

■ The Return of Draw Egan (producer), 1916, starring William S. Hart

When an outlaw-turned-lawman's past catches up with him, he finds himself torn between a barmaid and the pious daughter of the town reformer. Ince, with longtime partner William S. Hart, tried to portray a lifelike version of the western frontier. Although Hart demanded increasing control over his films—eventually going on to write, direct, and produce as well as acting in them—work with Ince continued until 1920.

Silent to Sound 1920–1929

"Wait a minute! Wait a minute! You ain't heard nothing yet!"

Alan Crosland: The Jazz Singer, 1927, USA,
starring Al Jolson
Quote: Al Jolson as Jakie Rabinowitz in *The Jazz Singer*

Silent to Sound

Major European Movements

German Expressionism, French Impressionism, and a number of smaller movements leave their mark on world cinema

p. 77

| 1920 | 1921 | 1922 | 1923 | 1924 |

Carl Theodor Dreyer
Sergei Eisenstein p. 64
Jean Epstein
Jacques Feyder
Abel Gance p. 70
Marcel L'Herbier
Fritz Lang p. 76
Karl Heinz Martin
F. W. Murnau p. 74
G. W. Pabst p. 80
Vsevolod Pudovkin
Dziga Vertov
Robert Wiene

American Slapstick Comedy

Physical humor attains an unmatched level of cleverness and complexity during the silent era

Charlie Chaplin p. 58
Buster Keaton p. 56
Harry Langdon
Laurel and Hardy p. 54
Harold Lloyd p. 55

p. 54

1920–1929

Hollywood Cinema

Directors in America—many of whom were European émigrés—develop their own "classic" style of cinema, often creating new genres

Frank Borzage
Michael Curtiz p. 122
Allan Dwan
John Ford p. 158

| 1925 | 1926 | 1927 | 1928 | 1929 |

Early Avant-garde Cinema

European artists push the limits of film style and content

Luis Buñuel p.63, p. 228
René Clair p.63, p. 146
Marcel Duchamp
Germaine Dulac
Viking Eggeling
Man Ray
Hans Richter
Walter Ruttmann

Ernst Lubitsch p. 112
Robert J. Flaherty p. 82
Victor Sjöström p. 66
Josef von Sternberg p. 136
Erich von Stroheim p. 78
King Vidor p. 52
William Wellman p. 50

p. 52

Silent to Sound

Developing Styles

Cinema achieved a new level of sophistication in the 1920s. Charlie Chaplin's career personified the move from experimentation to artistry. After becoming a star in short slapsticks, he began making features such as *The Kid* (1921), comedies that also satisfied his love of drama and interest in social issues. By the time *City Lights* was released, it was one of the last films without sound—and a prime example of the subtlety attained by directors in the final years of the silent era.

In France, the medium was elevated to a high art. Some filmmakers, like Abel Gance, even saw it as a culmination of all the arts. Gance was a French Impressionist, and sought to present emotion through technical means—lens and lighting effects, camera movements, and editing. In *La Roue* a man faces death, and his life flashes by in a series of one or two freeze frame shots.

■ **Charlie Chaplin: City Lights**, 1931, starring Charlie Chaplin and Virginia Cherrill

■ **Abel Gance: La Roue,** 1923, starring Séverin-Mars, Gabriel de Gravone, and Ivy Close

Experiments in Meaning and Purpose

Editing was further developed in the Soviet Union. By exploiting film's power to propagandize, Bolshevik directors like Sergei Eisenstein and Vsevolod Pudovkin aimed to educate with entertainment. Films like *Ten Days That Shook the World* combined Communist triumphs with innovative editing techniques, creating the montage. Non-fiction directors like Dziga Vertov produced the state's newsreels, and Esfir Shub reedited the Czar's home movies, creating the first "compilation" documentaries.

Outside the Soviet Union, avant-garde directors like Walter Ruttmann and Jean Vigo juxtaposed images of real life to make satirical, experimental, or ideological films.

Movements in European Film

European film industries never fully recovered the power they lost during World War I, but Germany came closest to dislodging Hollywood from its top spot. Supported by the extension of a wartime ban on imports, directors like Fritz Lang and F. W. Murnau developed an original and popular film style: German Expressionism. Inspired by distorted, highly subjective Expressionist art, they used elaborate, exaggerated mise-en-scène—sets, lighting, costumes, and acting—to suggest a world gone mad. This aesthetic had a great impact on world cinema, both in Hollywood and on other national styles such as French Impressionism, with films such as *L'Argent*.

Kammerspiel, another German film trend, presented a more realistic view of society. Its style was inspired by the theater of Austrian director Max Reinhardt, whose work influenced F. W. Murnau, Ernst Lubitsch, Otto Preminger, and many others.

■ **Marcel L'Herbier: L'Argent**, 1928, starring Pierre Alcover and Marie Glory

■ **F. W. Murnau: The Last Laugh**, 1924, starring Emil Jannings

Silent to Sound 1920–1929

Fred Niblo: The Mark of Zorro, 1920, starring Douglas Fairbanks

Raoul Walsh: Sadie Thompson, 1928, starring Gloria Swanson

Hollywood and Typecasting

Realizing the box-office value of foreign film styles, American producers lured many European directors to Hollywood with the promise of glamour, wealth, and (particularly for German filmmakers) social stability. This helped build Hollywood up to the powerful position it commanded at the outbreak of World War II.

The late 1910s and early '20s saw the rise of the first Hollywood stars. Actors such as Gloria Swanson amassed great popularity at the box office, which allowed them to demand creative control over their films, as well as vast salaries. These stars were often associated with a particular style of film and punished for any diversion from it. Douglas Fairbanks, for example, found his niche and kept to it, with colorful action films like *The Mark of Zorro*. When Rudolph Valentino—the original "Latin lover" of film—tried to diversify his image with *Monsieur Beaucaire* (1924), he was faced with a flop.

William Wellman

1896, Brookline–1975, Los Angeles

■ Won the first Academy Award for Best Picture ■ Nicknamed "Wild Bill" as a WWI fighter pilot, a moniker his film colleagues decided was equally well suited to his directorial style ■ Launched the careers of James Cagney and Gary Cooper ■ American ■ Drama, War ■ Directed 76 films

When William Wellman arrived in Hollywood after the war, his friend Douglas Fairbanks found him a job as an actor. It was not long before he switched to a position behind the camera—he considered acting to be a self-obsessed profession—and worked his way up to the director's chair. For the next four decades, he wrote, directed, and occasionally produced an average of two films a year. Wellman was known for his tough treatment of actors, even claiming to have put John Wayne in his place. He saw versatility as the key to cinematic integrity and adapted his shooting style to the content of each film. In *The Ox-Bow Incident* (1943), he conveyed the claustrophobia of gang mentality by using tight close-ups, while in *Wings* he attached cameras to fighter planes in order to present the vertiginous reality of air combat.

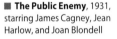

■ **The Public Enemy**, 1931, starring James Cagney, Jean Harlow, and Joan Blondell

James Cagney's performance as a feisty bootlegger in *The Public Enemy* made him the star of the gangster genre and started a fashion for unsentimental crime dramas. The love triangles and violence in the film were considered shocking, but audiences were especially alarmed by the gangster's unchivalrous brutality—at one point in the film he pushes a grapefruit into his girlfriend's face.

■ **Wings**, 1927, (above and below) starring Charles Rogers, Richard Arlen, Clara Bow, and Gary Cooper

Based on his experience in the Lafayette Flying Corps, *Wings* evoked the violence and camaraderie of military life with distinctive realism. Wellman claimed that he made films for entertainment, not art, but the battle scenes in *Wings* reveal his propensity for painterly long shots. Wellman revisited his wartime memories again with the film *Lafayette Escadrille* (1958), but the extensive cuts insisted on by his studio bosses disappointed him so much that he gave up filmmaking.

Other Works

A Star is Born, 1937, starring Janet Gaynor and Fredric March

Nothing Sacred, 1937, starring Carole Lombard and Fredric March

The Story of G. I. Joe, 1945, starring Robert Mitchum

The High and the Mighty, 1954, starring John Wayne, Claire Trevor, Laraine Day, and Robert Stack

William Wellman

King Vidor

1894, Galveston—1982, Paso Robles

■ The longest-working director in Hollywood ■ Worked in a wide range of genres ■ Pioneered the war film ■ Advanced the careers of many stars, including Gregory Peck, Barbara Stanwyck, Jennifer Jones, and Audrey Hepburn ■ American ■ Drama, Western, Musical ■ Directed 57 films

1894 Born in Texas
1919 Directs first feature
1922 Begins working for Goldwyn Studios
1928 Nominated for an Oscar for *The Crowd*
1939 Directs the Kansas scenes in *The Wizard of Oz*
1982 Dies in California

Introduced to film as a schoolboy working as a projectionist, King Vidor became one of the most popular American directors of the 1920s and '30s. Able to work within the confines of the studio system, he still managed to leave a distinctive stylistic mark on his films. From the focus on "female issues" in his melodrama *Stella Dallas*, to the sexual adventurousness of the western *Duel in the Sun*, he made genre films that dared to take on social issues. This strength could also be a drawback, as his work was often reedited. In the case of the social drama *The Crowd* (1928), the studio changed his realistic ending to a happy one. In 1978 Vidor received an Honorary Academy Award for lifetime achievement for his role as one of cinema's pioneers.

■ **The Big Parade**, 1925, starring John Gilbert

The Big Parade, the first non-propagandistic film about WWI to be made in Hollywood, embraces a strongly pacifist message. John Gilbert plays a soldier who falls in love with a French woman before being sent to the front, where he faces the democratizing horrors of war. Despite Vidor's depiction being grittily accurate, audiences loved the film.

Other Works
Stella Dallas, 1937, starring Barbara Stanwyck
The Fountainhead, 1949, starring Gary Cooper
War and Peace, 1956, starring Audrey Hepburn

■ **Hallelujah!**, 1929, starring Daniel L. Haynes and Nina Mae McKinney

In this early musical, Vidor controversially insisted on an all-black cast and a soundtrack comprised of Southern spirituals. African-American actors were largely ignored in the silent era and though they were featured more often after the arrival of sound, it was mainly in secondary roles, as subservient or humorous characters. In spite of its patronizing plot, *Hallelujah!* provided a rare arena for talent. It also launched the career of Nina Mae McKinney.

■ **Duel in the Sun**, 1946, starring Jennifer Jones, Joseph Cotten, and Gregory Peck

In *Duel in the Sun*, Vidor again approached the subject of race with a complexity that was rare for the times. Jennifer Jones stars as a part-Native American girl who struggles with her sexual desires and against the prejudice of those around her. The film suffered from extensive edits after the Hollywood censors rejected its frank treatment of rape and intermarriage, but sold more seats as a result.

King Vidor

Slapstick

■ Physical comedy ■ Small actions often lead to vast consequences ■ Fell out of favor as a genre with the advent of sound and animation ■ Aside from Charlie Chaplin, silent comedians were largely forgotten until film scholars revived their work in the 1960s

■ *left*: **Way Out West**, by James W. Horne, 1937, starring Stan Laurel and Oliver Hardy

■ **1895** *Tables Turned on the Gardener* marks the beginning of slapstick

1907 Max Linder makes *Max Learns to Skate*

1931 Charlie Chaplin releases *City Lights*, his last silent film, to popular and critical acclaim

1965 Buster Keaton's retrospective at the Venice Film Festival receives a standing ovation

1976 Mel Brooks makes *Silent Movie*, an homage to slapstick comedies

Until the arrival of sound, slapstick comedies were film's most popular genre and dominated filmmaking. The best performers exploited the medium with as much skill as any "serious" actor, devising stunts, special effects, complex editing techniques, and—in the case of Charlie Chaplin (p. 58) and Buster Keaton (p. 56)—sophisticated narratives. Today, Chaplin and Keaton are the most widely praised, but Harold Lloyd was also a major star during slapstick's heyday and Stan Laurel and Oliver Hardy continue to attract an international following. As dialogue became more important than action and animated characters without physical limits became popular, the golden age of slapstick came to an end.

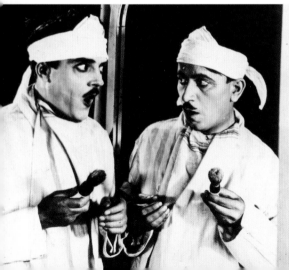

■ **Max Linder: Seven Years Bad Luck**, 1921

Max Linder's effect on cinema history was profound. In 1907, he invented the sophisticated and unlucky "Max," the first identifiable film personality and star of almost 200 shorts. Like the fortunes of the French film industry, his fame dwindled during WWI, but he retained the respect of Charlie Chaplin. The Tramp's physicality was inspired by Linder films like A *Champion Boxer* (1910) and *Max's Hat* (1913). Chaplin was far from alone in his admiration—the Marx Brothers used the mirror gag shown here in *Duck Soup* (1933).

Other Works

Speedy, by Ted Wilde, 1928, starring Harold Lloyd

A Night at the Opera, by Sam Wood, 1935, starring Groucho Marx, Chico Marx, and Harpo Marx

Abbott and Costello Meet the Mummy, by Charles Lamont, 1955, starring Bud Abbott and Lou Costello

■ **Fred Guiol: The Second Hundred Years**, 1927, starring Stan Laurel and Oliver Hardy

Laurel and Hardy bickered their way through nearly 30 years of cinema, an anomaly considering the fact that many of their contemporaries failed to make the transition to sound. Apart from rare tributes by comedians like Jacques Tati and Mel Brooks, slapstick never again reached the same level of artistry.

■ **Fred C. Newmeyer and Sam Taylor: Safety Last**, 1923, starring Harold Lloyd

While Buster Keaton delighted in mechanical devices, Harold Lloyd's comedy relied on a mix of straight athleticism and boyish charm. In *Safety Last* he scaled the front of an office building, performing with a minimum of stuntmen and a disabled hand. His injured hand, caused by a live "gag" bomb in 1919, rarely held him back and he made 29 more films.

Slapstick

Buster Keaton

1895, Piqua—1966, Woodland Hills

■ Called the "Great Stone Face" ■ One of the most popular and influential silent comedians ■ Combined physical stunts with technical trickery, including multiple exposures and intricate editing ■ Codirected most of his films ■ American ■ Comedy ■ Directed 48 films

1895 Born Joseph Frank Keaton IV in Kansas

1901 Harry Houdini renames him "Buster"

1917 Acts in *The Butcher Boy*

1917 Laughs on screen for the last time in *Fatty at Coney Island*

1920 Launches Keaton Studios with *One Week*

1923 The first Keaton Studios feature, *The Three Ages*, is released

1928 Gives up his independent production unit for a contract with MGM

1966 Dies in California

Buster Keaton learned his trade in his family's vaudeville act, where he learned that audiences laughed more when he performed with a solemn "stone" face. Fascinated by the technical possibilities of motion pictures, he gave up theater to direct and act in film. His first cinematic stunt—a bag of flour in the face in *The Butcher Boy*—opened the floodgates for his stunts. He often satirized other stars, such as Thomas Ince's (p. 40) fondness for screen credits in *The Playhouse* (1921), where Keaton plays every character. One of his most famous sequences occurs in *Sherlock Jr.*, as he dreams he is caught in a film montage of dramatically diverse locations, surrounded by lions one minute and a raging ocean the next. Keaton's career as both a director and actor faded after the popularization of sound and the rise of the studio system but renewed interest has revived his popular acclaim.

Silent to Sound 1920–1929

■ **Sherlock Jr.**, 1924, starring Buster Keaton, Kathryn McGuire, and Joe Keaton

When Keaton was three years old he began acting with his family's vaudeville troupe. In *Sherlock Jr.* he acts opposite his father. The film is about a love-struck projectionist who wants to become a detective, but his future plans and love life are thwarted when he is wrongly accused of theft. Buster Keaton's stunts had few rivals—the motorcycle he is riding on here ends up without a driver and Keaton stays on!

■ **The General**, 1927, starring Marion Mack, Glen Cavender, and Buster Keaton

Although *The General* is often featured on modern critics' Best Film lists, it was poorly received at the time of its release. Based on the true Civil War story of a Southern engineer's battle to save his train, it incorporated meticulous period detail. Keaton's zeal for historical accuracy—formerly unknown in comedies—can also be seen in his earlier film, *Our Hospitality* (1923), which is set in the early 1800s. *The General* was Keaton's magnum opus and his career went into decline a year later when he moved to MGM Studios.

◄ **The Navigator**, 1924, starring Buster Keaton

Directed with Donald Crisp, this seagoing farce was Keaton's biggest box-office success. About two socialites who find themselves marooned on an empty cruise ship, the film features many sight gags. Keaton viewed his work with professionalism, editing out one of his favorite moments because test audiences had not laughed at it enough.

Other Works

One Week, 1920, starring Buster Keaton

Hard Luck, 1921, starring Buster Keaton and Virginia Fox

Cops, 1922, starring Buster Keaton

Buster Keaton

Charlie Chaplin

1889, London—1977, Corsier-sur-Vevey

■ Wrote, directed, starred in, and sometimes composed the music to many of his films ■ The "Tramp" ■ Invented a physical presence that combined balletic grace with comic mannerisms ■ Mixed slapstick comedy with drama
■ British ■ Comedy, Drama ■ Directed 11 films

Comedy in the United States

1889 Born in the UK

1910 Visits the US

1914 Signs up with Keystone Studios; invents the "Tramp" character, first seen in *Kid Auto Races at Venice*

1917 Starts his own studio

1919 Cofounds United Artists

1952 Is accused of Communist sympathies and moves to Switzerland

1971 Honorary Academy Award for lifetime achievement

1977 Dies in Switzerland

Charlie Chaplin's "Tramp" rose from the rough styles of early slapstick to become the single most recognizable character ever created on film. As an impoverished child, Chaplin followed his parents into London's vaudeville scene. Mack Sennett (p. 28) saw Chaplin's rendition of a drunk in "A Night in an English Music Hall," a skit he played on a tour of the United States, and offered him his first film contract. Chaplin soon gained near-complete control of his productions and began adding intellectual and artistic elements to his comedies. *The Kid* mixed melodrama with humor. *Modern Times* was inspired by his anxiety with the machine age, while *The Great Dictator* was his response to anti-Semitism and the rise of fascism. It was this controversial attitude that led American anti-Communist groups to campaign against him, eventually forcing him into virtual exile.

Other Works

The Kid, 1921, starring Charlie Chaplin and Jackie Coogan

City Lights, 1931, starring Charlie Chaplin and Virginia Cherrill

Monsieur Verdoux, 1947, starring Charlie Chaplin

Limelight, 1952, starring Charlie Chaplin, Claire Bloom, and Buster Keaton

■ **The Gold Rush**, 1925, starring Charlie Chaplin

This was the film that Chaplin claimed he wanted to be remembered for. Inspired by the Klondike Gold Rush, he devised a scenario with classic moments including the "dance of the dinner rolls" and a scene where the starving Tramp eats his boot.

Silent to Sound 1920–1929

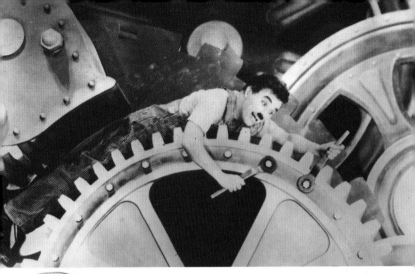

■ **Modern Times**, 1936, starring Charlie Chaplin and Paulette Goddard

Chaplin thought that talking pictures were only a temporary trend, but by the time he began to work on *Modern Times* he could no longer ignore them. *City Lights* had successfully featured sound effects, but his problem was two-fold: Not only did he believe that film was essentially a visual medium that would only be hampered by sound, but he was also conscious of the fact any voice he used would come as a shock to his many fans. In *Modern Times*, he eventually resolved the problem by speaking only once—to sing a song in Italian-style gibberish.

■ **The Great Dictator**, 1940, starring Charlie Chaplin and Paulette Goddard

A passing comment by producer Alexander Korda drew Chaplin's attention to the fact that the "Tramp" shared a physical likeness with Adolf Hitler. He decided to wage his own personal war against Nazi Germany by making *The Great Dictator*, a satire about a Jewish barber who bears a striking resemblance to an anti-Semitic dictator. In a typical Chaplin moment, the dictator denotes his aspirations of world domination by dancing with a globe. The problem of sound came up again, but this time Chaplin solved it by ending the film with a passionate speech in defense of freedom.

Charlie Chaplin

A Star Is Born

Greta Garbo claimed she wanted to be "left alone"—and she was not the only one. As stars became Hollywood's biggest product, audiences began to demand more and more information about their personal lives. Clara Bow's popularity was so widespread that using lipstick was described as "putting on a Clara Bow." Newspaper reports of her liaisons with men, her mental instability, and her fear of sound technology eventually ruined her career. Many American men felt threatened by the "exotic" nature of Rudolph Valentino's screen persona, and the press repeatedly accused him of effeminacy, which bothered the actor so much he challenged one journalist to a boxing match.

■ **Clara Bow**—sweet, vivacious and slightly naughty, she epitomized the 1920s-era "jazz baby." By the time she starred in the vastly successful *It* (1927), she was America's highest paid female actor, but her charm proved less advantageous in private; she was exploited by producers and snubbed by the Hollywood elite.

■ **Rudolph Valentino** was nicknamed the "Latin Lover" and he wooed and won thousands of fans when he danced the tango in *The Four Horsemen of the Apocalypse* (1921). Discovered by June Mathis—the first female film executive—Valentino presented a sensitive counterpoint to the action-oriented heroes of the day. After his early death, 100,000 people attended his funeral.

Silent to Sound 1920–1929

Greta Garbo's cool gaze and uninhibited passion brought a new, sophisticated sensibility to American cinema. Her refusal to cooperate with the Hollywood publicity mill of public appearances, autographs, and interviews only heightened the mystique around her—as did her fiery portrayals of doomed women in *Flesh and the Devil* (1926, pictured), *Anna Karenina* (1935), and *Camille* (1936).

Douglas Fairbanks began his career in drawing-room comedies, but will always be associated with the bold athleticism that made him a household name. In a series of showy action films—most notably *The Mark of Zorro* (1920), *The Three Musketeers* (1921), and *The Thief of Baghdad* (1924, pictured)—he became cinema's first "swashbuckler." He and his wife, actor Mary Pickford, were known as Hollywood royalty."

Avant-garde

- Approaches film as an art form ■ The genre was first developed by Dada and Surrealist filmmakers ■ Explores the aesthetic possibilities of cinema through abstract animation, Expressionism, Structuralism, lyrical documentaries, and many other styles ■ Often uses experimental narrative structures
- *left:* **The Golden Age**, by Luis Buñuel, 1930

- **1923** The last Dada soiree features Man Ray's *Return to Reason*
- **1943** Maya Deren's *Meshes of the Afternoon* begins the American avant-garde
- **1947** Oskar Fischinger makes *Motion Painting No. 1*
- **1950** Isidore Isou's *Venom and Eternity* screens at Cannes
- **1966** Michael Snow makes the influential formalist film *Wavelength*

Avant-garde cinema probes aesthetic, social, and politica boundaries. Kenneth Anger—who led the way for man directors, including Derek Jarman—dealt frankly wit homosexuality in films like *Fireworks* (1947). In *Empir* (1964) and *Poor Little Rich Girl* (1965), Andy Warhol simu taneously mocked and paid homage to Hollywood. Sta Brakhage physically manipulated film stock to make th *Dog Star Man* series (1961–64) and others. Many contem porary artists continue to use film, often in work exploring time and temporality, as in Tacita Dean *Fernsehturm* (2001).

■ **Derek Jarman: Caravaggio**, 1986

With *Jubilee* (1977) and *The Last c England* (1988), Derek Jarman provided a radical response to Margaret Thatcher's UK. With his contemporary Peter Greenaway, Jarman often referenced classica art. In *Caravaggio*, he recounts th artist's life in images taken direct from his paintings.

■ **Carl Boese and Paul Wegener: Der Golem**, 1920

Art influenced mainstream cinema. German Expressionist films like *Der Golem* owed

Silent to Sound 1920–1929

their skewed aesthetic the art movement of the same name, while many other films were influenced by montage styles and Dada.

■ René Clair: Entr'acte, 1924

Disturbed by the irrationality of WWI, Dada artists like Marcel Duchamp, Man Ray, and Hans Richter set out to underline human absurdity in senseless sound poems, ready-made artworks, and multi-disciplinary performances that almost always ended in riots. They employed film to convey this chaos. Films like *Entr'acte* used camera effects such as stop motion, odd angles, and slow motion with bizarre props such as a hearse pulled by a camel, and confused or nonexistent storylines to discombobulate the audience. Most Dada films are imbued with a sense of mischief—the ballerina pictured here is a bearded man.

■ Luis Buñuel: An Andalusian Dog, 1929

The Surrealists venerated the power of the subconscious. Their art combined Dada's illogical outlook on the world with a psyche-probing Freudian element. *An Andalusian Dog*, the most famous Surrealist film of all time, layers one disturbing image upon another—ants crawl out of a man's hand, a woman's naked back becomes a cello, a man slits a woman's eye with a razor. These images were intended to shock the audience into a state of free association.

Other Works

The Blood of a Poet, by Jean Cocteau, 1930

Reassemblage, by Trinh T. Minh-ha, 1983

A Place Called Lovely, by Sadie Benning, 1991

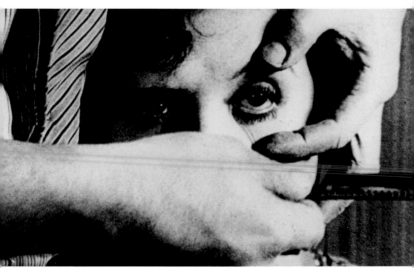

Avant-garde

Sergei Eisenstein

1898, Riga—1948, Moscow

■ Master of montage ■ Theorized about the power of film ■ Popularized editing techniques, including jump cuts and non-diegetic sound ■ Influenced many directors including Jean-Luc Godard and Francis Ford Coppola ■ Russian ■ Propaganda, Monumental, Soviet Montage ■ Directed 7 films

1898 Born in Latvia

1923 Inspired by Karl Marx, Eisenstein writes the manifesto "The Montage of Attractions" and makes *Glumov's Diary*, a short film

1928 Soviet critics denounce Soviet montage films as "formalist"

1929 Eisenstein leaves the USSR to travel in Europe and the United States

1931 Films the unfinished *¡Que Viva Mexico!*

1945 Wins the Stalin Prize for *Ivan the Terrible Part I*, but parts II and III are subsequently banned by Stalin

1948 Dies in Moscow

Born to cultured, middle-class parents in Riga, Sergei Eisenstein trained as an engineer. In 1917 he joined the Russian revolution, putting both his scientific skills and his artistic talents at the disposal of the Bolsheviks. He participated in many productions at Moscow's Proletkult Theater before directing *Enough Simplicity in Every Wise Man* (1923), a 19th-century play staged as a circus, and the film *Glumov's Diary*. After the international success of *Battleship Potemkin*, Eisenstein's career stalled under ideological pressure from the government. He ended a 10-year lull in his career with the anti-German fable *Alexander Nevsky*. His trilogy about Czar Ivan IV was well received until he showed the tyrant becoming increasingly bloodthirsty and afflicted. Eisenstein later had political problems and spent his last years writing theory.

■ Strike, 1925

Soviet montage films aimed to propagandize the masses. By juxtaposing images in a particular manner, and by carefully selecting the internal composition of those images, Eisenstein tried to stimulate thoughts and emotions. His first feature film, *Strike*, contains many examples of this, including a sequence that draws a comparison between the slaughter of workers and the butchering of animals.

Silent to Sound 1920–1929

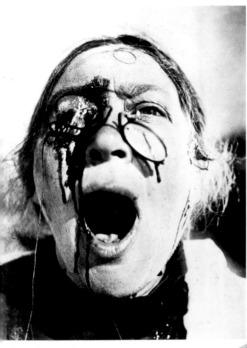

■ Battleship Potemkin, 1925

The Odessa steps sequence, in which mothers, children, and elderly people are massacred by the military, shocked contemporary audiences as much for its violence as for its powerful technique. The scene—an imagined moment in the failed anti-Czarist naval rebellion of 1905—is now one of film history's most famous. Instead of allowing any single character prominence in the film's narrative, Eisenstein depicted perceptible character types, often played by non-actors. These include a mother who berates the soldiers for shooting her son, a young woman who knocks her baby carriage down the steps, and an old lady with a terrified, bloody face who ends the sequence.

Alexander Nevsky, 1938

ger to do away with what they described as "formalism," tics of Soviet montage theory publicly condemned Eisen-ein's work. When *Bezhin Meadow* (1937), his first sound film, as censored by the state, Stalin gave him a second chance: *exander Nevsky*. With an uncomplicated plot about a easant-friendly hero, Eisenstein adhered to the Soviet yle, but managed to slip in some of his old editing chniques.

Other Works

Ten Days that Shook the World, 1928, starring Vladimir Popov	Ivan the Terrible Part I, 1944, starring Nikolai Cherkasov
Old and New, 1929, starring Marfa Lapkina	Ivan the Terrible Part II, 1946

Victor Sjöström

1879, Silbodal–1960, Stockholm

■ Father of Swedish cinema ■ Renowned for his finely composed shots and subtle performances ■ Emphasized the power of nature ■ Fate played a central role in his films ■ Inspired many directors, including Ingmar Bergman ■ Swedish ■ Drama, Horror, Comedy ■ Directed 55 films

1879 Born in Sweden

1912 Directs his first film, *The Gardener*

1923 Goes to Hollywood to work for MGM Studios

1930 After struggling with sound technology, he returns to Sweden

1942 Works as a producer at Svensk Filmindustri, where he fosters the career of Ingmar Bergman

1960 Dies in Sweden

Along with his compatriot Mauritz Stiller, Victor Sjöströ rose to prominence in the mid-1910s, during Sweden's ea film boom. Director Ingmar Bergman (p. 230) revere Sjöström, praising his "incorruptible demand for truth describing Sjöström's *The Phantom Carriage* as his "fi really big cinematic experience." Sjöström's style is chara terized by folkloric imagery and poetic movement. After th international success of *Ingeborg Holm* (1913)—a fil particularly admired for its realism—his directorial care both in Hollywood and Sweden became influential arour the world. Throughout his life, Sjöström also maintained career as an actor and h performance in Bergman *Wild Strawberries* (195 was well received by bo critics and audiences.

Other Works

A Man There Was, 1917, starring Victor Sjöström

The Outlaw and His Wife, 191 starring Victor Sjöström and Edith Erastoff

The Phantom Carriage, 1921, starring Victor Sjöström

■ **He Who Gets Slapped**, 1924, starring Lon Chaney and Norma Shearer

After luring Sjöström to Hollywood, Metro-Goldwyn-Mayer launched their newly formed

studio with his first American film, *He Who Gets Slapped*. Sjöström, who had spent his childhood in New York, managed to achieve commercial and artistic success in the

United States—a balancing a that some European directors including Mauritz Stiller, faile to accomplish. Dismayed by t constraints of sound, Sjöströ gave up directing in 1937.

Silent to Sound 1920–1929

The Wind, 1928, starring Lillian Gish

With one eye always on the box office, Sjöström explored many genres. He made dramas and comedies, as well as the horror classic *The Phantom Carriage*, which pioneered the use of flashbacks and double exposures. *The Wind* is Sjöström's version of a western. On a homestead in rural Texas, a delicate Southerner (Gish) kills and buries her rapist, only to have the crime discovered when the wind exposes his grave. Afraid that audiences would be repelled by such a grim story line, studio bosses created an optimistic ending—as they had done to Gish and Sjöström's first collaboration, *The Scarlet Letter* (1926). *The Wind* was not popular at the time of its release, but cinephiles now consider it one of the masterpieces of the silent era.

The Tower of Lies, 1925, starring Lon Chaney and Norma Shearer

Sjöström brought Lon Chaney and Norma Shearer together for a second time in *The Tower of Lies*, one of five films he directed that was based on the work of Nobel Prize–winning author Selma Lagerlöf. Another, *The Outlaw and His Wife*, is one of Sjöström's most celebrated films. In it he plays a man forced into thievery by starvation. Both films explore one of Sjöström's favorite themes: the futility of attempting to intervene with fate.

Victor Sjöström

The Passion of Joan of Arc

■ by Carl Theodor Dreyer, France, 1928, Drama

Danish director Carl Theodor Dreyer's Lutheran up-bringing strongly influenced the films he made. In his masterpiece, *The Passion of Joan of Arc*, he turned the French martyr's trial, torture, and execution into an austere Passion play. Intended to be screened in complete silence, the film owes its distinctive aesthetic to a mix of all three major contemporary movements—French Impressionism, German Expressionism, and Soviet montage. Dreyer used expressionistic sets, stark lighting, and dramatic camera angles.

Despite Joan of Arc only being Falconetti's second film role—and her last—her performance set a new standard for naturalistic acting. Filmed without makeup in extremely close shots, she delved into the psychology of the character. Dreyer asked her to portray the humanity of a young girl, rather than the grandeur of a historic martyr.

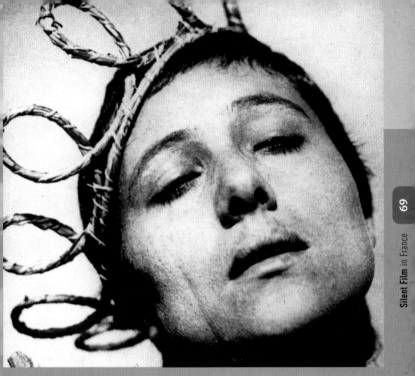

■ **The Passion of Joan of Arc**, 1928, starring Maria Falconetti

The presentation of Jeanne's harsh treatment by her captors and the parallels drawn between her and Christ sparked controversy—particularly in the UK, where the film was banned. The oppression of women by patriarchal societies was an issue close to Dreyer's heart: His unwed mother had been forced to give him up for adoption, then died while trying to induce an abortion. He revisited the theme throughout his career, most notably in *Day of Wrath* (1943) and *Ordet* (1955).

The Passion of Joan of Arc

Abel Gance

1889, Paris—1981, Paris

■ Leading director of French Impressionism ■ Advanced many techniques including the moving camera, rapid editing, complex double exposures, 3-D, and stereophonic sound ■ Influenced many filmmakers
■ French ■ Historical Drama ■ Directed 42 films

Abel Gance wanted the audience to feel like actors in his films. He strapped cameras to the chests of his cameramen or onto the backs of moving horses, and once allegedly hurled them through the air to mimic the path of a bullet. Aiming to capture a sense of immediacy and to render a strong sense of his characters' psychologies, he used quick-fire editing long before the Soviet montage filmmakers made it famous. Gance became obsessed with the theater at an early age, but by 1909 he had already started acting and writing for films. He continued to work on stage until the closure of the Paris theaters in 1914—and the cancellation of *Victoire de Samothrace*, his play for Sarah Bernhardt—led him to concentrate on cinema. He reached the pinnacle of his fame with *Napoléon*, but saw his career decline as film studios became increasingly controlling.

Napoléon, (above polyvision sequence and left), 1927, starring Vladimir Roudenko and Albert Dieudonné

The tale of Napoléon's young life, from his childhood (played by Roudenko) to the invasion of Italy in 1796 (Dieudonné), took four years for Gance to write, direct, act in, and edit. It originally ran six hours—the first installment of an intended six-part series. Gance constantly altered his style to suit the subject matter: For the terror scenes, he used quick cuts to express the chaotic violence of the crisis. In the climactic military sequences, he

filmed with three cameras to create "polyvision," widening out the screen to include three separate images at once. He began experimenting with battle scenes in *I Accuse!*, when he took the camera with him to the front during World War I, but the technical complexity of *Napoléon* reached a whole new level. Gance used quick, expressive editing for the first time in *La Roue* (1923), the film that inspired Sergei Eisenstein's technique. In *Napoléon*, he combined rhythmic editing with other effects, ranging from double exposures to elaborate moving-camera shots. He

Other Works

I Accuse!, 1919, starring Romuald Joubé and Séverin-Mars

The Battle of Austerlitz, 1960, starring Pierre Mondy and Martine Carol

created a living replica of Jacques-Louis David's 1793 painting *The Death of Marat*. For the finale, the left- and right-hand images were tinted blue and red to imitate the French flag. The film opened at the Opéra in Paris, a fitting tribute to a man who treated cinema as high art.

Abel Gance

The Cabinet
of Dr. Caligari

■ by Robert Wiene, Germany, 1920, Horror

Expressionism in Germany

The Cabinet of Dr. Caligari proclaimed the arrival of a new style of filmmaking: German Expressionism. The script, written by Hans Janowitz and Carl Mayer in the aftermath of World War I, related a horror story about a madman, a somnambulist, and a series of unsolved murders. When he decided to finance the film, producer Erich Pommer—who went on to become a central figure in the Expressionist movement—wanted Fritz Lang (p. 76) to direct. Lang declined, but he suggested an influential narrative framing device: that a final scene should make it clear that the film itself was a madman's vision. Insanity is hinted at in the stark colors, irregular sets, and in the stylized performances and exaggerated makeup of the actors. Conrad Veidt, the somnambulist, claimed Expressionist actors moved with the edgy forcefulness that the sets had.

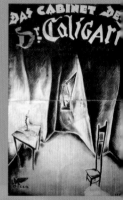

F. W. Murnau

1889, Bielefeld—1931, Los Angeles

■ One of the most celebrated silent directors ■ Popularized the moving camera with his film *The Last Laugh*, which included shots filmed from an elevator and on a turntable ■ Influenced John Ford and Terrence Malick ■ German ■ Drama, Horror ■ Directed 21 films

■ **1889** Born Friedrich Wilhelm Plumpe in Germany

1919 Directs *The Blue Boy*, his first film

1922 After losing a lawsuit to the Bram Stoker estate, all but bootleg copies of *Nosferatu* are destroyed

1924 *The Last Laugh* becomes famous

1927 Signs a contract with Fox Studios and moves to Hollywood

1931 Dies in an automobile accident; Fritz Lang, Emil Jannings, Greta Garbo, and Robert J. Flaherty are among the 11 people who attend his funeral

■ **Sunrise**, 1927, starring Janet Gaynor and George O'Brien

Sunrise is widely considered one of the best films ever made. For his first American film, Murnau used exaggerated, Expressionist sets, lighting, and acting to tell the story of an impoverished farmer's infatuation with city life. The oversize city set—meant to dwarf and dehumanize its residents—was so costly that, despite its success, the film did not make a large profit.

For years, Greta Garbo kept a death mask of F. W. Murnau on her desk. His other acolytes might not have been quite as dedicated, but Murnau's influence on Hollywood—and, indeed, on European filmmaking—was profound. After entering the business at the end of World War I, he became one of the leaders of German Expressionism. He went on to gain international reknown for the experimental "unfastened camera" movements in *The Last Laugh*, a Kammerspiel film. Kammerspiel, similar to the later New Objectivity movement, consisted of Social Realist "chamber pieces" inspired by Max Reinhardt's theater of the same name. Murnau was one of Germany's top directors when he left Berlin for Hollywood. After making *Sunrise*, he became increasingly disillusioned and ended his contract shortly before his death.

Other Works

The Haunted Castle, 1921, starring Arnold Korff

Phantom, 1922, starring Alfred Abel

The Last Laugh, 1924, starring Emil Jannings

Tartuffe, 1925, starring Hermann Picha

Faust, 1926, starring Gösta Ekman and Emil Jannings

Murnau embraced epic cinema when he filmed the myth of Faust, who sold his soul to the Devil in exchange for the opportunity to be young again. Inspired by the demonic paintings of Pieter Brueghel, the film was shot on a vast scale at the UFA studios in Berlin and featured many innovative special effects.

■ **Nosferatu**, 1922, starring Max Schreck

Shunning the studio-bound conventions of most contemporary films, Murnau shot his landmark horror film on location. Copyright issues resulted in its official withdrawal, but Nosferatu's eerie story and striking aesthetic made it an underground hit: Its many tributes include Werner Herzog's 1979 remake.

Fritz Lang

1890, Vienna—1976, Los Angeles

■ Explored humanity's darker side and complex morality of issues such as guilt and revenge ■ Employed subtle visual signals ■ Influenced Alfred Hitchcock, Tim Burton, and many others
■ Austrian-American ■ Drama, Fantasy, Film Noir ■ Directed 46 films

■ **1890** Born in Austria-Hungary
1919 First film, *The Half-Caste*
1920 Meets Thea von Harbou, co-writer and wife
1933 Leaves Germany after Goebbels asks him to lead new production studio
1936 *Fury*, his first Hollywood film
1944 Directs *Ministry of Fear* after Graham Greene's novel
1963 Plays himself in Jean-Luc Godard's *Contempt*
1976 Dies in Los Angeles

After running away from school, traveling in Asia an North Africa, fighting in World War I, and writing scripts Lang finally began directing films in 1919. With successe like *Dr. Mabuse: The Gambler*, he became the most popula filmmaker in Germany. His style was rooted in Expres sionism, but he showed an impressive versatility, makin crime dramas as well as fantasy and horror films. In 192C he started to collaborate with his future wife Thea vo Harbou, with whom he wrote *Metropolis* and *M*. They spl romantically and ideologically in the early 1930s, and i 1933 Lang left Germany to escape Nazism. He went on t have a diverse and prolific career in Hollywood.

■ **M**, 1931, starring Peter Lorre

This gritty drama about a child killer propelled actor Peter Lorre to international stardom. The film's dark, distinctive look and its focus on ambiguous morality and the criminal underworld made it one of the main inspirations for film noir, a genre Lang went on to master.

Other Works

Dr. Mabuse: The Gambler, 1922 starring Rudolf Klein-Rogge

Woman in the Moon, 1929, starring Willy Fritsch

Fury, 1936, starring Spencer Tracy and Sylvia Sidney

The Big Heat, 1953, starring Glenn Ford and Gloria Grahame

Silent to Sound 1920–1929

Metropolis, 1927, starring Brigitte Helm

With a vast and elaborate set, a two-year-long shooting schedule, 37,000 extras, an intricate female robot costume, and a large budget, *Metropolis* was the biggest film ever attempted in Germany. This early example of science fiction chronicled a workers' rebellion in a future totalitarian state. The version screened at the Berlin premiere lasted about 150 minutes, but later it was drastically reduced for distribution in the United States and much of the cut footage disappeared.

■ **Die Nibelungen: Siegfried**, 1924, starring Paul Richter

From an epic medieval poem, Lang created a spectacular world of misty primordial forests, medieval castles, dragons, and vengeful brides. The saga continued, with even more blood and gore, in *Kriemhild's Revenge* (1924). The film's costume and set design were elaborately detailed and set new standards for the industry.

Fritz Lang

Erich von Stroheim

1885, Vienna–1957, Paris

■ Nicknamed "the man you love to hate" for his charismatic portrayals of villains ■ Insisted on perfection in every detail, filming vast amounts of footage in order to achieve it ■ Often used visual metaphors
■ Austrian-American ■ Drama, Comedy ■ Directed 9 films

In *Sunset Boulevard* (1950) Erich von Stroheim plays Max von Mayerling—a forgotten director who once ranked alongside D. W. Griffith (p. 32) and Cecil B. DeMille (p. 36). The character is the devoted servant of an aging, demented film star. This was Billy Wilder's (p. 168) tribute to Erich von Stroheim, the actor and great cinematic auteur playing the butler. A fanciful self-publicist, Stroheim climbed up the Hollywood ranks after being Griffith's assistant on *Intolerance: Love's Struggle Throughout the Ages* (1916) and by playing dissolute Germans in postwar dramas. As writer, director, and star, his profligate spending quickly became as famous as his obsessive desire for authenticity. The fastidiously made *Greed*, his most famous film, greatly influenced the work of King Vidor (p. 52) and Josef von Sternberg (p.136). Though this attention to detail at any cost earned him popularity at first, both of these attributes eventually contributed to his undoing—after being fired from *Walking Down Broadway* (1932), his directing career was left in ruins.

■ **Foolish Wives**, 1922, starring Erich von Stroheim

Stroheim re-created Monte Carlo on the studio lot—right down to working bells in the grand hotel lobby. *Foolish Wives* was the third in a trilogy of dramas that depicted sexual politics with what many found to be scandalous frankness. His producers decided to capitalize on the director's spendthrift ways (including his insistence that real caviar and champagne be served in the relevant scenes) by proudly billing it as the "first million-dollar picture." It was a great success

■ **Greed**, 1924, starring Gibson Gowland

Greed is one of silent cinema's great lost masterpieces. Shooting on location, Stroheim filmed Frank Norris's epic novel *McTeague*—about the ruination of relationships because of money—in its entirety. He even insisted his actors fight in the intense heat of the Death Valley desert. The result of such hard work ran for more than nine hours, but the studio forced a drastic cut and the original footage was lost forever. When Stroheim watched the edited version years later, he said it "was like viewing a corpse in a graveyard."

◗ **The Merry Widow**, 1925, starring John Gilbert and Mae Murray

Studio boss Irving Thalberg's decision to replace Stroheim on the set of *Merry-Go-Round* (1923) changed the power structure of Hollywood forever: From then on, the producers had the final say over what films were made, and how—not the directors. This new, stricter regime made the perfectionist Stroheim miserable. *The Merry Widow*, a sharp comedy based on Franz Lehar's popular operetta, was the last film he managed to make almost entirely according to his own wishes, while also pleasing audiences, critics, and the studio.

Other Works	
Hearts of the World (as actor), 1918	The Wedding March, 1928, starring Erich von Stroheim and Fay Wray
Blind Husbands, 1919, starring Erich von Stroheim	The Honeymoon, 1928, starring Zasu Pitts

Georg Wilhelm Pabst

1885, Raudnitz (today Roudnice)—1967, Vienna

■ Leading New Objectivity and early German sound director ■ Used small details in costumes and props to convey key aspects of character ■ Directed with skill and empathy ■ Advanced the careers of Greta Garbo and Louise Brooks ■ German ■ Drama ■ Directed 31 films

1885 Born in what is today the Czech Republic

1923 Directs his first film, *The Treasure*, in the Expressionist style

1925 Achieves international success with *Joyless Street*

1928 Begins working with actor Louise Brooks

1939 Makes two films for the Nazi government

1948 Attacks Nazism and anti-Semitism in *The Trial*

1956 Retires from filmmaking

1967 Dies in Vienna

Georg Wilhelm Pabst made "street films" with such flair that his first attempt, *Joyless Street*, became the most popular film of the genre. Developed in part as a reaction to the excesses of Expressionism—a movement with which he was once associated—his street films and the larger artistic movement New Objectivity combined social criticism with explorations of the psychological effects of poverty in postwar Europe. The human mind fascinated Pabst and his next film, *Secrets of a Soul*, broke new ground by centering on Freudian psychology. His films featuring Louise Brooks are famous for their highly erotic characters. With the arrival of sound, he moved away from New Objectivity, but continued to be known for the sensitivity and the perceptiveness of his films.

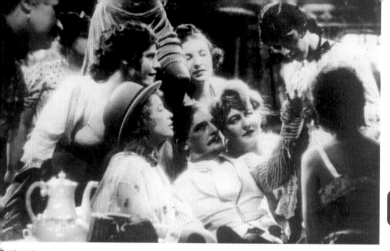

The Threepenny Opera, 1931, starring Lotte Lenya

After attaining new heights of artistry—and controversy—with Louise Brooks, Pabst turned to sound. Many consider his two pacifist films, *Comrades of 1918* (1930) and *Comradeship* (1931), to be among his best.

But his rendition of Bertolt Brecht and Kurt Weill's satirical operetta could not be bettered, from its topical aesthetic—despite being set in 1890s London, the film was a clear picture of Weimar-era Berlin—to its star, the great actor Lotte Lenya.

Joyless Street, 1925, starring Greta Garbo and Asta Nielsen

New Objectivity presented fatalistic and realistic views of life—which, in Germany and Austria in the early 1920s, was often a daily fight for survival. *Joyless Street* follows the decline of two women. The film's candid portrayal of crime, desperation, and prostitution in the wake of World War I in Austria caused an outcry.

Pandora's Box, 1928, starring Louise Brooks

Pabst's decision to cast an American as Lulu, the siren in Frank Wedekind's classic play was nearly as controversial as the performance he coaxed out of Louise Brooks: Brooks's Lulu was simply and sweetly without morals.

Other Works
Secrets of a Soul, 1926, starring Lili Damita
The Love of Jeanne Ney, 1927, starring Brigitte Helm
Diary of a Lost Girl, 1929, starring Louise Brooks

Robert J. Flaherty

1884, Iron Mountain—1951, Dummerston

■ Pioneered and popularized the feature-length documentary ■ *Nanook of the North*'s success led to a fashion for exotic documentaries in the 1920s
■ Inspired other documentary filmmakers, including Richard Leacock
■ American ■ Documentary ■ Directed 8 films

1884 Born in Michigan

1910 Begins work as a guide on expeditions to the Canadian Arctic

1922 *Nanook of the North* is released to great critical and popular acclaim

1926 British cinephile John Grierson creates the term "documentary" to describe *Moana*

1929 Works on *Tabu* with F. W. Murnau

1933 Makes government-sponsored *Industrial Britain*

1942 Releases his first "essay" film, *The Land*

1951 Dies in Vermont

In documentary filmmaking—a genre that is itself divisive—the role played by its most famous early practitioner continues to be contentious. The cinematic value of Robert J. Flaherty's films is unquestionable, but the methods he used to obtain those images have been criticized for more than 60 years. Flaherty staged many of the scenes of "real life" that he recorded. While filming an Inuit seal hunt for *Nanook of the North*, he told the hunter they might have to forgo capturing their prey in the interests of a good shot and they answered that "not a man will stir, not a harpoon will be thrown until you give the sign." The fact that they were using harpoons at all was an anomaly—at that time most Inuit hunted with rifles—but Flaherty wanted to document traditional customs and capture the imaginations of his audience.

■ **Louisiana Story**, 1948, starring Joseph Boudreaux and Lionel Le Blanc

Set amid the swamps and alligators of Cajun bayou country, *Louisiana Story* is one of Flaherty's narrative films and it tells a whitewashed story of the area's first contact with oil drillers. The film's loose narrative structure and focus on nature are characteristic of Flaherty's documentary style. He often depended on lyrical images of landscape to add coherence to his rambling story lines.

Nanook of the North, 1922

Flaherty's passion for the Canadian Arctic and the Inuit people inspired his first film, *Nanook of the North*. The documentary began as an amateur venture, when Flaherty, the son of a prospector, began bringing a camera with him on expeditions to the north. His feature-length portrait of a year in the life of Nanook contained many fictions (Nanook's real name was actually Allakariallak), but the charisma of the participants and the exoticism of their milieu made it immensely popular. Flaherty's reliance on commercial sponsors also caused controversy. The Revillon Frères fur company financed the film and *Louisiana Story* was made with money from Standard Oil. In both films, Flaherty painted his benefactors' businesses in a roseate hue: The fur trade is food, clothing, and a means of bartering for much-needed commodities to Nanook and his family, while the disruptions caused by the installation of an oil derrick in *Louisiana Story* are portrayed as merely transitory.

Other Works

Moana, 1926

Tabu: A Story of the South Seas (with F.W. Murnau), 1931, starring Matahi and Anne Chevalier

Industrial Britain, 1933

Man of Aran, 1934

Elephant Boy (with Zoltan Korda), 1937

The Land, 1942

Robert J. Flaherty

Color
and Sound

In the 1910s and '20s, black-and-white films were rarely without color, nor were they silent. Early filmmakers were successful with color: Many silent films were tinted blue for night sequences, yellow for daytime, or even hand-painted. When they finally managed to synchronize sound, there was a cinematic revolution, but throughout the silent era, live musicians played an integral role by providing "mood" music on the set and at the cinema. Recorded music arrived first, in the mid-1920s, and optical soundtracks—which translate the sound waves into an image that runs along the side of the film-strip—became the industry-wide standard.

■ **The Jazz Singer** (1927), starring Al Jolson, was a phenomenal success. The first "talkie," it paved the way for sound to take over Hollywood. Heavy sound apparatus and in-efficient microphones caused a dip in the quality of American films in the late 1920s—aside from a few exceptions such as Rouben Mamoulian's *Applause* (1929). Many European director solved this problem by filming silently and adding recorded sound later.

Color was used in early films to create mood and a greater sense of reality, but it was not until the 1920s that the technique of capturing color through film—rather than being added later—was developed. Epic cinema demanded color and the two-strip Technicolor techniques that were featured in films such as Cecil B. DeMille's *The Ten Commandments* (1923) captivated audiences. The invention, in the early 1930s, of three-strip Technicolor—a process that uses a prism to divide light—really made color filmmaking viable.

Cinema
During the War
1930–1945

"Here's looking at you, kid."

Michael Curtiz: Casablanca, 1942, USA, starring Humphrey
Bogart, Ingrid Bergman, and Paul Henreid
Quote: Humphrey Bogart as Rick Blaine in *Casablanca*

Cinema During

Europeans in Hollywood

Foreign-born directors bring elegance and innovation to Hollywood films

p. 112

American Mavericks

A new generation of directors challenge the limits of filmmaking

1930   1932   1934   1936

Hollywood Studio Masters

Versatile professionals span genres and define the classic Hollywood style

p. 108

the War 1930–1945

European Documentarians and Propagandists

Artists use reality-based film for political and social aims

John Grierson
Humphrey Jennings
Leni Riefenstahl p. 142
Dziga Vertov

p. 143

p. 146

Poetic Realism in France

French filmmakers create stylized parables of everyday life

Marcel Carné p. 148
René Clair p. 146
Julien Duvivier
Jean Renoir p. 144
Jean Vigo
Jean Cocteau

Cinema During the War

Hollywood Reality: Depression and War

While Europe was caught up in the struggle against Nazi Germany, the United States was suffering under the Great Depression. At the peak of the Depression, a quarter of the nation was out of work, but movie theaters were packed. Hollywood's films lifted audiences' spirits. Though studios produced socially relevant films like *I Am a Fugitive from a Chain Gang*, their profits came from escapist genres like musicals and comedies. In 1936, a Warner Brothers employee was killed by Nazis in Berlin. The studio retaliated by making *Confessions of a Nazi Spy*, alerting America to the fascist threat. After the Pearl Harbor attacks in 1941, the United States joined the fight and films told true tales of wartime heroism, using newsreel footage of the actual events.

■ **Mervyn LeRoy: I Am a Fugitive from a Chain Gang**, 1932, starring Paul Muni and Glenda Farrell

■ **Anatole Litvak Confessions of a Nazi Spy**, 1939, starring Edward G. Robinson, Francis Lederer, and George Sanders

Hollywood Escapism: Musicals and Comedy

Depression-era audiences flocked to see the lavish dance numbers of Busby Berkeley's musicals and the antics of the Marx Brothers. Backstage musicals of the early 1930s matured into sophisticated Technicolor masterpieces like Vincente Minnelli's nostalgic *Meet Me in St. Louis* (1944). Vaudeville comics like W. C. Fields and Mae West successfully transferred their acts to Hollywood, but the most successful escapist entertainment often included a dose of reality. When the chorus girls of *Gold Diggers of 1933* sang "We're in the Money," it was an ironic admission that cash was in short supply. The film's final number, "Remember My Forgotten Man," laments the plight of jobless World War I veterans. The screwball comedies of the 1930s turned a cynical eye on the foibles of the rich. *My Man Godfrey* (1936) mined comic gold when a socialite brought home a penniless "forgotten man" to be her new butler.

Women's Films and Prestige Pictures

Hollywood noticed that most moviegoers were female and made a series of women's films, also known as "tearjerkers" or "weepies." These films centered on strong women who overcame hardships like disease, poverty, or unrequited love and created strong female roles: Barbara Stanwyck in *Stella Dallas* (1937), Bette Davis in *Now, Voyager*, and Joan Crawford in *Mildred Pierce* (1945). In 1936, Irving Thalberg of MGM produced *Romeo and Juliet*. He knew the film would lose money, but argued it would bring prestige to his studio. Inspired by British films like *The Private Life of Henry VIII* (1933), Hollywood's "prestige pictures" included literary adaptations, historical dramas (*The Private Lives of Elizabeth and Essex*, 1939), and biographies (*The Life of Emile Zola*, 1937). MGM's literary tearjerker *Gone With The Wind* (1939) became the biggest box-office success at that time.

■ **George Cukor: The Personal History, Adventures, Experience, and Observation of David Copperfield, the Younger** 1935, starring Freddie Bartholomew, Edna May Oliver, and W. C. Fields

■ **Irving Rapper: Now, Voyager**, 1942, starring Bette Davis and Paul Henreid

Merian C.
Cooper and Ernest
B. Schoedsack:
King Kong, 1933,
starring Fay
Wray and
Robert Arm-
strong

Tex Avery's
Bugs Bunny
cartoon

Special Effects and Animation

Before CGI, filmmakers used smoke and mirrors, minia-
tures, and paintings to create the futuristic cities of
Things to Come (1936). Painstaking stop-motion animation was used to bring *King Kong* to life. Walt
Disney won respect for animated films with
Snow White and the Seven Dwarfs (1937). His
rival, the Fleischers Studio, produced Hollywood's second animated feature, *Gulliver's
Travels* (1939) and pioneered the use of
"rotoscoping" techniques—which involve
tracing live action film stills so animators
can use them as guides—in their stylish
Superman cartoon series. Tex Avery of
Warner Brothers introduced cartoon icon
Bugs Bunny in 1940. Three years later, MGM
created its own cartoon icons Tom the cat and
Jerry the mouse, who danced with Gene Kelly in
the 1945 musical *Anchors Aweigh*.

Introduction

Horror

■ Filmmakers use terror and suspense to thrill audiences ■ Universal Studios was the major producer of classic monster movies ■ Horror films helped advance special effects and makeup ■ Actors Boris Karloff, Vincent Price, and Christopher Lee became horror icons

■ *left:* **The Mummy**, by Karl Freund, 1932, starring Boris Karloff

1896 George Méliès directs *Le Manoir du Diable*, the first horror film

1925–48 Universal produces a series of iconic monster films

1951–57 Films tap into Cold War–inspired anxieties

1958–74 The UK's Hammer Films revive Dracula and Frankenstein's monster

1960 Hitchcock's *Psycho*, the first low-budget slasher

1966 The end of Hollywood's censorship code allows graphic violence

1999 Supernatural thrillers are repopularized by *The Blair Witch Project*

■ **George Romero: Night of the Living Dead**, 1968

Romero's low-budget classic updated the zombie film for the Vietnam War era with graphic violence and mysterious radiation that brings the dead back to life. Romero broke many unwritten rules of horror films by brutally killing off his protagonists and showing gruesome images of the zombies eating dismembered bodies.

Film is an ideal medium for conjuring nightmarish worl of suspense and terror. German directors pioneered t use of expressionistic sets and lighting in chilling classi like F. W. Murnau's (p. 74) early vampire film *Nosfera* (1922). American silent film star Lon Chaney used inve tive makeup techniques to create monster roles in *Th Hunchback of Notre Dame* (1923) and *The Phantom of t Opera* (1925). Universal cashed in on the success of a early sound version of *Dracula* with a series of titul movie monsters including *Frankenstein* (1931), *Th Mummy,* and *The Wolf Man* (1941). Special effects maste pushed the boundaries of their art in films like *King Kon* (1933). After World War II elements of science fiction we added to horror films, and sociopolitical anxieties we used to create spine-tingling films like *The Thing* (195 and *Invasion of the Body Snatchers* (1956). The 1960s ◐

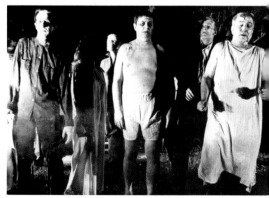

Cinema During the War 1930–1945

■ **Karl Freund: The Mummy**, 1932, starring Boris Karloff

Freund's atmospheric classic mixes horror with gothic romance. In the film archaeologists unearth the mummy of the Egyptian prince Imhotep, played by Boris Karloff. When he is unwittingly brought back to life, he sets about reviving the soul of his ancient love in the body of a modern woman.

■ **Tod Browning: Dracula**, 1931, starring Bela Lugosi

Browning's film of the gothic novel was the first in a string of horror classics for Universal Studios. Count Dracula (Lugosi) arrives in the UK and pursues the beautiful Mina Harker (Helen Chandler). Lugosi's thick accent and stark mannerisms influenced film portrayals of vampires for decades to come.

Horror

saw the revival of classic monsters Dracula and Frankenstein in gory Technicolor films starring Christopher Lee and Peter Cushing, while Vincent Price starred in a series of gothic horror films based on the writings of Edgar Allan Poe like *The Pit and the Pendulum* (1961). The loosening of film censorship rules led to increasingly explicit depictions of violence and gore in low-budget horror films like *The Texas Chainsaw Massacre* (1974). Alfred Hitchcock's (p. 186) groundbreaking thriller *Psycho* (1960) inspired a sub-genre of serial killer slasher films, which peaked in the 1980s with the *Halloween* and *Friday the 13th* film series. The subtler chills of supernatural terror movies like *Rosemary's Baby* (1968) and *The Exorcist* (1973) live on in *The Blair Witch Project* (1999) and J-horror (Japanese horror) films such as *The Grudge* (2004).

■ **Gore Verbinski: The Ring**, 2002, starring Naomi Watts

Gore Verbinski adapted Japanese director Hideo Nakata's *The Ring* (1998) for Western audiences. *Ringu* used elements of traditional Japanese ghost tales to tell the story of a television reporter (Watts) investigating a mysterious videotape whose viewers die of terror. After watching the tape, she has one week to solve its mystery or meet the same terrible fate. The film's success inspired other works in the J-horror subgenre that build suspense around themes of occult powers linked to folk religions. The vengeful spirit that haunts *The Ring* is a *yūrei*, or female ghost, whose white clothes and unkempt hair derive from Kabuki theater.

John Carpenter: Halloween, 1978, starring Donald Pleasence and Jamie Lee Curtis

This low-budget film inspired the subgenre of slasher films of the 1980s and '90s. On Halloween 1963, six-year-old Michael Myers discovers his sister having sex and kills her. After 15 years in a mental institution, Michael escapes and returns to his hometown. The local sheriff ignores the warnings of Michael's psychiatrist Dr. Loomis (Pleasence) and soon Michael resumes his killing spree. Teenage babysitter Laurie Strode (Curtis) discovers the bodies of her friends then fends off the knife-wielding killer herself. The film pays homage to Alfred Hitchcock's classic film *Psycho* with its low-budget aesthetic and first-person camera that takes the killer's point of view. Carpenter cast Jamie Lee Curtis, the daughter of *Psycho*'s star Janet Leigh.

James Whale

1889, Dudley—1957, Los Angeles

■ Injected irony and humor into tales of terror ■ *Frankenstein* inspired the horror classics of Universal ■ Influenced by German Expressionists ■ Made landmark early musicals in the US ■ Pioneered use of a moving camera ■ British-American ■ Horror, Drama ■ Directed 20 films

James Whale's talent as a stage director enabled him bring wit and irony to a string of successful films at U versal. He arrived in Hollywood in 1930 and began a fruit collaboration with producer Carl Laemmle Jr. His fil adaptation of Mary Shelley's *Frankenstein* was a huge but typecast him as a specialist in horror films. His films li *The Old Dark House* (1932) introduced many of the co ventions still in use in horror films today. Whale w inspired by German filmmakers like F. W. Murnau (p. 74) use expressionistic lighting and a moving camera, and brought stars like Claude Rains and Boris Karloff from t London stage to Hollywood. After the expensive flop T Road Back (1937), Whale's reputation suffered and he w unable to find work. His lonely later years inspired B Condon's *Gods and Monsters* (1998).

■ **The Bride of Frankenste**
1935, starring Boris Karloff

When Dr. Frankenstein (Colin Clive) discovers his monster (Karloff) is still alive, he joins forces with the eccentric Dr. Pretorius (Ernest Thesiger) to give the creature a bride. Wh resisted making a sequel to *Frankenstein* until he had com plete creative control and ma scenes that add playful humo while deepening Frankenstei emotional character. The brid (Elsa Lanchester) and her dra matic birth were based on Fri Lang's *Metropolis* (1927).

Showboat, 1936, starring Irene Dunne and Allan Jones

Whale's faithful adaptation of the Broadway classic is a land-mark Hollywood musical. Young Magnolia (Dunne) is an aspiring singer aboard her father's Mississippi River show-boat. Her romance and mar-riage to the gambler Gaylord (Jones) turn sour when they move to Chicago and hit hard times. The film was controver-sial for integrating black and white performers and for a sub-plot about a mixed-race singer named Julie (Helen Morgan).

The Invisible Man, 1933, starring Claude Rains, William Harrigan, and Gloria Stuart

A mysterious stranger, wrapped in bandages, appears in a small British town. Dr. Jack Griffin (Rains) has discovered a drug that makes him invisible but has also driven him insane. When the locals discover his secret, he goes on a murder spree. Whale used ingenious techniques and groundbreaking special effects—wires mysteriously lifted objects and footprints appeared in snow as if by magic.

Other Works

Waterloo Bridge, 1931, starring Mae Clarke, Douglass Mont-gomery, and Bette Davis

Frankenstein, 1931, starring Colin Clive, Mae Clarke, and Boris Karloff

The Man in the Iron Mask, 1939, starring Louis Hayward, Joan Bennett, and Warren William

James Whale

Gangster Films

- Depicted violent crime from criminal's point of view ■ Often inspired by real-life mobsters like Al Capone ■ Set in lurid big city underworlds ■ Violent gangster films led to strict Hollywood censorship codes ■ Chief stars James Cagney, Edward G. Robinson, and Humphrey Bogart
- *left*: **Little Caesar**, by Mervyn LeRoy, 1931, starring Edward G. Robinson

1912 D. W. Griffith's crime drama *Musketeers of Pig Alley*

1920 Prohibition in the US fuels criminal activity

1930–34 Hollywood produces string of gangster hits

1934 Hays Production Code enforced; violence censored in Hollywood

1940s Film noir borrows elements of gangster films

1972 Francis Ford Coppola's *The Godfather* reinvents the gangster genre

1983 Brian De Palma's brutal remake of *Scarface*

Though silent filmmakers such as D. W. Griffith (p. 32) told stories of violent criminals, the gangster genre ripened in the 1930s with the rise of real-life mobsters like Al Capone. The prohibition of alcohol in the United States fueled gangland violence and Hollywood studios used sensational stories from newspaper headlines. Audiences were fascinated by the brutal characters of the underworld. Filmmakers depicted violence and sex, then claimed they were doing a public service by bringing these amoral activities to light. Mervyn LeRoy's 1931 film *Little Caesar* set many of the conventions of the genre. The story follows small-time hood Rico Bandello (Robinson) as he shoots his way to the top of Chicago's criminal underworld, then dies in a hail of gunfire. Today, the gangster film's irresistible blend of amorality and brutal violence lives on in the work of Martin Scorsese (p. 320) and the Yakuza films from Japan.

■ **Howard Hawks: Scarface, the Shame of the Nation**, 1932, starring Paul Muni, Ann Dvorak, and George Raft

This brutal drama portrays the rise and fall of a Chicago mobster loosely based on Al Capone. Tony Camonte (Muni), an ambitious gang lord who eliminates his competition, is mean, ugly, and amoral. Tony's relentless ambition for power leads to a string of 28 murders before he meets his own violent end. The film uses dark humor to soften its brutality, but censors still felt it glorified violence and held up its release for two years.

Cinema During the War 1930–1945

William Wellman: The Public Enemy, 1931, starring James Cagney

In his first starring role, Cagney plays Tom Powers, a cocky thug who rises to the top of a Chicago bootlegging empire. He briefly enjoys his power before setting off a gang war and meeting a violent end. The film depicts Tom's childhood at the hands of an abusive father, and his family's sorrow at his turn to crime. The disturbing end shows the delivery of Tom's corpse to his mother. Cagney was chosen for the role despite his short stature and distinctive machine-gun speaking style. This first role secured him as one of history's most classic actors for the gangster genre.

Other Works
White Heat, by Raoul Walsh, 1949, starring James Cagney and Virginia Mayo
Miller's Crossing, by Joel Coen, 1990, starring Gabriel Byrne, Albert Finney, and John Turturro

Sergio Leone: Once Upon a Time in America, 1984, starring Robert De Niro, James Woods, and Elizabeth McGovern

This epic tale of New York City mobsters was the last film by the Italian director Sergio Leone. Elderly David "Noodles" Aaronson (De Niro) reflects on his life, first as a teenage gang member in the 1920s, then as a Prohibition-era gangster. The film jumps back and forth in time, building a complex portrait of men caught in a cycle of violence. As Noodles struggles to maintain his honor, De Niro's portrayal balances brutality with weariness and regret.

Stars of the Silver Screen

Spotlight on the Stars

102

In an era of rationing and uncertainty, the stars of Hollywood epitomized glamour and style. Louis B. Mayer and other studio moguls had the power to transform farm boys and waitresses into celluloid gods. Dramatic talent was a distant second to an ephemeral quality known as "screen presence." Each studio had a wealth of actors under contract and jealously protected its property. Publicity departments carefully molded the media image of each star, inventing names, histories, and even sex lives. Though the stars bristled at the control and yearned for independence, the fall of the studio system brought the golden age of Hollywood to an end.

Clark Gable was the King of Hollywood from the mid-1930s to the early '40s. Audiences—especially women—flocked to his roguish charm, which concealed a vaguely threatening manliness.

Bette Davis's unconventional beauty and brittle intensity allowed her to embody a striking range of dramatic roles from Queen Elizabeth I to mousey spinsters.

Cinema During the War 1930–1945

Shirley Temple's 1934 breakthrough in *Bright Eyes* shot her to fame and the curly-haired youngster became America's favorite child star. Her infectious optimism combined with singing and dancing skills won her legions of fans including President Roosevelt, who lauded her as a national treasure. As she grew older, Temple found the transition to adult roles difficult and her career faded.

Cary Grant personified Hollywood sophistication, but he began his career as Archibald Leach, an uneducated Cockney mime and acrobat. Grant's best roles display his physical dexterity and flawless comic timing. Known for his quick wit mixed with dry humor, Cary Grant bent Hollywood's censorship rules, but always maintained the image of a gentleman.

Marlene Dietrich was Hollywood's favored temptress—a cold beauty with no time for sentimentality or social taboos. After starring in seven lurid melodramas directed by her longtime collaborator Josef von Sternberg, she made a comeback in 1939 as a saloon singer, in George Marshall's western *Destry Rides Again*. In her later roles, she combined her exotic sensuality with a self-mocking sense of humor, but she faded from the limelight after WWII.

Stars of the Silver Screen

Musicals

■ Music and dance integrated into film's plot ■ Songs develop characters and the story ■ Dance sequences used spectacular sets ■ Backstage musicals framed songs in a theatrical plot ■ Broadway musicals adapted well to the screen ■ Diverse directors experimented with the genre

■ *left*: **42nd Street**, by Lloyd Bacon, 1933

The film musical is a beloved genre that has been reinvented by each generation. As soon as filmmakers could use sound, they added songs to enliven plots. Song and dance segments were added to films that were otherwise silent such as *The Jazz Singer* (1927). The first true movie musical, *The Broadway Melody* (1929), inspired a flood of backstage films in which songs were performed in a theatrical setting. *42nd Street* (1933) introduced audiences to the choreographer Busby Berkeley, whose spectacular dance numbers included lavish sets and showgirls dancing in geometric kaleidoscope patterns. Ernst Lubitsch (p. 112) directed operettas like *The Love Parade* (1929) in which characters first broke into song to further the plot. A boom in musicals in the 1930s brought a flood of talented songwriters such as Irving Berlin to Hollywood. Inspired by the success of the *The Wizard of Oz* (1939), MGM created a special production unit to make original musicals. Producer Arthur Freed gave directors Stanley ⭢

■ **Miloš Forman: Hair**, 1979, starring Treat Williams, John Savage, and Beverly D'Angelo

Miloš Forman transformed Broadway's tribal rock musical into the coming-of-age story of a young Vietnam draftee who, while on his way to boot camp is adopted by hippies and introduced to LSD and free love. Award-winning choreographer Twyla Tharp made the joyful musical numbers, filmed in the streets and parks of New York City.

■ **Robert Wise and Jerome Robbins: West Side Story**, 1961, starring Natalie Wood and Richard Beymer

Choreographer Jerome Robbins brilliantly adapted the groundbreaking Broadway musical, a modern retelling of *Romeo and Juliet*. The tragic love story of Tony (Beymer) and Maria (Wood) unfolds against a backdrop of street gang rivalry as the star-crossed lovers struggle to make peace between warring gangs. Much of the film was shot on location with the electrifying dance numbers restaged on real New York streets.

■ **Mark Sandrich: Top Hat**, 1935, starring Fred Astaire and Ginger Rogers

After first appearing in *Flying Down to Rio* (1933), Fred and Ginger became stars with a series of bubbly romantic musical comedies. Released during the Depression, the films were an escapist glimpse into a world of Art Deco glamor and carefree wealth. In *Top Hat*, romantic sparks fly when playboy Astaire meets spunky Rogers in London. They perform elegant dances to songs by Irving Berlin.

Donen and Vincente Minnelli (p. 166) unprecedented artistic freedom. Minnelli's masterpieces *An American in Paris* (1951) and *The Band Wagon* (1953) blend expressive camera work with spectacular music and dance. Despite the success of original movie musicals like *Singin' in the Rain* (1952), producers increasingly turned to Broadway shows like *The Sound of Music* for adaptations. Many contemporary directors have tried their hand at musicals, and a new generation of filmmakers continue to experiment with this enduring genre.

■ **Rob Marshall: Chicago**, 2002, starring Catherine Zeta-Jones, Renée Zellweger, and Richard Gere

Rob Marshall updated Bob Fosse's sultry satire on crime and celebrity with fresh casting and rapid-fire editing. A stage star and housewife are both arrested for murder. Awaiting trial, they become rivals and sensationalize their tales to grab headlines.

Other Works

■ Baz Luhrmann: Moulin Rouge!, 2001, starring Nicole Kidman and Ewan McGregor

Baz Luhrmann's wildly kinetic jukebox romance is a 21st-century ode to movie musicals of the past. An idealistic and penniless poet (McGregor) arrives in Paris in 1899. He is swiftly caught up in a bohemian underworld of artists and dreamers including the Impressionist painter Henri de Toulouse-Lautrec (John Leguizamo). He is charged with writing a musical production for the notorious nightclub and cabaret, the Moulin Rouge. He meets the club's enigmatic star (Kidman), and they fall madly in love, but she's been promised to a wealthy duke (Richard Roxburgh) whose money keeps the club afloat. As they act out their illicit affair through boisterous production numbers set to pop tunes by Elton John, T-Rex, and Nirvana, the stars bring a whole-hearted sincerity to their roles. Director Luhrmann was inspired by the energetic pacing of music videos and the colorful extravagance of Bollywood, and combines old-fashioned melodrama and humor at a dizzying pace.

Musicals

Victor Fleming

1883, Pasadena—1949, Cottonwood

■ Elegant craftsman whose films lack a signature style ■ Worked in silent film as a cameraman ■ Directed hit films at MGM studio ■ Won Best Director Oscar for *Gone With the Wind* ■ Favorite director of Clark Gable and Gary Cooper ■ American ■ Epic Drama, Western ■ Directed 45 films

1883 Born in California

1912 Hired as a stuntman

1916 Cameraman on D. W. Griffith's *Intolerance*

1919 Cameraman for President Wilson at the Versailles Peace Conference

1919 Directs first film *When the Clouds Roll By*

1932 Hired by MGM as a director

1939 Directs *The Wizard of Oz* and *Gone with the Wind*

1939 Wins Best Director Oscar for *Gone With the Wind*

1949 Dies in Arizona

■ **Gone with the Wind**, 1939, starring Vivien Leigh and Clark Gable

This epic romance, set during the US Civil War, is based on Margaret Mitchell's novel. The story follows the struggles of headstrong heroine Scarlett O'Hara (Leigh), an impoverished aristocrat, who is in love with Ashley Wilkes (Leslie Howard) and the roguish Rhett Butler (Gable). The film's vivid characters and events represent Hollywood craftsmanship at its best.

Fleming is best known for *The Wizard of Oz* and *Gone with the Wind*. A consummate storyteller and craftsman, his Hollywood career began as a stuntman in silent films. He cast the unknown Gary Cooper in his 1929 western *The Virginian*, making him a star. Fleming was a pragmatic outdoorsman and known as a "man's director." He was Clark Gable's favorite director and replaced "woman's director" George Cukor (p. 116) on *Gone with the Wind*. Fleming drew extraordinary performances from a wide range of actors. He directed Jean Harlow in her two biggest hits, *Red Dust* and *Bombshell* (1933), and Ingrid Bergman said of Fleming, "He got things out of me that were different from anything I had done before. What more can an actor want?"

Cinema During the War 1930–1945

The Wizard of Oz, 1939, starring Judy Garland

This musical fantasy is one of the most beloved films of all time. Dorothy Gale (Garland) is carried by a tornado to the magical land of Oz. With the help of the Scarecrow, the Tin Man, and the Cowardly Lion she defeats the Wicked Witch and meets the fabled Wizard who helps her return to Kansas. Seventeen-year-old Judy Garland became an instant star and the film and its theme song *Over the Rainbow* have become classics.

Other Works

Red Dust, 1932, starring Jean Harlow and Clark Gable

Treasure Island, 1934, starring Wallace Beery

Captains Courageous, 1937, starring Spencer Tracy and Mickey Rooney

Test Pilot, 1938, starring Clark Gable

A Guy Named Joe, 1943, starring Spencer Tracy

■ **Joan of Arc**, 1948, starring Ingrid Bergman

The story of Joan of Arc, a 15th-century peasant girl whose religious vision leads her to military victory, but who is betrayed and burnt at the stake. The film was reedited by the studio and viewed as a failure, but, in 1998, Fleming's original version was released to widespread acclaim.

Victor Fleming

Screwball Comedies

■ Romantic comedies with fast-paced, witty dialogue ■ Often mismatched pairs in sophisticated settings ■ Absurd plot twists and oddball characters ■ Sexual tension directed into barbed dialogue and slapstick violence ■ Key directors include Howard Hawks, Ernst Lubitsch, and Preston Sturges

■ *left:* **Pillow Talk**, by Michael Gordon, 1959, starring Rock Hudson and Doris Da[...]

1930 Hays Production Code restricts sexuality in Hollywood films

1934 First screwball comedy *It Happened One Night* is a huge hit

1934–42 Golden age of Hollywood screwball comedies

1941 Preston Sturges's *Sullivan's Travels* adds social consciousness to comic plot

1942 Hollywood comedies become graver during WWII

1988 *A Fish Called Wanda* has elements of screwball

2004 David Russell's *I ♥ Huckabees* brings genre to contemporary audiences

Hollywood produced a collection of romantic farc[es] between 1934 and 1942 known as screwball comedi[es]. These films drew from theatrical farces by Shakespea[re] and Oscar Wilde and added modern sexual tension a[nd] lunacy. In 1934, the Hays Production Code forbade ref[er]ences to sex in Hollywood films. That same year, Fra[nk] Capra's (p. 118) *It Happened One Night* was released. T[he] film redirected sexual energy into verbal sparring. I[n a] typical screwball comedy, a badly matched couple a[re] forced together by unusual circumstances. They tra[de] insults and even physical blows before falling into ea[ch] other's arms. World War II brought a new seriousness [to] Hollywood and the golden age of screwball comedi[es] came to an end. Despite this, several more recent fil[ms] have used fast-paced, screwball-inspired dialogue a[nd] other conventions, reinventing the genre.

■ **Gregory La Cava: My Ma[n] Godfrey**, 1936, starring Willi[am] Powell and Carole Lombard

Wealthy socialite Irene Bulloc[k] (Lombard) meets a charming hobo, Godfrey Smith (Powell[,]) and brings him home to wor[k] as her butler. Godfrey finds himself the only sane adult i[n] the eccentric Bullock family. [His] job gets even harder when Ire[ne] falls in love with him. Gregor[y] La Cava gave his actors the freedom to improvise their li[nes] but maintained a controlled mood of deadpan absurdity.

Cinema During the War 1930–1945

Other Works

Twentieth Century, by Howard Hawks, 1934, starring Carole Lombard and John Barrymore

Ball of Fire, by Howard Hawks, 1941, starring Gary Cooper and Barbara Stanwyck

Howard Hawks: Bringing Up Baby, 1938, starring Cary Grant and Katharine Hepburn

The night before his wedding, David Huxley (Grant) meets Susan Vance (Hepburn) a daffy but headstrong woman looking for her pet leopard, Baby. Their misadventures derail David's wedding plans and land him in jail. Hawks directed his actors at a breakneck speed, a technique that later became a trademark of the genre.

Rob Reiner: When Harry Met Sally..., 1989, starring Billy Crystal, Meg Ryan, Carrie Fisher, and Bruno Kirby

Harry (Crystal) and Sally (Ryan) are old friends who reunite in New York. Things become comedic as they try to stay friends without sex and love getting in the way. Reiner's hit film is a modern look at relationships that, through its witty banter, pays tribute to classic romantic comedies.

Screwball Comedies

Ernst Lubitsch

1892, Berlin—1947, Los Angeles

■ Comedic actor in Germany ■ Moved to Hollywood as a director ■ His comedies addressed controversial subjects ■ Stories revealed character with subtle actions ■ Witty dialogues inspired screwball comedies
■ German-American ■ Comedy ■ Directed 46 films

■ **1892** Born in Berlin

1913 Acts in short film comedies in Berlin

1914 First film as a director: *Fräulein Seifenschaum* (*Miss Soapsuds*)

1922 Moves to Hollywood

1923 First American film, *Rosita*

1929 Directs his first sound film, *The Love Parade*

1935–36 Production chief at Paramount Studios

1943 Earns his third Best Director Oscar nomination for *Heaven Can Wait*

1947 Dies in Hollywood while filming *That Lady in Ermine*

When Ernst Lubitsch stepped off the plane from German he brought European sophistication to Hollywood film Lubitsch created a new type of refined, adult comedy. H silent films showed a keen eye for small nuances of behavior that tell volumes about a character's thought His later comedies addressed difficult subjects like marit infidelity and totalitarianism with a bubbly style that be came known as the "Lubitsch touch." Though his comedies were often set in Europe among the idle rich, the had a distinctly American irreverence that influence screwball comedies. Fellow German Billy Wilder (p. 16 followed him to Hollywood to co-write Lubitsch's screw ball comedies *Bluebeard's Eighth Wife* and *Ninotchk* After Lubitsch's death in 1947, Wilder famously put a inspirational sign on his wall reading "What wou Lubitsch have done?"

Other Works

The Love Parade, 1929, starring Maurice Chevalier and Jeanette MacDonald

Design for Living, 1933, starring Gary Cooper, Fredric March, and Mariam Hopkins

Bluebeard's Eighth Wife, 1938, starring Gary Cooper and Claudette Colbert

The Shop Around the Corner, 1940, starring James Stewart

■ **Ninotchka**, 1939, starring Greta Garbo and Melvyn Douglas

This satire of Stalin-era Russia mocks both East and West. Nin (Garbo) is a stern official sent to Paris to sell jewels for the Russian government. French playboy Léon (Douglas) wants to stop the sale. He woos Nina, revealing her inner capitalist. In an early scene, Nina points to a absurd woman's hat in a store window as proof that capitalis is on its last legs. A few days lat she happily buys the same hat.

To Be or Not To Be, 1942, starring Carole Lombard and Jack Benny

A theater troupe led by Joseph Tura (Benny) and his wife, Maria (Lombard), take on the Nazis after they invade Poland. The actors help the Polish Resistance, but the Nazis discover their plan and take chase. In the resulting suspense the troupe is forced to impersonate Nazi officers and even Hitler himself. This dark comedy struck too close to home in 1942, and even Lubitsch's light touch could not make it a hit.

■ **Trouble in Paradise**, 1932, starring Herbert Marshall and Miriam Hopkins

Lubitsch's personal favorite among his own films, *Trouble in Paradise* is about a pair of jewel thieves, Gaston and Lily (Marshall and Hopkins) who meet in Venice and join forces. They travel to Paris where they plan to swindle wealthy perfume tycoon Mariette Colet (Kay Francis). They both get jobs in Mariette's household and gain her trust. Gaston falls in love with Mariette, Lily grows jealous, and the romantic triangle jeopardizes their scheme. The film epitomizes the Lubitsch style with a European setting and witty, fast-paced dialogue. After the creation of the Hays Code in 1930, the film's sexual innuendo was considered too risqué, and it was not shown again until 1968.

Preston Sturges

1898, Chicago—1959, New York

■ Writer-director of brash comedies ■ A brief string of comedy hits led to expensive flops ■ Made the last great screwball comedies of the era ■ Used a regular troupe of loyal actors ■ Ended his career as Hollywood exile
■ American ■ Comedy ■ Directed 12 films

1898 Born in Illinois

1920 Invents the first kiss-proof lipstick

1929 First play, *The Guinea Pig*, is a Broadway hit

1932 Moves to Hollywood as a writer

1940 Wins Best Original Screenplay Oscar for *The Great McGinty*

1941–44 Writes and directs six comedy hits

1944 Creates independent filmmaking company

1947 *The Sin of Harold Diddlebock* is an expensive flop

1955 Last film in France

1959 Dies in New York

Preston Sturges was known as an erratic genius who created several hit comedies, which were bracketed by flops and false starts. He spent years as a writer in Hollywood craving the esteem reserved for directors. He got it with his 1940 hit *The Great McGinty*—the first film with the credit "Written and Directed by"—which earned Sturges an Oscar for screenwriting. Over the next five years, he made six classic comedies marked by twisting plots and breezy, fast-paced dialogue. Unfortunately his later films such as *The Sin of Harold Diddlebock* (1947) were disappointments and Sturges became known as an expensive perfectionist. He moved to France to make his last film *The French, They Are a Funny Race* (1955), another flop. The ups and downs of Sturges's life rival the plots of his films. He died halfway through writing his memoirs.

■ **The Lady Eve**, 1941, starring Henry Fonda and Barbara Stanwyck

A screwball comedy inspired by the story of Adam and Eve *The Lady Eve* is set on a cruise ship where a pair of con artists Jean Harrington (Stanwyck) and her father, the Colonel (Charles Coburn), target "Hopsie" (Fonda), the dull-witted heir to a brewery fortune. Sturges mixes brilliant comic dialogue with slapstick humor, including playful sexual innuendo involving an escaped pet snake.

Cinema During the War 1930–1945

Sullivan's Travels, 1941, starring Joel McCrea and Veronica Lake

Sturges's biting satire on Hollywood features Joel McCrea as John Sullivan, a director of light comedies who vows to make a serious film. For research he dresses as a hobo and travels around America with an unemployed actress (Lake). The film mixes romantic farce and slapstick comedy with Social Realism, affirming the transcendent power of laughter.

The Palm Beach Story, 1942, starring Joel McCrea and Claudette Colbert

Tom and Gerry (McCrea and Colbert) are a pretty but penniless New York socialite couple who decide to divorce for financial reasons. To speed up the process, Gerry moves to Florida. On the train south, she meets millionaire John D. Hackensacker III (Rudy Vallee) who falls in love with her. Tom joins Gerry, bent on stopping the divorce, but Hackensacker's man-hungry sister falls for Tom. The film is a witty, active satire on the conventions of marriage as well as the conventions of screwball comedies—high-class protagonists caught in romantic dilemmas—marking the end of the genre's golden age.

Other Works

Christmas in July, 1940, starring Dick Powell

The Great McGinty, 1940, starring Brian Donlevy

Hail the Conquering Hero, 1944, starring Eddie Bracken

Unfaithfully Yours, 1948, starring Rex Harrison

Preston Sturges

George Cukor

1899, New York—1983, Los Angeles

■ Sophisticated and versatile director of classic Hollywood studio films ■ Fifty year career in filmmaking ■ Directed 21 actors in their Oscar-nominated roles ■ Fired from *Gone With the Wind* ■ Late career Oscar triumph with *My Fair Lady* ■ American ■ Comedy, Musical, Drama ■ Directed 55 films

1899 Born in New York

1926 Directs *The Great Gatsby* on Broadway

1929 Goes to Hollywood

1932 New star Katharine Hepburn plays in his *A Bill of Divorcement*

1933–38 String of "prestige pictures" at MGM

1933–50 Four nominations for Best Director Oscar

1939 Fired from *Gone with the Wind*

1964 Wins Best Director Oscar for *My Fair Lady*

1981 His last film, *Rich and Famous*

1983 Dies in Los Angeles

■ **The Philadelphia Story**, 1940, starring Katharine Hepburn, James Stewart, and Cary Grant

On the eve of her second marriage, socialite Tracy Lord (Hepburn) is torn between her dull fiancé, her playboy ex-husband (Grant), and a cynical reporter (Stewart). This screwball comedy's witty dialogue captivated audiences, reviving the normally aloof Hepburn's career with its romantic dilemma.

George Cukor's confident, stylish professionalism let him thrive in the Hollywood studio system for 50 years. He was known as a perfectionist and subtle innovator who helped define the look and style of classic Hollywood films. His works range from comedies like *Dinner at Eight* (1933) to dramatic "prestige pictures" like *David Copperfield* (1935) and *Gaslight* (1944). Despite being fired from two films in 1939, *The Wizard of Oz* and *Gone with the Wind*, his career did not suffer. Cukor is often referred to as a "women's director" for his ability to direct women to great performances, but he was more accurately an "actor's director" for direction of star performances. He directed Marilyn Monroe in two films, had a 47-year working relationship with Katharine Hepburn, and directed the highest number of male actors to Oscars.

Cinema During the War 1930–1945

The Women, 1939, starring Norma Shearer, Rosalind Russell, and Paulette Goddard

Cukor's reputation as a "women's director" was accentuated by this acidic comedy of manners in which all 130 speaking parts are played by women. Even the animal roles were played by females. Mary Haines (Shearer) is a happily married New York wife who hears that her husband is having an affair with a shopgirl (Joan Crawford). She heads west to Nevada to file for a quick divorce. There, Mary spends several weeks at a dude ranch surrounded by bitter, gossiping wives in the same boat. Cukor's cast included many of the top starlets of the day.

My Fair Lady, 1964, starring Rex Harrison and Audrey Hepburn

Henry Higgins is a misogynistic speech expert who bets a colleague he can transform cockney Eliza Doolittle into a well-mannered British gentlewoman. Cukor had a late career triumph with his adaptation of this Broadway musical, winning his only Oscar for Best Director.

Other Works

Little Women, 1933, starring Katharine Hepburn

Adam's Rib, 1949, starring Katharine Hepburn and Spencer Tracy

A Star Is Born, 1954, starring Judy Garland

Love Among the Ruins, 1975, starring Katharine Hepburn and Laurence Olivier

Frank Capra

1897, near Palermo–1991, La Quinta

■ Directed classic films with inspirational messages ■ Directed *It Happened One Night*, the first screwball comedy ■ Won three Best Director Oscars
■ Wartime documentaries *Why We Fight* are classics of propaganda
■ Italian-American ■ Comedy, Documentary ■ Directed 37 films

1897 Born in Sicily

1903 Moves with his family to California

1920 Works various jobs in silent films

1928 Hired as a director at Columbia Pictures

1934 Wins Best Director Oscar for *It Happened One Night*

1942–45 Directs eight war documentaries

1938 Wins third Best Director Oscar for *You Can't Take it With You*

1961 Directs last film, *Pocketful of Miracles*

1991 Dies in California

Frank Capra emigrated from Italy to America as a chil and discovered the American Dream. His best film express his faith in the value of hard work and the good ness of mankind. Capra began his career in silent come dies, then directed early sound films like *America Madness* (1932). A string of hits in the 1930s made hi the most successful director in Hollywood. Capra had a instinctive ability to stir the emotions of his audience. H applied this skill to propaganda with his World War II do umentary series *Why We Fight*. Critics saw his films as se timental and naive, labeling them "Capra-corn," but h serious films, like *The Bitter Tea of General Yen* (1933), we critical and box office failures. Frank Capra will be remen bered for his upbeat "feel good" films, a style of film making today known as Capra-esque.

■ **It Happened One Night**, 1934, starring Clark Gable and Claudette Colbert

Capra established the conventions of screwball comedies. An heir (Colbert) is on the run from her overbearing father. One night she crosses paths with a roguish reporter (Gable) who wants the rights to her story. They share a series of madcap misadventures, finally falling in love. Capra let his actors improvise to give the dialogue a more natural flow.

Cinema During the War 1930–1945

Mr. Smith Goes to Washington, 1939, starring James Stewart

This story of corruption in Washington DC is Capra's most political film. Jefferson Smith (Stewart) is a US Senator who appeals to his hometown supporters when his idealism puts him in conflict with crooked senior politicians. Though seen as feel-good Americana, the film takes a deeply cynical view of politics.

Other Works

You Can't Take It With You, 1938, starring James Stewart and Jean Arthur

Meet John Doe, 1941, starring Gary Cooper and Barbara Stanwyck

It's a Wonderful Life, 1947, starring James Stewart and Donna Reed

On Christmas Eve George Bailey (Stewart) is deep in debt and on the verge of suicide. An angel shows his friends' and family's lives without him. Capra's take on Charles Dickens's *A Christmas Carol* reaches its life-affirming finale by way of truly dark passages.

Censorship and the Hays Code

By the end of the 1920s, Hollywood was known as "Sin City." Sex and drug scandals gave the impression that the film community did not share the nation's high moral values. Films depicting prostitution, homosexuality, and violent crime enraged church leaders. Fearing government censorship, the studios created an office headed by Will H. Hays to set moral standards. In 1930 Hays drew up a list of "don'ts and be carefuls" that included nudity, mixed-race relations, drug use, and the ridicule of religion. The Hays Code was largely ignored until 1934 when the enforcement body, the Breen Office, clamped down. For 30 years, the Hays Code defined Hollywood morality, although filmmakers sometimes managed to sidestep rules by releasing films like *Some Like it Hot* (1959) and *Psycho* (1960) without official certification. In 1966, board chairman Jack Valenti scrapped the old code and replaced it with a rating system.

■ **Howard Hughes: The Outlaw**, 1943, starring Jane Russell

Hughes challenged censors by casting Russell because of her large breasts, and directing the film to ensure her assets were prominently showcased. When censors demanded cuts, he waged a media campaign and filed a lawsuit. He lost the case but the publicity helped turn opinion against the Hays Code.

■ **Maryland Board of Censors** reviewing movie scenes

Before the Hays Code, every film was reviewed by a myriad of local censorship boards and the all-powerful Catholic Legion of Decency. Hollywood made its code strict enough to satisfy all the groups. In 1952 and 1958, US Supreme Court rulings brought films under the protection of the First Amendment, making the codes illegal. Boards lost their authority to censor anything but genuine pornography,

**Wesley Ruggles: I'm No
Angel**, 1933, starring Mae West
and Cary Grant

In 1934, Mae West was
America's biggest box-
office draw, and she
owed much of her suc-
cess to censorship. She
shot to fame when her
Broadway play *Sex* was
raided by police and she
was jailed. Her notoriety
won her a contract in Hollywood where hit films *She
Done Him Wrong* (1933)
and *I'm No Angel* show-
cased her seductive
charms and bawdy
wit. When the Hays
Code was en-
forced, she
simply in-
creased the
number of
double
entendres
in her films.

Changes in the Film Industry

Censorship and the Hays Code

Michael Curtiz

1888, Budapest–1962, Hollywood

■ Prolific Hollywood craftsman ■ Master of many genres ■ Had a long career at Warner Brothers studio ■ Directed 12 films with Errol Flynn ■ Won Best Director Oscar for *Casablanca* in 1944
■ Hungarian-American ■ Adventure, Musical, Film Noir ■ Directed 160 films

1888 Born Mihály Kertész in Hungary

1912 Directs at the National Hungarian Theater

1913 Learns film directing at Nordisk studio, Denmark

1919–26 Directs 21 films in Vienna

1926 Hired by Warner Brothers and moves to Hollywood

1935–40 Directs a series of hit films with Errol Flynn

1943 Wins Best Director Oscar for *Casablanca*

1962 Dies in Hollywood

Michael Curtiz was a dynamic director whose enormou output ranged from gangster films and westerns t musical comedies. He left Hungary to learn filmmaking i Denmark, where his biblical epic *Moon of Israel* (192 caught the attention of producer Jack Warner wh brought him to Hollywood. Curtiz spent 18 years at Warne Brothers directing up to four films a year. His thriller *My tery of the Wax Museum* (1933) ranks among Hollywood horror classics. Curtiz directed Errol Flynn in a series o adventure films, making him a star. In 1943, Presiden Franklin Roosevelt wanted Curtiz to make the pro-Sovie propaganda film *Mission to Moscow*. Curtiz earned fou Oscar nominations for Best Director and won in 1943 fo *Casablanca*. In his later years, he directed Elvis Presley i *King Creole* (1958) and Bing Crosby i *White Christmas*. Curtiz was a perfec tionist who never stopped working an even complained when his crew took o for lunch. Today, his work epitomize the best of the Hollywood studio year

■ **Casablanca**, 1942, starring Humphrey Bogar and Ingrid Bergman

This classic film blends many genres. Set in Morocco during WWII, the film tells the love stor between Rick, a cynical nightclub owner played by Bogart, and Ilsa Lund (Bergman). Also a sus pense film, Ilsa pleads with Rick to help her hus band, a resistance fighter, escape from the Nazis Curtiz balanced these plots with elements of comedy and even musicals—he used several songs including the classic *As Time Goes By*.

Cinema During the War 1930–1945

Angels with Dirty Faces, 1938, starring James Cagney, ~~Humphrey Bogart, and Pat O'Brien~~

Rocky and Jerry are street-wise ~~kids growing up in the slums of New York's Lower East Side.~~ ~~years later~~, Rocky (Cagney) is a ~~hardened gangster while Jerry~~ (O'Brien) is a priest who runs a home for delinquent boys. When Rocky returns to the old neighborhood, the boys idolize him and the two former pals fight over the souls of the impressionable youths. After Rocky blackmails a corrupt lawyer (Bogart), Jerry's cam- paign against political corrup- tion unwittingly catches Rocky in its net. The film mixed wise- cracking gangster-film style with gritty Social Realism. Curtiz got powerful performances from the cast of adults and teens and earned his first Best Director Oscar nomination.

Other Works

The Sea Hawk, 1940, starring Errol Flynn and Brenda Marshall

Yankee Doodle Dandy, 1942, starring James Cagney

Mission to Moscow, 1943, pro-Soviet propaganda film

White Christmas, 1954, starring Bing Crosby, Danny Kaye, and Rosemary Clooney

■ The Adventures of Robin Hood, 1938, starring Errol Flynn, Olivia de Havilland, and Basil Rathbone

In 12th-century England, Sir Robin of Locksley (Flynn) becomes an outlaw to fight treacherous noblemen and win Maid Marian's heart. In his first Technicolor film, Curtiz packed each frame of this big-budget adventure with sweeping action and swordplay.

Michael Curtiz

William Wyler

1902, Mülhausen—1981, Los Angeles

■ Prolific Hollywood studio director with 45-year career ■ Wartime films helped Americans cope with hardships ■ Demanding perfectionist who wa hard on actors ■ Won three Best Director Oscars and nominated 12 times ■ German-American ■ Drama, Western, Comedy ■ Directed 61 films

1902 Born in Germany

1922 Moves to Hollywood to work at Universal Studios

1925 First film, *The Crook Buster*

1936 Hired by producer Samuel Goldwyn to direct big-budget films

1938–41 Directs Bette Davis in three Oscar-nominated roles

1942–45 Army service and makes propaganda films

1942 Wins Best Director Oscar for *Mrs. Miniver*

1961 Directs lesbian-themed *The Children's Hour*

1981 Dies in California

William Wyler began his Hollywood career as th youngest director at Universal Studios. His early film were low-budget B-movies, but in 1936 he became a big budget director with his adaptation of Sinclair Lewis novel *Dodsworth*—an unsentimental look at a dyin marriage that earned him his first Best Director Osc nomination. *Mrs. Miniver* (1942), about a middle-cla British family coping with World War II, helped America brace for war while Oscar-winning *The Best Years of Ou Lives* (1946) deals with American veterans returning fro the war. Wyler was notoriously demanding with h actors, often insisting on a dozen takes of a scene. H advice was often a terse "That was lousy," but his tech niques produced a record-breaking 36 Oscar-nominate performances and 14 winners.

■ **Wuthering Heights**, 1939, starring Merle Oberon and Laurence Olivier

Wyler's adaptation of Emily Brontë's novel made Laurence Olivier a star. Cathy (Oberon) is torn between her love for Edgar, a wealthy neighbor, and her brooding childhood friend Heathcliff (Olivier). The film omits nearly half of the novel, and producer Samuel Goldwyn added a sentimental ending showing Cathy and Heathcliff together in heaven that enraged Wyler.

Cinema During the War 1930–1945

Roman Holiday, 1953, starring Gregory Peck, Audrey Hepburn, and Eddie Albert

Princess Ann (Hepburn) arrives in Italy on a Royal Tour. She rebels against her sheltered life and breaks out to explore the city. American reporter Joe Bradley (Peck) finds her and plots to get an exclusive story. Wyler cast the unknown Audrey Hepburn based on her screen test, which revealed her playful charm.

Jezebel, 1938, starring Bette Davis, Henry Fonda, and George Brent

Set in 1850s New Orleans, *Jezebel* tells the story of a southern belle, Julie Mardsen (Davis), who begins to have trouble with her fiancé (Fonda) as she asserts her strength.

The famed waltz scene features a subversive Julie dancing in a shocking red dress—symbolizing her sexuality. Because color films were still uncommon and expensive at the time, the scene is shot in black and white and dialogue is used to fill in the color.

Bette DAVIS JEZEBEL
HENRY FONDA GEORGE BRENT
MARGARET LINDSAY DONALD CRISP FAY BAINTER
WILLIAM WYLER PRODUCTION
A WARNER BROS. PICTURE

Other Works

The Desperate Hours, 1955, starring Humphrey Bogart	Ben-Hur, 1959, starring Charlton Heston and Stephen Boyd
The Big Country, 1958, starring Gregory Peck and Charlton Heston	Funny Girl, 1968, starring Barbra Streisand

William Wyler

Orson Welles

1915, Kenosha—1985, Los Angeles

■ Directed his masterpiece *Citizen Kane* at age 25 ■ Used innovative story structure and camera effects ■ One of the most influential Hollywood directors ■ Studios reedited his later films ■ Struggled to fund projects ■ American ■ Literary Adaptation, Film Noir ■ Directed 14 films

1915 Born in Wisconsin
1931 Acts at the Gate Theater in Dublin
1938 Performs radio drama *War of the Worlds*, causing widespread panic
1941 Goes to Hollywood to make *Citizen Kane*
1948–56 Reputedly black-listed; moves to Europe
1970–85 Directs independent films
1985 Dies in Los Angeles

Welles was the great tortured genius of American film. H once said of himself, "I started at the top and worked m way down." He was already a star of Broadway and radi when he arrived in Hollywood to make *Citizen Kane* at th age of 25. The publisher William Randolph Hearst saw th film as an ugly portrait of himself and began a campaig to damage Welles's reputation. Though he directed handful of films after *Citizen Kane* (p. 128), they all su fered from studio interference or lack of funds. His secon feature, *The Magnificent Ambersons*, was taken away fro Welles and reedited by the studio. Unable to financ his films in the US, he moved to Europe where h directed Franz Kafka's *The Trial* and adaptations o Shakespeare including *Chimes at Midnigh* (1965). Restless and unpredictable, h never stopped working as an acto writer, and even magician. He le behind many unfinished film project

■ **Touch of Evil**, 1958, starring Charlton Heston and Janet Leigh

Touch of Evil was Welles's last Hollywoo film and one of the last great film noirs. Mexican police detective Mike Vargas (Heston) investigates the murder of a crime boss, putting himself and his new wife Susan (Leigh) in harm's way. Welles plays a corrupt Texas cop who challenges Vargas to a battle of wits. The film is renowned for its opening three-minute moving crane shot, but surrounded by controversy over the studio havin reedited the film in its rerelease.

The Lady from Shanghai, ?8, starring Orson Welles and ? Hayworth

?his quirky film noir, Welles ?ys Michael O'Hara, an Irish ?or hired by a wealthy couple to sail their yacht from New York to San Francisco. On the way, Michael begins an affair with the seductive wife (Hayworth) and they plot to run away together. Then Michael finds himself framed for murder. Welles used inventive camera work, particularly the concluding shoot-out in a house of mirrors. The studio reedited the film and left its plot incoherent.

Other Works

?he Magnificent Ambersons, ?942, starring Joseph Cotten, ?olores Costello, Anne Baxter, ?nd Tim Holt

?acbeth, 1948, starring ?rson Welles and Roddy ?cDowall

?he Trial, 1962, starring ?nthony Perkins

?ne Other Side of the ?ind, (unfinished), 1970–76, ?arring John Huston

■ **Othello**, 1952, starring Orson Welles

Welles plays the Moor whose scheming underling Iago plants seeds of jealousy against Othello's new wife, Desdemona, leading to her tragic death. Welles used his trademark depth of field and low camera angles to create a sense of foreboding. Unable to afford costumes, he relocated one scene to a bathhouse with the actors wearing sheets.

Orson Welles

Citizen Kane

■ by Orson Welles, USA, 1941, Drama

Often cited as the greatest film of all time, *Citizen Kane* was the first work by the ambitious young Orson Welles (p. 126). After Welles's radio drama *War of the Worlds* caused widespread panic, RKO Studios hoped to capitalize on the young director's notoriety. Welles collaborated with writer Herman Mankiewicz on a script loosely based on the life of newspaper tycoon William Randolph Hearst. The storytelling technique was revolutionary. The film opens with Charles Foster Kane's death then jumps back and forth in time to show Kane's life—from rural childhood, through his early newspaper triumphs, to his lonely old age. The audience pieces together Kane's tragic life. Angered by the film, Hearst pressured theaters not to show it and the film lost money. Welles won an Oscar for the screenplay, but his career and reputation were badly damaged by Hearst.

■ **Citizen Kane**, 1941, starring Joseph Cotten, Dorothy Comingore, Ruth Warrick, and Everett Sloane

Welles worked with cameraman Gregg Toland to create innovative new camera effects such as the use of a "deep focus." In normal camera shots only part of the image is in focus, however in *Citizen Kane* objects close to the camera are as clear as objects in the distance. Low camera angles—shooting up at the subject—were also used to give characters an imposing presence. Welles's radio experience led him to use sound in new ways: background noise subtly heighten emotions, while the soundtrack of one scene often continues into the next shot, creating a smooth transition between abrupt edits.

Cinema During the War 1930–1945

Citizen Kane

Walt Disney

1901, Chicago–1966, Los Angeles

■ Hollywood titan who pioneered animated films ■ Produced first animated feature film, *Snow White and the Seven Dwarfs* ■ Built family entertainment empire ■ Closely supervised his creative team ■ Developed new technologies ■ American ■ Animation ■ Produced 81 films

1901 Born in Chicago

1923 Moves to California and starts animation studio

1928 *Steamboat Willie* is a hit and he hires a staff of animators

1932 First Oscar for color short *Flowers and Trees*

1937 Release of *Snow White and the Seven Dwarfs*

1944 *The Three Caballeros* mixes animation with actors

1955 Disneyland opens in California

1961 First color TV series, *Wonderful World of Disney*

1966 Dies in Los Angeles

Walt Disney was a filmmaker and visionary who relentless pushed the limits of the art and technology of filmmakin After several false starts in the animation business, Disne had his first success with the short cartoon *Steambo Willie*. Disney moved up to the role of producer with ever-expanding staff of animators. His studio created th popular Mickey Mouse cartoons and the Silly Symphor shorts which included the Oscar-winning *Three Little Pi* (1933). These cartoons were a laboratory for new tec niques including Technicolor and the use of multiplar cameras to give the illusion of three dimensions. Disne took a big gamble in 1937 by releasing the first animate feature film ever, *Snow White and the Seven Dwarfs* (p. 13 Its success paved the way for a series of animated films

■ **Walt Disney and Ub Iwerks: Steamboat Willie**, 1928

Mickey Mouse made his screen debut in this short film, which was the first animated film with syn-chronized music and sound effects. Mickey is a mischievous tugboat sailor who disobeys his captain's orders, woos his girlfriend Minnie, and uses farm ani-mals as musical instru-ments. The combination of inventive animation with lively music and special effects made the film a sen-sation and Mickey a star.

Cinema During the War 1930–1945

Clyde Geronimi, Hamilton [Lu]ske, and Wilfred Jackson: [Cin]derella, 1950

[Dis]ney expanded this fairy tale [of a] girl and a glass slipper by [ad]ding a menagerie of comical [ani]mal friends and lively songs. [Cin]derella's stepmother forbids [her] from attending the Prince's [ball], but her Fairy Godmother [pro]vides the gown and acces[sor]ies if Cinderella gets home [by] the stroke of midnight. The [Prin]ce spots Cinderella as his [tru]e love, but she rushes out [lea]ving only a glass slipper.

[H]amilton Luske and Ben [Sh]arpsteen: Pinocchio, 1940

[Dis]ney chose a little-known [Itali]an children's tale for his [sec]ond animated feature. A wooden puppet is told he can become a real boy if he is "brave, truthful, and unselfish." He is tested by a series of mis-adventures and sly villains, only to find himself trapped in the belly of a whale. The film expands on the innovations of *Snow White*, with richer charac-ters and stunning animation.

Walt Disney

that were revolutionary for their subtle characterizations and their mix of comedy with dark, frightening passages. In 1940, Disney released his artistic *Fantasia*, a collection of short experimental animated segments set to classical music. Later animated features like *Sleeping Beauty* (1959) were criticized for softening the original fairy tales. His studio expanded into live action films and science documentaries, and later embraced television. Disney was actively involved with every step of the creative process. In 1955, he opened the first of many theme parks, Disneyland in California. Today, Disney's empire has spread to every corner of the globe. His company remains a hotbed of new ideas in the world of family entertainment and beyond.

Other Works

Alice in Wonderland, by Clyde Geronimi, Wilfred Jackson, and Hamilton Luske, 1951

20,000 Leagues Under the Se by Richard Fleischer, 1954, starring Kirk Douglas and Jame Mason

101 Dalmatians, by Clyde Geronimi, Hamilton Luske, and Wolfgang Reitherman, 1961

The Jungle Book, by Wolfgan Reitherman, 1967

■ **David Hand: Bambi**, 1942

Based Felix Salten's novel, the film tells the story of Bambi, a young deer destined to become Prince of the Forest. He is raised by his mother and learns the ways of the forest with help from his adorable animal friends. He even finds love with the doe Faline. The film's emotional punch comes halfway through when Bambi loses his mother to a hunter's bullet. The film had a powerful impact on children, and later Disney films shied away from provoking such primal fears favor of pure comedy. Disney animators achieved unprece dented realism by studying l fawns imported from Maine.

Cinema During the War 1930–1945

**Ben Sharpsteen:
Dumbo**, 1941

Disney's fourth animated
picture was this fable about
tolerance set against a circus
backdrop. Dumbo is a newborn
elephant ridiculed for having
large ears. Encouraged by his
friend Timothy the mouse, Dumbo
learns to use his ears as wings, and the
flying elephant is soon the hit of the big top. The film
balances touching scenes between Dumbo and his
mother with slapstick humor. The "Pink Elephants on
Parade" sequence is a surreal fantasy worthy of *Fantasia*.

Animation in the United States

■ **Robert Stevenson:
Mary Poppins**, 1964,
starring Julie Andrews
and Dick Van Dyke

This tale of a nanny with
magical powers was a technical and artistic breakthrough
for Disney. Julie Andrews
plays Mary Poppins, who
descends from the clouds over
Edwardian London to tame the
spoiled Banks children. They
share a series of adventures,
accompanied by the Cockney
chimney sweep Bert (Van
Dyke). In the process, Mary
teaches important life lessons.
The film was a first-class Hollywood musical with a script
that mixes comedy with heartfelt pathos. Disney's artists
used all the special-effects
tricks known at the time and
in one sequence, Mary and the
children drop into sidewalk
chalk paintings and interact
with animated characters.
This film made a star of Julie
Andrews and earned her a Best
Actress Oscar.

Walt Disney

Snow White and the Seven Dwarfs

■ by Walt Disney Productions, directed by David Hand, USA, 1937, Animation

In 1934, Walt Disney (p. 130) was a rising Hollywood sensation, but he was restless to do more. His goal was a full-length animated film that rivaled live-action films in both style and complexity. When he announced the production of *Snow White and the Seven Dwarfs*, critics dubbed the project "Disney's folly." Over the next three years, his studio grew from 300 to 700 employees and the original budget of $25,000 ballooned to $1.4 million. Disney even mortgaged his own home to finish the project. The film premiered in 1937 to rapturous praise. Disney's financial gamble paid off, and the creation of a new storytelling medium was realized.

Snow White's evil stepmoth is jealous of her beauty. She orders a woodsman to kill the girl, but she escapes and find shelter with dwarfs. The step-mother tricks Snow White int eating a poisoned apple and she falls into a coma-like slee After the death of the step-mother, a prince wakes her with love's first kiss.

■ **Snow White and the Seven Dwarfs**, 1937

To hold audiences for 83 minutes, Disney surrounded Snow White with a memorable supporting cast. Each dwarf had a distinctive personality and body language while the evil stepmother has become an iconic villain. Songs reveal the characters' thoughts and further the plot. Disney's animators created beautifully rendered water-color backgrounds and realistic effects to simulate rain and fire.

Snow White and the Seven Dwarfs

Josef von Sternberg

1894, Vienna–1969, Los Angeles

■ Expressionistic visual style ■ Wrote and directed romantic tales set in exotic locations ■ Used elaborate sets and costumes ■ Made seven films starring Marlene Dietrich ■ Created bold female characters who broke social taboos ■ Austrian-American ■ History, Drama ■ Directed 30 films

1894 Born in Austria

1916 Works as apprentice filmmaker in the US

1925 Directs first film *The Salvation Hunters* in Hollywood

1926 Charlie Chaplin hires him to direct a silent film

1927 Directs *Underworld*, the first modern gangster film

1930 Goes to Germany to film *The Blue Angel*

1930–35 Writes and directs six big-budget Hollywood melodramas starring Marlene Dietrich

1936 Fired by Ernst Lubitsch, head of Paramount Studios

1957 Last film, *Jet Pilot*

1969 Dies in Hollywood

Josef von Sternberg was one of Hollywood's greate visual stylists, best known for seven films he directed sta ring Marlene Dietrich. Born Josef Sternberg in Vienna, h adopted the aristocratic "von" when he arrived in Holl wood in the 1920s. Sternberg had a background in art ar theater and brought a painter's eye to his films. He use expressionistic lighting and production design and r created the exotic locations of his stories on Hollywoo sound stages using lavish sets and costumes. Sternber found his ideal collaborator in Marlene Dietrich. He said c her, "I am Marlene and Marlene is me." The provocativ female characters he wrote for her, often bot romantic and cynical, came to define he screen persona. Today, Sternberg's film can be read as cam melodrama o ironic commen tary on the genre

The Blue Angel, 1930, starring Marlene Dietrich and Emil Jannings

Filmed in Berlin, *The Blue Angel* was the first German-language talkie. Lola (Dietrich) is a cabaret singer who seduces a respectable teacher (Jannings). When the two marry, he loses his job and ends up a bit player in Lola's vaudeville act. The movie made Dietrich a star and led to more films with Sternberg.

Morocco, 1930, starring Marlene Dietrich, Adolphe Menjou, and Gary Cooper

Sternberg brought Dietrich to Hollywood to film this romance about Amy Jolly, a worldly nightclub singer who falls in love with a naive Foreign Legionnaire

Other Works

Shanghai Express, 1932, starring Marlene Dietrich, Clive Brook, and Anna May Wong

Blonde Venus, 1932, starring Marlene Dietrich, Herbert Marshall, and Cary Grant

The Devil is a Woman, 1935, starring Marlene Dietrich, Lionel Atwell, and Edward Everett Horton

(Cooper) while being pursued by a wealthy playboy (Menjou). In a groundbreaking scene, Dietrich performs her cabaret act dressed in a man's top hat and tails, then kisses a woman on the lips. The film is dense with atmosphere and sexual tension.

■ **The Scarlet Empress**, 1934, starring Marlene Dietrich

Dietrich plays Catherine the Great as an innocent princess who is corrupted. Transformed into a sexual predator, she pits rival lovers against each other. The film is Sternberg's most stylized.

Josef von Sternberg

John Huston

1906, Nevada–1987, Middletown

■ Maverick writer and director of Hollywood classics ■ Directed films about tough guys in moral dilemmas ■ *The Maltese Falcon* is considered first film noir ■ Defined screen persona of Humphrey Bogart ■ 14-time Oscar nominee ■ American ■ Film Noir, Drama, Adventure ■ Directed 38 films

■ **1906** Born in Missouri

1921 Leaves school to become a boxer

1925 Broadway acting debut

1937 Hired as a writer by Warner Brothers

1941 Directs first film, *The Maltese Falcon*

1943–45 Makes wartime documentaries

1949 Two Oscars for *The Treasure of the Sierra Madre*

1972 Revives career with boxing drama *Fat City*

1987 Last film, *The Dead*

1987 Dies in Rhode Island

■ **The Maltese Falcon**, 1941, starring Humphrey Bogart and Mary Astor

This detective film is considered the first example of film noir. Hired to locate the jewel-encrusted statuette of a falcon, private eye Sam Spade (Bogart) finds himself up against eccentric crooks and a classic femme fatale (Astor). Huston used daring camera work, including a seven-minute scene shot in a single take. Bogart's cynical role as Spade made him a star.

John Huston was an eccentric rebel whose adventurou life rivaled the stories of his films. His early work as a actor and screenwriter primed him for filmmaking and h directed both his father Walter and daughter Angelica their Oscar-winning roles. His own acting career includ films such as Roman Polanski's (p. 296) Neo-Noir *Chin town* (1974). Huston's films starred misfits caught in co plex moral dilemmas. He often wrote the lean, fast-pace scripts himself and had a disdain for happy ending Huston was renowned for his recklessness and hard livin He delayed the Uganda location shoot for *The Africa Queen* when he left to go elephant hunting. His care was revived in the 1970s with his adaptation of Kiplin adventure tale *The Man Who Would Be King* (1975).

Cinema During the War 1930–1945

Prizzi's Honor, 1985, starring Jack Nicholson and Kathleen Turner

Huston's career faltered in the 1960s, but he rebounded with a string of critical hits. This black comedy tells the story of two mafia assassins (Nicholson and Turner) who fall in love even though they have been hired to kill each other. The film's plot touches on classic Huston themes of moral dilemma and personal honor.

The Treasure of the Sierra Madre, 1948, starring Humphrey Bogart and Walter Huston

This classic adventure story set in Mexico focused on the corrosive power of greed. A penniless American, Fred C. Dobbs (Bogart), joins forces with two drifters to mine for gold. They strike it rich, but Dobbs starts to distrust the other men. His paranoia grows into madness, and the three partners turn on each other. Huston's light touch keeps the story moving through gripping sequences to a bitter and ironic conclusion.

Other Works

Key Largo, 1948, starring Humphrey Bogart and Lauren Bacall

The African Queen, 1951, starring Humphrey Bogart and Katharine Hepburn

The Misfits, 1961, starring Clark Gable and Marilyn Monroe

John Huston

Propaganda

■ Dramas and documentaries were to sway audience opinion ■ Used to build support for government policies ■ Often blended documentary footage with staged recreations ■ Music and narration magnified emotional response
■ Techniques later adopted by commercial advertisers
■ *left*: **Jude Süss**, by Veit Harlan, 1940, starring Ferdinand Marian

1915 D. W. Griffith's *The Birth of a Nation* honors the creation of the racist Ku Klux Klan

1917 Vladimir Lenin creates the Soviet office of propaganda

1918 US Army makes *America Goes Over* to build support for WWI

1925 Sergei Eisenstein's *Battleship Potemkin* dramatizes czarist repression

1935 Leni Riefenstahl's *Triumph of the Will* uses images and music to portray Hitler as a Nazi messiah

1939 The Ministry of Information is created in the UK to oversee wartime propaganda

1940 Charlie Chaplin attacks Hitler with comedy in *The Great Dictator*

1941–47 US Office of War Information makes over 200 propaganda films

Other Works

Reefer Madness, by Louis J. Gasnier, 1936, starring Dorothy Short and Kenneth Craig

Duck and Cover, by Anthony Rizzo, 1952

An Inconvenient Truth, by Davis Guggenheim, 2006

Propaganda films are designed to influence the opinion and behavior of their audience. The rise of totalitarian governments in the 1930s brought a golden age of propaganda filmmaking and Leni Riefenstahl's (p. 142) *Triumph of the Will* (1935) set a new standard. After the outbreak of World War II, Allied governments rushed to catch up. Alexander Korda produced his pro–UK feature *The Lion Has Wings* (1939) in less than a month to convince his government of the value of propaganda films. Soon after, the British and Americans created offices to produce wartime propaganda. Techniques developed during this time found their way into Cold War propaganda films and TV advertising. American director Michael Moore is leading a new generation of political filmmakers who often blur truth and fiction. Though his films are controversial, he won an Oscar for *Bowling for Columbine* (2002).

■ **Veit Harlan: Jude Süss**, 1940, starring Ferdinand Marian and Werner Krauss

The Nazi government produced this drama to justify their anti-Semitic policies. A greedy Jewish banker, Joseph "Süss" Oppenheimer (Marian), corrupts a duke with promises of riches. Süss embezzles funds and rapes a wholesome German girl. Director Veit Harlan shows Süss as a stereotyped Jew with hooked nose and greasy hair. The film sparked anti-Jewish violence when released in France.

Frank Capra and Anatole Litvak: Why We Fight: The Battle of Russia, 1943–45

This series of seven films was America's response to Nazi wartime propaganda. Capra enlisted Hollywood's finest to help convince the nation to join the fight against fascism. Dramatic narration and music were added to documentary footage and Walt Disney provided animated graphics. The first film, *Prelude to War,* won an Oscar.

Ilya Kopalin and Leonid Varlamov: Moscow Strikes Back, 1942, narrated by Edward G. Robinson

This Oscar-winning documentary records the Soviet army's counterattack that drove the invading Nazi army from Moscow in December 1941. The moving and sometimes gruesome footage was shot by frontline Russian cameramen and edited for American audiences. Soviet soldiers battle the Germans in the streets, while heroic Muscovites lend their support. The retreating Nazis leave a path of destruction with whole towns leveled and innocent civilians killed. The film includes shots of frozen, mutilated corpses. Many Americans distrusted their Soviet allies, so the film was designed to build sympathy and support for them, but during the postwar era the filmmakers were accused by a Senate committee of being Communist sympathizers.

Leni Riefenstahl

1902, Berlin–2003, Pöcking

■ Influential female director ■ Made landmark propaganda films for the Nazi Party ■ Pioneered techniques in sports photography ■ Used expressive camera angles ■ Nazi past thwarted her career ■ Directed last documentary at age 9* ■ German ■ Documentary, Drama ■ Directed 7 films

1902 Born Helene Bertha Amalie Riefenstahl

1926 Acts in first film, *The Holy Mountain*

1932 Directs *The Blue Light*

1932 Meets Adolf Hitler at a Nazi rally

1933–35 Films Nazi rallies

1936 Films the summer Olympic games in Berlin

1945–49 Held in a French prisoner of war camp

1949–2000 Unable to get funding for films due to her Nazi past, she takes up photography

2002 Last film, *Underwater Impressions*, premiers

2003 Dies in Germany

A former actress, Leni Riefenstahl turned to directing with the melodrama *The Blue Light*. Adolf Hitler admired the film and asked Riefenstahl to create the landmark documentaries *Triumph of the Will* and *Olympia*. In 1940, she directed the Spanish drama *Lowlands* (released in 1954) for which she used concentration camp inmates as extras. For 6 years, Riefenstahl's Nazi past prevented her from making films, but she managed to direct *Underwater Impressions*, at the age of 99.

■ **Olympia**, 1938

Riefenstahl called her documentary about the 1936 summer Olympic Games a celebration of the athletic body. She used low camera angles, slow motion, and even underwater cameras to catch nuances of movement. She also pioneered the use of tracking shots with cameras mounted on rails to follow alongside runners. The film is divided into two sections. *Part I: Festival of the People* opens with a poetic recreation of the ancient games in Greece with Riefenstahl herself as a nude runner. *Part II: Festival of Beauty* includes a montage of the diving competition using dramatic camera angles.

Cinema During the War 1930–1945

Triumph of the Will, 1935

[Ri]fenstahl's film portrait of the [193]4 Nazi Party rally in Nurem[ber]g is a milestone of propa[gan]da filmmaking. She had the [sta]dium designed as a giant [film] set and choreographed [row]s of soldiers to her camera's [mo]vements. Riefenstahl used [30] cameras to record the event, [som]e mounted on airplanes [and] rolling tracks to capture [dra]matic angles. Sixty-one [hou]rs of footage were edited [into] a two-hour film. Hitler's [spe]eches are cut with shots of [his] adoring listeners, backed by [stir]ring Wagnerian music. The [film] won top prizes at festivals [but] was banned in many coun[trie]s for promoting the Nazis.

Olympia, 1938

The 1936 Olympic Games were meant to celebrate the Third Reich, and *Olympia* is seen by many as Nazi propaganda. However, the film also documents the athletic triumphs of African-American runner Jesse Owens and Hitler's shock as Owens wins his fourth gold medal.

Other Works

The Blue Light, 1932, starring Leni Riefenstahl and Mathias Wieman

The Victory of Belief, 1933

Lowlands, 1954, starring Leni Riefenstahl and Bernhard Minetti

Underwater Impressions, 2002

Leni Riefenstahl

Jean Renoir

1894, Paris–1979, Los Angeles

■ Lyrically examined social struggles in his novels and films ■ Revealed character through subtle details ■ Used extended takes and deep focus
■ One of the masters of Poetic Realism
■ French-American ■ Drama, Comedy ■ Directed 37 films

1894 Born in France

1925 Directs first film, *Whirlpool of Fate*

1935–39 Writes and directs a string of classic films in France

1941 Escapes France during German invasion and settles in the US

1945 Collaborates with William Faulkner on Hollywood film *The Southerner*

1962 Publishes memoir, *Renoir, My Father*

1971 Last film, *The Little Theater of Jean Renoir*

1979 Dies in Los Angeles

Jean Renoir is among cinema's greatest filmmakers. A writer, actor, and director, he examined the great soc struggles of his times with a gentle, lyrical style. In *Bou Saved from Drowning*, a Parisian bookseller brings hor a tramp who wreaks havoc in the bourgeois househo Renoir's support for the left-wing Popular Front par inspired his film *The Crime of Monsieur Lange* (1936) abc a worker punished for creating a labor union. His Wo War I drama *Grand Illusion* (1937) shows how the conf changed Europe's social order. Renoir used subtle came movements and long shots to give a sense of intima and reveal character. In his later years, he retired fro filmmaking and wrote novels, plays, and the definiti biography of his father, the Impressionist painter Pier Auguste Renoir.

Cinema During the War 1930–1945

he Rules of the Game, 9, starring Nora Gregor and cel Dalio

romantic farce is a subver-portrait of the French g class. The film unfolds ng a week at the country or of Robert, a Jewish aris-at, and his wife, Christine. ove triangles develop, oir's camera glides through house revealing the inter-ng stories, often showing plots unfolding in a single e. In the end, love forces of the players to break the es of the game."

■ **The Human Beast**, 1938, starring Jean Gabin and Simone Simon

Adapted from a novel by Émile Zola, *The Human Beast* antici-pates the 1940s' film noirs.

Other Works

Boudu Saved from Drowning, 1932, starring Michel Simon

French Cancan, 1954, starring Jean Gabin

The Doctor's Horrible Experiment, 1959, starring Jean-Louis Barrault

Jacques (Gabin) falls in love with Séverine (Simon), the wife of his co-worker. After the seduction, Séverine tries to convince Jacques to murder her husband. Renoir used plot devices and character types later found in the Hollywood film noirs—Séverine is a classic femme fatale, manipu-lating men with her sexuality and Jacques is an innocent man who commits terrible crimes because of his lust. The film is foreboding and has dramatic shots of roaring trains, symbol-izing the forces of destiny driving Jacques toward self-destruction.

Jean Renoir

René Clair

1898, Paris—1981, Neuilly-sur-Seine

■ Revered screenwriter and director with lyrical style ■ Directed classic romantic tales set in Paris ■ Inventive use of music and sound ■ Fled to Ame to escape Nazi occupation ■ Directed hit films in the UK and Hollywood
■ French ■ Drama, Comedy ■ Directed 24 films

■ **1898** Born in Paris
1924 Collaborates with Dada artist Francis Picabia on *Entr'acte*
1930–34 Directs seven romantic films that are set in Paris
1935 Makes his first English language film, *The Ghost Goes West*
1942 Moves to Hollywood and directs five films
1947 Returns to France
1965 Directs last film, *The Lace Wars*
1981 Dies in France

René Clair was French cinema's first great auteur v wrote and directed films with his own romantic, lyr style. His first short film was the surrealist collage images *Entr'acte*. The silent film was created to acco pany a ballet, and Clair later incorporated music a singing into his early sound films. In his satire on m ernization, *Freedom for Us* (1931), his characters surrounded by music, including commentary fr singing flowers. Rather than recreating naturalistic sou Clair used both music and sound effects as counterpo to his visuals. Clair set his early films in Paris and portra the city in a sweet and romantic light. After France invaded by Nazi Germany in World War II, Clair flec

Hollywood where he had a succes career. He returned to France a he and today the prestigious film aw from the Académie Française be his name.

■ **Under the Roofs of Paris**, 1930, starring Albert Préjean and Pola Illéry

A collection of romantic vignettes set in the crowded tenements of Paris. Two men vie for attention of a beautiful woman, Pola. Albert is street singer and Fred is a petty thief, but Albe gets arrested instead of Fred and Pola falls in l with Albert's best friend. Clair rebelled against technical restrictions of early sound technolo and shot most scenes silently, later adding a musical score. Silent films could use moving c eras as they weren't weighed down by the ne technology, and he created several imaginati tracking shots.

Cinema During the War 1930–1945

I Married a Witch, 1942, starring Veronica Lake, Fredric March, and Susan Hayward

the 1690s, a Massachusetts landowner condemns a witch to burn at the stake. About 250 years later, she returns in the form of sultry Veronica Lake to take revenge on his descendant, Wallace Wooley (March). Fate turns the tables on the vengeful witch and soon the two are married. Clair enlivened the plot with fast pacing and clever special effects.

Other Works
Entr'acte, 1924, starring Francis Picabia, Man Ray, and Marcel Duchamp
The Crazy Ray, 1925, starring Henri Rollan and Charles Martinelli
The Million, 1931, starring Annabella and René Lefèvre
The Ghost Goes West, 1935, starring Robert Donat and Jean Parker

Bastille Day, 1933, starring Annabella and George aud

modest flower seller falls in e with her neighbor, a taxi driver. They spend an idyllic evening together at Paris's Bastille Day festivities, but dark secrets in his past come back to haunt him. The film is a poetic elegy to young romance with a loose, free-flowing plot. Clair found humor and pathos in the lives of ordinary Parisians and their daily struggles.

René Clair

Marcel Carné

1906, Paris–1996, Clamart

■ Master of Poetic Realism ■ Used metaphor and symbolism to comment on daily life ■ Made films critical of German occupation during WWII ■ Worked with screenwriter Jacques Prevért ■ Later criticized by the French New Wave ■ French ■ Drama, Fantasy ■ Directed 20 films

1906 Born in France

1929 Directs the short documentary *Nogent, Eldorado du Dimanche*

1930 Assists René Clair on *Under the Roofs of Paris*

1936–46 Works with Jacques Prévert on seven films

1944 Directs *Children of Paradise* during Allied bombing

1946 *Gates of the Night*, his last film with Prévert, is a failure

1958 Last hit, *The Cheaters*, is critiqued by François Truffaut

1996 Dies in France

With Jean Renoir (p. 144) and René Clair (p. 146), Marcel Carné was a master of Poetic Realism. Beginning with *Hôtel du Nord*, he romanticized the struggles of everyday life with symbolism and theatrical artifice. His 10-year collaboration with the poet and screenwriter Jacques Prévert resulted in a series of stylish classics, culminating in the masterpiece *Children of Paradise*. Carné produced his best films during the German occupation of France and the hardships of World War II. While working under the Nazi-installed Vichy government, he managed to subvert their attempts to control his art. By using subtle metaphors in his films, he supported the struggle for liberation. After the war, Carné fell out of fashion and his films lost their popular appeal. The young generation of New Wave film makers rebelled against Carné's style of artificial, studio-bound films in favor of confrontational realism.

■ **Children of Paradise**, 1945, starring Arletty, Jean-Louis Barrault, and Pierre Brasseur

This romantic epic, set in the theater world of Paris around 1835, tells several interlocking stories and shows the interplay between theater and real life. Garance (Arletty) is caught in a love triangle with the naive mime Baptiste (Barrault) and the roguish actor Frédérick (Brasseur). Despite filming during WWII, Carné managed to build elaborate sets and fill them with costumed extras.

■ **The Devil's Envoys**, 1942, starring Arletty, Marie Déa, and Alain Cuny

Two emissaries of the devil, Gilles (Cuny) and Dominique (Arletty), arrive at the castle of Baron Hugues to steal the souls of his family. The Baron's daughter Anne (Déa) is so pure of heart that she turns Gilles against the devil (Jules Berry). This fairy tale was a metaphor for France's struggle against Hitler. Carné used slow motion to create a dreamlike feel that centers around the troubles of love and loss—typical of Poetic Realism.

Other Works

enny, 1936, starring Françoise Rosay and Albert Préjean

Hôtel du Nord, 1938, starring Annabella and Jean-Pierre Aumont

Port of Shadows, 1938, starring Jean Gabin and Michel Simon

Daybreak, 1939, starring an Gabin, Jules Berry, and letty

is moody contemporary agedy established Carné's distinctive visual style. The plot nters around a good-hearted risian factory worker (Gabin), no commits murder to free a ung woman he loves from r aging seducer. He waits in s apartment to be arrested at ybreak. Filled with romantic spair, the film is an expres- n of the spiritual turmoil in ance on the eve of WWII.

Marcel Carné

Postwar Cinema and the 1950s

"Apparently the only performance that will satisfy you is when I play dead."

Alfred Hitchcock: North by Northwest, 1959, USA, starring Cary Grant
Quote: Cary Grant as Roger Thornhill in *North by Northwest*

Postwar Cinem.

Masters of Noir

Steeped in wartime pessimi
film noir's directors pictured
femme fatales and dogged
tectives playing cat-and-mo
games in its shadowy scene

Robert Aldrich
Henri-Georges Clouzot
Jules Dassin
Edward Dmytryk
Charles Laughton
Ida Lupino

p. 165

1944　　　　1946　　　　1948　　　　1950

Hollywood Directors

Genre films made in Hollywood during the
postwar era feature exuberant dancing, desert
shoot-outs, thrillers, and trapped housewives

and the 1950s

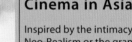

Cinema in Asia

Inspired by the intimacy of Neo-Realism or the grand scale of the western, the work of Asian directors revealed sensibilities that tantalized critics and directors worlds away

Postwar Cinema and the 1950s

A New Beginning

European directors, cinematographers, and screenwriters fled the Nazi regime and took refuge in the United States, often bringing an Expressionist style, characterized by dramatic shadows, deep focus, and a less black-and-white approach to morality. Their film noirs were cheap B-movies, but their heroes were not immediately sympathetic and their villains not as obviously identified. Darker motivations were at work as protagonists found themselves led by sexual desires and obsessions. Noir filmmakers were often influenced, as Alfred Hitchcock was, by Freudian psychoanalysis. The cold-blooded femme fatales and tough-talking detectives in *The Maltese Falcon* (1941), *Double Indemnity*, and *In A Lonely Place* (1950) became icons, inspiring Neo-Noirs and enriching Hollywood characterization.

■ **Billy Wilder: Double Indemnity**, 1944, starrin Fred MacMurray and Barbara Stanwyck

■ **John Wayne**, actor and icon

Douglas Sirk:
Imitation of Life,
1959, starring Lana
Turner

Ed Wood Jr.:
Plan 9 from Outer
Space, 1959,
starring Maila
"Vampira" Nurmi
and Bela Lugosi

Reinventing Genres

With the success of drive-in cinemas, low-budget film-makers started making inventive horror films, such as Jacques Tourneur's *I Walked with a Zombie* (1943), and also misbegotten horror/science-fiction hybrids such as Ed Wood Jr.'s *Plan 9 from Outer Space*. Threatened by TV, studios used bigger, brighter canvases. The wide-screen and Technicolor formats boasted biblical epics like Henry Koster's *The Robe* (1953) and came alive with Gene Kelly's exuberant musicals and John Ford's later, more desolate work. Whereas the western genre, and its greatest star, John Wayne, once provided harmless entertainment at history's expense, the genre took a darker turn in the 1950s. Hollywood's "women's pic-tures" also became more subversive; Douglas Sirk's unrealistically happy endings signaled for the first time, as David Lynch and Tim Burton would in the 1980s, that something was rotten in pastel-hued suburbia.

Postwar Europe

In Europe, the postwar devastation inspired film-making. French filmmakers, like Jean-Pierre Melville, Louis Malle, and Henri-Georges Clouzot, started to make excruciatingly tense, dark thrillers. Their precursor Jean Cocteau's films reached back into Georges Méliès's bag of tricks to create sumptuous films about the power of illusion. His *Beauty and the Beast* is a miraculous cinematic experience, much more Freudian than Disney's. The Beast's castle and Jean Marais's sultry performance slowly charm Belle to the point that she seems disappointed when she is confronted with the prince at the film's end. Marlene Dietrich agreed, shouting at one screening: "Give me back my Beast!" In response to flashy performances, director Robert Bresson's much drier style, exemplified in *Pickpocket*, called for his actors to stop acting, and simply model his parables about redemption.

New Realities

In Italy, Roberto Rossellini and Vittorio De Sica similarly created a new kind of cinema. Their Neo-Realist style was informed by a need to document the stories of regular Italians. After Rosselini's influential *Rome, Open City*, about Rome's resistance fighters, Federico Fellini and Luchino Visconti went on to make more stunningly styled films. Rossellini, with his muse Ingrid Bergman, made films like *Europa '51* (1952) and *Journey to Italy*

(1954), which only later were recognized as masterpieces of understatement. In India, Satyajit Ray made Neo-Realism his own while Mehboob Khan and Raj Kapoor launched Bollywood. Japan's industry was also reborn and Western audiences were introduced to the fluid films of Kenji Mizoguchi and Akira Kurosawa. Yasujiro Ozu had been making films since the 1920s, but his portraits of the modern Japanese family have proven timeless.

John Ford

1895, Cape Elizabeth–1973, Palm Desert

■ Won six Oscars, more than any other director ■ Made silent and sound film
shorts, and documentaries ■ Immigrant background influenced subject matt‹
■ Worked with John Wayne on 24 films ■ Greatly influenced Orson Welles
■ American ■ Western, Drama ■ Directed 122 films

1895 Born Sean Aloysius O'Feeney to immigrants

1915 Uncredited role as an actor in D. W. Griffith's *The Birth of a Nation*

1917 Directs his first feature for Universal, *The Tornado*, as Jack Ford

1923 First uses the professional name John Ford for *Hoodman Blind*

1934 Lieutenant commander of the US Naval Reserve, beginning his important association with the military

1935 Wins his first Oscar for *The Informer*

1966 Last film, *7 Women*

1973 Dies in California

A true veteran of the film business, John Ford made
large number of silent films, of which but few survive, a
won Oscars in the 1930s and '40s (for *The Grapes of Wra*
and the Welsh coal-mining saga *How Green Was I
Valley*). His best remembered works, however, are ›
westerns with John Wayne, who worked with him for o‹
35 years on 24 films such as *Stagecoach* and *The Man W‹
Shot Liberty Valance*. Ford's work was thus most influe‹
tial in the techniques he introduced in that most Am‹
ican of genres, the western. He was a master of t‹
extreme long shot, a panoramic style perfectly suited
the dramatic desert setting of Ford's favorite locatic‹
Utah's Monument Valley. Though his early work suff‹
from a simplistic, offensive portrayal of Native Americ‹
his message was always sympathetic to immigrant s‹
tlers, perhaps stemming from his Irish background.

Other Works

Stagecoach, 1939, starring Claire Trevor and John Wayne

How Green Was My Valley, 1941, starring Walter Pidgeon and Maureen O'Hara

The Quiet Man, 1952, starring John Wayne and Maureen O'Hara

The Man Who Shot Liberty Valance, 1962, starring John Wayne, James Stewart, and Vera Miles

■ **The Grapes of Wrath**, 1940
starring Henry Fonda and Jane
Darwell

Based on John Steinbeck's boo‹
set during the Great Depressio‹
this film follows the Joad famil‹
on their trek from dusty Oklaho‹
to the promised land of Californ‹
The film, though naturalistically
shot, lacks the biting social awa‹
ness and political edge of the
book, and instead creates a mo‹
neutral homage to simple peop‹
and their struggles, which was
in keeping with Ford's humanis‹
ideology.

◀ My Darling Clementine, 1946, starrring Henry Fonda and Victor Mature

When the Earp brothers take a break during their cattle drive to California in the lawless town of Tombstone, their cattle are stolen and their youngest brother is killed. Wyatt Earp, played by the elegant Henry Fonda, vows to avenge his brother and takes the position of sheriff in an attempt to bring order to this lonely corner of the Wild West. Unlike Ford's *The Searchers*, this revenge story, which is centered around the famous shoot-out at the OK Corral, focuses less on violent plot mechanics than on the romance between Earp and bank robber Doc Holliday's old flame Clementine from Boston. The film's central juxtaposition of civilization and primitivism is reenacted in her choice between the sheriff and the robber.

The Searchers, 1956, starring John Wayne and Natalie Wood

Ford's most morally complex film, John Wayne stars as Ethan, a bitter Civil War veteran who returns home to find that his brother has married the woman Ethan loved. When a Comanche attack kills his entire family, Ethan is driven on an epic quest to find his abducted niece (Wood), vowing to kill her should she have become an "Indian." When finally confronted with his niece, he scalps her Indian chief husband Scar, but can not bring himself to kill her. Realizing the extent of his racist hate, Ethan wanders into the desert at the end, alone again. Ford's study of the dangerous lure of revenge is considered his masterpiece, and the film was his first to really address racism against Native Americans.

John Ford

Fred Zinnemann

1907, Vienna–1997, London

■ Won four Oscars and directed 19 Oscar-nominated performances ■ Inspired by documentary filmmaker Robert J. Flaherty ■ Strived for authenticity through location shooting and use of nonactors ■ Brought Neo-Realism to studio films ■ Austrian-American ■ Varied genres ■ Directed 22 films

1907 Born into a Jewish family
1929 Works with Billy Wilder and Robert Siodmak in Germany
1935 First feature film
1945 Is replaced by Vincente Minnelli on *The Clock*
1948 Postwar Germany on-location shooting of *The Search*
1951 Wins his first Oscar for his short film *Benjy*
1955 Pioneers the widescreen Todd-AO format for *Oklahoma!*
1982 His final film as director, *Five Days One Summer*
1997 Dies in London

After seeing the films of King Vidor (p. 52), Sergei Eisenstein (p. 64), and Erich von Stroheim (p. 78), Fred Zinnemann left Vienna to enroll in the Technical School for Cinematography in Paris. Trained as a cameraman, he moved to Hollywood where he met documentary filmmaker Robert J. Flaherty (p. 82) and discovered his calling as a director. In 1935, Zinnemann filmed *The Wave* in Mexico, an affecting tale of a fisherman who pays with his life when he sets out to start a union. Shot with only nonactors, this film predates Luchino Visconti's (p. 208) similar Neo-Realist *The Earth Trembles* by 13 years, but shares its commitment to Social Realism. The film attracted the attention of MGM, where Zinnemann began directing shorts, alongside future greats such as Jacques Tourneur and Jules Dassin, and went on to make his most famous films applying his Neo-Realist style to just about any genre.

■ **From Here to Eternity**, 1953, starring Burt Lancaster, Montgomery Clift, and Deborah Kerr

Set on the eve of the Pearl Harbor attack, *From Here to Eternity* depicts the intersecting lives of a scrupulous outsider, his best friend (Oscar-winner Frank Sinatra), their sergeant, and a promiscuous armywife (Kerr, cast against her usual "type"). The iconic love scene on the beach and a long take of a knife fight in an alley showcase Zinnemann's masterful editing and pacing.

Postwar Cinema and the 1950s

Other Works

The Search, 1948, starring Montgomery Clift and Aline MacMahon

The Nun's Story, 1959, starring Audrey Hepburn and Peter Finch

A Man for All Seasons, 1966, starring Paul Scofield, Wendy Hiller, Robert Shaw, and Orson Welles

Oklahoma!, 1955, starring irley Jones and Rod Steiger

sed on the 1943 musical by dgers and Hammerstein no also worked on *The Sound Music*) about cowboys

High Noon, 1952, starring y Cooper and Grace Kelly

ntier marshal Will Kane, yed by Gary Cooper, is about resign and go on his honey- on when he learns a criminal n his way to settle a score h him. Even though the ire town deserts him, he ooses to stay and fight, and film turns into a tense, ost real-time countdown to n. Adding to the tension, oper's Quaker wife (Kelly) mately has to choose ween her pacifist religion her husband's life. Zinne- nn's favorite subject is the is of conscience, whether it tains to the public or the pri- e sphere. Among the film's Oscars was one for Cooper, another for the expert ting, which deftly speeds up slows down the film's sup- edly real-time pacing, show- ed in the film's climax.

courting farm girls, *Oklahoma!* is Zinnemann's only musical. Though it was the first film shot using the high-definition 70 mm Todd-AO wide-screen camera, Zinnemann also shot the film on 35 mm Cinema-

Scope to ensure that all thea- ters would be capable of screening it. Unlike most screen musicals of the time, the orig- inal play was not cut for time and instead was so long that it included an intermission.

Fred Zinnemann

Nicholas Ray

1911, Galesville—1979, New York

■ His formal training as an architect infused his films with a strong sense of space ■ Preferred stories about outcasts and loners ■ Revered by French directors Jean-Luc Godard, François Truffaut, and Jacques Rivette ■ American ■ Film Noir, Drama, Western ■ Directed 20 films

■ **1911** Born Raymond Kienzle in Wisconsin

1929 Studies architecture at Frank Lloyd Wright's art colony

1945 Assists Elia Kazan on his *A Tree Grows In Brooklyn*

1946 His only musical for stage, Duke Ellington's *Beggar's Holiday*

1961 First big-budget epic *King of Kings*

1963 Collapses on the set of *55 Days at Peking*, his last studio film

1973 His experimental, unfinished *You Can't Go Home Again* screens at Cannes

1979 Dies in New York

Other Works

They Live by Night, 1948, starring Farley Granger and Cathy O'Donnell

The Lusty Men, 1952, starring Susan Hayward, Robert Mitchum, Arthur Kennedy, and Arthur Hunnicutt

Run for Cover, 1955, starring James Cagney and Viveca Lindfors

King of Kings, 1961, starring Jeffrey Hunter and Siobhan McKenna

"Cinema is Nicholas Ray" wrote Jean-Luc Godard (p. 2 in the film magazine *Cahiers du Cinéma*. The French N Wave directors appreciated Ray's expressionistic, a often far from realistic, use of color and framing more th American audiences, who criticized Ray's blending genres. His films usually feature loner protagonists, su as James Dean in *Rebel Without a Cause* or Joan Crawfo in *Johnny Guitar*. With regards to style, Ray said training as an architect made him more aware of t importance of space during his 15-year career. His stu ning use of the wide-screen CinemaScope format—whi allowed for the width of the picture to be twice as wide usual—exemplifies his strong sense of horizontal co position. Ray was often pressured to direct certain typ of films by his studio, but his personal projects a renowned for their fluidity and subversive visual force

■ **Johnny Guitar**, 1954, starrin Joan Crawford and Mercedes McCambridge

Crawford plays a saloon owner who refuses to be driven out of town by a jealous frontier town woman who incites an angry m against her for a murder she di not commit. Though Crawford assisted by the title character, P focuses on the battle between two women. Modern critics and filmmakers like Martin Scorsese praise this proto-feminist weste for its flamboyant imagery and innovative characterizations.

Rebel Without a Cause,
[19]55, starring James Dean and
[Na]talie Wood

[In] *Rebel Without a Cause* Dean
[sta]rs as a troubled teenager
[ne]w to Los Angeles. After an
[arr]est for drunkenness, he
[bo]nds with Natalie Wood and
[th]e adoring Sal Mineo at the
[po]lice station. After a fight with
[th]e school bully, who gets killed
[in t]he film's famous game of
[chi]cken, the three teens hide at
[an] abandoned mansion, briefly
[pla]ying at being a family,
[be]fore events conspire to the
[film]'s tragic showdown. From
[the] film's tilted opening shot,
[Ra]y composes his story beauti-
[full]y, making dramatic use of
[Cin]emaScope's wide-screen.

■ **In a Lonely Place**, 1950,
starring Humphrey Bogart and
Gloria Grahame

Bogart plays a jaded screenwriter
accused of murder. His neighbor,
played by Ray's estranged wife

Gloria Grahame, gives him an
alibi, and he falls for her. When
she starts to doubt his innocence, tempers flare. Typical of
film noir, the characters cannot
escape their own troubled
psyches.

Nicholas Ray

Singin' in the Rain

■ by Stanley Donen and Gene Kelly, USA, 1952, Musical

Singin' in the Rain traces the evolution of the film industry from silent to sound. Set in Hollywood, 1927, Gene Kelly plays Don Lockwood, a talented entertainer who grows to be a successful silent film actor, costarring with the dim-witted Lina Lamont (Jean Hagen). One night, he meets the down-to-earth showgirl Kathy Selden (Reynolds) and soon they fall in love. The success of the first talking picture, *The Jazz Singer* (1927), forces the studio to convert the latest Don and Lina film into a talkie. After a series of hilarious difficulties, a test screening proves that Lina's shrill voice grates the audience. Despite Kathy being unknown in Hollywood, Don and his friend Cosmo Brown (O'Connor) suggest Kathy dub Lina's voice for the film, and they set about writing a new musical version of the script that will prove a triumph for sound, and make Kathy a star.

Singin' in the Rain, 1952, starring Gene Kelly, Donald O'Connor, and Debbie Reynolds

Conceived as a "catalogue" musical of the composers' work, the writers framed the film around the arrival of sou[nd] in Hollywood. This decision w[as] enriched by the fact that ma[ny] of the film's crew had actuall[y] lived through this change in the industry.

Gene Kelly's prolific Hollywo[od] career reached its apex with [the] performance of the song *Sin[-] gin' in the Rain*, one of the m[ost] famous and vivacious acts in film history. The editing and c[a-] mera work emphasize how h[is] style is rooted more in pure athleticism than in Fred Asta[i-] re's learned style. O'Connor a[lso] shines in his hilarious "Make 'Em Laugh" dance, which us[es] little cutting and editing to accentuate the actor's athlet[ic] ability as a circus performer. In an ironic turn Debbie Reynolds's singing voice was actually dubbed for the film.

Postwar Cinema and the 1950s

Singin' in the Rain

Vincente Minnelli

1903, Chicago—1986, Los Angeles

- Highly aesthetic use of set design and choreography ■ Sets were inspired by modern art and his flowing camera work by Max Ophüls ■ Often worked with Gene Kelly, Fred Astaire, and Judy Garland ■ Admired by the French New Wave ■ American ■ Musical, Drama, Romantic Comedy ■ Directed 33 films

1903 Born into Illinois revue-show family

1931 Becomes a set and costume designer on Broadway

1943 Directs his first feature film, *Cabin in the Sky*

1945 After collaborating on *Meet Me in St. Louis*, he marries Judy Garland

1946 Daughter Liza is born

1951 Divorces Judy Garland

1958 Wins his only Oscar and Golden Globe, for *Gigi*

1976 First directs Liza in *A Matter of Time*, his last film

1986 Dies in California of Alzheimer's

Vincente Minnelli began his career performing in h family's touring revue from the age of three until he w eight. The lure of the theater drew him first to Chicag and later to New York's Broadway. He soon found work a set and costume designer on Broadway—an experienc that would greatly influence his films. In 1933, he starte working at Radio City Music Hall where he would make new show each month as producer and art director. Th talent for lavish entertainment is evident in his Hollywoo musicals, which epitomized the colorful escapism assoc ated with the genre. Inspired by Max Ophüls's flowin tracking shots, Minnelli used a crab dolly when filmin enabling his camera to turn in all directions, tracking h elaborate fantasy ballets (like in *Yolanda and the Thi* 1945, starring Fred Astaire) for which he often foun inspiration in modern and Surrealist art.

■ **The Bad and the Beautiful**, 1952, starring Lana Turner and Kirk Douglas

Told through flashbacks, Minnelli's most bitter, personal film deals with Hollywood hypocrisy and brutal ambition. Douglas's character was inspired by calculating movie producers and he plays a producer willing to do anything to get his film made—alienating his star, his director, and his screenwriter in the process.

Postwar Cinema and the 1950s

Designing

oman, 1957,
arring Gregory Peck, Lauren
call, and Dolores Gray

esigning Woman is about an
matched couple (Peck and
call) who only realize their
compatibility after they have
arried. Their story is further
mplicated by Peck's involve-
ment in a boxing promoter's
scam and Bacall's job as a
high-end fashion designer.
Screenwriter George Wells
won an Academy Award for
the screenplay and French
New Wave critic and director
Eric Rohmer praised Minnelli's
lavish work in this screwball
romantic comedy.

Other Works

The Pirate, 1948, starring Gene
Kelly and Judy Garland

An American in Paris, 1951,
starring Gene Kelly

Gigi, 1958, starring Leslie Caron

Some Came Running, 1959,
starring Frank Sinatra

■ **The Band Wagon**, 1953,
starring Fred Astaire and Cyd
Charisse

Minnelli's musical revolves
around an aging star making a
comeback in a Broadway version of *Faust*, in which he stars
opposite an upstart young ballerina. This classic film includes
the surreal "Triplets" number, as
well as "Girl Hunt Ballet," which
was inspired by Mickey
Spillane's hard-boiled detective
stories. Its song "That's Entertainment!" embodies Minnelli's
passion for show.

Vincente Minnelli

Billy Wilder

1906, Sucha—2002, Los Angeles

■ Winner of six Oscars ■ Introduced taboo subjects such as cross-dressing, alcoholism, and prostitution ■ Pioneered film noir techniques such as voice-over narration and chiaroscuro lighting
■ Austrian-American ■ Comedy, Drama, Film Noir ■ Directed 26 films

Though Wilder is perhaps best known for his witty and riotous romantic comedies starring Marilyn Monroe (like *The Seven Year Itch* and *Some Like It Hot*) and Audrey Hepburn (such as the 1954 *Sabrina* and 1957's *Love In The Afternoon*), his mastery extended far beyond that genre. Apart from a pioneering portrait of a tortured addict, *The Lost Weekend* (1945), a tense whodunit set in a World War II POW camp, *Stalag 17* (1953), and a terse satire about media exploitation, *Ace In The Hole* (1951), Wilder authored many of the key aspects of film noir in *Double Indemnity*. This film, about an insurance man conned into murder by a femme fatale (played with relish by Barbara Stanwyk), introduced the sardonic voice-over narration and the claustrophobic chiaroscuro lighting (creating high contrast images rich with mood and shadow), that came to typify the genre and are still used in Neo-Noirs.

Postwar Cinema and the 1950s

■ **The Apartment**, 1960, starring Jack Lemmon and Shirley MacLaine

A lonely office worker (Lemmon) is forced by a chain of superiors to lend them his apartment for their liaisons. When he finds elevator operator Shirley MacLaine passed out in his bed from an overdose, he cares for her and preserves his boss's secret. Even though its plot features an overdose and rampant adultery, Wilder's sad comedy was a wild success and won five Oscars.

■ **Sunset Boulevard**, 1950, starring Gloria Swanson and William Holden

Silent-film star Swanson stars as a deluded diva who kills the young screenwriter she hired to script her comeback. Upon her arrest, she mistakes the news cameras for a film set, saying "All right, Mr. DeMille, I'm ready for my close-up." Wilder co-wrote the film, which is narrated by Holden's character after his death. This noir is an indictment of the film industry and was an attempt at breaking down the illusions therein.

Other Works

Double Indemnity, 1944, starring Fred MacMurray, Barbara Stanwyck, and Edward G. Robinson

The Seven Year Itch, 1955, starring Marilyn Monroe and Tom Ewell

Irma La Douce, 1963, starring Jack Lemmon and Shirley MacLaine

Some Like It Hot, 1959, starring Tony Curtis and Marilyn Monroe

Two broke musicians attempt to escape pursuing gangsters by dressing up as women and joining an all-girl band. Things get complicated when Curtis falls for Monroe, the band's singer. Wilder uses gender confusion for full comedic effect. Now praised, the film was condemned for its sexual perversions.

Robert Wise

1914, Winchester—2005, Los Angeles

■ Orson Welles's editor on *Citizen Kane* ■ Influenced by B-movie producer ar[...]
screenwriter Val Lewton to embed a message in genre films ■ Remembered
for being an excellent craftsman, not an auteur ■ Mastered many genres
■ American ■ Musical, Science Fiction, Film Noir ■ Directed 39 films

1914 Born in Indiana

1933 Moves to California, where he finds work as a sound effects and music editor for RKO Studios

1935 Is sound editor on John Ford's *The Informer*

1942 Edits and reshoots parts of Orson Welles's *The Magnificent Ambersons* for RKO Studios while Welles is in Brazil

1944 Co-directs his first film, *The Curse of the Cat People*, with Val Lewton

1961 Wins his first Oscar for *West Side Story*

1965 Second Oscar for *The Sound of Music* after taking over from William Wyler

2000 His last film, *A Storm in Summer*, is made for TV

2005 Dies in Los Angeles

Starting out in Hollywood as a sound effects editor on *T[...]
Hat* (1935), Robert Wise worked his way up to editing filr[...]
by greats such as John Ford (p. 158), Orson Welles (p. 12[...]
and William Dieterle (*The Devil and Daniel Webste[...]
Despite learning several valuable lessons from these ma[...]
ters, Wise's greatest influence was always the producer [...]
his early genre films, Val Lewton, who was originally RH[...]
Studios' head of horror pictures. Lewton's knack for lo[...]
budget horror films with a strong dramatic and psych[...]
logical basis and sumptuous noir style, guided Wise in h[...]
dramatically and stylistically strongest early works wi[...]
dubious titles like *The Curse of the Cat People* (a 19[...]
sequel to Jacques Tourneur's luminous horror tale [...]
sexual repression *Cat People*) or the Boris Karloff–starri[...]
The Body Snatcher (1945). Widely acknowledged to be [...]
master editor and a chameleon of any genre, Wise's ea[...]
films carry the strongest authorial stamp, whereas h[...]
later blockbusters, like *West Side Story* (1961) and *T[...]
Sound of Music* lack an identifiable cohesive style.

■ **The Sound of Music**, 1965, starring Julie Andrews and Christopher Plummer

The story of the von Trapp fami[...]
and their governess resonates
with Rodgers and Hammerstein[...]
songs, while the constant threa[...]
of the Nazi regime creates a cou[...]
terpoint. Shot on location in Au[...]
tria, the film was Wise's most
enduring success and enabled
him more creative freedom.

Postwar Cinema and the 1950s

American Masters

The Day the Earth Stood Still, 1951, starring Michael Rennie and Patricia Neal

An alien lands on earth to warn humanity of the dangers of nuclear proliferation. Shot and wounded before he can pass along his peaceful message, he is forced to flee a government hospital. A few sympathetic humans at a boarding house understand his plight and help him send out his warning. Wise masterfully used the science fiction genre to package a cautionary tale about the arms race and its potentially disastrous effects. Bernard Herrman provided the film's futuristic score.

The Set-Up, 1949, starring Robert Ryan and Audrey Totter

After directing the classic film noir *Born to Kill*, Wise helmed this tense thriller about a has-been boxer unwilling to throw a match, oddly based on a long prose poem by Joseph Moncure March. Running almost in real time, the film is praised for its European-standard Realism and the tight editing of the fight scenes. Its influence can be felt in the storylines and settings of Quentin Tarantino's *Pulp Fiction* (1994), Martin Scorsese's *Raging Bull* (1980), and Stanley Kubrick's *The Killing* (1956).

Other Works

Born to Kill, 1947, starring Claire Trevor, Lawrence Tierney, and Walter Slezak	**I Want to Live!**, 1958, starring Susan Hayward, Simon Oakland, and Virginia Vincent
Blood on the Moon, 1948, starring Robert Mitchum and Barbara Bel Geddes	**Star Trek: The Motion Picture**, 1979, starring William Shatner and Leonard Nimoy

Robert Wise

TV, 3-D, and Drive-In Theaters

Experiments in the transmission of moving images started around the beginning of the 20th century, resulting in the first successful demonstration in London's Alexandra Palace in 1936. By 1945, TV had gained a foothold in the US, with nine stations on the air and about 7,000 sets in homes. By 1952, the number of sets had exploded to 20 million in the UK alone, and cinemas were noticing a marked drop in attendance. The success of the device and its programming caused Hollywood to counter with gimmicks such as Smell-O-Vision and 3-D, but also more lasting techniques such as wider screens (Cinema-Scope), better stereophonic sound, and wider screen storytelling. Still, the movie industry would never be as all-powerful as in 1930, when weekly attendance came to 65 percent of the entire population.

Long considered the Holy Grail of cinema, research in 3-D film is as old as film itself. The brain creates depth when two images are viewed separately and simultaneously by each eye. Projected images use stereoscopic film. Often thought as a fad, recent experiments by Steven Spielberg and James Cameron suggest a future for 3

The way we watch was further revolutionized with the drive-in theater. Invented in 1933, drive-ins thrived after World War II, and at the height of their popularity the US counted about 4,000. Drive-ins made moviegoing easier for both families with children and teenagers eager for privacy. At first the technology was simple—a sheet nailed to some trees, a radio blasting sound from behind—but in later days the theaters were outfitted with stereophonic sound transmitted via a low-power radio transmitter into each individual car. Television and sensitivity to weather later led to their drastic decline.

Postwar Cinema and the 1950s

DIE ZEITSCHRIFT FUR DEN HERRI

TV. 3-D. and Drive-In Theaters

Dramas

■ Term based on the word *melodrama* ■ Not so much a genre as a focus on humanity and its struggles ■ Heightened emotions and character development are central themes ■ Biographical dramas gained in popularity at the end of the 20th century

■ *left:* **Camille**, by George Cukor, 1936, starring Greta Garbo and Robert Taylor

1912 The first full-length drama, *Queen Elizabeth*, screens in New York

1919 Lillian Gish tragically falls for a Chinese man in D. W. Griffith's *Broken Blossoms*

1939 Bette Davis plays a dying socialite in the classic tearjerker *Dark Victory*

1959 John Cassavetes uses improvisation in his drama *Shadows*

1979 Sally Field tearfully receives her Oscar for *Norma Rae*

1985 Whoopi Goldberg performs in *The Color Purple*

1996 Tom Cruise apologizes in *Jerry Maguire*

Though the term *drama* now covers a spectrum of film as broad as the label *fiction* does in the world of literature, the current use derives from *melodrama*, a story in which emotions are heightened and character development is crucial. This broad definition mainly excludes genres like horror and action, but can include literary adaptations, costume films, or musicals, yet there are commercial tearjerkers whose stories are packed with breakdowns and good-byes. Contemporary world cinema features many dramas that simply deal with the struggles and joys of life. Often considered a "women's genre," dramas are indeed often set in the home and have complicated romantic plots, but just as often play out in courtrooms, locker rooms, or in army barracks. Though traditionally created with happy endings, bittersweet or unresolved endings are equally common today.

Other Works

Hiroshima, Mon Amour, by Alain Resnais, 1959, starring Emmanuelle Riva and Eiji Okada

Kramer vs. Kramer, by Robert Benton, 1979, starring Meryl Streep and Dustin Hoffman

The Shawshank Redemption, by Frank Darabont, 1994, starring Tim Robbins and Morgan Freeman

You Can Count on Me, by Kenneth Lonergan, 2000, starring Laura Linney

■ **Douglas Sirk: All That Heaven Allows**, 1955, starring Jane Wyman and Rock Hudson

This wildly successful drama explores the controversial love affair between an upper-class widow and her younger gardener. Though her college-age children and her suburban friends disapprove, she ultimately chooses love over conventionality. The film's tentatively happy ending does not hide the critique Sirk embedded in its portrayal of postwar suburbia. his style, with its pointed color-coding, emphasizes this.

Todd Haynes: Far From Heaven, 2002, starring Julianne Moore and Dennis Haysbert

Whereas older dramas could only hint at things the censors thought too controversial, Haynes reveals the full complexity of 1950s suburbia, making what Roger Ebert called "best and bravest movie of '57." Moore plays a housewife whose idyllic world crumbles when she sees her husband kissing another man. When she finds comfort in the arms of an African-American gardener, her community's ideas about relationships tear her life apart. Haynes's tribute extends beyond his choice in subjects to the film's look, which luminously reproduces Sirk's Technicolor studio sets and Ophüls's crane shots without a trace of irony.

■ **Max Ophüls: Letter from an Unknown Woman**, 1948, starring Joan Fontaine and Louis Jourdan

Letter from an Unknown Woman is about a woman's tragic, life-long love for a self-absorbed pianist, whose path she crossed three times. Told through her deathbed letter to him, flash-backs reveal her story, as he slowly realizes her identity. Famed for fluid long tracking and complex crane shots, Ophüls's style influenced Kubrick and Paul Thomas Anderson.

Dramas

Elia Kazan

1909, Constantinople (today Istanbul)—2003, New York

■ Co-founded New York's Actors Studio for Method acting ■ Introduced a masculinity that was vulnerable and powerful ■ Infamously denounced peop to McCarthy's anticommunist House Un-American Activities Committee ■ Turkish-American ■ Drama, Literary Adaptation ■ Directed 150 films

■ **1909** Born Elia Kazancıoğlu in what is today Istanbul

1913 Kazan's family moves to New York

1932 Apprentices at Lee Strasberg's Group Theater

1947 A bad review causes him to give up acting

1947 Wins his first Oscar for *Gentleman's Agreement*

1952 Testifies for McCarthy and denounces several so-called communists in the film industry

1976 Takes over for Mike Nichols on *The Last Tycoon*

1998 Honorary Academy Award for lifetime achievement gets mixed applause

2003 Dies in New York

A hugely successful stage director of the works of Te nessee Williams and Arthur Miller, Elia Kazan was a prop nent of a new, more naturalistic kind of acting. I co-founded the Actors Studio, whose "Method"—know as Method acting—was rooted in lived experiences, cr ating performances that might be less pretty and contr lable, but more vivid and unexpected. Kazan's legacy w to be forever soiled when he, a one-time ex-communi testified at McCarthy's hearings of the House Un-Am ican Activities Committee, effectively blacklisting eig Hollywood talents. Though he defended himself by d nouncing the horrors perpetrated by the Soviet Unio the liberal progressive director still felt misunderstoo *On the Waterfront* can be read as a reaction to the events, as Brando's protagonist is also ostracized f standing up for what he believes is right.

Other Works

A Tree Grows in Brooklyn, 1945, starring Dorothy McGuire

The Sea of Grass, 1947, starring Katharine Hepburn and Spencer Tracy

Gentleman's Agreement, 1947, starring Gregory Peck, Dorothy McGuire, and John Garfield

A Face in the Crowd, 1957, starring Andy Griffith

Splendor in the Grass, 1961, starring Natalie Wood and Warren Beatty

■ **East of Eden**, 1955, starrin James Dean and Jo Van Fleet

Two brothers struggle under domineering father and the revelation that their mother i prostitute. This lyrical Cinema Scope retelling of the biblical story of Cain and Abel featur a Method performance by James Dean as Cain, or Cal. Though some critics deemed the film too old-fashioned, se eral scenes seethe with a rag that is powerfully at odds wit the film's sumptuous tones a slow pacing.

On the Waterfront, 1954, starring Marlon Brando and Eva Marie Saint

...ndo plays the role of a former ...king champ who becomes ...olved with his brother's ...arious work. After Eva Marie ...nt's brother is killed for ...eatening to rat out the cor- ...t union leaders, she galva- ...s Brando to expose the ...pant corruption. Brando's ...hod acting shows in a scene ...which he improvised after ...nt's white glove falls on the ...und. By tenderly picking it ...and even trying it on, the ...cess of Brando's conversion ...n collaborating goon to so- ...y responsible man is beau- ...ly apparent. His transition ...minates in the classic scene in ...ch he and his brother under- ...edly debate Brando's deci- ... to speak out. Their Method ...formances turn what could ...e been a routine gangster ...ne into one rich with nuance ...d ingenuity.

FROM HORIZON PICTURES
AND
Columbia

**MARLON BRANDO
ON THE WATERFRONT**

AN ELIA KAZAN PRODUCTION

co-starring KARL MALDEN · LEE J. COBB

with ROD STEIGER · PAT HENNING and introducing EVA MARIE SAINT

Produced by SAM SPIEGEL

Screen Play by BUDD SCHULBERG · Music by LEONARD BERNSTEIN

Directed by ELIA KAZAN

■ **A Streetcar Named Desire**, 1951, starring Marlon Brando and Vivien Leigh

After Stella's sister Blanche arrives on her doorstep in steamy New Orleans, old secrets are revealed and slow-burning desires saturate the characters. Though the play was edited to avoid controversy, the final cut suffered even more edits. Still, Brando's performance and Tennessee Williams's words are powerful and its controversial topics of homosexuality, lust, and rape remain intact.

Elia Kazan

Richard Brooks

1912, Philadelphia–1992, Los Angeles

■ Nominated for eight Oscars ■ Contributed many scripts including several for Jules Dassin and John Huston ■ Admired for his Social Realist style and dependable budgeting ■ His work often deals with what drives people to viole[nce] ■ American ■ Drama, Film Noir, Literary Adaptation ■ Directed 24 films

Before serving for two years with the Marines in Wo[rld] War II, Brooks worked as a sports reporter for NBC a[nd] later branched out to stage directing and serial writing[.] Hollywood, after the war, he became a screenwriter [of] B-movies like Robert Siodmak's *Cobra Woman* (1944) a[nd] Jules Dassin's *Brute Force* (1947). The success of his d[i]script for John Huston's (p. 138) noir *Key Largo* (19[48]) enabled him to direct his own material. A Social Rea[list,] he often dealt with complex issues like free speech or c[ap]ital punishment and recurrently examined the moti[ve] behind violence. A true studio director at heart, Bro[oks] was known for never going over budget or over time [on] his films. Later in his career he went independent, mos[tly] adapting popular novels like Dostoevsky's *The Broth[ers] Karamazov* and Joseph Conrad's *Lord Jim*, but he ne[ver] quite reached the success he had before.

■ **In Cold Blood**, 1967, starring Robert Blake and Scott Wilson

Based on the nonfiction boo[k] by Truman Capote, *In Cold Blood* reconstructs the lead-[up] to the brutal murder of a Kan[sas] family and its dramatic aftermath. The stark black-and-wh[ite] visuals and geometric comp[osi]tions are by cinematographe[r] Conrad Hall. To reach a high[er] level of realism, Brooks filme[d] at original locations, casting actual hangman and original jury members.

Postwar Cinema and the 1950s

Cat on a Hot Tin Roof, [19]58, starring Elizabeth Taylor [an]d Paul Newman

[Bo]th Taylor and Newman were [Os]car-nominated for this [So]uthern drama about an alco[hol]ic (Newman) and his unful[fill]ed wife (Taylor) who are [for]ced to appear at the [bir]thday party of the dying [pa]triarch Big Daddy. To Ten[nes]see Williams's great dismay, [the] Pulitzer Prize–winning play [di]rected on the stage by Elia [Ka]zan) was censored in its film [ver]sion to draw attention away [fro]m the taboo topics of homo[sex]uality and suicide.

■ **The Blackboard Jungle**, 1955, starring Glenn Ford and Sidney Poitier

Brooks based his screenplay on the autobiographical novel by Evan Hunter, later known as crime author Ed McBain. An ambitious teacher tries to instill a sense of morality in his troubled inner-city New York high school, where a gang led by Poitier wreaks havoc. With its frank treatment of juvenile delinquency, sexuality, and racial tensions, the film became a hot topic, inspiring both controversy and admiration. Not only did this film introduce Sidney Poitier as a talent, it also was the first film to include a rock 'n' roll song, *Rock Around The Clock* by Bill Haley & The Comets.

Richard Brooks

Thrillers

■ Loss of identities, dangerous pursuits, or the threat of captivity ■ Suspense is often achieved by the manipulation of time ■ Film noir introduced the dangerous erotic power of the femme fatale ■ Stylistic depiction of dark subject matter ■ Protagonist and viewer are forced to question truth and reality
■ *left:* **The Night of the Hunter**, by Charles Laughton, 1955

1945 Hitchcock's *Spellbound* introduces psychoanalytical ideas to film

1955 The French coin the term "film noir" to describe dark American thrillers

1968 Faster cars and new camera angles enabled the first modern car chase in *Bullitt*

1974 Watergate inspires political thrillers

1990 Tim Robbins unwinds psychologically in *Jacob's Ladder*

1992 Sharon Stone revives the dangerous and icy femme fatale in *Basic Instinct*

The best thrillers put audiences on the edge of their seats by first breaking down protagonists' notions of reality and then disorienting them, ultimately revealing the evildoer behind the plot. First appearing around World War II, spy films became thrillers of treason, pitting spy against spy and questioning the nature of evil. Later, the pessimistic perspective of film noir (Delmer Daves's *Dark Passage*, 1947), and the Neo-Noirs (John Dahl's *Red Rock West*, 1992) mixed confusion, crime, and seedy settings to unnerve the audience while the engrossing, simple entertainment of the action thriller (Jan de Bont's *Speed*, 1994) uses the energy of chases and races. Another subgenre is the psychological thriller, which unsettles the protagonists' minds, making them question reality and often resulting in devastating twist endings.

Postwar Cinema and the 1950s

■ **Henri-Georges Clouzot: Diabolique**, 1955, starring Simone Signoret

A fragile woman suffering under her abusive and philandering husband teams up with his lover to do away with him. After they succeed, his corpse disappears, and the woman is terrorized by what seems to be his ghost. An influence on Hitchcock's *Psycho* (1960), the twist ending remains shocking, as the director deceives the viewer in exactly the same manner as the tragic wife.

Film Genres

Other Works

Cape Fear, 1962, by J. Lee Thompson, starring Gregory Peck and Robert Mitchum

The Fugitive, by Andrew Davis, 1993, starring Harrison Ford and Tommy Lee Jones

The Game, by David Fincher, 1997, starring Michael Douglas and Sean Penn

Carol Reed: The Third Man, 1949, starring Joseph Cotten and Orson Welles

Set in the iconic ruins (and sewers) of postwar Vienna, Reed brought Graham Greene's original screenplay about counter-espionage to life with the help of cinematographer Robert Krasker. His Expressionist images are characterized by extreme camera angles and dramatic shadows, both characteristic of film noir, which reflect the murkier morality and confusing political landscape of the postwar world.

■ **Christopher Nolan: Memento**, 2000, starring Guy Pearce and Carrie-Anne Moss

In this dizzying Neo-Noir, Nolan created a unique protagonist—one without a long-term memory. Through tattooing his body and taking Polaroid photos, he is daily reminded of his quest for revenge. As the film's random chronological structure tantalizingly reveals, the other characters in his life might not be who they say they are, and the main character is forced to reinterpret the facts in an attempt to figure out whom he is really after. This thriller is especially effective in its questioning of the filmic truth, asking viewers to see beyond the surface.

Thrillers

Otto Preminger

1906, Vienna—1986, New York

■ Largely independent from studios ■ Celebrated by the French New Wave ■ Marketer's eye for controversial material ■ The success of his unrated work helped bring down the Production Code ■ Austrian-American ■ Drama, Film Noir, Musical ■ Directed 37 films

■ **1906** Born into a Jewish family in Vienna

1931 His first film, *Die Grosse Liebe*, is released

1935 Directs his first Broadway play, *Libel*

1944 Takes over directing duties from Rouben Mamoulian on *Laura*

1953 As an actor he plays a Nazi in Billy Wilder's *Stalag 17*

1966 Success of his unrated *The Moon Is Blue* ends the reign of the Production Code

1980 Directs his last film, *The Human Factor*, based on the novel by Graham Greene

1986 Dies in New York

Early in his career, Otto Preminger directed a string of film noirs for 20th Century Fox that still stand as his master pieces (and were hailed as such by British critics and directors of the French New Wave), but his most lasting contribution to film history lies in his role in bringing about the fall of the Production Code, which censored studio films in order to prevent condemnation by the Catholic Legion of Decency. His independently produced and distributed films were untouched by the Code, and therefore included banned words such as "virgin" and "pregnant" (in *The Moon Is Blue*, 1953), and dealt with taboo subjects such as rape and addiction (like in the Frank Sinatra–starring *The Man with the Golden Arm*, 1955), but still earned money at the box office, leaving the censorial power of the Code powerless and ultimately up for revision in 1966. His later films are graced by the iconic poster and title designs of Saul Bass.

■ **Anatomy of a Murder**, 1959, starring James Stewart and Lee Remick

Stewart plays an ex-prosecutor who defends a man who has murdered his wife's rapist. Like Preminger's other portraits of institutions (government in 1962's *Advise & Consent* or the church in *The Cardinal*, 1963), the film presents the justice system in an honest light, with all its flaws. Duke Ellington's jaunty score adds to the film's ambivalent air.

Postwar Cinema and the 1950s

Carmen Jones, 1954, starring Dorothy Dandridge and Harry Belafonte

Oscar Hammerstein's 1943 stage update of Bizet's opera changes the story's setting from Spain to the United States. Preminger cast the story with only African Americans. Though both Dandridge and Belafonte were trained singers, their singing was dubbed.

River of No Return, 1954, starring Robert Mitchum and Marilyn Monroe

Rugged outsider Matt Calder (Mitchum) has just been released from prison. When he is forced to take sultry saloon singer Kay Weston (Monroe) and his own young son on a dangerous river journey they must learn to get along. Both Preminger and Monroe were

contractually obliged to do this film (his last for the studio), yet the film was created with care. The successful result was praised for its pacing and the smart CinemaScope compositions, a first in the western genre. Preminger got the actors to do most of their own stunts—at times putting their lives in grave danger—so as to get realistic performances.

Other Works

Angel Face, 1952 , starring Robert Mitchum and Jean Simmons

Porgy and Bess, 1959, starring Sidney Poitier and Dorothy Dandridge

Exodus, 1960, starring Paul Newman and Eva Marie Saint

Otto Preminger

Sinners and Saints

The golden age of Hollywood was characterized by an almost total control of the production and distribution of films by the Hays Code. Stars were coached and molded by the studios and their tame exploits written up in fan magazines in a fierce battle aimed at drawing fans away from television and into theaters. A 1952 court case forced studios to end their control of theaters, enabling films that didn't have the Hays Code stamp of approval to be shown to the greater public.

■ **James Dean** only appeared in a few features but his portray of loners and ou ders made him an icon for rebellious teenagers. His attit and behavior both c and offscreen were revolutionary.

■ **Rock Hudson and Doris D** were the studios' ideal wholesome couple and they made three romantic comedies together. The public images o reserved, yet vivacious actors Day were shaped by studios s as to conform to the Hays Cod Grace Kelly also exuded an innocent and clean image, bu had to abandon acting when s married Rainier III, Prince of Monaco and some of her roles like in *Butterfield 8* (1960), were taken on by Elizabeth Taylor.

▶ **Elizabeth Taylor** was the iconic passionate and emotion ally volatile woman, and her sultry attitude helped moderni Hollywood women. Though h career as a child-star was shaped by studios, her own personality made her a legen

Postwar Cinema and the 1950s

Marilyn Monroe: Born Norma Jean Mortenson, she was transformed into an iconic sex symbol. Monroe appeared in 19 films before breaking through in 1953, when she starred in *Niagara* as Rose, a woman plotting to kill her husband. The same year she was featured in the first *Playboy* magazine. Monroe brought female sexuality to the screen.

Sinners and Saints

Alfred Hitchcock

1899, London—1980, Los Angeles

■ Master of suspense ■ Pioneered the audience's role as a voyeur
■ Praised by French New Wave directors ■ Films he directed earned
several Oscar nominations but never won
■ British-American ■ Thriller, Suspense, Horror ■ Directed 58 films

1899 Born into a middle-class Catholic family in east London
1920 Starts work at a film studio, designing titles for silent movies
1925 His first directed silent film, shot in Germany, flops
1926 *The Lodger*, his second film, is a commercial success
1929 Directs his first sound film, *Blackmail*
1940 Oscar nomination for first American film, *Rebecca*
1960 *Psycho* shatters box office records worldwide
1980 Dies at home in Los Angeles

One of the few directors to have made successful silen
sound, and color films in a career spanning six decade
Alfred Hitchcock was still plagued by a sense of unde
appreciation for most of his life. At first, American criti
did not value his decision to lend his name to a series (
popular TV mysteries or his work in commercial gen
films. It was not until his work was championed b
French New Wave directors like Eric Rohmer, Claud
Chabrol (p. 234), and François Truffaut (p. 236) in th
late 1950s that Hitchcock was hailed as an *auteur*, a tru
cinema artist with a singular visual style.

Always looking for a fresh angle, Hitchcock looked fo
ways to avoid clichés or subvert the familiar. He wou
challenge himself (and his audiences) by making film
set solely on a small rowboat (*Lifeboat*, 1944), seeming
shot in a single, endless take (*Rope*, 1948), or by c

■ **The Birds**, 1963, starring Tippi Hedren

This film's villains are animals
a first for Hitchcock. Tippi
Hedren plays a socialite who
arrives at a small coastal village, only to become the sub
ject of increasingly vicious
avian attacks. After she escape
their first attempts, the film's
open-ended final scenes are
haunting, with flocks of birds
descending menacingly on t
California coast, seemingly ju
waiting to begin their onslaug
in earnest.

Vertigo, 1958, starring James Stewart and Kim Novak

James Stewart stars in this complex psychological thriller, set in San Francisco, as a retired police detective who falls for Kim Novak, a troubled woman he has been hired to shadow. After he saves her from suicide, he remains plagued by nightmares. When he takes her to the bell tower that she keeps dreaming about, she runs up but he is unable to follow due to his crippling vertigo (fear of heights). From the ground, he watches her jump to her death. Depressed, he starts to visit the places she used to go, where he spots a woman who looks strikingly like her (also played by Novak). Though she claims to be a simple country girl, new to the city, he soon finds out the truth, a shocking revelation that takes him to the top of the bell tower. Hitchcock subverts the mystery genre by revealing the puzzle in the middle of the film—thus, it becomes more about the complex character of the detective than a simple

whodunit. To show Stewart's fear of heights, Hitchcock developed the dolly zoom. The camera moves away from the actor while zooming in. The foreground stays the same but the background closes in substantially. This distortion of perspective has a disorienting effect that the director would later reuse in *Marnie* (1964) to signify a sudden, shattering realization.

Other Works

Dial M for Murder, 1954, starring Ray Milland, Grace Kelly, and Robert Cummings

The Man Who Knew Too Much, 1956, starring James Stewart and Doris Day

Torn Curtain, 1966, starring Paul Newman and Julie Andrews

Family Plot, 1976, starring Karen Black and Bruce Dern

Alfred Hitchcock

killing off the leading actress early on in the film (*Psycho*, p. 190). Playing with his audience's expectations was an important way of building the suspense characteristic of Hitchcock, a slowly growing feeling of tension that ends in a climax. In his 1936 film *Sabotage*, suspense is achieved through showing an innocent boy carrying an innocuous-looking package that the audience knows actually contains a ticking bomb.

Hitchcock saw film as a primarily visual medium, so he often emphasized the image over sound or dialogue in his most crucial scenes. All his films were meticulously storyboarded, with each shot's composition hand-drawn in advance.

■ **North by Northwest**, 195 starring Cary Grant

After advertising executive Cary Grant finds a murdered man at the UN, he is mistake for the murderer and pursue in a thrilling chase across the United States by mysterious agents looking for a piece of microfilm. The wrongfully accused man is a recurring motif in Hitchcock's work, also appearing in *The 39 Step The Wrong Man*, and both versions of *The Man Who Kne Too Much*.

Rear Window, 1954, starring James Stewart and Grace Kelly

When a photographer (Stewart), is incapacitated by a broken leg, he begins to spy on his neighbors for entertainment. He soon believes that he has witnessed a murder in an opposite apartment. With his girlfriend (Kelly), he devises a way to bring the murderer to justice, only to have to fight him himself when the man spots the glint of his spyglass and comes after him. Hitchcock creates a parallel between his protagonist, fixed in a spot in his wheelchair, and the audience, stuck in their theater seats. The neighbors' windows become individual cinema screens, allowing Stewart and the viewer to compose their own story based on

what they see. The audience shares Stewart's point of view, so they know what he knows and are directly involved in solving the mystery. As Kelly investigates the suspense becomes unbearable—Stewart can see her but is unable to

alert her. Through cunning editing and point-of-view shots, Hitchcock develops the idea of the viewer as a voyeur, one who receives pleasure from watching others, making the audience complicit and thus more invested in the story.

Alfred Hitchcock

Psycho

■ by Alfred Hitchcock, USA, 1960, Thriller

Based on the book by Robert Bloch, which in turn was loosely based on the crimes of serial killer Ed Gein, *Psycho* deals with a cross-dressing murderer in a seedy motel. At first the studio thought the story was too gory, so Hitchcock scaled down the budget to $1 million, and used the crew from his TV show. After the Technicolored *Vertigo* (1958) and *North by Northwest* (1959), he chose to film in black and white to prevent the shower scene from looking too bloody.

Janet Leigh's shower scene occurs roughly a third of the way into the film. Its 90 shots were storyboarded by design Saul Bass, who also worked c many of Hitchcock's opening credits. The manic editing ar Bernard Herrmann's shriekin violins suggest more bloodsh than the scene actually show

Psycho, 1960, starring Janet Leigh and Anthony Perkins

Uniquely, Hitchcock kills off the protagonist, Janet Leigh, early in the film, leaving the audience in shock until the psychoanalyt-

ical resolution. Though ostensibly a horror film, the gore was kept to a minimum; instead *Psycho* teased the audience into suspense with a twisting narrative and cunning editing.

The *Psycho* house and the Ba Motel were built at Universa Studios, where they remain and, as a historic first, Gus Va Sant made a shot-for-shot co remake of the film in 1998.

Fugitive Marion Crane (Leigh) stops at the Bates Motel during a storm. At first, the hotel's owner, Norman Bates's (Perkins) and his harsh mother's eccentricites seem harmless, but when Marion is killed while showering in her motel room and Bates tries to hide the evidence so as to save his mother, suspicions mount.

Psycho

Historical Films & Costume Dramas

■ Characterized by lush set designs and costuming ■ Lavish visualization of historic, literary, or biblical stories gives weight to the films' stories ■ Often depicting the higher classes, royalty, or famous artists

■ *left*: **The Adventures of Robin Hood**, by Michael Curtiz and William Keighley, 1938, starring Errol Flynn and Olivia de Havilland

1925 MGM releases silent version of *Ben-Hur*, then the most expensive film

1939 The Civil War epic *Gone with the Wind* breaks box office records

1956 Cecil B. DeMille remakes his own *The Ten Commandments* from 1923

1976 34 million Americans watch the first network screening of *Gone with the Wind*

1997 *Titanic* breaks box-office records

2002 Zhang Yimou directs *Hero*, China's most successful film export to date, set in 220 BCE

The first American historical feature, D. W. Griffith's (p. controversial *The Birth of a Nation* (1915), was dee influenced by the earlier Italian epics *Quo Vadis?* (191 and the spectacular *Cabiria* (1914). These films visua overwhelm the viewer, thereby inducing a feeling luxury, as well as an immersion in history. The genre's su ject matter ranges from the biblical (the first wide-scre CinemaScope film, *The Robe*, 1953, or Mel Gibson's *Passion of the Christ*, 2004), to adaptations of biograph or the works of esteemed authors like William Shak speare, Jane Austen, E. M. Forster, or Henry James. Sty also vary; where the films of Merchant Ivory (*A Room w a View*, 1985) recreate the past as accurately as possib other films, such as Baz Luhrmann's *Romeo + Juliet* (199 take a more irreverent approach.

Postwar Cinema and the 1950s

■ **Joseph L. Mankiewicz: Cleopatra**, 1963, starring Eli beth Taylor and Richard Burt

Though *Cleopatra* won four Oscars and was the highest-grossing film in the United States that year, the produci studio Fox still barely made a profit from it. Originally budgeted at $2 million, producti difficulties soon raised this to staggering $44 million (equiv lent to $300 million today). T film's original cut was six hou long; this was scaled down to four for the premiere, and ag for distribution to three hour

■ **Shekhar Kapur: Elizabeth**, 1998, starring Cate Blanchett and Joseph Fiennes

England's powerful and iconic virgin queen has been portrayed on the screen by some of film's greatest actors—Judi Dench in *Shakespeare In Love* (1998), Bette Davis twice (1939, 1955), Glenda Jackson in *Mary, Queen of Scots* (1971)—and even by an actor, Quentin Crisp in Sally Potter's *Orlando* (1992). Costume dramas have proven fertile in exploring issues of female empowerment. The worldwide success of Kapur and Blanchett's version prompted the 2007 sequel *Elizabeth: The Golden Age*.

Other Works

Queen Christina, by Rouben Mamoulian,1933, starring Greta Garbo and John Gilbert

Great Expectations, by David Lean, 1946, starring Alec Guinness

Howards End, by James Ivory, 1992, starring Emma Thompson and Anthony Hopkins

William Wyler: Ben-Hur, 9, starring Charlton Heston

ning 11 Oscars, *Ben-Hur* er three hours of epic bib- story set in the time of s. Charlton Heston plays -Hur, a Jewish merchant, ngly imprisoned by his lhood friend, the Roman er Messala. After years on ley ship, he escapes and rs a spectacular chariot against Messala to get evenge.

Historical Films & Costume Dramas

Michael Powell & Emeric Pressburger

1905, Bekesbourne–1990, Avening (Powell)
1902, Miskolc–1988, Saxstead (Pressburger)

■ Inspired by technical innovations ■ Wrote, directed, and produced
■ British/Hungarian ■ Musical, Fantasy, War ■ Directed 19 films together

1902 Pressburger born in Hungary

1905 Powell born in the UK

1932 Powell directs seven "quota quickies" (subsidized British B-movies)

1935 Pressburger emigrates to the UK

1939 First collaborative work on *The Spy in Black*

1942 Joint director credit for the first time on *One of Our Aircraft is Missing*

1943 Form the production company The Archers

1956 The Archers dissolves

1984 Powell marries editor Thelma Schoonmaker

1988 Pressburger dies in the UK

1990 Powell dies

■ **Peeping Tom**, 1960, starring Carl Boehm and Anna Massey

After parting ways with Pressburger, Powell directed this tale of a perverse mild-mannered serial killer who films his victims as he murders them in order to capture the look of real terror in their faces. The usually princely Boehm is cast against type in this dark psychoanalytical masterpiece.

Though Michael Powell was already an able and talent[ed] filmmaker (making many subsidized "quota quickies" British B-movies, in the 1930s) before he met the H[un]garian screenwriter Emeric Pressburger (active in Be[rlin] before 1933, in Paris until 1935), it was to be their coll[ec]tive efforts that proved most lasting in both their care[ers.] Their first few films, all set in the army, captured the att[en]tion of both the British and American wartime pub[lic,] giving them the opportunity to self-produce their m[ost] ambitious works as The Archers. These uniquely Brit[ish] films (credited as written, produced, and directed by b[oth] Powell and Pressburger) are characterized by their in[no]vative technical mastery, subtle but powerful use of co[lor] and intelligent, understated writing.

Postwar Cinema and the 1950s

Black Narcissus, 1947, starring Deborah Kerr and Kathleen Byron

Two nuns struggle to establish a convent in the Himalayas, they face difficulties and one is driven to madness. Though the set is strikingly realistic, the entire film was shot at Pinewood Studios and expertly uses dramatic mattes and landscape paintings for the scenery.

The Red Shoes, 1948, starring Moira Shearer, Anton Walbrook, and Marius Goring

A talented ballerina joins a prestigious ballet troupe, taking the lead in a dance adaptation of Hans Christian Andersen's *The Red Shoes*. The ballet is about a girl with magical red shoes that have been bewitched by a shoemaker so that they will not stop dancing. The ballerina finds herself tragically attracted to the composer and is ultimately forced to choose between her life and her art. When she decides too late, the ballet hauntingly goes on without her. Real dancers were transformed into actors under Powell and Pressburger's masterful direction and the film is still praised for its lyrical set design, lush Technicolor images, rhythmic editing, and soundtrack.

Other Works

49th Parallel, 1941, starring Laurence Olivier

The Life and Death of Colonel Blimp, 1943, starring Roger Livesey and Deborah Kerr

A Canterbury Tale, 1944

The Elusive Pimpernel, 1950, starring David Niven

The Tales of Hoffmann, 1951, starring Moira Shearer

Michael Powell & Emeric Pressburger

Louis Malle

1932, Thumeries—1995, Beverly Hills

■ Often made sexually explicit films ■ Directed documentaries as well as
fiction films and shorts ■ Worked with Jacques Cousteau and Robert Bresson
■ Active as a director in both the United States and France
■ French ■ Drama, Historical, Comedy ■ Directed 21 films

■ **1932** Born in France

1956 Shoots and co-directs Jacques Cousteau's *The Silent World*

1958 *The Lovers* is tried for obscenity before the United States Supreme Court

1967 Shoots enough footage for seven BBC documentaries about India

1975 Moves to the United States

1981 *My Dinner with Andre* is a success in the United States

1992 Makes the racy film *Damage*

1994 His last film, *Vanya on 42nd Street*

1995 Dies in California

Born to a half-Jewish father in the French countryside
Louis Malle survived World War II in France, an experience
that would later fuel his autobiographical film *Goodbye,
Children*. After the war, Malle studied political science and
film in Paris, but soon decided to learn his craft on the set.
He became a cameraman for legendary oceanographer
Jacques Cousteau and later worked with Robert Bresson
on *A Man Escaped* (1956). His first directorial efforts were
different from those of his contemporaries—the French
New Wave filmmakers. Malle mainly tried to make immersive, elegant films and had no interest in subverting
or deconstructing the language of cinema. His visually
sumptuous, yet politically probing documentaries—
especially his film on India, *Calcutta* (1969), and his
street interview experiments in the Direct Cinema style,
Place de la République (1974)—show his documentarian
roots and aesthete's soul.

■ **Pretty Baby**, 1978, starring
Susan Sarandon, Brooke Shields
and Keith Carradine

Set in New Orleans' red light
district in 1917. Shields, 12 at
the time, daringly portrays a
prostitute's daughter whose
virginity is auctioned off. Carradine plays the photographer
who documents the women's
lives, becoming obsessed with
Shields. Malle was often controversial; his frank *The Lovers*
prompted an obscenity court
case in the US Supreme Court.

Postwar Cinema and the 1950s

Elevator to the Gallows,
1958, starring Jeanne Moreau
and Maurice Ronet

A self-confident young man
plots to kill his lover's husband,
but when he gets stuck in an
elevator, his car and identity are
stolen by two juvenile delinquents and he is accused of two
different murders. While he
attempts to escape from the
elevator, his lover, Jeanne
Moreau in her first major film
appearance, wanders the rainy
streets of Paris looking for him.
Though the plot seems a
traditional noir, in which a
crime goes horribly wrong,
the strangely aloof performances and the hypnotic, improvised jazz score by Miles Davis,
a first in the world of soundtracks, create a more medita-
tive mood.

■ **Zazie in the Subway**, 1960,
starring Catherine Demongeot
and Philippe Noiret

Forced to spend a weekend
with her uncle in Paris, all Zazie,
a foulmouthed young girl,
wants to do is ride the subway.
When a strike makes this impossible, she decides to unhinge
the lives of the adults around
her with her anarchic interventions. Malle's strangest work is
an adaptation of a book by lin-
guistic Raymond Queneau.
Though Malle was never a New
Wave filmmaker, this homage
to slapstick (using sped-up film
and other older tricks from the
genre) was applauded by
François Truffaut.

Other Works

The Lovers, 1958, starring
Jeanne Moreau

Viva Maria!, 1965, starring
Brigitte Bardot

The Thief of Paris, 1967,
starring Jean-Paul Belmondo

Atlantic City, 1980, starring
Burt Lancaster

Goodbye, Children, 1987

Jean-Pierre Melville

1917, Paris–1973, Paris

■ Deeply influenced by Hollywood and film noir ■ Strong emphasis on silence and visuals over dialogue ■ Directed, produced, designed, wrote, sho and acted ■ His independence inspired the French New Wave directors ■ French ■ Crime, War, Drama, Literary Adaptation ■ Directed 12 films

1917 Born Jean-Pierre Grumbach into a Jewish family

1937 Begins service in the French army

1940 Inspired by the author of *Moby Dick*, takes on the surname Melville while in the French Resistance

1943 Sees *Citizen Kane*

1946 First film as director

1948 Without owning the rights, films Vercors's *Le Silence de la Mer*

1967 His studio burns down

1973 Dies of a heart attack

Obsessed with American film, Melville spent his chil hood watching films in Paris's cinemas and would la adopt a Stetson hat and sunglasses in tribute to Ame ican masters, like John Huston (p. 138), Howard Hawl and John Ford (p.158). Quite different from his Fren contemporaries, he combined studio and location shoc to create meticulously composed, yet uniquely urb gangster films. In *The Godson*, for instance, he focused the killer's ritualistic routes through Paris. The film bleached aesthetic and emphasis on silence make th thriller as exciting as it is pensive. His films were all bo office hits, but they were also the work of an auteur, wi a unique authorial hand in all facets of production. Th independence as well as his precise use of sound an geography later inspir the French New Wa Quentin Tarantino (p. 41 and Michael Mann.

■ **The Godson**, 1967, starrin Alain Delon and François Péri

After a solitary contract killer, played by a nearly silent Delo is almost caught by the police he is chased by the gangsters who ordered the murder and the cops who do not trust his too-perfect alibi. This medita-tive gangster tale would later inspire John Woo's *The Killer* (1989) and Jim Jarmusch's *Ghost Dog: The Way of the Samurai* (1999).

Postwar Cinema and the 1950s

The Strange Ones, 1950,
starring Nicole Stéphane and
Édouard Dermithe

After seeing his adaptation of
Vercors's Resistance novel *Le
Silence de la Mer*, author Jean
Cocteau asked Melville to make
this film, also known as *Les En-
fants Terribles*. Cocteau, himself
an accomplished filmmaker
(*Beauty and the Beast*, 1946), felt
inspired by Melville's combination of voice-over narration and
silence to depict his protagonists' inner lives and outer
struggles. This innovative use of
sound typified Melville's later
crime films. To film Cocteau's
story of an incestuously close
brother and sister who drive
each other to ruin, Melville
made some interesting choices,
casting a female actor to play
both the brother's male high-
school crush, as well as the girl
who pines after him later on.
The remarkable camera effects
were all improvised on a low
budget—a crushing final crane
shot filmed from an elevator and
other shots on the mobile stages
of the Théâtre Pigalle.

Other Works

Fever Heat, 1955, starring
Roger Duchesne

Leon Morin, Priest, 1961,
starring Jean-Paul Belmondo
and Emmanuelle Riva

Doulos: The Finger Man, 1962,
starring Jean-Paul Belmondo
and Serge Reggiani

Army of Shadows, 1969,
starring Lino Ventura

The Red Circle , 1970, starring
Alain Delon and Yves Montand

Dirty Money, 1972, starring
Alain Delon

Jacques Tati

1908, Le Pecq–1982, Paris

■ Specialist in visual slapstick that gently poked fun at the absurdities of tech nology and modern life ■ Played the lead in all his films ■ His long shots left it to the viewer to find the smart sight gags
■ French ■ Comedy, Short Films ■ Directed 6 full-length films

1908 Born west of Paris

1932 Directs and acts in his first short film

1939 Is drafted for WWII and misses his scheduled performance at Radio City Music Hall in New York

1958 Oscar for *Mon Oncle*

1964 The set of *Playtime* is badly damaged in a storm

1967 *Playtime* is a commercial failure

1971 Almost bankrupt, Tati borrows money to make *Trafic*

1974 His last film, a semi-documentary, *Parade*, is made for Swedish TV

1977 A Swedish distributor pays off Tati's debts and rereleases his work

1982 Dies in Paris

Tati's passion for sports led him to an early career as mime. In the 1930s his successful routine enabled him act in, write, and direct several comedic shorts. Tati's stag career was cut short by army duty and after the war became a film director. *Jour de Fête*, his first feature fil was an elaboration of one of his own satirical shorts abo an overzealous postal worker. Though intended to be t first French color moving picture, the processing of t film failed. Luckily, Tati had simultaneously shot in bla and white, and was able to release it to both critical ar commercial triumph. His first three films (two of whi star himself as M. Hulot) were international critical ar box-office successes. Tati's ambitious decision not to re on his laurels—simply directing sequels to his Hul cycle—led him into financial ruin. All his films share gentle style of slapstick comedy, in which Tati hims plays a straight man in a comic world, the inverse Buster Keaton's (p. 56) and Charlie Chaplin's (p. 58) filn

■ **M. Hulot's Holiday**, 1953, starring Jacques Tati and Nathalie Pascaud

This film introduced the worl to Tati's signature character, the serious, technologically clueless Monsieur Hulot, who bumbling, well-intended actions cause mayhem. In thi gently satirical work, Monsieu Hulot goes to the beach, wre ing havoc at his boarding hou as well as among his fellow vacationers.

Postwar Cinema and the 1950s

■ Playtime, 1967, starring Jacques Tati and Barbara Dennek

M. Hulot and a group of American tourists spend a day in an anonymous and hypermodern city. Shot on 70 mm, Tati took advantage of the high definition format's clear depth of field by placing sight gags in corners of the screen.

Other Works

L'École des Facteurs (short), 1947, starring Jacques Tati

Jour de Fête, 1949, starring Jacques Tati and Guy Decomble

Trafic, 1971, starring Jacques Tati

Parade, 1974, starring Jacques Tati

Mon Oncle, 1958, starring Jacques Tati and Alain Bécourt

Introducing the technophobic elements that would be the main theme of his masterpiece, Playtime, Mon Oncle is Tati's most successful film. Tati contrasts the lives of Hulot and his young nephew, who lives with his dull parents in a technologically advanced and Modernist house. Their culture of efficiency and materialism contrasts Hulot's bohemian lifestyle, leading to hilarious technological malfunctions. Though most of Tati's dialogue is peripheral, he also shot an English version of the film, in which signs were translated and some speech was dubbed.

Jacques Tati

Vittorio De Sica

1901, Sora–1974, Paris

■ Began Neo-Realism through location shooting, episodic plotting, and filmi[ng] ordinary subjects ■ Though he had a light comic touch, his work was often sentimental ■ Worked well with child actors ■ Admired Charlie Chaplin ■ Italian ■ Drama, Comedy ■ Directed 26 films

1917 Acts in his first film, *The Clemenceau Affair*

1940 Co-directs first film, *Rose Scarlatte*

1949 *The Bicycle Thief* wins an honorary Oscar

1953 Acts in Max Ophüls's romantic drama *The Earrings of Madame de...*

1957 Oscar nomination for his supporting role in *A Farewell to Arms*

1968 Becomes a French citizen

1974 Directs his last film, *Il Viaggio*, before dying

Though Vittorio De Sica was a glamorous stage a[nd] cinema teen idol in his early 20s, his lasting fame com[es] from his directorial work and creation of the Neo-Real[ist] style, which influenced filmmakers worldwide. Af[ter] World War II the Italian Cinecittà studio was used as [a] refugee center, forcing De Sica to shoot on location. [He] turned this obstacle into a virtue, recording on the stree[ts] and dubbing sound and dialogue later. His documenta[ry] style and casting of nonactors complemented his sto[ry] lines' focus on tragedies affecting normal, flawed peop[le.] His films are often episodic in style, with events that a[re] not causally linked, emphasizing a greater sense [of] realism. His work with children and his subtle themes [of] hope are his films' signature aspects.

Postwar Cinema and the 1950s

■ **Umberto D.**, 1952, starrin[g] Carlo Battisti

This is the heartrending story [of] a retired professor who, unab[le] to pay his rent, slowly realizes [that] he might no longer be able to afford his beloved dog. We follow the man as he desperately tries to sell his meager possessions, lets himself be hospitalized, even contemplates suicide, but ultimately cannot leave his dog. Made according to the Neo-Realist credo, this film might be De Sica's most bittersweet, as th[e] audience knows the ending's reunion of man and dog can only be temporary.

he Bicycle Thief, 1948,
ring Enzo Staiola

r a long-unemployed worker
s a job posting flyers, his
cle becomes his most
ortant possession. When it
olen, he goes out to look
t with his young son. Shot
rely on location in Rome,
g nonprofessional actors
depicting the lives of ordi-
y people, *The Bicycle Thief*
ame the best-known Italian
-Realist film. Its touching
ing became emblematic of
movement.

Other Works

racle in Milan, 1951, starring
ancesco Golisano

arriage Italian Style, 1964,
arring Sophia Loren and
arcello Mastroianni

e Garden of the Finzi-
ntinis, 1970, starring
lmut Berger

■ **Shoeshine**, 1946, starring
Rinaldo Smordoni and Franco
Interlenghi

Two homeless orphans try to
make enough money off soldiers to be able to buy a horse.
After the rowdy boys resort to
crime, they are thrown into a
squalid prison. If De Sica's first
studio films show only a hint of
the humanity that would make
him an Italian icon, his seventh
film, *Shoeshine*, displayed all of
his compassion and Neo-Realist
characteristics—documentary-
style location shooting, nonprofessional actors, and loose,
episodic plotting.

Vittorio De Sica

Federico Fellini

1920, Rimini–1993, Rome

- Famed associative, surreal style and personal storytelling ■ Recurring moti
are the circus, the church, and the sea ■ Worked with Roberto Rossellini and
Michelangelo Antonioni ■ Composer Nino Rota created his most famous scor
- Italian ■ Drama, Comedy ■ Directed 19 films

- **1920** Born in a small coastal town in Italy
- **1938** Moves to Rome
- **1939** Tours the country with a vaudeville troupe
- **1943** Marries his muse, the actor Giulietta Masina
- **1945** Co-writes Rossellini's *Rome, Open City*
- **1952** Directs his first film, *The White Sheik*
- **1974–75** *Amarcord* is nominated for three Oscars
- **1990** Directs his last film, *The Voice of the Moon*
- **1993** Dies in Rome

■ **La Strada**, 1954, starring Giulietta Masina and Anthony Quinn

Fellini's first international hit, *La Strada* features his wife as a young woman who is sold to a circus performer. Despite being rooted in the Neo-Realist tradition, the film introduced a few of the momentarily surreal scenes that came to define Fellini's work.

Federico Fellini's name has become synonymous w
opulent, phantasmal, and intensely personal films, but
started his work with the famed Neo-Realist Robe
Rossellini, writing raw and realistic stories set in ravag
postwar Italy. Though Fellini's style changed from matt
of-fact Neo-Realism, his storytelling remained rooted
the associative, episodic plotting of those earlier fil
    As his work became m
fragmentary and perso
    his three recurri
    motifs—the circus,
    sea, and the Cath
    church—came
    symbolize freedo
    redemption, a
    repression, resp
tively. His later w
divided critics, so
calling films such
Satyricon indulge
while oth
hai
them
vision.

a Dolce Vita, 1960, starring
cello Mastroianni

olce Vita is a unique docu-
ntation of the years when
breakdown of the studio
em in Hollywood and the
lyzing effects of black-
ng sent international talent
ome's film industry. Over
n days and nights, and
ugh many scenic episodes,
cello Rubini (Mastroianni),
loid reporter, follows
news on the streets of
e, all the while struggling
the women in his life
ong them Anouk Aimée
Anita Ekberg). Nominated
Best Director Oscar, the
ranks among the greatest
made and has been cited
e source of the word
arazzi.

Other Works	
I Vitelloni, 1953, starring Franco Fabrizi and Alberto Sordi	**Satyricon**, 1969, starring Martin Potter and Hiram Keller
Juliet of the Spirits, 1965, starring Giulietta Masina	**Amarcord**, 1973, starring Bruno Zanin

■ **Nights of Cabiria**, 1957, starring Giulietta Masina, François Périer, and Amedeo Nazzari

Fellini's wife, Giulietta Masina, returns as Maria "Cabiria" Ceccarelli, a naive girl in this tragic tale of a prostitute who searches for love and endures hardships. The film's plot is firmly grounded in the Neo-Realist style through its gritty settings and tragic story lines, but *Nights of Cabiria* combined Fellini's earlier style with hints of the visual freedom and dreamy atmospheres that would become prominent in his later work. The film was awarded an Oscar for Best Foreign Film.

Federico Fellini

8½

■ by Federico Fellini, Italy, 1963, Drama

Hounded by his producers, attacked by critics, and pleaded with by scores of actors, Guido Anselmi (Mastroianni) is a filmmaker suffering from what film critic Roger Ebert called "director's block." He flees to a remote spa only to find a whole circus following him. When his stern wife and flighty mistress inadvertently collide at the spa, his personal life falls apart as well. Told in a surrealist, associative style, most of the film consists of a chain of encounters in which conversations are started and continued, but never finished. The more the struggling director is confronted with the demands of life, the more he retreats into a dreamworld of other lives and memories of his past existence. The definitive film about the creative process, 8½ examines the way any successful artist has to juggle scrutiny from the media, commercial concerns, and artistic integrity, all the while maintaining a healthy personal life.

The final circus scene was originally set in a moving traincar. Though filmed, the entire sequence is now lost. Guido Anselmi's ultimate redemption at the hands of women in his life is staged in virginal white. Since Guido's womanizing protagonist is based on Fellini himself, the then forms a kind of creative manifesto for the director's work; struggling with the limitations of the Neo-Realist form, he decided to infuse his nostalgic, but raw tales with the surrealist power of dreams, the revelatory influence of memory, and symbolism.

½, 1963, starring
cello Mastroianni, Claudia
dinale, Anouk Aimée, and
dra Milo

delirious fantasy, the
ale characters
ear in the
ctor's harem,
pering him and
tly bickering
ng themselves.
rlesque per-
ner, Jacqueline
bon (Yvonne
adei), is sent away
ause she is too old.
tic, she tries to con-
e the director, and the
er women, that her
ale form has not lost its
ctive powers.

8 ½

Luchino Visconti

1906, Milan—1976, Rome

■ Lavish set design and costumes ■ Successful stage and opera director
■ Despite his aristocratic background he was an avowed Marxist ■ His la[te]
films are studies of the decadence and decay of the aristocracy
■ Italian ■ Drama, Historical, Literary Adaptation ■ Directed 14 films

1906 Born into aristocracy in Italy

1936 Assists director Jean Renoir in France

1939 Visits Hollywood

1942 Directs his first film, *Ossessione*

1954 Directs his first Maria Callas opera

1960 Returns to Neo-Realism for *Rocco and His Brothers*

1963 Palme d'Or for *The Leopard*

1969 Receives his only Oscar nomination for *The Damned*

1976 Dies while editing *The Innocent*

Other Works

The Earth Trembles, 1948, starring Alfio Fichera

White Nights, 1957, starring Maria Schell and Marcello Mastroianni

Rocco and his Brothers, 1960, starring Alain Delon, Renato Salvatori, and Annie Girardot

The Damned, 1969, starring Dirk Bogarde

Ludwig, 1972, starring Helmut Berger and Romy Schneider

Postwar Cinema and the 1950s

Born into a wealthy Italian family, Visconti was the idea[l] [di]rector to not only accurately portray the luxurious live[s of] the rich, but also the emotional and political consequen[ces] of excess and decadence. His experience working with J[ean] Renoir (p. 144) and his skills as an opera director are evid[ent] in his powerful historical films that often span charact[er] lifetimes. Unique in his oeuvre is his debut, *Ossessi[one]* (1942), a lurid tale of erotic obsession that first sees a wo[man] and her lover kill her husband, then destroy each other. [The] first of three films based on James M. Cain's *The Postm[an] Always Rings Twice*, its release was first delayed by the M[us]solini dictatorship, then by the fact that Visconti did not o[wn] the rights. Though commonly hailed as Neo-Realist fo[r its] location shooting and focus on the underclass, the film'[s] plot seems too causally determined and lacks the social c[on]science of directors like Vittorio De Sica (p. 202).

Senso, 1954, starring Alida Valli and Farley Granger

A stunning Venetian countess is charged with the safekeeping of the financial reserves of the Italian partisan resistance. When she embarks on an illicit affair with an officer from the oppressing Austro-Hungarian forces, she gets carried away by her passions and squanders the money on him, only to have him desert her. Visconti theatrically stages her fall from grace in gorgeous, broad strokes, from the elaborate colors of her own lush palace, to the dark shades of the Venetian backstreets she is forced to wander, hopelessly looking for her lover.

Death In Venice, 1971, starring Dirk Bogarde and Björn Andrésen

Instead of the writer protagonist of Thomas Mann's famous novel, Visconti turned his into a composer very loosely based on Gustav Mahler, whose tumultuous compositions underscore the film's most dramatic turns. In Venice to cure his ailing health, the composer falls for a luminous youth staying in the same hotel. As his obsession grows stronger, his health fails and the opulent Venetian facades turn ugly and dilapidated.

he Leopard, 1963, starring Lancaster, Alain Delon, and dia Cardinale

d Sicily's rough landscape, ristocratic patriarch strug- with his declining fortunes. gain his position, he allows on to marry the daughter of merchant. Visconti's admi- n for Kenji Mizoguchi's d but fluid staging is ob- s in the 40-minute ball that s the film. Vicente Min- s influence is also apparent e production design and ibrant use of Technicolor.

Pier Paolo Pasolini
Bologna, 1922–Ostia, 1975

■ Inspired by painters such as Giotto, Mantegna, and Bosch ■ Influenced by Carl Theodor Dreyer and Robert Bresson ■ Stylized staging modeled on sile films ■ His most successful films had rather explicit subjects
■ Italian ■ Drama, Satire, Historical ■ Directed 12 films

1922 Born in Italy

1950 Moves to Rome with his mother

1954 Publishes his first book of poetry, *La Meglio Gioventù*

1957 Writes the screen-play for Fellini's *Nights of Cabiria*

1961 Makes his first film, the Neo-Realist *Accattone*

1962 Directs Orson Welles in the short *La Ricotta*

1963 Films the documentary *Sopralluoghi in Palestina*

1975 Murdered on a beach in Ostia

A true universal artist, Pasolini was a writer, critic, po actor, painter, and filmmaker. Though his first films firmly rooted in Neo-Realist style with political und tones, his later films take a much more stylized and stract approach that is reminiscent of the rigorous cine of Robert Bresson and Carl Theodor Dreyer. His lyr background especially shows in this later work, which is rife with references to art history. His commercially s cessful *Trilogy of Life*, *The Decameron* (1971), *The Can bury Tales* (1972), and *The Arabian Nights* (1974), sexually frank and emblematic of its era. His perso struggle with his homosexuality can be read in most of films, as well as his preoccupation with death, which of subsumes his young protagonists.

■ **Mamma Roma**, 1962, starring Anna Magnani

Loosely based on his own fi years in Rome, Pasolini tells story of a mother (Magnani) who, after regaining custod of her teenage son, is force back into prostitution when son fails to hold a job. Her ni time diatribes, delivered to expansive Roman streets, a the few hustlers and custom that come to her are movin and powerful. Pasolini effec tively used the lines in Magn aging face to more poignan illustrate his titular characte descent into degeneration.

Postwar Cinema and the 1950s

The Gospel According to Matthew, 1964, starring ᵣique Irazoqui

ᵢs successful adaptation of ᵣist's life was shot entirely in ₑ stunning hillside town of ₜera. Despite Pasolini's atheism ₑd Marxist ideas the film is ₚrisingly venerable.

■ Salo, or the 120 Days of Sodom, 1975, starring Paolo Bonacelli

This brutal adaptation of the infamous Marquis de Sade novel transposes the story to 1940s fascist Italy. The film shows how four powerful men subject captured teenagers to unspeakable degradations over 120 days. With very few close-ups, Pasolini's stylistic choice for frontality and simplicity is reminiscent of the limitations of silent film.

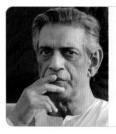

Satyajit Ray

1921, Calcutta—1992, Calcutta

■ Inspired by Italian Neo-Realism and Jean Renoir ■ Few of his films are available outside India ■ His small-scale, poetic stories defy the excesses of Hollywood and Bollywood ■ Most of his films are in the Bengali language
■ Indian ■ Drama, Comedy, Musical, Historical, Crime ■ Directed 31 films

1921 Born in West Bengal

1949 Assists Jean Renoir on the Indian location scouting for *The River*

1950 Of the about 100 films he sees while in Europe, *The Bicycle Thief* inspires him the most

1956 First film, *Pather Panchali,* honored at Cannes

1956–81 Makes a film a year

1992 Dies after accepting an Honorary Academy Award for lifetime achievement

Indian cinema bears few revelations as unexpected as t films of Satyajit Ray. A self-taught filmmaker, his debut fi *Pather Panchali*, was made with only amateur actors. T film's international success enabled Ray to make a film year, including two sequels to his debut. Portraying the liv of just one family, the *Apu* trilogy still retains its quiet for Deeply influenced by Italian Neo-Realism, they tell simp stories of a marginalized underclass without the opuler and song-and-dance commonly associated with Bol wood. This new kind of film was also hinted at in Kapoor's Chaplinesque *The Tramp* (1951) and Mehbo Khan's *Mother India* (1957). Because of his use of the Beng language Ray's films are rarely shown in the rest of India

Postwar Cinema and the 1950s

Manahagar, 1963, starring dhabi Mukherjee and Anil atterjee

o called *The Big City*, this film te innovatively deals with men's rights. When her hus-nd fails to fully provide for his ily, a young wife gets a job ing sewing machines, even ugh this is frowned upon by ir community. The husband so convinced she should t, until he is fired. Now her ily's sole breadwinner, the e is faced with a choice after English friend and col-gue is fired because of her nic background: stay on, or t in solidarity and try her k elsewhere in the big city.

■ **Days and Nights in the Forest**, 1969, starring Soumitra Chatterjee and Sharmila Tagore

Four arrogant young men leave Calcutta and head to the coun-tryside in search of calm. There they meet a few other city folk and awkwardly mingle with the locals. Largely plot-less, the

Other Works
Pather Panchali, 1955, starring Subir Bannerjee and Chunibala Devi
Aparajito, 1956, starring Smaran Ghosal
The World of Apu, 1959, starring Soumitra Chatterjee and Sharmila Tagore

narrative resembles that of Renoir's *The Rules of the Game* (1939) and could be described as a "fugue"—a musical term that denotes a series of repeti-tions and variations on a theme—in this case, the com-parison of city folk and their rural counterparts and their comical misadventures. The moral center of this film, Sharmila Tagore, can be considered one of the world's best actors of her time and she shines brightest in Ray's *The World of Apu* (1959), in the role of Apu's unexpected young wife and in *The Goddess* (1960), where she plays a woman whose father-in-law believes she is a Hindu goddess.

Satyajit Ray

Kenji Mizoguchi

1898, Tokyo–1956, Kyoto

■ More than half of his black-and white-films were lost ■ Style consisted of long takes and few close-ups ■ Subject matter was progressive, even feminis[t] identifying with destitute women ■ Admired by the French New Wave ■ Japanese ■ Costume Drama, Literary Adaptation ■ Directed 88 films

■ **1898** Born in Japan
1905 His sister is sold into prostitution
1907 Meets Matsutaro Kawaguchi, who later co-writes with him
1909 His father forces him to drop out of school
1923 Directs his first film, *The Resurrection of Love*
1930 Makes one of the first Japanese sound films, *Home Town*
1952 *Oharu* wins the International Award at Venice
1956 Dies in Japan

Unlike the flashy panache of Akira Kurosawa's (p. 21[?] editing and camerawork, Kenji Mizoguchi's work preser[ve] meditative tracking shots that create a lasting effect a[nd] long takes that show the aftermath of dramatic outburs[t]. His films rarely have close-ups, prolonging the tension his scenes. His career was mostly devoted to costu[me] dramas that exuded a quietly tragic humanism, focus[ing] on the sufferings of women in an undemocratic a[nd] patriarchal society. His films often feature brutal violen[ce] portrayed with a calm distance and striking poignancy. later became popular with international critics and w[on] at the Venice Film Festival for *The Life of Oharu*, *Uget[su]* and *Sansho the Bailiff*. His exotic style and hypnotic use the camera appealed many and can be seen the work of Michelange[lo] Antonioni (p. 238) and Nic[h]olas Ray (p. 162).

■ **Sansho the Bailiff**, 1954, starring Yoshiaki Hanayagi

One of Mizoguchi's most power[ful] costumed melodramas, or *jidai g[eki]* it is a dramatic tale of a provincia[l] governor's family thrown to the winds when he is exiled. The children are forced into slavery, whereas their mother is put to w[ork] as a prostitute. Mizoguchi's epic scope shows the grown-up son escaping his enslaver and trying redeem his family by calling for a[n] end to slavery.

Postwar Cinema and the 1950s

Postwar Cinema in Japan

Ugetsu, 1953, starring Masayuki Mori and Machiko Kyô

Mizoguchi's international success gave him free creative rein on this project, also known by the poetic title *Tales of the Pale and Silvery Moon After the Rain*. The film's haunting images and epic story are shot with a constantly moving camera on a crane, emphasizing the story's flow and supernatural moments. *Ugetsu* deals with the lives of two couples suffering in a state of civil war; its men are fueled by greed and ambition to ultimately ruin their families. One of the men, a potter, falls in love with a spectral aristocratic lady, whom he escapes after learning she is really a ghost. Upon returning home, he finds his wife's warm welcome is also a cruel dream.

Street of Shame, 1956, starring Machiko Kyô

Mizoguchi's last film (and biggest box-office success) deals with the dreary lives and thwarted dreams of five prostitutes in contemporary Tokyo's Dreamland brothel. The director's sympathy for the precarious position of women in Japanese society was most likely formed by his sister's fate as a child prostitute, and *Street of Shame*'s sensitive portrayal influenced political debate on this issue.

Other Works	
The Story of the Last Chrysanthemums, 1939, starring Shôtarô Hanayagi	Miss Oyu, 1951, starring Kinuyo Tanaka
The 47 Ronin, 1941, starring Yoshizaburo Bashi	The Life of Oharu, 1952, starring Kinuyo Tanaka and Tsukie Matsuura

Kenji Mizoguchi

Akira Kurosawa

1910, Tokyo—1998, Tokyo

■ Pioneered deep-focus photography, which allows all characters to be in focus
■ Worked with actor Toshirô Mifune on 16 films ■ Inspired by westerns, US crim
films, and the work of John Ford and Jean Renoir ■ Revered by many directors
■ Japanese ■ Drama, Samurai, Crime, Literary Adaptation ■ Directed 31 film

1910 Born in Japan

1943 Debut film, *Judo Saga*

1948 First directs Toshirô Mifune, in *Drunken Angel*

1950 Oscar for *Rashomon*

1980 *Kagemusha* wins the Palme d'Or

1982 Publishes his *Something Like an Autobiography*

1990 Wins Honorary Academy Award for lifetime achievement

1997 Toshirô Mifune dies

1998 Dies in Tokyo

After earning international recognition with *Rashom*
in 1950, Akira Kurosawa produced a series of films s
hailed as some of the world's best. His steady style is cha
acterized by the use of telephoto lenses, which expand
a shot's range and flattened the frame. They also enabl
him to keep his camera far from his actors, not interferi
with their performance. A perfectionist, Kurosawa w
known to have roofs removed, streams reversed, a
hundreds of horses imported to make his epically scal
films look just right. His actors were often provided wi
their costumes weeks in advance to make sure they h
the lived-in appearance he desired. After the indulge
two-year shoot of *Red Beard*, the director broke with C

Ran, 1985, starring Tatsuya Nakadai and Mieko Harada

ing (Nakadai) divides his gdom among his sons and ir greed sparks a brutal war. n was awarded an Oscar for its gant costumes. Before this aptation of Shakespeare's g Lear, Kurosawa also adapted e story of Macbeth as *Throne Blood* (1957). Literary adapta- ns from various cultures, xed with Japanese styles, cul- e, and history were a popular nre for the director. He also ned versions of Russian clas- s including *The Lower Depths* 957) by Gorky, and *The Idiot* 951) by Dostoyevsky.

■ **Seven Samurai**, 1954, starring Takashi Shimura and Toshirô Mifune

This intriguing blend of samurai lore and Hollywood western was hugely influential in the rest of the world and was even remade by John Sturges in the US under the name *The Magnificent Seven* (1960). By using several cameras to film the action sequences from different angles at once, Kurosawa could create more dynamic scenes in the editing room, all the while preserving continuity. By choosing lenses longer than 150 mm, the image became a bit flattened, enabling greater clarity at a

grander scale. Kurosawa's sharp editing and brilliantly orchestrated action would inspire a new, almost balletic type of martial arts film that would stylistically plunder *Seven Samurai* for years to come.

Other Works
No Regrets for Our Youth, 1946, starring Setsuko Hara
Stray Dog, 1949, starring Toshirô Mifune
Red Beard, 1965, starring Toshirô Mifune
Kagemusha, 1980, starring Tatsuya Nakadai

Akira Kurosawa

Toshirô Mifune, his star of 16 films, and Japanese funding became hard to come by. With the help of his American director friends, and even Soviet producers for *Dersu Uzala* (1975), the director went on to make films at a slower pace until the age of 83. At the time he was accused by Japanese critics of catering to Western audiences, but in retrospect his films seem to explicitly deal with foreign cinematic influences and technological advances. If he used Western vernacular from the work of John Ford (p. 158) or the hard-boiled crime novels of Ed McBain, he always juxtaposed it with Japanese history or culture, creating a powerful dynamic. American directors such as Arthur Penn and Francis Ford Coppola (p. 314) acknowledge his influence, and George Lucas (p. 358) even transposed the plot of *The Hidden Fortress* (1958) to form the narrative base of *Star Wars*.

■ **Rashomon**, 1950, starring Toshirô Mifune and Machiko K...

This radical telling and retellin... of an alleged rape offers four different storytellers' points o... view and allows their subjecti... takes to coexist in the audien... mind, giving them the choice ... choose which one is "true." Th... story technique was also used... Bryan Singer's *The Usual Suspe...* *Rashomon*'s international suc... cess coincided with the growi... confidence of the Japanese ec... omy, and soon its film industr... was making 500 films a year.

Dreams, 1990, starring Akira
...ao and Martin Scorsese

...s film in eight segments, all
...ed on dreams Kurosawa
..., was the only film he wrote
...e. His admirers, George

Lucas, Francis Ford Coppola,
and Steven Spielberg helped
secure funding for the project.
The *Crows* segment stars
Scorsese as Vincent Van Gogh
who guides an art student

(based on the young Kurosawa)
through his paintings. Other,
grimmer segments like *Mount
Fuji Red* warn against nuclear
proliferation and warfare, but
are just as painterly.

■ **Yojimbo**, 1961, starring Toshirô Mifune and Tatsuya Nakadai

After a prolific 1950s, Kurosawa started the new decade with a black comedy that is rooted in both American gangster and western films. Mifune plays a rogue samurai who plays a town's two warring gangs against each other, until he is the last man standing. *Yojimbo* was remade, almost shot for shot, by Sergio Leone as his spaghetti western *For a Few Dollars More* (1964), with Clint Eastwood in the lead role.

Akira Kurosawa

New Impulses
1960–1974

"What the hell is wrong with freedom?
That's what it's all about."

Dennis Hopper: Easy Rider, 1969, USA, starring Dennis
Hopper, Peter Fonda, and Jack Nicholson
Quote: Dennis Hopper as Billy in *Easy Rider*

New Impulse

French New Wave

In the late 1950s through the '60s, a group of free-spirited directors have a lasting influence on generations of filmmakers with radical film language and techniques

p. 228

American Cinema

New methods of storyt that used more comple characters, ambiguous sages, and innovative s

Robert Aldrich
Hal Ashby p. 294
John Frankenheimer
George Roy Hill p. 274
Norman Jewison

1960   1962   1964   19

Claude Chabrol p. 234
Jean-Luc Godard p. 232
Chris Marker
Jacques Rivette
Eric Rohmer
François Truffaut p. 236
Agnès Varda

European Avant-garde

Three icons revolutionized world cinema with their enigmatic and compelling works

Michelangelo
Antonioni p. 238
Ingmar Bergman
p. 230
Luis Buñuel
p. 228

Stanley Kubrick p. 246
Sydney Lumet p. 268
Mike Nichols p. 276
Sam Peckinpah p. 270
Arthur Penn
Sydney Pollack p. 278

p. 233

p. 274

960–1974

European Cinema

Intellectual architects of contemporary cinema

Bernardo Bertolucci p. 240
John Boorman
David Lean p. 244
Sergio Leone p. 264
Joseph Losey p. 284
Roman Polanski p. 296
Nicolas Roeg p. 288

The Independents

Radical realism with a vision of independent cinema

John Cassavetes p. 292
Dennis Hopper
Glauber Rocha

223

1968   1970   1975

ritish Free nema

om 1956 until the mid-
50s, a semi-documen-
y style with political
nsciousness set against
leak social background

dsay Anderson p. 282
k Clayton
hard Lester
n Loach
ny Richardson

Ken Russell
John Schlesinger p. 286
Andrei Tarkovsky p. 298
Andrzej Wajda
Peter Yates

p. 256

p. 297

Comedy in the United States

The heirs of slapstick and screwball comedy

Mel Brooks p. 258
Blake Edwards p. 260
Jerry Lewis p. 256

New Impulses

Fresh Ideas and New Realities

In the 1950s, one of the most profound and influential movements, the French New Wave—a group of critics writing for the magazine *Cahiers du Cinema*—called for a radical breach with classic moviemaking and hailed new approaches such as Italian Neo-Realism. According to their "auteur theory," film should carry the director's inimitable style—as epitomized by John Ford and Alfred Hitchcock. Another source of inspiration was the experimental Nouveau Roman, exemplified in Alain Resnais's *Hiroshima Mon Amour*. New stylistic and narrative techniques such as improvised dialogue, rapid changes of scene, and jump cuts were used in an attempt to revolutionize viewing patterns.

■ **Agnès Varda**
Cléo from 5 to 7
1962, starring
Corinne Marchand

■ **Alain Resnais**
Hiroshima Mon Amour, 1959, starring Emmanuelle Riva and Eiji Okada

Richard Lester:
A Hard Day's
Night, 1964, star-
ring the Beatles

Mike Hodges:
Get Carter, 1971,
starring Michael
Caine and Britt
Ekland

European Cinema: Icons and Iconoclasts

Europe was home to three outstanding directors, whose
idiosyncratic signatures and characteristic styles influenced generations of filmmakers, though they cannot
be attributed to any particular movement: Michelangelo Antonioni with his sense of alienation and manipulation of time; Ingmar Bergman, whose works are
characterized by a philosophical profundity; and Luis
Buñuel, famous for his surreal takes on the bourgeoisie.
Alongside these icons of European cinema and the
French New Wave, other national movements developed, such as British New Wave, which focused on
working-class topics in a stark, semi-documentary
style. While classical crime thrillers like *Get Carter*
depicted urban tristesse, Richard Lester showed a more
cheerful vision of the UK's "swinging sixties" in his
Beatles films. The ongoing attraction of big Hollywood
productions can be seen in the CinemaScope epics by
David Lean, Bernardo Bertolucci, and Sergio Leone.

American Cinema: A New Spirit

While new movements exploring different portrayals of realism developed in Europe, Hollywood was forced to face the decline of its studio system, which was triggered by the spread of TV technology and financial problems within the film industry. More liberal approaches to sex and violence, which already characterized European cinema, were introduced with the abolishment of the Production Code and filmmakers pushed this new freedom to the limits. The graphic violence of Sam Peckinpah or the explicit language used in Bob Fosse's biopic *Lenny,* about comedian Lenny Bruce, are symptomatic of this new attitude.

Tackling concepts of reality in the United States also meant dealing with deep-seated racial issues and conflicts and questions of conscience, which were treated in a variety of films ranging from the crime thriller *In the Heat of the Night* to Robert Mulligan's poignant literary adaptation of the American

■ **Norman Jewison: In th Heat of the Ni** 1967, starring Sidney Poitier a Rod Steiger

■ **Robert Mulligan: To K Mockingbird,** 1962, starring C ory Peck and M Badham

Bob Fosse:
Lenny, 1974,
starring Dustin
Hoffman

Jack Clayton:
The Great Gatsby,
1974, starring
Robert Redford and
Mia Farrow

classic, *To Kill a Mockingbird*, whose protagonist, the moral lawyer Atticus Finch (Gregory Peck), to this day is hailed as the "greatest hero of American film" and even influenced the ethics of the American legal system.

The mix of cultural and political turmoil during the 1960s and early '70s led to counterculture movements and a liberal spirit that is evident in box-office hits like Mike Nichols's *The Graduate* (1967) as well as in the works of young directors such as Hal Ashby and Arthur Penn, all of which portray unorthodox characters that broke the "types" that had featured so prominently in American films up until that time. Their films also pay tribute to the aesthetics of the French New Wave filmmakers. While the glamour and illusion of Jack Clayton's *The Great Gatsby* exemplified the lingering influence of classic Hollywood style, the experimental films of John Cassavetes paved the way for independent directors.

Luis Buñuel

1900, Calanda–1983, Mexico City

■ Father of cinematic Surrealism ■ Made most of his movies in Mexico and France ■ Critical of organized religion and the bourgeoisie ■ Won the Palme d'Or in Cannes twice as well as 29 other film awards
■ Spanish-Mexican ■ Surrealist, Avant-garde, Drama ■ Directed 32 films

■ **1900** Born into a bourgeois family and raised in a repressive Jesuit school in Spain
1920 Studies literature and philosophy in Madrid; meets Salvador Dalí and García Lorca
1933–35 Dubs American films in Paris and Spain
1938–42 Employed in the Museum of Modern Art in New York
1944–46 Works for Warner Brothers in Hollywood
1947 Moves to Mexico
1949 Mexican citizenship
1983 Publishes autobiography, *My Last Sigh*
1983 Dies in Mexico City

An auteur and a provocateur at heart, Buñuel began h directing career infiltrating reality with surreal image His oeuvre can be split into three creative periods. Th groundbreaking short *An Andalusian Dog* (1928), whic he created with Salvador Dalí, made him part of the Su realist movement, reinforced by the even more sca dalous *The Golden Age* (1930). After the provocati documentary short *Land Without Bread* (1932), Buñuel le Spain and did not direct for 15 years. His Mexican peri covered a couple of commissioned works for the Mexic market which nonetheless bear his iconoclastic hallmar *Viridiana* (1961), the only feature film he made in h native country, was banned in Spain for its anticleric images, among which was a parody of the Last Supp His later French movies combined his deep-felt Su realism with even more subversive and satirical image

New Impulses 1960–1974

Other Works	
Nazarín, 1959, starring Francisco Rabal	The Phantom of Liberty, 1974, starring Jean-Claude Brialy, Michel Piccoli, and Monica Vitti
Diary of a Chambermaid, 1964, starring Jeanne Moreau	

■ **The Discreet Charm of the Bourgeoisie**, 197 starring Fernando Rey and Stéphane Audran

This Surrealist masterpiece unfolds like a series comical and inescapable dreams. Six stoic upp class friends try in vain to have dinner togethe but are constantly interrupted by absurd happenings. This hilarious satire on capitalism received an Oscar for Best Foreign Film.

Belle de Jour, 1967, starring Catherine Deneuve, Michel Piccoli, and Pierre Clémenti

Deneuve plays the wife of a wealthy doctor whose repressed sexual desires lead her to prostitution. While her masochistic nature becomes obvious in a series of erotic daydreams, she starts a more serious love affair with a client, a seedy gangster who shoots her husband out of jealousy and then gets killed himself.

The Young and the Damned, 1950, starring Alfonso Mejía and Roberto Cobo

Set in the slums of Mexico City, the film follows the violent lives of a group of juvenile delinquents. Inspired by Vittorio De Sica's *Shoeshine* (1946),

Buñuel took a bleak and unapologetic stand to strengthen what he called an "attack on the sadness that ruins children before they have a chance." A young boy, neglected by his mother, joins a gang. When

he witnesses a murder by the gang leader, he decides to look for a job, but harsh circumstances lead to a fatal ending. The prophetic heritage of the film was reflected half a century later in the Brazilian movie *City of God* (2002).

Luis Buñuel

Ingmar Bergman

1918, Uppsala–2007, Fårö

■ Won the Palm of Palms at Cannes ■ Architect of psychological-existential films ■ Wrote the scripts for most of his films ■ Won 60 film awards plus nine Academy Award nominations
■ Swedish ■ Avant-garde, Drama, Chamber Cinema ■ Directed 40 films

1918 Born into a rigorous Lutheran family in Sweden

1937 Studies art and literature at Stockholm University

1945 Directs first movie, *Crisis*

1963 Director at the Royal Dramatic Theatre, Stockholm

1976–85 Self-imposed exile in Munich; makes *The Serpent's Egg* (1977)

2007 Dies in Sweden; all his films are included in UNESCO's Memory of the World archive

Ingmar Bergman ranks among the most prolific directors of all time; those he has influenced include directors Stanle Kubrick (p. 246), Andrei Tarkovsky (p. 298), Woody Alle (p. 326), and David Lynch (p. 350). Trained in theater, h profoundly intellectual and sensuous films deal with met physical issues such as mortality, loneliness, faith, and th clash between adolescents and adults. Films such a *Summer with Monika* (1953) deal with his signature topi women and their identity, while his 1960s' trilogy *Throug a Glass Darkly, Winter Light,* and *The Silence* examines th nonexistence of God. Throughout his work, the complexi ties of human nature are depicted with an unmatche magical camera style, inspiring his actors to improvise.

■ **Wild Strawberries**, 1957, starring Victor Sjöström and Ingrid Thulin

An old professor travels to his former university to receive a honorary degree. Various encounters on the road alternate with flashbacks and surre dreams that forecast his death and make him aware of his life time failings and loneliness.

Other Works

The Seventh Seal, 1957, starring Bibi Andersson and Max von Sydow

Scenes from a Marriage, 1973, starring Liv Ullmann and Erland Josephson

The Silence, 1963, starring
[Ingr]id Thulin and Gunnel
[Lin]dblom

[Tw]o sisters and a ten-year-old are
[liv]ing in a hotel in a foreign
[cou]ntry where they do not under-
[stan]d the language. Isolation and
[the] impossibility to communicate

are the main topics of this dark
and disturbing movie with
explicit sex scenes. Cinematographer Sven Nykvist
realized Bergman's radically
claustrophobic
picture with
extreme depth
of focus.

[F]anny and Alexander, 1982, starring Pernilla
[All]vin and Bertil Guve

[Ber]gman called this autobiographical work,
[whi]ch received four Academy Awards, a
[sum]mary of his life as a filmmaker. Siblings
[Fan]ny and Alexander grow up in a pros-
[per]ous household in Sweden. After the
[fath]er's sudden death, the mother
[mar]ries the bishop and moves to his
[asc]etic chancery, where the children
[suff]er from isolation and hardship.

Jean-Luc Godard

1930, Paris

- The ultimate intellectual of cinema history ■ Leading figure of the Nouve
Vague (French New Wave) ■ Invented new film aesthetics, styles, and tech-
niques ■ Won 30 film awards
- French-Swiss ■ Avant-garde, Drama, Satire ■ Directed 40 Films

■ **1930** Born into a wealthy French-Swiss family

1950 Establishes film magazine with Jacques Rivette

1954 First short movie, *Operation Concrete*

1968 Forms the Dziga Vertov Group, a Marxist film-production company

1988–89 *History(s) of the Cinema*, a video project about the concept of cinema and 20th-century history

2007 European Film Award for Lifetime Achievement

Godard is by far the most radical figure of the French N Wave, with no other modern director having broken many cinematic conventions. His search for new arti expression and his relentless way of transferring left politics to the screen are legendary. The prototype of auteur, he bravely exercised social criticism and used screen like an artist. His early, most influential films are ch acterized by their neglect of classical narrative structu and their mixed genres. Many directors have remarked classics like *Band of Outsiders* (1964) and *Pierrot le I* (1965). After an intense political period, he concentrated distinguished film essays for TV before returning to screen with provocative films such as *Hail Mary* (1985).

■ **Contempt**, 1963, starring Brigitte Bardot, Michel Piccoli, Jack Palance, and Fritz Lang

Contempt is a critical discourse about filmmaking. Steeped in bright Mediterranean colors and composed in three acts like a Greek tragedy, the film is an oppressive picture puzzle of reality, fiction, and ennui.

Other Works

Week-End, 1967, starring Mireille Darc and Jean Yanne

Détective, 1985, starring Laurent Terzieff and Jean-Pierre Léaud

Notre Musique, 2004, starring Sarah Adler and Nade Dieu

Breathless, 1960, starring
n-Paul Belmondo and Jean
berg

sed on an idea by Truffaut,
key film of the French New
ve is fresh and spontaneous.
mondo plays a hoodlum
who mimics the mannerisms of
Humphrey Bogart. Having accidentally shot a policeman he
plans to flee Paris with his girlfriend (Seberg). A restless
thriller whose point is not suspense, it portrays a young
couple searching for a new
definition of love. The film references pop culture and rose to
fame for its lightness, improvised dialogues, inventive jump
cuts, natural sets, and handheld camera work.

Alphaville, 1965, starring Eddie Constantine
d Anna Karina

combining science fiction and film noir into a
real thriller, Godard pays homage to Fritz Lang
well as foreseeing Kubrick's vision of a future
rld where computers rule over humankind.
tead of using special effects to create the
pistic town of Alphaville, Paris is transformed
o a nightly urban landscape full of neon signs
d bleak concrete. The film follows a secret
ent as he fights a fictitious technocracy with
th weapons and witty language.

Jean-Luc Godard

Claude Chabrol

1930, Paris

■ Pioneer of French New Wave ■ Master of suspense, following in the tradition of Alfred Hitchcock ■ Intelligent analysis of the bourgeoisie ■ European Film Academy Lifetime Achievement Award, 2003
■ French ■ Thriller, Film Noir, Drama, Comedy ■ Directed 54 films

■ **1930** Born to a pharmacist

1958 First movie, *Le Beau Serge*, marks the beginning of French New Wave

1959 Wins Golden Bear in Berlin for *The Cousins*

1964 Starts a series of spy thrillers

1978 *Violette Nozière*, a successful adaptation of a 1930s murder case, starring Isabelle Huppert

1988 *Story of Women*, a gripping portrait of a back-street abortionist in Nazi-occupied France

2007 Critic's Award for *A Girl Cut in Two*, Venice Film Festival

Like many of his fellows of the Nouvelle Vague (French New Wave), Chabrol started as a film critic for the magazine *Cahiers du Cinéma*. In the early 1950s he wrote a book about Alfred Hitchcock (p. 186), who greatly influenced Chabrol's suspenseful style. His early films are characterized by an improvised Realism, typical of the French New Wave and which is charmingly executed in *The Good Time Girls* (1960). Most of Chabrol's meticulously crafted later movies explore murder and obsession while chronicling French society. His films are sardonic observations of the bourgeoisie and its hypocritical morals—like Hitchcock with a social consciousness. Chabrol often put actress Stéphane Audran (his wife from 1964 to 1980) in the leading role and, after their divorce, often worked with Isabelle Huppert.

■ **Hell**, 1994, starring Emmanuelle Béart and François Cluzet

Adapted from a 1964 script by Henri-Georges Clouzot, another master of the French suspense thriller, *Hell* is a prime example of a psychological study. Paul, happily married to stunningly beautiful Nelly, becomes more and more jealous. Driven far more by delusion than reality, he gets increasingly suspicious about everything his wife does and slowly turns into a mentally ill monster. With masochistic loyalty, Nelly endures all suffering

New Impulses 1960–1974

French New Wave

**Innocents with Dirty
Hands**, 1975, starring Romy
Schneider, Rod Steiger, and
Paolo Giusti

Innocents with Dirty Hands tells
the story of Schneider con-
spiring with her lover, young
Paolo Giusti, to kill her alcoholic
and impotent husband Steiger.
Afterward the dead body
mysteriously vanishes with his
money and Giusti. The wryly
humorous plot twists between
reality and amorality, deliv-
ing a series of unexpected
surprises.

🔲 **This Man Must Die**, 1969, starring Michel Duchaussoy and
Jean Yanne

Charles (Duchaussoy) is seeking revenge on his son's hit-and-run
killer. When he finds the suspect—garage owner Paul (Yanne)—
Charles seduces his sister-in-law to gain access into the family.
He notes his murderous plans in a diary but, despite the culprit's
monstrous behavior, finds himself unable to act. When Charles
realizes that Paul's son wishes his father dead as well, the forces
of destiny and vengeance collide. Luminous narrative
structure, tense performances, and subtly
evocative cinematography make this
one of Chabrol's most convincing thrillers—one
that owes more to
Fritz Lang than
to Hitchcock.

François Truffaut

1932, Paris—1984, Neuilly-sur-Seine

■ Leading figure of the French New Wave ■ Advocate of the author's cinem
■ Pioneer of art-house cinema ■ Greatly influenced by Jean Renoir and Alfre
Hitchcock ■ Won 28 film awards, nominated for three Academy Awards
■ French ■ Drama, Film Noir, Comedy ■ Directed 21 films

■ **1932** Born as an illegiti-
mate child in Paris

1955 First short films with
Jacques Rivette and Alain
Resnais

1960 Producer for Jean
Cocteau and Jacques
Rivette

1967 Publishes a long interview with Hitchcock

1974 *Day for Night* wins an
Academy Award

1977 Acts in Spielberg's
*Close Encounters of the
Third Kind*

1984 Dies in France

Truffaut was a notorious lover of cinema. After a diffic
childhood, he worked as a film critic for *Cahiers du Ciné*
with the support of publisher André Bazin. He so
became one of the leading figures of the French N
Wave, though he was more radical as a critic than as a fi
maker. Truffaut worked on the scripts of all his mov
often showing a deep affection for the crime novels
adapted for the film noirs *Shoot the Piano Player* (1960) a
Mississippi Mermaid (1969). Another common feature
the presence of children, best exemplified in *The Wild Cl*
(1970) and *Small Change* (1976). The driving force of
creative output was the romantic notion of sharing
passion for cinema with his audience.

Other Works

The Bride Wore Black, 1968, starring Jeanne Moreau	The Last Metro, 198C starring Gérard Depa dieu and Catherine Deneuve
Day for Night, 1973, starring Jacqueline Bisset and Valentina Cortese	Confidentially Yours 1983, starring Fanny Ardant

■ **Jules and Jim**, 1962, starring Jeanne More
Oskar Werner, and Henri Serre

The lightness of being characterizes this accou
a ménage à trois between a German, Jules
(Werner), a Frenchman, Jim (Serre), and unfath-
omable Catherine (Moreau), but passion turns i
melancholy. Outstanding performances, brillia
montage, an anamorphic lens, and the lyrical mu
of George Delerue makes this homage to Chap
and Renoir a timeless masterpiece of poetic cine

New Impulses 1960–1974

he 400 Blows, 1959, star-
 Jean-Pierre Léaud

 of the most intense and
ping portraits of adoles-
ce ever banned on celluloid,
aut's debut awarded him
 Director in Cannes. Remi-
ent of the director's own

deprived childhood, the film
tells the story of his alter ego
Antoine Doinel (Léaud) who
seeks love from his mother and
stepfather but is rejected. He
regularly runs into trouble at
school, is caught stealing, and is
sent to a reformatory school. He

flees to the seaside, where the
movie, shot in vivid documentary style, ends ambiguously
with a landmark freeze-frame
close-up of the boy. *The 400
Blows* started the Antoine
Doinel series that includes films
on marriage and divorce.

ahrenheit 451, 1966,
ing Oskar Werner and
 Christie

aut's foremost intention
to make a film about books.
red by Ray Bradbury's sci-
-fiction novel, he creates a
-future world where books
orbidden. Werner plays a
ghter whose task is burning
ks but who begins to doubt
n he starts a romance with
egal book lover (Christie).

François Truffaut

Michelangelo Antonioni

1912, Ferrara—2007, Rome

■ Pioneer of postwar cinema ■ Aesthetically one of the most influential a
cinema directors ■ Elliptical and open-ended films ■ Won the lifetime
achievement Academy Award ■ Recieved 35 International Film Awards
■ Italian ■ Drama, Experimental ■ Directed 17 movies

■ **1912** Born in Italy

1936 Studies economics; works as a film critic

1942 Scriptwriter for Roberto Rossellini, assistant director for Marcel Carné

1943 *People of the Po Valley*, first of his Neo-Realist short documentaries

1983 Golden Lion, Venice, Lifetime Achievement

1995 *Beyond the Clouds*, episodic film, co-directed by Wim Wenders

2007 Dies on the same day as Ingmar Bergman

A pessimistic view of the world pervades the wor
Antonioni, especially the films he directed in the 19
which defined a new aesthetic that influenced art-ho
cinema for generations. His suggestive, stylized fi
examined people's incapability to understand their c
lives. Antonioni's renowned "Italian trilogy" is cente
on one of his major topics: alienation. Images of archit
ture and landscapes, presented with long camera sh
are as important as his characters. His later works por
his mastership of composition with brilliant mise-
scene that mix light and color. Devoid of classical lin
causality, his movies offer enigmatic stories whose va
endings are nonetheless perfect in their incompleten

New Impulses 1960–1974

Other Works	
Cronaca di un Amore, 1950, starring Lucia Bosé and Massimo Girotti	The Passenger, 1975 starring Jack Nichols and Maria Schneider
Il Deserto Rosso, 1964, starring Monica Vitti and Richard Harris	Identification of a Woman, 1982, starrir Tomas Milian

■ **Eclipse**, 1962, starring Monica Vitti and Alain Delon

After *L'Avventura* (1960) and *La Notte* (1961), A
nioni ends his Italian trilogy with *Eclipse*. Vitti's
affair with a materialistic broker suffers becaus
her ennui, which is visually enforced by geome
cally framed shots and symbolism. A triptych in
black and white, these unforgettable images, c
bined with a detached mood, created a new ci
matic language. Antonioni said, "Nothing app
as it should in a world where nothing is certain

Blowup, 1966, starring David Hemmings and Vanessa Redgrave

A vibrant portrait of London in the 1960s, the film captures a day in the life of a selfish but disillusioned fashion photographer, who accidentally witnesses a crime when photographing an unknown couple. The woman tracks him to his studio and begs him to give her the film. He becomes suspicious and makes blowups of the photos—the developing process becoming a meditation on the line between reality and imagination—until he finally identifies a dead body. When he eventually finds the body in the park, he is without his camera. Later, the body is gone, as are the film and photos. In his unlikely hero's strange odyssey, Antonioni incorporates parties, liberated teenagers, rock music, and hippies into an artificially colorized urban landscape saturated with bleak Pop Art colors. Ultimately, *Blowup* is about reality and how we perceive it, or think we perceive it.

■ **Zabriskie Point**, 1970, starring Mark Frechette and Daria Halprin

An essay on American counterculture in the 1960s that flirts with psychedelic art and romantic notions, the film, with an amateur cast, tells the story of two idealistic lovers. A scene in Death Valley multiplies into a stunning vision of sexual liberation, and the criticism of consumerism is symbolized by an explosion filmed in slow motion and scored with the music of Pink Floyd. Unfortunately, the film was a commercial failure.

Michelangelo Antonioni

Bernardo Bertolucci

1940, Parma

■ Films focus on the analysis of the human soul and psyche ■ Influenced b
Jean-Luc Godard and Pier Paolo Pasolini ■ Inspired New Hollywood directc
■ Career Golden Lion, Venice, 2007 ■ 27 Film Awards
■ Italian ■ Drama, Epic Drama ■ Directed 15 Films

1940 Born to a well-known
Italian poet and film critic

1960 Publishes poetry
book, the prize-winning
In Search of Mystery

1961 Assistant director for
Pier Paolo Pasolini on
Accattone

1962 First film, *The Grim
Reaper*

1964 *Before the Revolution*
wins Max Ophüls Prize

1968 Scriptwriter for
Sergio Leone's *Once
Upon a Time in the
West*

1971 Directs elec-
tion campaign
film for Commu-
nist party

1989 Features
Bologna for
1990 FIFA
World
Cup
film

The works of Bernardo Bertolucci are characterized
Marxist politics, Freudian psychoanalysis, a deep love
the arts, and an obsession with sex. Growing up in
intellectual circles of his artistic father, he started exp
menting with home movies in his adolescence. His e
feature films already showed strong characteristics
time-transcending narrative structure, expressive light
and inventive camera moves. While the greatest crit
response was reserved for *The Conformist* (1970), the en
cism of *Last Tango in Paris* (1972) caused a worldw
sensation. The five-hour epic *1900* (1976), about c
struggle, was followed by the more commercial, lo
trilogy about isolation, containing the critic
hailed *The Last Emperor* (1987), *The Shelter
Sky* (1990), and *Little Buddha* (1993). In
Dreamers, Bertolucci returned to the—rom
tically transfigured—turmoil of the 196
further exploring sex, cinema, and politi

■ **Last Tango in Paris**, 197
starring Marlon Brando and
Maria Schneider

The highly controversial box-
office hit about an anonymo
sexual relationship of Americ
Paul (Brando) and young Par
enne Jeanne (Schneider) was
banned in Italy and censored
elsewhere. While the interior
were inspired by the visionar
paintings of Francis Bacon, it
Brando's intense performanc
that made the film a success.

he Last Emperor, 1987,
ing John Lone, Joan Chen,
Peter O'Toole

unmatched historical epic
assive proportions boasts
ptional costumes, exotic
and impressive central

perspectives that create a kalei-
doscopic effect. It won nine
Academy Awards and Ber-
tolucci was the first director
ever to be permitted to film in
the Forbidden City, where the
story of China's last monarch

unfolds. The child emperor is
raised in isolation, later dis-
pelled by the Communists,
used as a shadow puppet by
the Japanese, imprisoned by
the Soviets, and ends up as a
gardener in Beijing.

■ **The Conformist**, 1970,
starring Jean-Louis Trintignant

Told in flashbacks in a stream of
consciousness, Bertolucci's
intellectual story about the
mechanisms of fascism features
cinematographer Vittorio
Storaro's exceptional visual
style, which transformed the
ambivalent story about patri-
cide, homosexuality, and
treason into a mind-bending
feast for the eye and the mind.

Other Works

The Spider's Stratagem, 1970,
starring Giulio Brogi and Alida
Valli

Tragedy of a Ridiculous Man,
1981, starring Ugo Tognazzi
and Anouk Aimée

Stealing Beauty, 1996, starring
Liv Tyler and Jeremy Irons

The Dreamers, 2003, starring
Michael Pitt and Eva Green

Bernardo Bertolucci

Angry and Adventurous

The Vietnam War and the counterculture of the 1960s had a lasting impact
young American directors and actors. The decline of the old Hollywood stu
system and the abolishment of the Production Code were further evidenc
change. As films became more violent, film heroes got more vicious. Paul Newr
was a role model for cleverly courageous parts while Clint Eastwood (p. 3
epitomized the rough cowboy. Their European counterpart, French actor A
Delon, starred in *The Godson* (1967) and *The Sicilian Clan* (1969) and incarna
European cool. Jean-Paul Belmondo of *That Man from Rio* (1964) was Fran
sunnier action hero. Meanwhile, Jane Fonda's performance in *Barbarella* (19
was the female equivalent to the hard-action heros of the 1960s and early '7

■ **Easy Rider's** (1969) Dennis
Hopper and Peter Fonda popularized the American road movie.
Hopper was already a rebellious
actor and Hollywood misfit by
the time he directed his first
feature, the low-budget
production *Easy*

Rider. The biker's odyssey
features Billy (Hopper) and
Wyatt (Fonda), wittily named
after western heroes, and
encompasses the trinity of 1960s
counterculture: sex, drugs,
and rock 'n' roll. The

protagonists' search for free
ends in their disillusioning de
The improvised plot, fresh di
logue, and stunning landsca
provide for the ultimate roac
movie—a timeless masterpi

■ **Sean Connery's role as James Bond** made the debonair secret agent iconic. The longest running film series in cinema history, Ian Fleming's British Secret Service agent 007, first made it onto the screen in *Dr. No* (1962, left). The spy has experienced multiple incarnations—Sean Connery, Roger Moore, Pierce Brosnan, and Daniel Craig are some of actors who have played the part. Characterized by dry British humor, heroism in every situation, state-of-the-art cars and gadgets, villains who long for world domination, and the notorious Bond girls, the Bond series has paved the way for numerous new "types."

Peter Yates's *Bullitt* (1968) s Steve McQueen, himself a sionate biker and racing car er, in a leading role that tailor-made for him. For greater part of the film, this ce thriller shows him ind the wheel as the dom of the road is captured m's first legendary car se. The visual brilliance of high-speed chase through Francisco was as influential he action genre as the cha-erization of a waywardly bedient police officer ose legacy is seen in films *Dirty Harry* (1971) and *The ch Connection* (1971).

Angry and Adventurous

David Lean

1908, Croydon–1991, London

■ Editor and director ■ Famous for epics of cinematographic grandeur
■ Greatly influenced by John Ford ■ Admired by Steven Spielberg, Marti[n]
Scorsese, and George Lucas ■ Won 2 Oscars and 24 other Film Awards
■ British ■ Drama, Epic, Romance ■ Directed 16 films

■ **1908** Born to Quakers who think films are a sin
1930 Editor of newsreels
1934 Edits feature films
1942 Directs first film, In Which We Serve, co-directed with Noël Coward
1984 Is knighted
1990 American Film Institute's Lifetime Achievement Award
1991 Dies in London

If there ever was a British director whose knightly accol[ade] was reflected in his screen adventures, it is Sir David Le[an]. With only a couple of epics he made cinema history. A[fter] miscellaneous jobs in the British film industry, L[ean] became an editor in the 1930s. Before winning multitu[de] of international awards for his monumental films, [he] directed nearly a dozen notable films in the 1940 and '[50]. His first feature films were intimate dramas such as [the] classic romance *Brief Encounter*, one of a few collaborati[ons] with playwright Noël Coward. His screen adaptation[s of] Charles Dickens's novels *Great Expectations* (1946) a[nd] *Oliver Twist* (1948) already showed a tendency [for] historical accuracy and visual perfectionism. These ch[ar]acteristics grew to artistic heights with his [later] cinematic monuments, time-absorbing superla[tive] enterprises covering continents and the comp[lex] scale of human existence.

Other Works

Brief Encounter, 1945, starring Celia Johnson	*A Passage to India*, 1984, starring Judy Davis, Victor Banearjee, and Peggy Ashcroft
Ryan's Daughter, 1970, starring Robert Mitchum	

■ **The Bridge on the River Kwai**, 1957, starring Alec Guinness

This war drama contains a minimum of combat but a lot of psychology. Captured in a Japanese prison camp, British colonel Nicholson (Guinness) is forced to build a bridge. Th[e] task turns into a question of honor for him, and when the Allies plan to destroy the bri[dge] the story heads for a fatal cli[max]. The exciting epic won seven Academy Awards, including [Best] Picture and Best Director.

Doctor Zhivago, 1965, starring Omar Sharif and Julie Christie

e lush adaptation of Boris sternak's novel took three ars to make. It was—regards of five Academy awards— lled to pieces by critics, but diences were overwhelmed this gargantuan love story. e film chronicles Russian iety and history of the early h century, focusing on the nance between Yuri Zhivago arif) and Lara (Christie). urice Jarre's title theme sically immortalized *Zhivago*.

Lawrence of Arabia, 1962, rring Peter O'Toole, Omar arif, Alec Guinness, and :hony Quinn

jarded as one of the best vies ever, this winner of seven demy Awards has lost ie of its magic. Briton T. E. vrence's autobiography iis Arabian adventures s the foundation for visually poetic sterpiece :

showed the desert as never seen before. Lawrence (O'Toole) is an enigmatic and eccentric British officer who helps Arabian Bedouins. His knowledge of politics and

culture, love for the desert, and homoerotic relation with Sherif Ali (Sharif) form a superb character study. In 1989 Steven Spielberg and George Lucas helped restore the film to its original length.

Stanley Kubrick

1928, New York–1999, Childwickbury Manor

■ Perfected every genre movie he realized ■ Absolute artistic control
■ Influenced by Max Ophüls ■ Influential to many directors including Stev
Spielberg, Ridley Scott, and James Cameron ■ Won 31 film awards
■ American/British ■ Drama, Science Fiction, War, History ■ Directed 13 fil

- ■ **1928** Born to a doctor
- **1946** Apprentice photographer
- **1951** First short documentary, *Day of the Fight*
- **1953** First feature film, *Fear and Desire*
- **1968** Starts working intensely on magnum opus *Napoleon*, which never materializes
- **1997** Lifetime Achievement Award, Directors Guild of America; Career Golden Lion, Venice
- **1999** Dies in the UK

Having trained his eye as a photographer, Stanley Kub
became one of the great maverick artists of mod
cinema. The passionate chess player gained the status c
obsessive filmmaker by working meticulously on ev
detail of his films, often repeating scenes numerous ti
during shooting until he deemed them to be perfect. Si
his adaptation of Nabokov's *Lolita*, he took artistic con
over every step of the production from start to finish, e
the marketing and public projection. With each new
terprise, which often took years of preparation, the re
sive director tried to tackle and incorporate a differ
genre. His insatiable curiosity frequently led to techn
innovations. Besides utilizing numerous special-effe

devices for *2001: A Sp
Odyssey* (p. 250), he a
obtained a special l
(originally made for

■ **Lolita**, 1962, starring Sue
Lyon, James Mason, and She
Winters

Kubrick turned Nabokov's sc
dalous novel into a psycholo
ical tour de force. The story
middle-aged, pedophilic pr
fessor (Mason) who falls in l
with a nymphet (Lyon) and
marries her mother (Winters
to stay close to her, depicts
alienation and obsession,
beguilement and dependenc
in a tragic farce—a source o
inspiration for David Lynch.

New Impulses 1960–1974

A Clockwork Orange, 1971, starring Malcolm McDowell

This satire is about a gang led by Alex DeLarge (McDowell), who loves Beethoven, killing, and raping until he is caught and has to undergo reeducation.

This leads to the overall question: If human beings are deprived of the ability to choose evil, are they necessarily good? The first Dolby film, it was so shocking in the UK that it was taken out of distribution.

Spartacus, 1960, starring Kirk Douglas, Laurence Olivier, Charles Laughton, and Jean Simmons

Spartacus was Kubrick's one and only affair with the American studio system. Having replaced Anthony Mann, he impressively showed for the first time what he could do as director on a huge scale. Though he achieved a convincing historical epic, he was upset by the power and influence of the producer, Kirk Douglas. Shot in 70 mm super Technirama, the film tells the story of rebellious slave Spartacus (Douglas) who leads fellow gladiators in a revolt against the Roman Empire. The revolt becomes the controversial subject in the political struggle between two senators, Crassus (Olivier) and the more temperate Gracchus (Laughton).

NASA) to present the world of the 18th century in *Barry Lyndon* in natural candlelight. Other strong characteristics included the customary use of a narrator and a strong emphasis on music, particularly classical, to enforce the sequence of events. The central motif of his work is the decision-making ability of an individual in an ambivalent world, the fallibility of man driven by fears and desires. His longtime friend Steven Spielberg (p. 354) called him "a complete illustrator of human condition." His worldview might have been pessimistic but his legacy of cinema masterpieces comforts us with the assurance of living in the most compelling of all worlds.

■ **The Shining**, 1980, starring Jack Nicholson and Shelley Duvall

The chase scenes through the hotel's long hall corridors and garden maze, where the barbarous horror story takes place, demonstrated the efficiency of the recently invented Steadicam. Kubrick transformed Stephen King's novel into a roller-coaster ride of sheer madness. Nicholson was in stunning form, while the director reportedly brought Duvall close to a nervous breakdown.

■ **Full Metal Jacket**, 1987, starring Matthew Modine

After graphic Vietnam War movies like Cimino's *The Deer Hunter* (1978) and Coppola's *Apocalypse Now* (1979), Kubrick's effort looked more like a te assembly. The humiliating training of the recruit by a vicious sergeant builds the first part of the story which continues in Vietnam.

Other Works	
The Killing, 1956, starring Sterling Hayden	Barry Lyndon, 1975, starring Ryan O'Neal
Paths of Glory, 1957, starring Kirk Douglas	Eyes Wide Shut, 199 starring Tom Cruise and Nicole Kidman

■ **Dr. Strangelove or: How I Learned to Stop Worrying and Love the Bomb**, 1964, starring Peter Sellers, George C. Scott, and Sterling Hayden

This subversive comedy, directed at the height of the Cold War, has delighted generations of art-house viewers. Peter Sellers, in a triple role as a British officer, US president, and the mysterious adviser Dr. Strangelove, had funny lines, but the implied nuclear threat underscored the seriousness of the issue.

Stanley Kubrick

2001: A Space Odyssey

■ by Stanley Kubrick, UK, 1968, Science Fiction

Kubrick (p. 246) based *2001: A Space Odyssey* on a sh[ort] story by Arthur C. Clarke and worked with the author [to] expand the plot into a philosophical discourse abo[ut] space, time, and the prospect of extraterrestrial life. T[he] film starts with apes finding an enigmatic black mo[no]lith and learning to use tools. In a legendary match c[ut] the film jumps forward three million years as a flyi[ng] bone turns into a spaceship. In 2001, a scientist flies [to] the moon to examine another mysterious monol[ith] followed by a mission to Jupiter 18 months later. The intelligent computer Hal 9000 kills the crew except astronaut Bowman, who manages to disconnect it. The mythological space adventure still inspires much speculation.

For Dawn of Man, the first of the film's four parts, Kubrick's Academy Award–winning special-effects team developed a front-projection system that allowed filming in the studio. A unique projector threw the image of an African waste-land onto a mammoth screen without the image being visible on the cast in the foreground. Another inventive technique was the Slit-Scan machine, made for the Star Gate sequence, of psychedelic light and shapes evoking infinity. Today CGI has made both techniques obsolete.

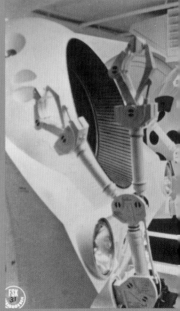

001: A Space Odyssey, 1968, starring ' Dullea and William Sylvester

prick consulted scientists, com-er designers, and aeronautical isers. The spacecrafts, most notably Ferris-wheel spaceship *Discovery* ame NASA later adopted), were istic. Flatscreens, biometrics, voice recognition are also ured before their time.

2001: A Space Odyssey

Science Fiction

- One of the earliest film genres ■ Topics include space and time travel; utopia and dystopia; aliens, androids, and apocalypse ■ Sophisticated special effects ■ Classics include *Metropolis*, *2001: A Space Odyssey*, and the *Alien*, *Star Wars*, and *Matrix* series
- *left:* **Planet of the Apes**, by Franklin J. Schaffner, 1968, starring Charlton Hesto

1902 *A Trip to the Moon*, by Georges Méliès, starts the genre

1927 Fritz Lang's *Metropolis* has a dystopian society

1966 *Fantastic Voyage*, by Richard Fleischer, is a trip inside the human body

1973 *Westworld*, by Michael Crichton, first film with CGI

1982 *Blade Runner* launches cyberpunk

1999 *Star Wars* series resumes with release of *The Phantom Menace* after a 16-year break

Science-fiction films are as old as the film industry. The first boom for the genre came in the wake of nuclear fission in the 1950s when numerous B-movies were made l cult heros such as Jack Arnold (*The Incredible Shrinking Man*, 1957) and Roger Corman (*Day the World Ende* 1955). Aliens, another favorite topic, were exemplified Robert Wise's (p. 170) *The Day the Earth Stood Still* (195 Stanley Kubrick's *2001: A Space Odyssey* (1968) was turning point toward more serious efforts. From apoc lyptic scenarios like *Mad Max* (1979) to fairy-tale spa adventures like *Star Wars* (1977), the popularity of scien fiction continues. In the 21st century, CGI has infinite multiplied special-effects opportunities.

Other Works

Invasion of the Body Snatche by Don Siegel, 1956, starring Kevin McCarthy and Dana Wyn

Johnny Mnemonic, by Robert Longo, 1995, starring Keanu Reeves

V for Vendetta, by James McTeigue, 2005, starring Natalie Portman

■ **Richard Fleischer: Soyle Green**, 1973, starring Charlto Heston and Edward G. Robins

Describing severe climate changes, this dystopian film al depicts the greenhouse effect, overpopulation, food shortag euthanasia, and ambiguous S lent Green wafers for the mass

Roland Emmerich: Independence Day, 1996, starring [...] Smith and Jeff Goldblum

[...]n invasion was put on a big [...]e in this $70-million-epic inspired by the classic *War of the Worlds*. A colossal alien mothership enters the orbit of earth deploying huge spacecrafts that attack major cities worldwide. The United States successfully leads a counterattack, installing a computer virus and implanting a nuclear bomb in the mother ship.

■ **Douglas Trumbull: Silent Running**, 1972, starring Bruce Dern

Silent Running used many of the special effects originally developed for Kubrick's *2001: A Space Odyssey*. Trumbull's directorial debut tells the story of the *Valley Forge*, a spaceship transporting earth biotopes. When ordered to abandon the project, rebellious astronaut Lowell (Dern) kills the other crew members to save his beloved plants and animals. Trumbull later worked on many other science-fiction classics.

Steven Spielberg: A.I.: Artificial Intelli-gence, 2001, starring Haley Joel Osment

[...]rick's legacy to Steven Spielberg was this [...]osophical and sentimental film that com-[...]d the signatures of both directors. Using [...] motif of *Pinocchio*, it is the futuristic tale [...] world in which highly advanced robots [...]e been developed, including a copy of [...]y (Osment), who wants to be human.

Special Effects

In 1966 when Stanley Kubrick (p.246) set out to make his science-fiction epic *2001: A Space Odyssey*, special effects had changed little since the days of silent films. Every studio had in-house technicians who specialized in mechanical effects (for example, a man in a Godzilla suit destroying a miniature Tokyo) and optical effects (overlaying footage of actors with a matte painting of a medieval city). Kubrick's own team, headed by Douglas Trumbull, improved on time-honored methods and developed new ones to give unprecedented realism to *2001*. The film inspired a new generation of independent special-effects masters. John Dykstra designed computer-guided cameras to film *Star Wars* (1977) and founded Industrial Light & Magic.

New Impulses 1960–1974

**n Close Encounters of
Third Kind** (1977) Steven
berg worked with Doug-
rumbull—engineer of
: *A Space Odyssey*'s special
ts. Trumbull filmed minia-
alien spacecrafts in smoky

roma-key effects are an
al technique used to super-
se images that are filmed
rately. An actor or object is
d in front of a blue or
n backdrop. The colored
can be replaced with shots
y background the director
ses. First used in the 1940
The Thief of Baghdad,
ma-key effects have been
ly enhanced by computer
nology. Today, entire films
hot using the technique.

rooms, deliberately allowing
lens flare, an effect caused by
lights reflecting inside the
camera's lens. The footage was
superimposed on shots of a
miniature Devil's Mountain
and a full-size landing strip set.

▶ **Michael Crichton's
Westworld** (1973) is set in an
amusement park where guests
interact with realistic android
characters like Yul Brynner's
Gunslinger. The film was the
first to use computers to create
optical effects. Two minutes of
footage were pixelated to
depict the android's point of
view. To show acid burning the
Gunslinger's face, ground Alka-
Seltzer was wiped on Brynner's
skin and splashed with water.

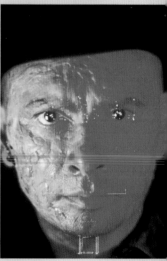

Special Effects

Jerry Lewis

1926, Newark

■ Master of slapstick comedy ■ Actor, writer, director, and producer ■ Influenced by silent-movie stars such as Charlie Chaplin, Stan Laurel, and Harold Lloyd ■ Inspired Woody Allen and Steve Martin ■ American ■ Slapstick Comedy ■ Directed 13 films

■ **1926** Born Joseph Levitch into a family of show people
1946 First appearance with Dean Martin is an immediate success
1949 Screen debut, *My Friend Irma*
1956 Martin and Lewis split
1971 Cult hero in France, culminating in 16 sold-out nights at the Olympia, Paris
1977 Nominee for the Nobel Peace Prize for his charity activities
1982 Autobiography published

A born facial contortionist, Jerry Lewis, who first appea on stage at age five, was an experienced but emp handed stand-up comedian until he started to w with Dean Martin. Lewis interested himself in the prod tion process, in camera work, lighting, and editing. learned much from director Frank Tashlin, whose id corresponded with Lewis's surreal slapstick madn Incorporating all technological possibilities, from visu light, and sound to editing, Lewis made films ab childish, multifaceted outsiders who observe the biz world around them. His moviemaking ideal was a "t filmmaker"—director, actor, scriptwriter, and produce one person, such as Charlie Chaplin (p. 58). Lewis step down from directing owing to poor he but performed convincingly character roles in films of Ma Scorsese (p. 320), Emir Kustu (p. 458), and Peter Chelsom.

■ **The Bellboy**, 1960, starring Jerry L

This is the first film that Lewis direc wrote, and produced himself. Since he had an engagement in Miami's Fontainebleau Hotel, he quickly dev a story that could be filmed on the spot, u technology to better stage the physical g Lewis plays hotel employee Stanley, a m figure comparable to Jacqu Tati's Monsieur Hulot, and h sequences of bizarre escapa often triggered by everyday hotel situations, pay homac to silent-film stars.

■ **Jerry Lewis and Dean Martin**—a perfect match

In 1946, New York's comedy scene was conquered by a new team: Dean Martin and Jerry Lewis. Their happy-go-lucky and irreverent slapstick gags were just what people needed after the war. The structure was relatively simple, with Martin playing the smart romantic with a great talent for singing and Lewis the clownish, energetic live wire. Three years later they were the US's most popular TV and live comedy team and a guaranteed box-office hit. From 1949 to 1956, the couple made 16 feature films as well as appearing regularly on TV and touring the most fashionable nightclubs.

Other Works

Cinderfella, 1960, starring Jerry Lewis and Count Basie

The Ladies Man, 1961, starring Jerry Lewis

The Family Jewels, 1965, starring Jerry Lewis

Which Way to the Front?, 1970, starring Jerry Lewis

The Nutty Professor, 1963, starring Jerry Lewis

...e, clumsy, and a lovable ...—Professor Kelp is a typical ...mple of Lewis's characters. A ...of respect from his students leads him to use a potion that turns him into a Dean Martin–style ladies' man. The double personality motif alludes to Mamoulian's *Dr. Jekyll and Mr. Hyde* (1931), with a thoughtful twist.

Mel Brooks

1926, New York

■ Director, screenwriter, actor, producer, composer, and lyricist ■ Influence
by Buster Keaton, Charlie Chaplin, and the Marx Brothers ■ Only director wh
won Oscar, Grammy, Emmy, and Tony awards
■ American ■ Comedy, Slapstick, Parody ■ Directed 11 films

1926 Born Melvin
Kaminsky in Brooklyn

1949–59 Gag writer and
performer for TV programs
(*Your Show of Shows*)

1960 Records *The 2000-
Year-Old Man*

1963 Makes the animated
Academy Award–winning
short, *The Critic*

1965 Co-creates spy spoof
TV series *Get Smart*

1980 Founds production
company, Brooksfilms

2001 Directs a Broadway
musical version of his
own big success, *The
Producers*

2008 *Get Smart* is turned
into a feature film

■ **The Producers**, 1968,
starring Zero Mostel and
Gene Wilder

Brooks's first feature film
was also his greatest
triumph. A take on the
financial backside of
show business, it
tells the story of a
scheming producer
(Mostel) and his
accountant (Wilder),
who hope to make
money by producing
an intentional flop
musical about Hitler.

New Impulses 1960–1974

There is hardly a film genre that Mel Brooks left
touched. From western and horror to epic, science ficti
and adventure, Brooks fired off hard-hitting gags, e
making movie pastiches in the typical styles
Alfred Hitchcock (p. 186) and Frank Capra (p. 118). Alo
side corny jokes and zany action, the compulsive co
also stands out for the meticulously detailed way in wh
he referred to original films of the various genre
shooting at original sites, using original props and de
rations, even adopting specific styles, camera work, a
perspectives. Recurring issues in Brooks's films are fath
son relationships and the influence of one's orig
Although hugely successful with mainstream audien
he regularly faced controversy in his profession, perh
because of his disrespectful, even mali-
cious parodies of renowned classics,
such as Ernst Lubitsch's (p. 112) *To Be or
Not to Be* (1942), which in 1983 he
turned into a musical starring Anne Bancroft.

Blazing Saddles, 1974, starring Cleavon Little and Gene Wilder

The ultimate parody of the time-honored western, *Blazing Saddles* tells the story of a governor who appoints a black sheriff (Little), hoping that this will lead the stubborn citizens of a racist town to finally leave their homes, thus paving the way for a new railway line. Iconoclastic Brooks mixed and redefined the classic western ingredients, from characters to typical campsite songs, three of which he composed and wrote the lyrics for himself. The film features a short appearance of Count Basie in the desert.

Other Works

Young Frankenstein, 1974, starring Gene Wilder, Peter Boyle, and Gene Hackman	**High Anxiety**, 1977, starring Mel Brooks, Madeline Kahn, and Cloris Leachman

Silent Movie, 1976, starring Mel Brooks and Marty Feldman

Simultaneously a parody of the US star system and a loving homage to the leading figures of early filmmaking, *Silent Movie* tells of three aspiring filmmakers planning to produce the first silent movie in many decades. To make the film more marketable, they try to cast some top names, including Burt Reynolds, James Caan, Paul Newman, Anne Bancroft, and Liza Minnelli. There is only one word spoken in the entire film, voiced by legendary mime Marcel Marceau.

Blake Edwards

1922, Tulsa

■ Was both the scriptwriter and producer for most of his films ■ Famous for his *Pink Panther* series ■ Influenced by the comedic styles of Laurel and Hardy ■ Wins 22 film awards
■ American ■ Slapstick Comedy, Drama, Romance ■ Directed 37 movies

■ **1922** Born the son of a stage director and movie production manager in Oklahoma

1942–48 Acts in minor roles in more than 20 Hollywood B-movies

1948 Writes TV series

1954 Starts to direct TV series

1958 Creates, produces, and directs popular TV series *Peter Gunn*

1972 Exiles himself to the UK after feuds with American studios

1979 Returns to United States for box-office hit *10*

1995 Successfully adapts *Victor/Victoria* starring Julie Andrews as a Broadway musical

2003 Receives Honorary Academy Award in recognition of his writing, directing, and producing of extraordinary films

Other Works

The Great Race, 1965, starring Jack Lemmon

Darling Lili, 1970, starring Julie Andrews and Rock Hudson

That's Life!, 1986, starring Julie Andrews

Blake Edwards started his career as an actor and scri writer for screen and radio plays. Although best known his comedies such as the *Pink Panther* series, he also c ated a notable drama about alcohol abuse. Through his career, he cooperated with composer Henry Manc who won several Academy Awards for the scores Edwards's films. His unique sense of humor, often go and ludicrous slapstick, is unmatched in his works w actor Peter Sellers in films such as *The Party* (1968). Ju Andrews, to whom he has been married since 19 starred in several of his movies, including the Hollywo satire *S.O.B.* (1981) and the gender-bending come *Victor/Victoria* (1982).

■ Days of Wine and Roses
1963, starring Jack Lemmon and Lee Remick

This melodrama about a coup growing alcoholism was base on a successful television pro duction. Joe (Lemmon) marrie innocent Kirsten (Remick) and introduces her to the socially accepted alcohol buzz. It is no long before the party drink becomes a daily necessity and the two risk their lives. With th help of Alcoholics Anonymou Joe tries to get sober. Lemmo Remick, and Edwards drank heavily during the shooting a the movie made all three reco sider their drinking habits.

■ **Breakfast at Tiffany's**, 1961, starring Audrey Hepburn and George Peppard

Based on the novella by Truman Capote, this comedy highlights the life of playgirl Holly Go-lightly (Hepburn), implicitly questioning the tra-ditional postwar role of women and showing their search for a new, self-determined identity. An eccentric socialite and naive girl at the same time, Holly and her cat live in the same apart-ment block as aspiring young author Paul Varjak (Peppard), who also makes his living by going out with elderly paramours. The restlessness and superficiality of New York life proves unsatisfac-tory to both. Whereas Capote's story remains unresolved, there is a happy ending for Holly and Paul in the film. The opening sequence with Holly in an evening gown, wearing sunglasses and glancing at the jewels displayed at Tiffany's, turned Audrey Hepburn into an icon of style. Henry Mancini won an Academy Award for Best Song ("Moon River") and for Original Music Score.

he Pink Panther, 1963, starring Peter ers, David Niven, and Claudia Cardinale

first *Pink Panther* movie was the commercially cessful start of a series of films, six of which red Peter Sellers playing the clumsy French ce detective, Inspector Jacques useau. The original movie a cheerful crime drama sing on Sellers and en, a jewel thief ut to steal the infa-us diamond called "Pink Panther." animated ning sequence Henry ncini's leg-ary title theme turned into a oon series. The ake of the film 006 by Shawn featured Steve tin as Clouseau was again a hit.

Blake Edwards

Martial Arts

■ Action films centered on displays of traditional Asian combat techniques
■ Originated in China and Hong Kong ■ Incorporated elements of historical drama, comedy, and fantasy ■ Brought to international popularity by American-born actor Bruce Lee ■ Jackie Chan and Jet Li crossed over to Hollywood stardom
■ *left:* **The Fearless Hyena**, by Jackie Chan and Kenneth Tsang, 1979

Film Genres

1973 Bruce Lee's mysterious death makes him a cult figure
1973–83 Hong Kong produces classic martial arts films starring Jackie Chan, Sammo Hung, and Gordon Liu
1991–97 Director Tsui Hark's six-part *Once Upon a Time in China* film series makes Jet Li an international star

China and Hong Kong already had flourishing film industries before the American-born kung fu star Bruce Lee gained worldwide attention in the early 1970s. His brand of bare-handed combat ended the era of swordplay spectacles and ushered in a golden age of martial arts film. Hong Kong stars Jackie Chan and Jet Li followed in Lee's footsteps, crossing over to Hollywood and paving the way for non-Asian martial-arts stars Chuck Norris and Steven Seagal. Though focused on artfully choreographed fight scenes, the genre often incorporates elements of historical drama or comedy and Ang Lee blended fantasy and romance in his hit film *Crouching Tiger, Hidden Dragon* (2000).

Stephen Chow: Kung Fu Hustle, 2004, starring Stephen Chow and Yuen Wah

Comic homage to martial arts' classic stars, Chow plays a crook who is caught in a battle between the Axe Gang and the aging residents of a slum, played by kung fu stars of the 1970s.

Lo Wei: Fist of Fury, 1972, starring Bruce Lee and Nora Miao

Before his death, Bruce Lee revolutionized the film industry by popularizing martial arts films in the West. In his second film, Lee played a martial arts student in 1930s Shanghai who does battle with a rival Japanese karate school to avenge the death of his master. Lee's kung fu skills and his portrayal of the abuse of the Chinese by occupying Japan were groundbreaking.

Andrzej Bartkowiak: Romeo Must Die, 2000, starring Jet Li, Aaliyah, and Delroy Lindo

An action-packed Romeo and Juliet tale set amid urban gang warfare. Han Sing (Li) sets out to avenge the death of his brother but falls in love with the daughter of a rival gang leader.

Other Works

Enter the Dragon, by Robert Clouse, 1973, starring Bruce Lee and John Saxon

Drunken Master, by Yuen Woo-Ping, 1978, starring Jackie Chan

The Shaolin Temple, by Chang Hsin-Yen, 1982, starring Jet Li

Martial Arts

Sergio Leone

1929, Rome–1989, Rome

■ Most important director of spaghetti westerns ■ Influenced by Akira Kurosawa and western classics ■ Inspired Sam Peckinpah, Quentin Tarantino and pop culture ■ Celebrated for the soundtracks of Ennio Morricone ■ Italian ■ Spaghetti Western, Epic Drama ■ Directed 7 films

● **1929** Born to film pioneer Vincenzo Leone (aka Roberto Roberti) and actress Bice Waleran
1947 Starts to work in the Cinecittà studios in Rome
1959 Assistant director for *Ben-Hur*
1961 Directorial debut with *The Colossus of Rhodes*
1973 Produces the spaghetti western comedy *My Name is Nobody*
1989 Dies in Rome

With just a fistful of movies, Sergio Leone reinvented t forlorn western genre. The "Italo," or spaghetti weste began in the early 1960s with low-budget productions l Sergio Corbucci's *Django* movies. Leone had worked in t film business from his early teens and was an experienc scriptwriter when he started to direct. *A Fistful of Doll* (1964), based on Akira Kurosawa's (p. 216) samurai fi *Yojimbo* (1961) and the first in his *Dollars* trilogy, set t tone for Leone's version of the American western. The fa of the characters, with Clint Eastwood (p. 384) leading t way, are as weather-beaten as the landscape. Leone's ar heroes are usually tough, independent outlaws who fig dirty, shoot first, and have a self-defined sense of justi Leone was a visionary who orchestrated his movies l stage operas. The director-composer relationship w Ennio Morricone proved to be one of t most rewarding in cinema histo Leone's stylistic influence is omnipres in cinema and TV commercials.

■ **Once Upon a Time in America**, 1984, starring Robert De Niro and James Woods

In 1968, after 35 years in exile, David "Noodles Aaronson (De Niro) returns to Brooklyn remi-niscing about his life of crime. In a series of fla backs a gangster story unfolds. In the 1920s h and his friend Max (Woods) began their crimin career and, following his prison term, continu in the 1930s during Prohibition, when their ga made a fortune. The hypnotic tale peaks wher he finds out that his presumed dead friend Ma is still alive and wants to settle an old score.

New Impulses 1960–1974

■ **Once Upon a Time in the West**, 1968, starring Charles Bronson, Henry Fonda, Claudia Cardinale, and Jason Robards

Leone's unmatched masterpiece unfolds its cleverly interwoven story of love and murder, treason and revenge at a painstakingly slow pace. The innovative film design offers screen-filling close-ups on the main characters alternating with majestic panorama shots. Stylized scenes of violence are shown in slow motion and sparse dialogue complements the unforgettable music of Ennio Morricone, who gave each character a signature melody. Never was the story of the conquest of the American West demystified more artfully.

he Good, The Bad and Ugly, 1966, starring Clint wood, Lee Van Cleef, and /allach

highlight of the *Dollars* gy (aka *The Man With No ne* trilogy) and the arche-l spaghetti western ined the most surreal ges. Never before were the er-than-life images more ent than in this western mid the American Civil . Eastwood (The Good), Van f (The Bad), and Wallach Ugly) are on the hunt for a une in gold. They meet in a

final showdown in which the audience can feel the heat and tension. Leone emphasized the pictures with sparse, often rudimentary dialogue. Nonetheless, he succeeded in building strong characters in Eastwood, with his cigarillo-smoking habit and sardonic humor, Wallach, with his comical and rampant temper, and Van Cleef, with his menacing behavior.

Other Works
For a Few Dollars More, 1965, starring Clint Eastwood
A Fistful of Dynamite, 1971, starring James Coburn and Rod Steiger

Spaghetti Westerns

Exploitation Films

■ Feature transgressive or provocative themes and material including sex, dr
use, and violence ■ Often made on a limited budget ■ Gained popularity i
the 1960s ■ Focus on content rather than production quality ■ Aim to mak
a quick profit ■ Use sensationalized advertising

■ *left:* **Undercover Brother**, by Malcolm D. Lee, 2002, starring Eddie Griffin

Film Genres

■ **1953** *The Wild One* popularizes the defiant motorcycle films

1959 *The Immoral Mr. Teas*
is the first nonporno-
graphic film to show
female nudity

1968 *Night of the Living
Dead* has graphic violence

1971 *Shaft* pioneers the
blaxploitation genre

2007 Release of *Grindhouse*
double feature *Planet Terror*
and *Death Proof*

From the drug-use-depicting *Reefer Madness* (1936)
pseudo-snuff films like *Faces of Death* (1978), filmmak
have cashed in on shock value throughout the history
film. Generally made on a low budget and without conc
for production quality, exploitation films consist
provocative material such as excessive violence, s
mayhem, and drug use. Often borrowing stylistic eleme
from other genres such as documentary and hor
exploitation films can be divided into many subgen
including sexploitation, blaxploitation, mondo, spagh
westerns, and splatter. Exploitation films gained popula

in the 1960s, when restrictions s
rounding film content were lesser
and back-alley grind-house cinem
gained popularity. Directors who ha
worked within the genre include Geo
Romero, Quentin Tarantino (p. 4
John Waters (p. 346), and Jack Smith.

■ **Mario Bava: The Bay of Blood**, 1971, star
Claudine Auger, Isa Miranda, Claudio Camaso,
and Luigi Pistilli

Also known as *Twitch of the Death Nerve*, this
Italian horror film pioneered the slasher genre
and had an immense influence on horror film
that followed, including *Friday the 13th*. A non
stop bloodbath featuring impressive gore and
a chilling atmosphere, *The Bay of Blood* is a
carefully constructed film that focuses on a se
of murders that ensue as the result of a furiou
bayside property war. Widely regarded as one
the greatest slasher-horror films of all time, it
cult classic.

New Impulses 1960–1974

Russ Meyer: Beyond the Valley of the Dolls, 1970, starring Dolly Read, Marcia McBroom, and Cynthia Myers

The projected sequel to 1967's *Valley of the Dolls*, *Beyond the Valley of the Dolls* is a frenzied satirical comedy that focuses on the adventures of The Carrie Affair—an all-girl rock band that sets out for Hollywood only to find themselves in a world of sleaze, drugs, and sex. An underground cult classic, the film is camp and provocative, and influenced many subsequent directors, including John Waters.

■ **Gordon Parks: Shaft**, 1971, starring Richard Roundtree

Widely considered a pioneer of the blaxploitation genre, *Shaft* is an influential action/crime film set in New York, centering on the charismatic private detective, Shaft (Roundtree). Featuring a funk/soul soundtrack and incorporating elements of film noir, it is a clever film that spawned a number of sequels: *Shaft's Big Score*, *Shaft in Africa*, and 2000's remake, starring Samuel L. Jackson.

Other Works

Blood Feast, by Herschell Gordon Lewis, 1963, starring William Kerwin

Caged Heat, by Jonathan Demme, 1974, starring Juanita Brown

Planet Terror, by Robert Rodriguez, 2007, starring Rose McGowan

Exploitation Films

Sidney Lumet

1924, Philadelphia

■ Archetypal actor's director ■ Most of his movies are situated in New York
■ Honorary Academy Award in 2004 for lifetime achievement ■ Earned 28
awards and 36 nominations
■ American ■ Drama, Crime, Cop Thriller, Court Drama ■ Directed 43 films

● **1924** Born into a family of
Jewish theater actors

1929 First appearance as
child actor

1939 Actor in *One Third of
a Nation*

1947 Establishes The
Actor's Workshop

1950 TV director for serials
(*Danger*)

1970 Co-directs documentary about Martin
Luther King with Joseph
L. Mankiewicz

1974 Directs Agatha
Christie's *Murder on the
Orient Express* in the UK

1995 Publishes in-depth
film knowledge book
Making Movies

■ **Network**, 1976, starring
Faye Dunaway, Peter
Finch, and William Holden

Howard Beale (Finch), an
aging news anchor, threatens to commit suicide on
air after being fired by his
TV station for poor ratings.
This generates huge ratings, making him an asset
but, in the end, also a
victim of a contract killer.
Ten Academy Award nominations and four wins
illustrate the impact of this
still valid media satire.

New Impulses 1960–1975

Lumet ranks as one of the most prolific and versatile directors of our time. He is technically profound, possesses a good sensitivity for handling actors, and favors New York as a film location. Some of his most notable films focus on crime and corruption, such as the portrayal of a bizarre bank robbery in *Dog Day Afternoon*, the cop thriller *Prince of the City* (1981), or the courtroom dramas *Q & A* (1990) and *Night Falls on Manhattan* (1997). Lumet handles intricate scripts with ease and his characters reveal complex personalities in a manner that greatly influenced art house cinema. Having realized his latest films in HD instead of celluloid, this true luminary shows an admirable openness for new techniques. The sublime cutting he innovatively employed in his classic *The Pawnbroker* (1965) became a standard in TV commercials and modern cinema.

12 Angry Men, 1957, starring Henry Fonda

Henry Fonda stars in this gripping courtroom drama as a juror who tries to convince the other members of his reasonable doubt, to save a young murder suspect from the death penalty. Lumet used his theater experience to turn the jury room into a crowded stage. Using deep-focus camera lenses, he created a tense, sometimes claustrophobic atmosphere. Besides the film being quoted on TV innumerable times, Russian director Nikita Mikhalkov recently released a highly praised remake.

Serpico, 1973, starring Al Pacino

The true story of NYPD officer Frank Serpico is convincingly portrayed by Pacino in one of his lead roles. Filmed in a style that suggests a documentary, the movie depicts the struggle of the idealistic cop's undercover work against a corrupt system where criminals and colleagues are one and the same. His work eventually leads to a committee being summoned and his stigmatization.

Other Works	
Dog Day Afternoon, 1975, starring Al Pacino	Guilty as Sin, 1993, starring Rebecca De Mornay
The Verdict, 1982, starring Paul Newman and Charlotte Rampling	Before the Devil Knows You're Dead, 2007, starring Philip Seymour Hoffman

Sam Peckinpah

1925, Fresno—1984, Inglewood

■ Called "Bloody Sam" for his explicit depictions of violence ■ Regular subj[...] included moral ambiguity and western myths ■ His close-ups and slow mo[...] scenes later influenced Quentin Tarantino and John Woo
■ American ■ Western, Drama, Crime ■ Directed 15 movies

■ **1925** Born David Samuel Peckinpah to a judge and is raised on a ranch

1950s Screenwriter and director of TV western series *Gunsmoke*, *The Rifleman*, and *The Westerner*

1954 Assistant for film director Don Siegel in *Riot in Cell Block 11*

1961 Directs first film, *The Deadly Companions*

1965 Loses control of his film *Major Dundee*, which is severely reedited by the studio; the director's cut is later released in 2005

1973 *Pat Garret and Billy the Kid* is changed by MGM and goes on to fail commercially

1984 Dies in California

■ **Straw Dogs**, 1971, starring Dustin Hoffman and Susan George

A timid American mathematician moves with his wife to the UK. Tensions between the couple and locals rise, leading to an outbreak of violence. Despite its controversial rape scene, *Straw Dogs* is a fine case study on the mechanisms of aggression.

New Impulses 1960–1974

Sam Peckinpah was a passionate film maverick who of[...] ran into trouble with the studio bosses. His marked p[...]erence for vivid scenes of violence and harsh mascu[...] values overshadows his brilliance in creating charac[...] with psychological depth. His protagonists were mo[...] male outsiders confronted with changes in society. [...] early TV works already expressed a great affection [...] westerns, and his reputation grew in this genre. [...] subtle portraits of a hapless entrepreneur in *The Ballad of Cable Hogue* (1970) and rodeo rider *Junior Bonner* (1972) contrast with other, more violent works. Even in his most creative phases the famously stubborn Peckinpah was plagued by alcoholism, which he suffered from since his military service.

e Getaway, 1972, starring
 McQueen and Ali MacGraw

 on a novel by Jim
npson, *The Getaway* was
npah's biggest commercial
ess. In a classic lovers-on-
un setting, it tells the story
e imprisoned criminal Doc
oy whose wife, Carol, con-
s with a seedy businessman
b a bank if Doc is released.
couple is double-crossed
e and is forced to flee to
co. The film is a triumph of
n and suspense with high-
d chases and escape scenes.

Other Works

■ **The Wild Bunch**, 1969,
starring William Holden, Ernest
Borgnine, Warren Oates, and
Ben Johnson

One of the most uncompro-
mising films of the 1960s, *The
Wild Bunch* is the story of an
aging gang facing changing
times during the Mexican revolution. The complex portrait of
the main characters with its
underlying theme
of betrayal is
framed by
legendary
outbursts

of violence, which are foreshad-
owed in the opening sequence
with children amusedly watching
ants feasting on scorpions—a
metaphor for the brutal mas-
sacres featured in this three-
hour epic. The gang's famous
final walk as they calmly go to
meet their fate, has been
quoted regularly by other directors—the bizarre bloodbath
ballet in slow motion has
stood the
test of
time.

New Hollywood

Bonnie and Clyde

■ by Arthur Penn, USA, 1967, Drama

Based on a true story, director Arthur Penn brought the legendary gangsters Bonnie Parker (Dunaway) and Clyde Barrow (Beatty) to the screen with visual panache. Like *The Graduate* (1967) and *Easy Rider* (1969), *Bonnie and Clyde* is a landmark movie of the new American cinema that emerged in the late 1960s. On the surface, the film chronicles the rise and fall of two outlaws and their gang as they rob banks, grocery stores, and gas stations. Always on the run through different southern states in the Depression-ridden early 1930s, they end up in an ambush where Bonnie and Clyde are shot in an unprecedented scene of aesthetisized graphic violence. The movie was not only exemplary for the change of Hollywood politics regarding censorship, but also reflected the social upheaval felt by many during the Vietnam era.

■ **Bonnie and Clyde**, 1967, starring Faye Dunaway and Warren Beatty

The film's opening sequence is a brilliant example of cinematic mastery. Penn introduces a frustrated Bonnie in a series of intimate shots that imply ennui as well as eroticism. The staccato editing preludes the restless pace of the movie, which was influenced by the playfulness of the French New Wave. In fact, the film was offered at first to François Truffaut. Without leaving its classic narrative structure the film finely uses edited long takes, location shots, jump cuts, slow motion, and freeze-frame—efficiently fusing classic American and artistic European cinematic styles, winning the Academy Award for Best Cinematography. The difficult sexual relationship between Bonnie and Clyde, who is portrayed as impotent, was played out convincingly by Dunaway and Beatty. The film launched gender discussions for years and was a benchmark for complex portraits of cinema heroes.

Bonnie and Clyde

George Roy Hill

1922, Minneapolis–2002, New York

■ Stage actor, director, writer, producer ■ Missing link between Hollywood's Golden Age and New Hollywood directors ■ Won one Academy Award and five other film awards
■ American ■ Drama, Western, Gangster, Comedy ■ Directed 14 movies

274

Drama in the United States

■ **1922** Born to a newspaper publisher
1948 Stage debut in Dublin
1950 Serves as a pilot in Korea
1957 Begins directing Broadway plays, including *Look Homeward, Angel*
1962 First feature, *Period of Adjustment*
1964 First big success: *The World of Henry Orient*, starring Peter Sellers
2002 Dies in New York

George Roy Hill, whose humorous and lighthearted fil made him a favorite of audiences and critics alike, h plenty of stage acting experience before he start making ambitious TV films. The passionate Navy pilot v equally driven by his love of music, which he studied Yale and in Dublin. In 1967 Hill directed the musi comedy *Thoroughly Modern Millie*, starring Julie Andre and James Fox, which was nominated for seven Acade Awards and won the Award for Best Original Music Scc

His two most successful films with P Newman and Robert Redford are *Bu Cassidy and the Sundance Kid* and *The St The signature style of this versa director is elegantly brisk and lig usually featuring smart soun tracks and witty dialogue.

■ **Butch Cassidy and the Sundance Kid**, 19 starring Paul Newman, Robert Redford, and Katharine Ross

A tragicomic western ballad where the bad guys' charm and humor surpasses the threat the crimes they commit. In this fi life seems to be one long picn as the unforgettable bicycle sc with Burt Bacharach's hit song *Raindrops Keep Fallin' on My He* proves. Hill and his dream tea Newman and Redford won fou Academy Awards for this film, which alludes playfully to the 1967 milestone of gangster e *Bonnie and Clyde*.

■ **The Sting,** 1973, starring Paul Newman and Robert Redford

classic comedy, ded into four sections, is ut a couple of con artists ng to deceive a mob boss 930s-era Chicago. The garnered seven Academy ards, including Best Picture Best Director. *The Sting* ved Hill's versatility, popularized his breezy signature style, and attracted attention for his fantastic deployment of unforgettable tunes for the soundtrack, such as Scott Joplin's piano rag *The Entertainer*. For some time, Hill was the only director with two films in the top ten of the most commercially successful films ever.

The World According to p, 1982, starring Robin iams, Mary Beth Hurt, and nn Close

d on John Irving's novel, this edy was an international -office hit. With twisted nor, Hill shows the alleged sings of Western society from ferent angle.

Other Works

e **Great Waldo Pepper,** 1975, rring Robert Redford and an Sarandon

e **Little Drummer Girl,** 1984, rring Diane Keaton and Klaus ski

George Roy Hill

Mike Nichols

1931, Berlin

■ Director, producer, comedian ■ Influenced Sam Mendes, Wes Anderson, Spike Jonze, Steven Soderbergh, and the Coen brothers ■ Won numerous awards for both film and theater
■ German-American ■ Drama, Romance, Comedy, Satire ■ Directed 20 film

1931 Born as Michael Igor Peschkowsky, son of a Russian Jewish doctor

1938 Family emigrates to the United States

1956 Part of improvisational actors group The Compass Players, tours with Elaine May, nationally acclaimed for social satire

1963 Debut as Broadway director, *Barefoot in the Park*

1993 Co-produces *The Remains of the Day*

2003 Directs four episodes of 33-time award-winning TV series *Angels in America*

Before turning to film, German-born Mike Nichols w a hugely successful theater satirist, making fun of typi American middle-class issues and basic male-fem dynamics. His first two features, the adaptation Broadway hit *Who's Afraid of Virginia Woolf?* and t Oscar-winning *The Graduate*, instantaneously ranked h as one of the best directors of the 1960s. In the traditi of European filmmakers, he employed highly styliz visual flourishes, innovative editing and cinematograp and production design. In the mid-1970s, Nichols cc centrated on stage productions, but he returned cinema ten years later with films voicing social a political issues, such as *Silkwood* (1983) and *Prim Colors* (1998). Nichols's recent films have been m intimate, showing individuals in tragicor everyday struggles.

■ **The Graduate**, 1967, starring Dustin Hoffman, Anne Bancroft, and Katharine Ross

To this day, this icon of 1960s movies is seen as a symbol of adolescent alienation, subtly displaying the difficulty of rebellion. The story of

Benjamin's development fr college preppy to self-deter mined man introduced Hoi man as a new kind of male protagonist and Bancroft a highly erotic older seductre With his stylized mix of zoc cross-fading, and distance camera perspectives, flanke by the hallmark songs by Simon & Garfunkel, Nichols won an Academy Award fc Best Director and became Holly-wood A-list directo

loser, 2004, starring Natalie
man, Julia Roberts, Jude
, and Clive Owen

laborate character study
vo London couples
aged in a game of partner
pping and wreaking emo-
al damage, and with
ols's hallmark intelligent

dialogue and the actors'
convincing performances,
Closer was a great success and
proved Nichols's versatility.
The 73-year old director turned
Patrick Marber's prize-winning
stage drama into an intense
showpiece of contemporary
cinema.

harlie Wilson's War, 2007, starring Tom
ks, Julia Roberts, and Philip Seymour Hoffman

film is based on the experiences of a Texas con-
sman who tries to help people in Afghanistan
rganizing weapons for the mujahideen. Hanks
d Nichols to direct the film, which depicts the
elopment and changes of its protagonist.

■ **Who's Afraid of Virginia Woolf?**, 1966,
starring Elizabeth Taylor and Richard Burton

Nichols's directorial debut was this brutal analysis of
a corrupted marriage, with the real-life couple Taylor
and Burton delivering explosive abuse that broke
Hollywood's morality taboos. Its film noir style and
changes of perspective were a great success.

Mike Nichols

Sydney Pollack

1934, Lafayette—2008, Los Angeles

■ Actor, director, and producer ■ Actor in films of Woody Allen, Robert Altman, and Stanley Kubrick ■ Producer for Ang Lee, Anthony Minghella, ar Tom Tykwer ■ Winner of two Academy Awards and 18 other awards ■ American ■ Drama, Western, Thriller, Romance ■ Directed 21 films

- **1934** Born son of Russian-Jewish Americans
- **1952** Studies acting
- **1961** Dialogue coach on Frankenheimer's *The Young Savages*
- **1965** First feature film, *The Slender Thread*
- **1980** Increasingly involved as producer
- **2007** Actor in *Michael Clayton*
- **2008** Dies in California

Sidney Pollack is renowned for his exceptionally go handling of actors. His films often depict characters str gling against the conventions of society and the sea for an alternative way of living. Pollack was inspired political crises in the United States, from the McCar era (*The Way We Were*), to Watergate (*Three Days of Condor*, 1975), to consumerism and environmental top (*The Electric Horseman*, 1979). A lifelong friendship him with Robert Redford, whom he met during his f Hollywood assignment as an actor for *War Hunt* in 1 and who starred in seven of Pollack's films.

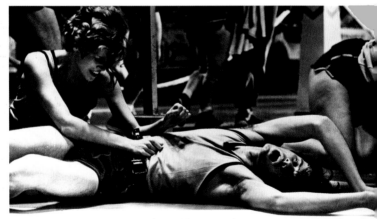

■ **They Shoot Horses, Don't They?**, 1969, starring Jane Fonda, Susannah York, and Gig Young

New Impulses 1960–1974

Nominated for nine Academy Awards, this film depicts the bitter Depression years without mercy. In the film,

contestants fight through th torture of one of America's infamous dance marathons a $1,500 prize.

Out of Africa, 1985, starring Robert Redford, ˻ryl Streep, and Klaus Maria Brandauer

˻s adaptation of Karen Blixen's autobiography ˻ut her life in Kenya before and during WWI ˻n the Academy Award for Best Picture and Best ˻ector. Sweeping landscapes and exceptional ˻formances by Redford, playing an aviating ˻venturer, and Streep, an equally unconven-˻al lady trying to run a coffee plantation, ˻de this film an all-time classic romance.

˻eremiah Johnson, 1972, starring Robert ˻dford and Will Geer

˻lack presented a meditative and thoughtful ˻stern about an ex-soldier who seeks peace and ˻uge in the mountains. While learning the trap-˻ life, revealed in vast landscape shots, he unwit-˻ly becomes involved in an Indian vendetta.

Other Works	
˻e Way We Were, ˻973, starring ˻rbra Streisand and ˻bert Redford	**Tootsie**, 1982, starring Dustin Hoffman
	The Firm, 1993, starring Tom Cruise

Sydney Pollack

John Frankenheimer

1930, New York—2002, Los Angeles

■ Director and producer ■ Director of in-depth political thrillers ■ One of Hollywood's leading craftsmen ■ Influenced by Carol Reed and Orson Welle ■ Famed for his innovative camera work
■ American ■ Drama, Political Thriller, Action ■ Directed 29 films

■ **1930** Born to a German-Jewish stockbroker and an Irish mother

1953/4 Assistant director at CBS-TV

1954 Takes over directing *You Are There* series from Sidney Lumet

1956 First feature, *The Young Stranger*

1961 Second feature, *The Young Savages*

1968 Directs campaign films for Robert F. Kennedy

2002 Inducted into the Television Hall of Fame

2002 Dies in Los Angeles

John Frankenheimer learned the techniques of filming the army, where he made several documentary shorts. then pursued a career as a TV director, directing more th 125 shows, and stayed with TV even after completing well-received first feature. Thrillers set in the 1960s such *Seven Days in May* (1964) firmly placed him as a top Hol wood director who closely observed American social a political issues while retaining a documentary approac Frankenheimer also spent a decade in Europe, from whe his experiences influenced *French Connection II* (1975), o of the first popular film sequels after World War II. T dominant topics of his work are the individual struggli against hostile surroundings and society, questions identity, and the reliability of perception.

■ **Birdman of Alcatraz**, 1962, starring Burt Lancaster and Karl Malden

Based on the real-life story of Robert Stroud (Lancaster), this is one of the most moving and intimate prison films. Sentenced to life in solitary confinement, Stroud became one of the world's leading experts on avian diseases. Lancaster is convincing in one of his best leading roles, transforming from a misanthrope into a humane and thoughtful individual.

New Impulses 1960–1974

The Manchurian Candidate, 1962, starring
[Fra]nk Sinatra, Laurence Harvey, Angela Lansbury,
[and] Janet Leigh

[A] political thriller unmasks several clichés of
[Col]d War-era America, painting a society ridden
[with] corrupt and submissive politicians, scheming
[com]munists, and unwitting terrorists. The film
[is fa]mous for its 360-degree camera work.

Other Works	
[Gr]and Prix, 1966, [sta]rring James Garner	Ronin, 1998, starring Robert De Niro
[Bla]ck Sunday, 1977, [sta]rring Robert Shaw	Reindeer Games, 2000, starring Ben Afleck

The Train, 1964, starring Burt Lancaster, Paul
[Scof]field, and Michel Simon

[At L]ancaster's request Frankenheimer replaced
[Art]hur Penn as director of this gripping movie set
[in W]orld War II. *The Train*'s story is based on
[eve]nts that actually occurred during the end of
[the] Nazi occupation,
[whe]n Paris railroad
[wor]kers saved the
[Mu]sée du Jeu de
[Pau]me's collection
[of m]odern art from
[bein]g taken
[to G]er-
[man]y.

Drama in the United States

British Free Cinema

- Key figures are Lindsay Anderson, Tony Richardson, and Karel Reisz
- Semi-documentary and realistic film style ■ Working-class topics and literary source material ■ Influenced by Italian Neo-Realism and French New Wave ■ Influential on Ken Loach, Mike Leigh, and Michael Winterbottom
- *left:* **The Loneliness of the Long Distance Runner**, by Tony Richardson, 196

1947 Lindsay Anderson and Karel Reisz cofound groundbreaking film journal *Sequence*

1956 British Free Cinema movement founded by Anderson, Reisz, Richardson, and Lorenza Mazzetti

1958 John Osborne and Tony Richardson launch film production company, Woodfall

1963 *This Sporting Life,* debut feature by Anderson, combines two innately British topics: coal mining and rugby

Founded in 1956, the British New Wave or British Fr Cinema movement can be called the artistic and li minded counterpart to Italian Neo-Realism and the Fren New Wave. Free Cinema initially consisted of a series short documentaries, most of which were realiz between 1956 and 1959, most famously Linds Anderson's *Every Day Except Christmas* (1957), which w the award for Best Documentary at the Venice Film F tival. Social relevance and realistic human behavior we some of the main elements of the feature films Anderson and his fellows Karel Reisz and Tony Richards British Free Cinema directors showed a preference working-class stories and shot many films on origin locations. John Schlesinger's (p. 28 early films are associated with the Brit New Wave, as are the films of socia maverick filmmaker Ken Loach. Too British directors such as Mike Lei (p. 466) and Michael Winterbottom a the artistic heirs of the movement, co tinuing to portray individuals and soc struggles as close to reality as possib

■ **Lindsay Anderson: If....**, 1968, starring Malcolm McDowell

McDowell starred in two other anarchic films made by Anderson, *O Lucky Man!* (1973) and *Britannia Hospital* (1982). *If....* was made during international student uprisings and portrays th story of a rebellious schoolboy from an elite sch fighting a stubborn class system. The film's pro- tagonist became a symbol of disaffected youth

Karel Reisz: Saturday [Ni]ght and Sunday Morning, [19]60, starring Albert Finney and [Sh]irley Anne Field

[Ba]sed on the social realist novel [by] Alan Sillitoe, the film is con-[sid]ered as the first kitchen-sink [dr]ama of the 1960s, [in] which all

exteriors were shot entirely on location. Arthur Seaton (Finney), a hard-headed young Nottingham factory worker, has an affair with the wife of a co-worker. When she gets pregnant he insists on an abortion while starting a romance with a young girl.

■ **Tony Richardson: Look Back in Anger**, 1958, starring Richard Burton and Claire Bloom

John Osborne's internationally acclaimed stage drama coined the term "angry young man." In Richardson's furious screen adaption, Jimmy Porter (Burton), a failure in his professional life, rages against the world, mistreats his pregnant wife, and starts an affair with her best friend. This well-observed tyrannical behavior, an orgy of psychological violence, was relentlessly criticized by feminist groups.

Other Works

Room at the Top, by Jack Clayton, 1959, starring Laurence Harvey and Simone Signoret

A Kind of Loving, by John Schlesinger, 1962, starring June Ritchie and Alan Bates

Joseph Losey

1909, La Crosse—1984, London

■ Worked in film, radio, and on stage ■ Influenced by Sergei Eisenstein, Berto[lt?]
Brecht, Fritz Lang, and Italian Neo-Realism ■ Worked with Nobel Prize–winne[r]
Harold Pinter ■ Cult figure of intellectuals
■ American ■ Drama, Thriller ■ Directed 31 films

1909 Born to a lawyer of Dutch origin in Wisconsin

1935 Attends classes by Sergei Eisenstein in Moscow

1936 Innovative stage production *Living Newspaper*

1947 Stages Brecht's *Galileo Galilei* starring Charles Laughton

1948 First feature, *The Boy with Green Hair*

1951 Political exile in the UK

1971 Wins the Palme d'Or for *The Go-Between*

1976 Moves to France

1979 Directs screen version of *Don Giovanni*

1980 Stages *Boris Godunov* in Paris

1984 Dies in London

■ **The Servant**, 1963, starring Dirk Bogarde, Sarah Miles, and James Fox

The Servant is an unusual class study in which the mysterious and sinister valet Barrett (Bogarde) turns the tables on his aristocratic master Tony (Fox) and exerts increasing, slightly erotic power over his superior. The film, characterized by Losey's typical mirror shots, won seven awards.

New Impulses 1960–1974

Joseph Losey began as a director of radical plays in Ne[w]
York in the 1930s. The self-proclaimed "romantic Marxi[st]"
and opera lover refused to testify in 1951 before the an[ti]-
Communist board and was blacklisted in Hollywood. [He]
left for the UK and became one of the leading figures [in]
European cinema in the 1960s. He pessimistically analyz[ed]
social issues, depicting figures under emotional and phy[s]-
ical pressure, victims of frailty and corruptibility, violen[ce]
and erotic power plays. His angry and powerful films are characterized by stark symbolism that illustrates his protagonists' minds.

Modesty Blaise, 1966, starring Monica Vitti, Terence Stamp, and Dirk Bogarde

The girl-power satire set in colorful and jaunty 1960s London, an adaptation of the popular comic strip by Jim Holdaway. A secret agent (Vitti) teams up with her friend (Stamp) to prevent a diamond heist planned by Gabriel Fothergill (Bogarde). A homage to Jean-Luc Godard's *Breathless*, it was nominated for the Palme d'Or.

Other Works

Eva, 1962, starring Jeanne Moreau

The Go-Between, 1970, starring Julie Christie and Alan Bates

Mr. Klein, 1976, starring Alain Delon and Jeanne Moreau

Accident, 1967, starring Dirk Bogarde, Stanley Baker, Michael York, and Jacqueline Sassard

A collaboration with Harold Pinter, this sharp-witted analysis of British society explores the emotional turmoil of Oxford professor Stephen (Bogarde), who, feeling constrained by social mores, starts a tragic love affair with Anna (Sassard), a student.

Joseph Losey

John Schlesinger

1926. London—2003. Palm Springs

■ Favored intimate dramas ■ Key figure of the British Free Cinema ■ Joined New Hollywood movement in the late 1960s ■ Received the Lifetime Achievement Award from the Directors Guild of Great Britain, 2002
■ British ■ Drama, Thriller, Romance ■ Directed 17 films

1926 Born into an intellectual middle-class family

1953–58 Acts in minor roles in British movies and TV series

1961 Wins British film award and Golden Lion in Venice for BBC documentary *Terminus*

1962 Debut film, *A Kind of Loving*

1970 Becomes a Commander of the British Empire

1998 Adapts *Sweeney Todd* for TV

2003 Dies in California

In an acceptance speech held one year before his death John Schlesinger said, "I was privileged to make films at a time when cinema dared to deal with people and their relationships to each other and society." This applies to most of his films realized on both sides of the Atlantic. His early feature films were straightforward dramas in the tradition of the British Free Cinema and frequently examined gender roles. While these intimate dramas reflected his middle-class perspective, his Oscar-winning debut in the United States, *Midnight Cowboy*, empathically concentrated on outsiders. His most personal film, *Sunday Bloody Sunday* (1971), depicted Jewish religion and homosexuality, an issue he established for mainstream cinema.

■ **Midnight Cowboy**, 1969, starring Jon Voight and Dustin Hoffman

A naive Texan, Joe Buck (Voight), moves to the city to become a hustler. With a tubercular small-time crook, Ratso Rizzo (Hoffman), they are one of the oddest couples in cinema history. This disillusioning New York City ballad, with its unique character study and merciless dissection of urban society, earned Schlesinger three Academy Awards and was an unexpected contribution to the New Hollywood movement.

New Impulses 1960–1974

arathon Man, 1976, star-
Dustin Hoffman, Laurence
er, and Roy Scheider

andmark thriller is unfor-
ble for its agonizing dental
re scene. Thomas "Babe"
(Hoffman) spends his spare
running in marathons. He is
untarily tangled up in an
nage plot and kidnapped
vicious ex-Nazi, Szell
er), who kills his brother
Scheider), an American
t agent. The complex story
ture with its references to
emporary topics influenced
ern thrillers.

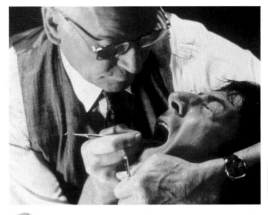

■ **Darling**, 1965, starring Julie Christie and Dirk
Bogarde

In an unconcerned conversational tone,
capricious model Diana Scott (Christie),
who takes every career opportunity to
climb up the social ladder, tells the various phases of her erratic life. She leaves
her true love, literate TV journalist
Robert Gold (Bogarde), only to end
up disillusioned as the wife of a
wealthy Italian prince. This early
and well-observed portrait of
fashionable swinging London
earned three Academy awards,
including Best Actress.

Other Works

Billy Liar, 1963, starring
Tom Courtenay and Julie
Christie

Sunday Bloody Sunday,
1971, starring Peter
Finch and Glenda
Jackson

**The Day of the
Locust**, 1975, starring
Donald Sutherland
and Karen Black

John Schlesinger

Nicolas Roeg

1928, London

■ Started his career as a cinematographer ■ As a director he is famous for linear narrative structures and cut-up techniques ■ Influenced by Michael Powell ■ Influential to Ridley Scott and François Ozon
■ British ■ Drama, Science Fiction, Mystery ■ Directed 14 films

● **1928** Born in London

1950 Starts working at MGM studio; camera assistant from 1951

1962 Second unit photographer for David Lean's *Lawrence of Arabia*

1964 Cinematographer for Roger Corman's *The Masque of the Red Death*, in 1966 for Truffaut's *Fahrenheit 451*, and in 1967 for John Schlesinger's *Far from the Madding Crowd*

1970 Directorial debut, *Performance*

1999 Lifetime Achievement Award from the British Independent Film Awards

Nicolas Roeg's versatile engagements as a cinemato pher during the 1960s built a fruitful foundation for to become one of the most visionary British directo all time. Roeg's films are marked by nonlinear narra constructions, convoluted editing, and superb colors choppy style, which regularly makes use of flashbacks flash-forwards, became the trademark of his 1970s' fi The intuitive mix of past, present, and future, as well a use of famous musicians as actors, is expressed skill in the science-fiction film *The Man Who Fell to Earth*, w pop star David Bowie played an alien struggling with italism and civilization, as well as in *Bad Timing* (19 where Art Garfunkel was convincing as a sexually sessed professor. Even upcoming directors quote hi a major inspiration.

■ **Don't Look Now**, 1973, starring Donald Sutherland Julie Christie

A constant subliminal threa through this atmospheric m terpiece. In Venice, Laura (Christie) and John Baxter (Sutherland) try to overcom death of their daughter. Joh who is unknowingly clairvo is restoring old churches wh Laura meets two elderly sist who say they have seen her daughter. At the same time murderer upsets the city. Th film's fatal climax is as famo its intense love scene.

New Impulses 1960–1974

Performance, 1970, starring ...s Fox, Mick Jagger, and ... Pallenberg

...rected with avant-garde ... Donald Cammell, Roeg's ...torial debut still reigns ...ng his most enigmatic ... combining associative ...tive techniques with mon-tage. In London in the swinging '60s, Chas (Fox), a vicious gangster on the run from his colleagues after having killed one of them, finds refuge in the guesthouse of an aging rock star (Jagger). Sex, drugs, and an identity crisis fuel this cult classic.

Other Works

Walkabout, 1971, starring Jenny Agutter and Luc Roeg

The Man Who Fell to Earth, 1976, starring David Bowie

Insignificance, 1985, starring Theresa Russell and Tony Curtis

■ **Eureka**, 1984, starring Gene Hackman, Theresa Russell, and Rutger Hauer

Eureka is Roeg's most expensive and most underrated film. Gold-miner Jack McCann (Hackman) comes into wealth, and, as the richest man in the world, moves to a Caribbean island but cannot find peace of mind. With references to Welles's *Citizen Kane* and Chaplin's *Gold Rush* the film drifts through genre sequences. With rapid editing and stylish zooms it was Roeg's last classic of free-form storytelling.

Nicolas Roeg

Disaster Films

■ Depict cataclysmic or devastating events ■ Use dramatic special effects
■ Gained popularity in the early 1970s ■ Perform well at the box office
■ Have widespread audience appeal ■ Often feature ensemble casts and popular actors ■ Regained popularity in the 1990s
■ *left:* **Godzilla, King of the Monsters!**, by Ishiro Honda and Terry O. Morse, 19

■ **1933** *King Kong* uses new special effects to depict a giant gorilla in New York

1937 *In Old Chicago* re-makes the Great Chicago Fire

1953 *The War of the Worlds* portrays a galactic battle for survival

1970 The release of *Airport* marks the beginning of a golden age for disaster film

1972 *The Poseidon Adventure* is the highest-grossing film of the year

1996 *Independence Day* wins an Academy Award for visual effects

1997 *Titanic* becomes the highest-grossing film ever

Disaster films typically focus on a group of characters w must overcome the effects of a devastating or catastrop event that often threatens all of humankind. With emphasis on special effects and spectacular act sequences, disaster films often feature star-studd ensemble casts and have wide audience appeal, there performing well at the box office—top box-office hits often among this genre. The early 1970s saw the po larity of films such as *Airport* and *The Towering Inferno*, disaster films have long been a part of cinema culture, v early apocalyptic films such as *The War of the Wor Godzilla, King of the Monsters!*, and *The Day the E Caught Fire* (1961). The 1990s saw a revival of the disa film genre, with big-budget titles such as *Independe Day* and *Titanic* dominating popular cinema.

■ **Mark Robson: Earthqu** 1974, starring Charlton Hes George Kennedy, and Ava Gardner

Hideously detailed and trem dously frightening, *Earthqu* a vivid disaster film that sho the destruction and chaos s rounding a 9.9-magnitude earthquake in Los Angeles. cutting-edge special effect unique marketing strategie (including the use of "Sensu round") it was a triumphant success at the box office, ar received five Academy Awa nominations.

■ **Ronald Neame: The Poseidon Adventure**, 1972, starring Gene Hackman, Ernest Borgnine, and Red Buttons

The Poseidon Adventure follows a group of travelers aboard the stately Poseidon—an aging cruise ship on its final ill-fated voyage. The film's breathtaking visual effects and Oscar-winning soundtrack fuel the suspense, making for an exhilarating escape film that became the highest-grossing film of 1972 and strongly influenced James Cameron's 1997 box-office smash, *Titanic*.

Other Works

Airport, by George Seaton, 1970, starring Burt Lancaster

The Towering Inferno, by John Guillermin and Irwin Allen, 1974, starring Steve McQueen and Paul Newman

Twister, by Jan de Bont, 1996, starring Helen Hunt

Roland Emmerich: The Day After Tomorrow, 2004, starring Dennis Quaid, Jake Gyllenhaal, and Emmy Rossum

The Day After Tomorrow is an apocalyptic science-fiction adventure depicting the catastrophic effects of global warming. Featuring iconic footage and suspenseful action sequences, it blends classic disaster elements with modern issues.

John Cassavetes

1929. New York—1989. Los Angeles

■ Actor, director, and scriptwriter ■ Influenced New Hollywood and Europe
Dogme directors ■ American pioneer of independent cinema ■ Famous fo
uncompromising character studies and social commentary
■ American ■ Drama, Thriller ■ Directed 12 Films

1929 Born to Greek immigrants; spends his early childhood in Greece

1950 Graduates from the American Academy of Dramatic Arts

1956 Teaches method acting in New York

1957 Directs his first version of *Shadows*, but re-releases it as his debut in 1959

1964 Lead role in *The Killers* by Don Siegel

1968 Roman Polanski casts him in the lead role in *Rosemary's Baby*

1989 Dies in California

■ **Shadows**, 1959, starring Ben Carruthers, Lelia Goldoni, and Hugh Hurd

Financed by his family and friends, Cassavetes's low-budget directorial debut intimately reflects the spirit of the Beat Generation and is of major importance for independent cinema. The mainly improvised film follows three African American siblings, meandering like the Charles Mingus jazz score, while the 16 mm handheld camera captures all the spontaneity.

New Impulses 1960–1974

John Cassavetes coyly called himself a professional ac and amateur filmmaker. As an actor, he shone brightly an intelligent villain, best remembered in movies ▮ *Saddle the Wind* (1958), *The Dirty Dozen* (1967), and *Fury* (1978). As a director he preferred frank films with co plex characters—reflections of the entire range of ▮ human condition, realized with brilliant immediacy. *Fa* (1968), for example, profoundly analyzed a disintegrat marriage and was nominated for three Academy Awar Known as an "actor's director," Cassavetes worked re larly with the same actors, including his muse and w Gena Rowlands. Despite having earned a reputation a free-spirited, spontaneous director, he didn't improv very much but worked meticulously on every script. artistic influence on younger generations carries on.

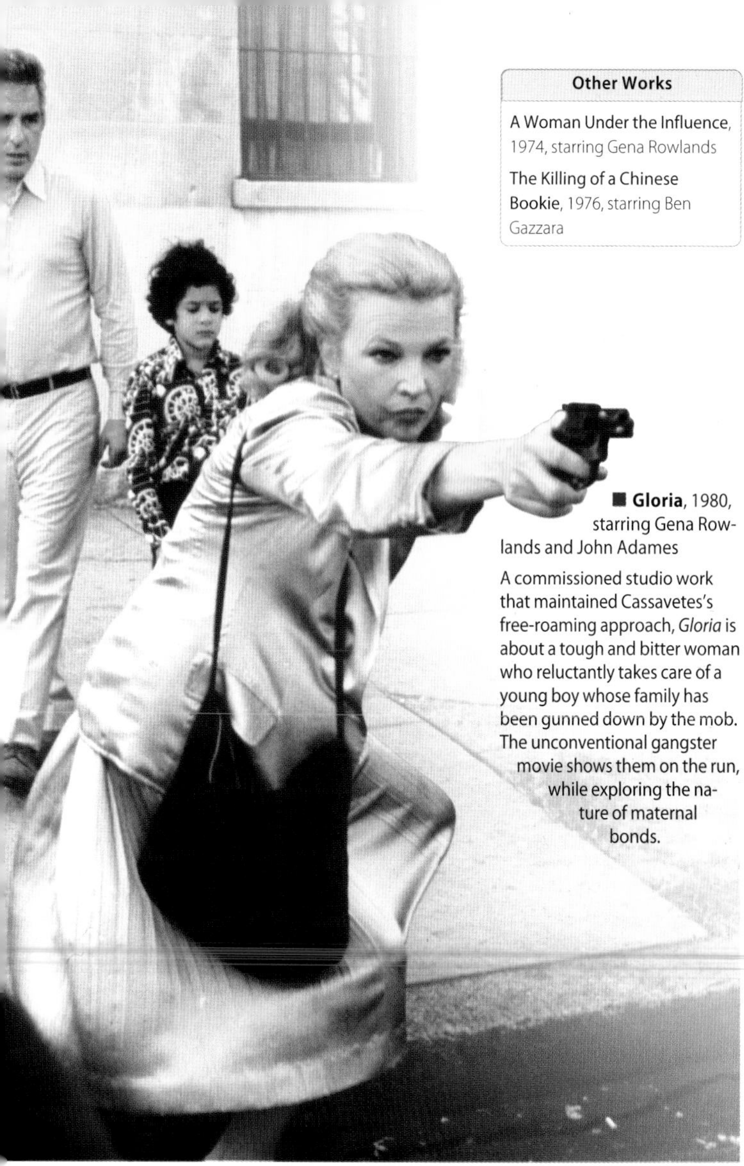

Other Works

A Woman Under the Influence, 1974, starring Gena Rowlands

The Killing of a Chinese Bookie, 1976, starring Ben Gazzara

■ **Gloria**, 1980, starring Gena Rowlands and John Adames

A commissioned studio work that maintained Cassavetes's free-roaming approach, *Gloria* is about a tough and bitter woman who reluctantly takes care of a young boy whose family has been gunned down by the mob. The unconventional gangster movie shows them on the run, while exploring the nature of maternal bonds.

Hal Ashby

1929, Ogden–1988, Malibu

■ Accomplished editor and director ■ Satirist with sociopolitical messages
■ Influential on directorial works of Sean Penn and Wes Anderson ■ Instigator of the New Hollywood movement
■ American ■ Drama, Black Comedy, Biopic ■ Directed 12 films

1929 Born into a Mormon family in Utah

1950 After two failed marriages he hitchhikes to Los Angeles

1956–65 Assistant editor for William Wyler and George Stevens

1965–69 Editor for films of Tony Richardson and Norman Jewison

1970 Directorial debut, *The Landlord*

1976 Directs the biopic *Bound for Glory* about the life of folk legend Woody Guthrie—the first motion picture filmed with a Steadicam

1988 Dies in California

After a difficult childhood Hal Ashby moved to California, where he began his career as a film editor and won an Oscar in 1967 for Norman Jewison's *In the Heat of the Night*. His debut as director, *The Landlord*, was the first of several intelligent dramas. Ashby's work in the 1970s earned many Academy Award nominations, but the reclusive talent could not cope with success and became a drug addict. He broke down during the shooting of the Rolling Stones documentary *Let's Spend the Night Together* (1982) and he is often unjustly dismissed.

Other Works

The Last Detail, 1973, starring Jack Nicholson and Otis Young

Shampoo, 1975, starring Warren Beatty, Julie Christie, and Goldie Hawn

Bound for Glory, 1976, starring David Carradine

Coming Home, 1978, starring Jane Fonda, Jon Voight, and Bruce Dern

Second-Hand Hearts, 1981, starring Robert Blake

■ **Harold and Maude**, 1971, starring Bud Cort and Ruth Gordon

Harold (Cort), a morbid youth, meets elderly Maude (Gordon) at a funeral. She shows him the beauty of life. Initially a flop, this satire about the constrictions of convention, one of the most unusual love stories in film history, developed a cult following. Ashby used long shots and gloomy interiors to mirror Harold's worldview.

Being There, 1979, starring
Peter Sellers, Shirley MacLaine,
and Melvyn Douglas

In one of his last roles Sellers bursts as gardener Chance, who
has spent his life isolated in the
house of an elderly gentleman,
gathering all his knowledge of
the world from the TV. When his
employer dies, Chance is turned
out into a world foreign to him
and runs into a car, whose
owners, Eve (MacLaine) and Ben
Rand (Douglas), take him home.
He applies his gardening princi-
ples to human matters and becomes a universally acclaimed
political adviser, even possible
presidential candidate. *Being
There* is both poignant and
utterly comical.

Roman Polanski

1933, Paris

■ Director, actor, scriptwriter, and producer ■ Influenced by playwrights Samuel Beckett, Eugene Ionesco, Harold Pinter, and Franz Kafka, and by directors Luis Buñuel and Alfred Hitchcock
■ Polish-French ■ Drama, Thriller, Horror, Comedy ■ Directed 17 films

■ **1933** Born in France to Polish-Jewish parents
1936 Moves to Kraków
1955 Acts in *A Generation*, by renowned Polish director Andrzej Wajda
1947 Works as stage actor, then in films
1969 Polanski's pregnant wife, actress Sharon Tate, is murdered
1975 Obtains French citizenship
1993 Career Golden Lion, Venice

A technical virtuoso, Roman Polanski's work is defined an atmosphere of obsession and fear, alienation, violen horror, and human aberration. He survived a terrify childhood in Kraków, during which his mother died i Nazi concentration camp and he was forced to flee ghetto and seek refuge in the Polish countryside. The p sionate cinema lover later studied at the renowned F School at Lodz. His first feature, *Knife in the Water* (19 immediately brought him international acclaim and Oscar nomination. Polanski has experimented with kind of genres, showing a preference for absurd a gothic themes.

New Impulses 1960–1974

■ The Pianist, 2002, starring Adrien Brody and Thomas Kretschmann

Due to Nazi oppression, famed pianist Wladyslaw Szpilman (Brody) has to earn his living as a bar musician in the Warsaw ghetto. He flees from a labor camp and eludes deportation, roaming the ruined city, hiding in an abandoned villa that has a piano. One day, his playing gives him away and a Nazi officer finds him. An international success, it won three Academy Awards and the Palme d'Or.

Rosemary's Baby, 1968, starring Mia Farrow and John ssavetes

young couple moves into a house that is rumored to ve a dark history. When the elderly neighbors e care of pregnant Rosemary (Farrow), her life ns into a nightmare. Following the Surrealist vel by Ira Levin, Polanski draws the dience into a world where dream, obses- n, and reality merge. *Rosemary's Baby* compelling satanic horror thriller where ery scene and situation consequently forces the subversive atmosphere.

Other Works

Repulsion, 1965, starring Catherine Deneuve

The Tenant, 1976, starring Roman olanski

Oliver Twist, 2005, starring Barney lark and Ben Kingsley

Chinatown, 1974, starring Jack holson, Faye Dunaway, and John Huston

s detective thriller set in 1930s Los geles was nominated for 11 Academy ards and won Best Script for Robert vne. It is an all-time classic of its genre, an homage to the film noir–heroes ip Marlowe and Sam Spade, though h more humor and disillusionment.

Andrei Tarkovsky

1932, Moscow–1986, Paris

■ Director and scriptwriter ■ Internationally acclaimed as Russia's most unorthodox filmmaker ■ Co-wrote most of his films ■ Influenced by Luis Buñuel and Ingmar Bergman ■ Won 19 awards
■ Russian ■ Avant-garde, Drama, History, Science Fiction ■ Directed 7 films

■ **1932** Born to a well-known Russian poet

1951 Studies Arabic

1954 Studies filmmaking at the Soviet State Film School

1961 Prize-winning diploma film *The Steamroller and the Violin*

1962 First film, *Ivan's Childhood*

1983 In London, directs stage production of *Boris Gudonov* at Covent Garden

1984 Officially defects from the Soviet Union to the West

1987 Publishes the book *Sculpting in Time* about the art, aesthetic, and poetics of films

1986 Dies in Paris

Other Works

Ivan's Childhood, 1962, starring Nikolai Burlyayev

Nostalgia, 1983, starring Oleg Yankovsky, Erland Josephson, and Domiziana Giordano

The Sacrifice, 1986, starring Erland Josephson and Susan Fleetwood

Even with his first feature film, *Ivan's Childhood*, whi won the Golden Lion at the Venice Film Festival, And Tarkovsky's lyrical and visionary language was not oper accepted in his home country. Whereas the debut had socialist vision, his next films became increasingly inn vative and uncompromising. Despite a growing reputa tion abroad he had to face severe obstacles at home in t Soviet Union. In the autobiographical *Mirror* (1975), quoted verses written by his poet father. This film shock Russian audiences with its open-ended, nonlinear str ture, and revolutionary Western cinematographic tec niques. Tarkovsky's idiosyncratic stories told of yearni and isolation, of spiritual commitment, and the role of t individual in improving life on earth.

■ **Andrei Rublev**, 1969, starring Anatoli Solonits and Ivan Lapikov

This controversial episod portrait of a medieval ico painter was banned in Russia and only interna tionally released in 1971 after having won a prize at Cannes. Tarkovsky explained: "An artist nev works under ideal condi tions. If they existed, his work wouldn't exist... Th artist exists because the world is not perfect... Ar born out of an ill-design world. This is the issue i *Rublev*."

alker, 1979, starring
sandr Kaidanovsky and
Frejndlikh

ast film Tarkovsky realized
ssia, *Stalker* is based on a
ella by Boris and Arkadi
gatzky and deals with the
's main topics: the cleft
between science and religion
and the future of humankind
in the face of nuclear
threats. The stalker
leads people to a
room inside
a fenced-off
zone,
where their secret hopes and
dreams come true. He meets
his greatest challenge when
trying to lead two people at
once, a burned-out writer and
a scientist.

olaris, 1972, starring
lya Bondarchuk and
atas Banionis

ned "the Russian answer to
rick's *2001*," it is a philo-
ical science-fiction parable
ve and life. A space mission
re human thoughts take on
ical form, the film's breadth
e Tarkovsky the most out-
ding of Russia's filmmakers,
ring Steven Soderbergh to
a remake in 2002.

Politics and Blockbusters 1975–1989

"I think we're going to need a bigger boat."

Steven Spielberg: Jaws, 1975, USA, starring Roy Scheider, Robert Shaw, and Richard Dreyfuss
Quote: Roy Schneider as Police Chief Martin Brody in *Jaws*

Politics an

302

New Hollywood

The mid-1970s saw young generation of filmmakers combine auteurism with the financial backing of Hollywood studios

1975   1980

Blockbusters

ockbusters

italizing on new
nology and marketing
niques, blockbusters
ress audiences and
sh box-office records

p. 351

1985   **1990**

hael Bay
es Cameron p. 366
rge Lucas p. 358
Rietman
ven Spielberg p. 354
ert Zemeckis p. 362

p. 359

New Independent Films

Produced without funding from Hollywood studios, Independent films challenge the conventions of mainstream cinema

Politics and Blockbusters

A tumultuous decade of upheaval and innovation, the 1970s were characterized by political and social changes. From the sexual revolution, Black Power, and counterculture movements to the Vietnam War and neoconservative politics, filmmakers were inspired by reality. The early 1970s saw the emergence of a new generation of German filmmakers. Influenced by the French New Wave, New German Cinema used nonactors, low budgets, and unpredictable narratives. From the visionary *The Tin Drum* to Werner Herzog's epic *Aguirre: The Wrath of God* (1972), New German Cinema's treatment of modernity, war, and history was praised for its reliance on artistic rather than commercial motives.

■ **Eric Rohmer: The Marquise o O**, 1976, starring Edith Clever

■ **Andrzej Waj Man of Marble,** 1976, starring Kr tyna Janda

■ **Volker Schlö dorff: The Tin Drum**, 1979, sta ring Mario Ador and Angela Win

New Hollywood

A young generation of Hollywood directors shaped a
movement of their own. Buoyed by greater control
over their projects, New Hollywood directors used their
freedom and financial security to produce scores of
challenging and stimulating films that were both artis-
tically groundbreaking and commercially successful.
From Peter Bogdanovich's poignant *The Last Picture
Show* (1971) to Woody Allen's cerebral romance *Annie
Hall* (1977), American screens were dominated by a daring and provocative collection of films throughout the
late 1970s. New Hollywood directors such as Francis
Ford Coppola and Martin Scorsese utilized big budgets
and reputations to experiment with form and convention, creating spectacular and epic films that appealed
to an increasingly savvy generation of filmgoers.

Well educated and closely knit, New Hollywood
directors were not content to stay within genre boundaries and freely borrowed from film history to create
complex, referential films like 1976's *Carrie*.

■ George Mill
and George
Ogilvie: Mad M
Beyond Thun
dome, 1985, sta
ring Mel Gibson
and Tina Turner

The Birth of the Blockbuster

Equal parts coming-of-age movie, horror film, high-school drama, and thriller, *Carrie*'s clever pastiche of successful elements exploded genre conventions and cleverly exploited new areas of audience appeal. This led to films such as *Mad Max*, whose similarly ground-breaking combination of road movie, postapocalyptic drama, and action film gained critical attention and became a central figure in the popularization of Australian cinema.

In 1975, Steven Spielberg's thriller *Jaws* ushered in a new era of filmmaking when it transformed the usually low-earning period of the summer break into a prime time for profit making. Featuring a highly visible, nationwide marketing campaign and released simultaneously in 675 theaters across the United States, *Jaws* became the first film in motion picture history to earn over $100 million, marking the end of the New Hollywood movement and the dawn of the summer blockbuster.

■ Wes Craven
A Nightmare
Elm Street, 19
starring Robert
Englund

Ted Kotcheff: *First Blood*, 1982, featuring Sylvester Stallone and Richard Crenna

Joe Dante: *Gremlins*, 1984, featuring Zach Galligan and Phoebe Cates

The Film Boom of the 1980s

Encouraged by the box-office sensations of films from the late 1970s such as *Jaws,* as well as the new market that emerged with the drop in VCR and home-entertainment prices and the subsequent rise of video rentals, films produced during the early 1980s strove for dominance through special effects, big-budget aesthetics, and wide audience appeal. Innovative marketing and merchandizing techniques were used and the popularity of films was used to create sequels. Era-defining hits such as *First Blood,* the first of the *Rambo* series, launched a new generation of superstars with actors such as Arnold Schwarzenegger and Sylvester Stallone becoming synonymous with emerging genres, creating new types for stars and films and spearheading box-office hits. Meanwhile, Wes Craven began making horror films that revolutionized the genre.

Introduction

As 1980s cinema exploded with high-paced action films and family-oriented blockbusters like *Gremlins* (1984) and *ET: The Extra-Terrestrial* (1982), Tim Burton offered a humorous and inventive take on mainstream fare with *Beetlejuice* (1988)—an occasionally grotesque film that capitalized on the rise of the fantasy and comedy genres and innovations in special effects. Combining clever comedy, groundbreaking animation techniques, and a unique, expressionistic vision, Burton's films gave new treatments to classic Hollywood plots and were a well-received screen staple throughout the decade.

■ **Stephen Fre** **My Beautiful Laundrette**, 19 starring Daniel Lewis and Gord Warnecke

■ **Lasse Hall-ström: My Life as a Dog**, 1985 starring Anton Glanzelius

Filmmakers capitalized on their rich knowledge of film history by using familiar conventions in a drastically new way, awing audiences and creating a new form of film culture.

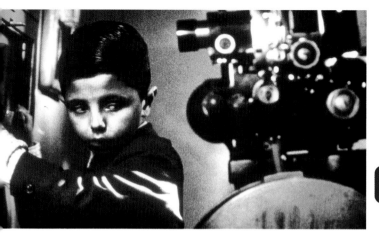

Underground and Independent

Meanwhile, the divide between Hollywood's super-directors and underground filmmakers widened, as an innovative, often provocative new generation of independent directors emerged, challenging their Hollywood contemporaries. In 1985, Stephen Frears's *My Beautiful Laundrette* was heralded for its lo-fi aesthetic, flawed characters, and politically charged narrative. It represented a new type of independent cinema. On the other side of the Atlantic, Jim Jarmusch's unique, painterly films, such as *Down by Law* (1986), fused beat cinematography, meandering narratives, and eclectic music, finding new audiences and proving a lasting influence on a generation of young directors to come. In 1988, the success of the literate and self-reflexive drama *Cinema Paradiso* breathed life back into Italian cinema, collecting an Oscar for Best Foreign Language film and paving the way for a new decade of socially conscious international cinema.

William Friedkin

1935, Chicago

■ Made one of the highest grossing horror films of all time ■ Iconic membe
of the New Hollywood movement ■ Influenced by European cinema ■ Mas
of suspense and action ■ Controversial subject matter and imagery
■ American ■ Thriller, Drama, Action ■ Directed 18 films

■ **1935** Born in Chicago

1955 Begins working in a TV studio

1965 Moves to Hollywood

1967 Produces his first feature, *Good Times*

1968 Produces and directs *The Birthday Party* in the UK

1973 Films *The Exorcist*

1985 *To Live and Die in LA* is released

2000 Rerelease of *The Exorcist* with previously unseen footage

William Friedkin began his film career in a TV station m
room before being promoted to studio floor manager.
directed several TV programs and documentaries bef
the release of his first feature film, the Sonny and C
comedy spoof *Good Times*. In 1968, Friedkin travelec
the UK to direct *The Birthday Party*, but it was 1971's
French Connection that earned him an Academy Aw
for Best Director, impressing critics with its susper
style, and on-screen tension. Friedkin's biggest succ
came with *The Exorcist* in 1973, a disturbing and provo
tive horror film that cemented his reputation among N
Hollywood's elite.

The Exorcist, 1973, starring
n Burstyn and Linda Blair

Exorcist follows 12-year-old
an MacNeil (Blair), whose
ther hires two priests to per-
m an exorcism when she
ws signs of demonic posses-
n. A classic horror film that
nbines a tension-driven plot
h highly innovative special
cts and subliminal images,
Exorcist is a nightmarish
k that earned 10 Academy
ard nominations and
ame one of the highest
ssing horror films of all time.

■ **The French Connection**,
1971, starring Gene Hackman
and Roy Scheider

The French Connection draws
inspiration from French New
Wave cinema and combines it
with a gritty Brooklyn aesthetic.
Two renegade detectives
(Hackman and Sheider) follow a
narcotics hunch in an action-
packed and tumultuous search
for a group of international
criminals. Carefully written,
acted, and choreographed, *The
French Connection* is a suave
film that keeps audiences on

edge through spectacular
chase scenes, tense stakeouts,
and nail-biting pursuits, making
it one of cinema's greatest
detective films.

Other Works

Sorcerer, 1977, starring Roy
Scheider and Bruno Cremer

Rules of Engagement, 2000,
starring Tommy Lee Jones and
Samuel L. Jackson

Bug, 2006, starring Ashley
Judd, Michael Shannon, and
Harry Connick Jr.

William Friedkin

Peter Bogdanovich

1939, Kingston

■ Pioneering member of the New Hollywood movement ■ Master of coming-of-age films ■ Often sets films in rural America ■ Interested in changing sexual and social politics
■ American ■ Drama, Comedy ■ Directed 17 films

1939 Born in New York

1955 Begins his career as an actor and writer

1966 Moves to Los Angeles

1966 Assistant director of Roger Corman's *The Wild Angels*

1971 Directs *The Last Picture Show*

1972 Joins the Directors Company with William Friedkin and Francis Ford Coppola

1974 *Daisy Miller* is a box-office flop

1999–2007 Guest stars in the critically acclaimed TV series *The Sopranos*

Beginning his career as a writer and actor, Peter Bogdanovich was frequently surrounded by Hollywood elite. He took the position of assistant director on Roger Corman's *The Wild Angels* in 1966, before directing own landmark film, *The Last Picture Show* in 1971. Bogdanovich's early films were character-based studies that dealt with social and sexual politics in the United States disappearing Golden Age. Set in rural America, *Paper Moon* and *The Last Picture Show* gained much critical acclaim for their complex characters and social commentary, but Bogdanovich's later films received largely lackluster reviews. In 2000, Bogdanovich won back the favor of critics with his work on the long-running HBO TV series *The Sopranos*.

■ **The Last Picture Show**, 1971, starring Timothy Bottoms and Jeff Bridges

A nostalgic coming-of-age drama, the film follows two friends on a journey of self-discovery. Praised by critics for its depiction of a changing social and sexual milieu, *The Last Picture Show* earned eight Academy Award nominations and put Bogdanovich at the center of the New Hollywood movement.

Other Works

ey All Laughed, 1981,
rring Audrey Hepburn and
rothy Stratten

xasville, 1990, starring Harvey
ristiansen and Pearl Jones

What's Up Doc?, 1972,
rring Barbra Streisand, Ryan
eal, and Madeline Kahn

at's Up Doc? is a screwball
nedy that centers on the
ners of four identical suit-
es. Notable for its homage to
ier films such as Bringing Up
y (1938), What's Up Doc?
tures iconic shots of the San
ncisco area and a memo-
e performance by Barbra
isand. A well-written and
rconnected tale full of
on and quirky dialogue,
as one of the biggest film
cesses of 1972.

■ **Paper Moon**, 1973, starring
Ryan O'Neal, Tatum O'Neal,
and Madeline Kahn

Shot in black and white and
filmed on location, *Paper Moon* is
a feel-good comedy about an
unlikely pair of con artists trying
to make a new beginning. The
film playfully examines ideas of
family and commitment. Tatum
O'Neal earned an Academy
Award for Best Supporting
Actress—the youngest winner
in Academy Award history.

Peter Bogdanovich

Francis Ford Coppola

1939, Detroit

■ Pioneer of American auteurism ■ Influenced by French New Wave ■ Key
figure of New Hollywood movement ■ Depicted controversial social issues
■ Directed one of the highest grossing films of all time
■ American ■ Gangster, War, Drama ■ Directed 23 films

■ **1939** Born into an artistic
family in Detroit
1961 Begins filmmaking at
Roger Corman's studio
1963 First film, *Dementia 13*
1969 Founds American
Zoetrope production
company
1972 *The Godfather* is
released and becomes a
major success
1973 Produces *American
Graffiti*
1979 *Apocalypse Now*
wins Palme d'Or
1997 Co-founds literary
magazine, *Zoetrope: All Story*
2007 *Youth Without Youth*

One of the most influential and iconic members of
New Hollywood movement, Francis Ford Coppola's fil
are often political and social commentaries that mas
fully capture the feeling of a time and era. Born in Detr
Coppola studied filmmaking at UCLA before joining Ro
Corman's movie factory where he made his first fi
Dementia 13. In 1969, Coppola directed *The Rain Peopl*
film that aligned him with the counterculture movem
and was successful enough for him to create his own p
duction company, American Zoetrope. In 1972, Copp
directed *The Godfather* (p. 316), which secured his p
tion among Hollywood's top directors and broke b
office records. Coppola again found success in the 198
with a number of "Brat Pack" films featuring clever casti
well-written scripts, and controversial themes.

■ **Rumble Fish**, 1983, starr
Matt Dillon, Mickey Rourke,
Diane Lane

A coming-of-age drama, *Rum
Fish* follows Rusty James and
notorious older brother The
Motorcycle Boy. Dealing wit
family, competition, disconr
tion, and power, *Rumble Fish*
was shot using high-contras
black-and-white film and fea
tures expressionistic cinema
raphy and an experimental
score by Stewart Copeland.
Drawing inspiration from the
French New Wave, it is one o
Coppola's most stylized films

Politics and Blockbusters 1975–1989

■ **Apocalypse Now**, 1979, starring Martin Sheen, Robert Duvall, Marlon Brando, Frederic Forrest, Laurence Fishburne, and Dennis Hopper

A group of American soldiers in Vietnam find themselves plunging deeper and deeper into anarchy as they move upriver in search of the dissident Colonel Kurtz. Sweeping aerial shots, explosive action, and spine-chilling performances make it an iconic study of fear and power and one of the most provocative war films in cinema history. Based on Joseph Conrad's colonial novel, *Heart of Darkness*, the film was also influenced by Werner Herzog's 1972 film, *Aguirre: The Wrath of God*.

The Conversation, 4, starring Gene ckman, John Cazale, Allen Garfield

Conversation is a vocative, myste- us thriller that fol- s the story of a anoid surveillance

expert caught in a moral dilemma between his life and his work. Nominated for three Academy Awards, the film is a dark, Orwellian story that examines politics, power, and control.

Other Works

he Rain People, 1969, arring James Caan d Robert Duvall

ne from the Heart, 982, starring Frederic orrest and Teri Garr

The Cotton Club, 1984, starring Richard Gere and Gregory Hines

Youth Without Youth, 2007, starring Tim Roth and Bruno Ganz

Francis Ford Coppola

The Godfather

■ by Francis Ford Coppola, USA, 1972, Drama

A rich, layered epic, *The Godfather* is much more than just a Mafia film. An analysis of American postwar politics and an intimate study of family and power, *The Godfather* is Francis Ford Coppola's most celebrated film and one of the high points of New Hollywood. Shot in a limited palette of color and shadow and utilizing largely continuous action, *The Godfather* features pitch-perfect performances by Marlon Brando and Al Pacino as the patriarch and reluctant son of the powerful Corleone crime family. Enormous and operatic in scale, *The Godfather* was met by an equally overwhelming reception, earning 11 Academy Award nominations and breaking box-office records.

The Godfather features an immense ensemble cast, with a number of the actors retaining their roles in the sequels that followed. Cinematographer Gordon Willis' use of long, slow zooms and pans provide an epic and grandiose aesthetic without sacrificing detail, while the dramatic score, a co-project between classical composer Nino Rota and Coppola's father Carmine Coppola, add authenticity and complexity

he Godfather, 1972,
ring Marlon Brando, Al
no, James Caan, Diane
ron, and Robert Duvall

Godfather spawned two
els, in 1974 and 1990. Both
e well received by audi-
es, and *The Godfather II* has
described as the best
el of all time. Earning six
demy Awards including
Picture, *The Godfather II* is
quel and prequel, contin-
the events of the first film
e detailing Vito Corleone
his family's rise to power.
third installment

introduced the Corleone family
to a new generation of filmgoers and blended fictionalized
real-life events with the family's
saga. The trilogy confirmed the
partnership between director
Francis Ford Coppola, writer
Mario Puzo, and
cinematogra-
pher Gordon

Willis as one of American
cinema's richest and most
critically
acclaimed
collabora-
tions.

The Godfather

Brian De Palma

1940, Newark

■ Influenced by French New Wave ■ Pioneered new shot techniques ■ Use[s] elements from film history and combines them with new technologies ■ Par[t of] the New Hollywood movement ■ Masterful control of pace and plot revelati[on] ■ American ■ Thriller, Gangster, Action ■ Directed 28 films

Influenced by the French New Wave, Brian De Palma [turned] out to be the Jean-Luc Godard (p. 232) of Americ[an] cinema. He began filmmaking in 1966 with the docum[en]tary *The Responsive Eye*, and although his oeuvre began [to] take shape with 1968's *Greetings*, it was not until [the] release of *Carrie* that De Palma shot to stardom. In [the] 1980s, De Palma directed *Scarface* and *The Untouchab[les]*, both rich with bullets, gore, and a new gangster aesthe[tic] while the 1990s and 2000s saw more mainstream fi[lms] such as *Mission: Impossible* and *The Black Dahlia*. [De] Palma's films are often characterized by a saturated co[lor] palette, sweeping shots, and themes of revenge and [ex]cess. A master of pastiche, he often borrows eleme[nts] from film history, revitalizing them for a new generati[on.]

■ **Scarface**, 1983, starring Al Pacino and Michelle Pfeiffer

Tony Montana (Pacino) is a ruthless and volatile gangster rising through the ranks of the Miami underworld. Featuring graphic violence and drug use, *Scarface* was originally given an X rating by the MPAA, but it was later reduced to an R. Scarface was an enormous success with audiences and critics alike and the film revived interest in the gangster genre.

he Untouchables, 1987,
ing Kevin Costner, Sean
nery, and Robert De Niro

e officers are hired to break
Chicago crime ring headed
e infamous Al Capone.
d on the biography of Eliot
, *The Untouchables* is a gritty
e drama that faithfully cap-
s the Prohibition era with
essive sets and Connery's
r-winning performance.

Other Works

Carrie, 1976, starring Sissy
Spacek and Piper Laurie

Blow Out, 1981, starring John
Travolta

Raising Cain, 1992, starring
John Lithgow and Lolita
Davidovich

Carlito's Way, 1993, starring Al
Pacino and Sean Penn

■ **Mission: Impossible**, 1996,
starring Tom Cruise, Jon Voight,
and Emmanuelle Béart

Mission: Impossible is a classic
international espionage movie
that was 1996's summer blockbuster. Following CIA agent
Ethan Hunt through a web of
conspiracy, the film is an action-
packed thriller, praised for its
special effects and multi-
layered narrative.

Martin Scorsese

1942, New York

- Founding member of New Hollywood ■ Influenced by John Cassavetes
- Depicts controversial subject matter ■ Interested in religion and cultural identity ■ Uses saturated color, long tracking shots, and expressionistic light
- American ■ Gangster, Thriller ■ Directed 20 films

One of the most powerful and recognizable directors modern American cinema, Martin Scorsese famously tr his hand at priesthood before studying filmmaking NYU Film School. Born in New York to Italian-Americ parents, Scorsese's consideration of his cultural ident was integral in shaping his success as a director, a resulted in classic films such as *Raging Bull* and *Goodfel*. In the 1970s, Scorsese became associated with the N Hollywood movement when he befriended Francis F Coppola (p. 314), Brian De Palma (p. 318), Steven Sp berg (p. 354), and the man who would star in his most s cessful movies, Robert De Niro. During this period, he a met independent director John Cassavetes (p. 292),

aging Bull, 1980, starring
ert De Niro, Cathy Moriarty,
Joe Pesci

La Motta (De Niro) is a
sic underdog battling what
hrows his way—yet the
lessness that makes him a

success in the ring makes him a
failure in his personal life. Using
dizzying tracking shots, stills,
slow motion, and home-movie
footage, *Raging Bull* was an
innovative but challenging hit
that won two Oscars.

Goodfellas, 1990, starring
Ray Liotta and Robert De Niro

A brutal biopic of a pair of
unrepentant gangsters rising
through the ranks of the mob,
Goodfellas features epic tracking
shots and gritty dialogue.

axi Driver, 1976, starring
ert De Niro and Jodie Foster

liro gives a career-best
ormance as Travis Bickle, a
tile taxi driver pushed fur-
and further toward the
e by modern city life. Fea-
g clever pacing and dra-
c catalysts, *Taxi Driver* was a
roversial success with audi-
s and critics. A pivotal film
he New Hollywood move-
t, it is an intimate study of
tion, alienation, violence,
morality in the underbelly of
rican society.

Martin Scorsese

whose punchy, gritty style had a great impact on the young director and influenced films such as *Mean Streets*. Scorsese's interest in the music industry aligned him with the counterculture movement throughout the 1970s and spawned the music documentaries *The Last Waltz* (1978) and later, *No Direction Home* (2005). Scorsese's films are often characterized by the use of slow motion, jump cuts, a strong focus on character, and unusual and expressive lighting. Most comfortable dealing with themes of masculinity, cultural identity, religion, and crime, Scorsese has also shown his flexibility by directing romance films and period dramas. An iconic and respected public figure, Scorsese's works have been an integral and successful part of American cinema since the 1970s, receiving critical acclaim and numerous awards, including an Oscar for Best Director in 2006 for *The Departed*.

322

Politics and Blockbusters 1975–1989

The Age of Innocence, 1993, starring Daniel Day-Lewis, Michelle Pfeiffer, and Winona Ryder

The Age of Innocence is a Victorian-era drama that follows the story of a wealthy lawyer (Day-Lewis) who questions his upcoming marriage after developing feelings for another woman. Based on the 1920 novel by Edith Wharton, the film is a complex romance about morality and scandal that won an Academy Award for its opulent costume designs.

The Departed, 2006, starring Leonardo DiCaprio, Matt Damon, Jack Nicholson, and Mark Wahlberg

The Departed was a highly anticipated film that impressed audiences. Featuring a star-studded cast and a popular soundtrack of iconic music from the 1970s and '80s, it is a clever crime thriller that appealed to a wide audience. *The Departed* is an English-language remake of the Hong Kong blockbuster, *Infernal Affairs* (2002). Set in Boston, it dramatizes ideas of identity and masculinity.

The Last Temptation of Christ, 1988, starring Willem Dafoe and Harvey Keitel

Working with scriptwriter Paul Schrader, this dramatic change of direction shocked some of Scorsese's fans and outraged religious communities upon its release. An epic and contemplative film, *The Last Temptation of Christ* is not only a retelling of a familiar story, but is a study of commitment, fear, and temptation that features seemingly endless tracking shots, wide views, and expressionistic lighting.

Martin Scorsese

Battlers and Bon Vivants

With the explosion of the action and blockbuster genres came a new generation of Hollywood heroes. From the neurotic, troubled characters of *Rain Man*, to the macho, high-intensity heroes of *The Terminator* (1984, far right), the 1970s to the '80s was the era of the superstar. Actors starred in seemingly endless sequels while at the same time becoming the subject of clever merchandising, including action figures, video games, and TV series. Capitalizing on the growth of mass media and wide releases, these new superstar movies became international box-office hits.

■ **Dustin Hoffman**, a dual Academy Award winner, first became known as a versatile and literate star when he portrayed a college student seduced by an older woman *The Graduate* (1967). Hoffmar costar in *Rain Man* (1988, abo was Tom Cruise who became major heartthrob of the 1980 and '90s, wooing audiences with his smooth on-screen cl risma and sincere performan

■ **Jack Nicholson**, one of H lywood's most famous figur has frightened and seduced audiences for almost 50 yea with his eclectic portrayals c neurotic killers and debona Casanovas, becoming the m nominated male actor in Academy Award history.

◀ **Sylvester Stallone's** rippling physique and deadpan delivery made him an action hero and a formidable on-screen force. With *Rocky* (1976) and *Rambo* (1982, left), Stallone's career exploded in the 1980s, making him one of America's most recognizable actors and a symbol of machismo.

■ **A former bodybuilder, Arnold Schwarzenegger's** mountainous physique made him a staple of blockbuster action films. Equally popular as a fearsome villain and gallant hero, his hard body was the physical manifestation of 1980s budgets. With a string of hugely successful films, Austrian-born Schwarzenegger became the world's most iconic action star.

Battlers and Bon Vivants

Woody Allen

1935, New York

- Prolific American auteur ■ Made iconic and influential romantic comedies
- Interested in relationships and psychoanalysis ■ Uses black humor, parody
and highly innovative cinematography to challenge cinematic conventions
- American ■ Comedy, Drama ■ Directed 36 films

- **1935** Born Allen Stewart Konigsberg in New York
- **1954** Writes gags for the *Ed Sullivan* show and *The Tonight Show*
- **1961** Begins performing as a stand-up comedian in Greenwich Village
- **1969** First film as auteur, *Take the Money and Run*
- **1977** Wins Academy Award for Best Director for *Annie Hall*
- **2002** Receives lifetime achievement award at Cannes Film Festival

Beginning as a comedian and playwright, Woody Allen wrote for the *Ed Sullivan* and *Tonight* shows and performed his own stand-up material at comedy clubs in New York. His literate humor quickly earned him notoriety, and he was able to direct and star in his film *Take the Money and Run* in 1969. Imaginative and perceptive, his films are often bookish, psychological forays into contemporary relationships, featuring self-deprecating humor and quirky, lovable characters. His two most successful films, *Annie Hall* and *Hannah and Her Sisters*, set benchmarks for romantic comedies and performed exceptionally well at the box office. Allen has been nominated for an abundance of Academy Awards and has won three Oscars. Although many critics argue that his best work took place in the 1970s, Allen has also received acclaim for some of his more recent films such as *Melinda and Melinda* (2004) and *Match Point*

Hannah and Her Sisters, [19]86, starring Woody Allen, Mia [Far]row, and Michael Caine

[Ha]nnah and Her Sisters is a [ro]mantic comedy that traces a [tu]multuous year in the lives of [thr]ee women. When Hannah's [hu]sband becomes dissatisfied [wit]h their marriage, he seeks [co]mfort in an adulterous rela-[tion]ship with her sister, Lee. [Me]anwhile, a younger sister, [Ho]lly, battles addiction, a floun-[der]ing career, and string of

Manhattan, 1979, starring [Wo]ody Allen, Diane Keaton, [and] Michael Murphy

[Wh]en Isaac Davis's young girl-[frie]nd fails to stimulate him [inte]llectually, he falls for a high-[fly]ing journalist and cabaret [sing]er who is having an affair [wit]h one of his closest friends. [Ma]nhattan is a clever study of [inte]rwoven relationships, fea-[turi]ng interesting cinematog-[rap]hy, creative dialogue, and [an e]mphatic Gershwin score.

Other Works

Sleeper, 1973, starring Woody Allen, Diane Keaton, and Mews Small

Annie Hall, 1977, starring Woody Allen, Diane Keaton, and Tony Roberts

failed romances. A web of disil-lusionment, humor, and love, it was praised by critics and audi-ences, and received seven Academy Award nominations.

Match Point, 2005, starring Scarlett Johansson and Brian Cox

Match Point focuses on Chris Wilton, a failing tennis cham-pion seeking a new direction in life. A film about luck, murder, and wealth, Match Point features iconic imagery, witty dialogue, an ensemble cast, and an excellent perform-ance by Johansson. Nominated for an Oscar and receiving largely positive reviews, it was a tremendous comeback success.

Woody Allen

Robert Altman

1925, Kansas City—2006, Los Angeles

■ Used innovative editing techniques ■ Frequently worked with ensemble casts ■ Emphasized character and dialogue rather than plot ■ Used improvisation in his films ■ Relied heavily on the postproduction process ■ American ■ Satire, Comedy, Drama ■ Directed 35 films

■ **1925** Born in Kansas
1943 Serves in WWII
1947 Writes film scripts
1957 First feature film *The Delinquents*
1970 Awarded Best Film at the Cannes Film Festival for *M*A*S*H*
1976 Founds production company Lionsgate Films
1992 Directs *The Player*
1993 *Short Cuts* wins Golden Lion at the Venice Film Festival
2005 Receives the Honorary Academy Award for lifetime achievement
2006 Dies in California

Known for his ingenuity, humor, and ability to make sh. statements on American society, Robert Altman's car spanned 50 years. After returning from service a bomber pilot during World War II, Altman began career by writing scripts and working in television. early experience in the television studio had a great i pact on his style of filmmaking, and can be seen throu unusual techniques such as linking two or three came simultaneously and zooming in on characters mid-c versation. Altman also encouraged his actors to imp vise dialogue and actions during filming, making postproduction process—in which the film's scenes edited to create cohesion—a pivotal part of the directi process. His most acclaimed films were kaleidosco views of everyday American life that emphasized development of characters—and overall atmosphere of the settings and uations they find themselves in. greatest commercial success was his d 1970 comedy, *M*A*S*H*.

■ **M*A*S*H**, 1970, starring Donald Sutherland and Elliott Gould

Deeply cynical and sharply antiestablishment, *M*A*S*H* quickly aligned itself with a counterculture audience and became one of the most successful comedies of its time.

Set amid the Korear War, the film traces dramas and follies c group of unlikely medics. A perfectly delivered comedy, i features witty dialogue, complex cha ters, inventive came work and innovative editing.

Short Cuts, 1993, starring
d Ward, Andie MacDowell,
ce Davison, Tim Robbins, June Moore, and Jack Lemmon

ed on Raymond Carver's
ok of the same name, *Short*
s is an interwoven tale of 22
racters living in Los Angeles.
turing an immense ensemble
t, *Short Cuts* is an ambitious
 that focuses on relation-
s, love, and isolation, using
provised dialogues, repeti-
, and setting to bind the
kely characters together.

Prêt-à-Porter, 1994, starring
rcello Mastroianni, Sophia
en, Julia Roberts, and Kim
inger

-à-Porter brings together a
t of models, celebrities,
orters, photographers, and
igners at Paris Fashion Week.

When a body is found, two
reporters are hired to investi-
gate the murder. A witty parody
and bold comment on the
fickle nature of the fashion
industry, the film splices documentary footage with narrative
scenes, focusing on fame and
insecurity.

Robert Altman

Michael Cimino

1939, New York

■ Made one of the most successful war films of all time ■ Relishes in spectac and ritual in epic stories ■ Directed films of many different genres ■ Memb of the New Hollywood movement ■ Often depicts working-class characters ■ American ■ War, Action ■ Directed 7 films

New Hollywood

■ **1939** Born in New York
1963 MFA from Yale University
1972 Co-writes the screenplay *Silent Running*
1974 *Thunderbolt and Lightfoot* is picked up by Clint Eastwood's production company, Malpaso
1978 *The Deer Hunter* wins him the Academy Award for Best Director
1980 *Heaven's Gate* flops
1985 *Year of the Dragon* earns him the title of Honorary Colonel of Thailand's Royal Air Force
1987 *The Sicilian* leads to controversy
2001 Authors the novel *Big Jane*

Trained in architecture, Michael Cimino's big break i the film industry came when his film *Thunderbolt a Lightfoot* was accepted by Clint Eastwood's (p. 3 studio. Although his debut was not an outstanding fin cial success, it did allow Cimino the chance to make *Deer Hunter*—a well-received and poignant film awarc Oscars for Best Picture and Best Director. Attempting follow his success, Cimino put together *Heaven's Ga* which, although it possessed an impressive cast a scope, fell dramatically short of its intended target. T financial loss of *Heaven's Gate* caused United Artists to Cimino and rein in the freedom they had given to you directors throughout the 1970s, a measure that so argue ended the New Hollywood movement. His repu tion tarnished, Cimino went on to make several inc pendent films, but unfortunately none of these would to the fame of *The Deer Hunter*.

Other Works

Thunderbolt and Lightfoot, 1974, starring Clint Eastwood

The Sicilian, 1987, starring Christopher Lambert and Terence Stamp

Desperate Hours, 1990, starring Mickey Rourke and Anthony Hopkins

Sunchaser, 1996, starring Woody Harrelson

■ **Year of the Dragon**, 198 starring Mickey Rourke, Aria Koizumi, and John Lone

Exploring ideas of crime and ethnicity and relishing in jux positions and graphic violer *Year of the Dragon* was sur rounded by controversy whe it was released in 1985. Dubb racist and stereotypical, this gritty cop drama received largely poor reviews despite script by Oliver Stone and a convincing performance by Mickey Rourke.

Politics and Blockbusters 1975–1989

■ **The Deer Hunter**, 1978, starring Robert De Niro, Christopher Walken, John Savage, and Meryl Streep

The Deer Hunter is a relentless and sincere portrayal of friends torn apart by politics, the world, and themselves. Christopher Walken and Robert De Niro are at their best as two steel workers united and divided by love, fear, and war. Epic in its scale and plot, *The Deer Hunter* delivers a big-budget aesthetic that manages not to overshadow the personal dramas that unfold. A masterfully written tale revealed with a clever hand, the film is an in-depth study of the psychological effects of war that extols color, ritual, and spectacle.

eaven's Gate, 1980, ~~r~~ing Kris Kristofferson, ~~ll~~elle Huppert, and ~~ri~~stopher Walken

~~R~~eating the success of *The ~~Deer~~ Hunter* would have been a ~~dau~~nting task, but ~~Hea~~ven's Gate was an ~~un~~precedented flop. ~~Ep~~ic western ~~feat~~uring a ~~mo~~nolithic, star-~~stu~~dded cast, it ~~was~~ largely ~~con~~sidered by ~~criti~~cs to be self-~~indu~~lgent and ~~over~~zealous. Its ~~$44~~ million produc-~~tion~~ costs, of which ~~only~~ $12 million would be ~~sal~~vaged, obliterated United ~~Arti~~sts, forcing them to quash

the creative freedom of auteurs. Nevertheless, *Heaven's Gate* is a cinematically bold and

picturesque film that painstakingly focuses on love, honor, and ideology.

Michael Cimino

Saturday Night Fever

■ by John Badham, 1977, USA, Drama

The success of *Saturday Night Fever* is inexorably tied with the success of its chart-topping soundtrack and singular performance by John Travolta. A cult classic, the film is a drug-and-alcohol fueled portrayal of the ritual of Saturday night that exploded disco and rein-vigorated the dance-film genre. Tony Manero (Tra-volta) and his friends are working-class youths who release their frustrations on the dance floor at club 2001 Odyssey. Dealing with issues such as competi-tion, supremacy, and escapism, *Saturday Night Fever* is a troubled coming-of-age movie that expertly tapped into a generation of filmgoers wooed by the bright lights of disco.

■ **Saturday Night Fever**, 1977, starring John Travolta and Karen Lynn Gorney

Originally rated R, the film w recut to remove nudity, expl language, and drug use and rereleased in 1978 with a PG rating. Featuring a wealth o by the Bee Gees, the soundt reached platinum sales 15 ti becoming the most success film soundtrack of all time. C verly timed and marketed, th film reached a generation cc ming of age in the late 1970

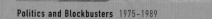

333

Saturday Night Fever

Rainer Werner Fassbinder

1945, Bad Wörishofen—1982, Munich

- Prolific and prominent member of New German Cinema ■ Worked as direct
producer, composer, and actor ■ Influenced by Bertolt Brecht and Douglas Sir
- Used heightened color ■ Influenced many independent directors
- German ■ Drama ■ Directed 41 films

- **1945** Born in Germany
  1964 Studies theater at Fridl-Leonhard Studio in Munich
  1964 Meets actress Hanna Schygulla
  1969 First feature-length film, *Love is Colder Than Death*, using the pseudonym Franz Walsch
  1972 Joins West German Television Studio and begins a partnership with Peter Märtesheimer
  1974 Directs *Fear Eats the Soul*
  1977 A festival of Fassbinder's films is held in Manhattan
  1978 The first in the *Germany* trilogy, *The Marriage of Maria Braun*
  1980 Directs *Berlin Alexanderplatz*
  1982 Dies in Munich, Germany

Other Works

Love Is Colder Than Death, 1969, starring Rainer Werner Fassbinder and Hanna Schygulla

Chinese Roulette, 1976, starring Anna Karina and Margit Carstensen

Rainer Werner Fassbinder was a prolific and flamboya figure of New German Cinema. Fassbinder endured a ficult childhood in postwar Germany before becomin theater director for the avant-garde Munich Action T ater. Influenced by Brecht, the French New Wave, a director Douglas Sirk, he moved into filmmaking a found major success in 1974 with *Fear Eats the Soul*. Fa binder led a colorful and controversial life that was t subject of much media attention. His visionary use tragic characters, improvised dialogue, and comp themes earned him immense respect amongst fi makers and influenced directors such as Krzysztof Ki lowski (p. 342) and John Waters (p. 346). After Fassbind death Hans Günther Pflaum made the document. *I Don't Just Want You to Love Me* about his life and wor

■ **Fear Eats the Soul**, 1974 starring Brigitte Mira, El Hed ben Salem, Barbara Valentin and Irm Hermann

A sincere drama that follows the unlikely romance betwe a middle-aged German won and a young Moroccan gues worker, *Fear Eats the Soul* is earnest and sober story of d crimination, isolation, and affection. Featuring clever dialogue and an extensive u of close-ups, *Fear Eats the So* Fassbinder's most accessibl film and a celebrated symbc of New German Cinema.

■ The Marriage of Maria Braun, 1978, starring Hanna Schygulla, Ivan Desny, and Klaus Löwitsch

A troubled portrait of postwar Germany, *The Marriage of Maria Braun* is an authentic study of love amid chaos. Following the romantic and financial endeavors of the hastily married girl, Fassbinder uses dramatic scenery, vivid juxtapositions, and symbolic cultural references to comment on Germany's struggle to rebuild itself in the aftermath of a devastating war.

a Year with 13 Moons, 8, starring Volker Spengler, d Caven, Gottfried John, Lilo Pempeit

binder wrote, directed, gned, shot, and edited *In a with 13 Moons*, making it of his most nsely biog- ical

intimate films. The tragic story of Elvira Weishaupt—a transgender woman with a difficult past—the film blends melo-

drama, tragedy, and humor and features a unique visual poetry and clever narrative. Alongside his *The Third Generation* (1979), it belongs to a period of low-budget and per- sonal films.

Rainer Werner Fassbinder

Werner Herzog

1942, Munich

■ Iconic member of New German Cinema ■ His films are usually of an enorm■ scale ■ Uses expressionistic cinematography ■ Landscape features as a char■ acter ■ Worked closely with Klaus Kinski ■ Sets films in remote destinations ■ German ■ Opera, Documentary, Horror ■ Directed 19 films

1942 Born in Germany

1954 Meets Klaus Kinski

1962 Studies at the University of Munich

1962 Makes *Herakles*, with a stolen camera

1963 Founds his own production company

1968 First feature film, *Signs of Life*

1975 *The Enigma of Kaspar Hauser* wins the Jury Prize at Cannes Film Festival

1978 Is the subject of the documentary, *I Am My Films: A Portrait of Werner Herzog*

2006 Directs *Rescue Dawn*

Visionary and nonconformist, Werner Herzog is an ico■ New German Cinema. Alongside his famous contem■ raries Rainer Werner Fassbinder (p. 334) and Wim W■ ders (p. 338), Herzog's films are ambitious and express■ and feature tales of extraordinary lives and places. La■ scapes often play important roles in Herzog's films, a■ act as catalysts for motivation and action—a the■ exemplified in his 1982 masterpiece, *Fitzcarraldo*, a■ which has led him to shoot on every continent. Wer■ Herzog has worked with an eccentric and volatile crew■ actors, most famously with the irascible Klaus Kinski. T■ frenzied, tumultuous relationship was the subject ■ Herzog's 1999 documentary, *My Best Fiend*. With ■ exception of 2006's *Rescue Dawn*, Herzog has produ■ mostly documentary films since 1987.

■ Aguirre: The Wrath of G■ 1972, starring Klaus Kinski a■ Helena Rojo

In search of the fabled El Dorado, a maniacal explorer sets out on a voyage into the Peruvian Amazon. Filmed in three weeks with a cast of 50 and a small budget, *Aguirre: The Wrath of God* was plague■ by production problems including floods, treacherous rapids, and impenetrable ju■ gles. Nevertheless, the film earned a cult following and went on to influence many high-profile directors.

The Enigma of Kaspar Hauser, 1974, starring [Brun]o S.

[An] expressionistic period drama detailing the life [of a] mysterious young man raised in captivity, *[The] Enigma of Kaspar Hauser* is a study of differ[enc]e and isolation. Bruno S. (who had spent most [of h]is life in institutions) is fascinating as the [mis]fit Kaspar Hauser, struggling against the [colo]nial attempts of the medical establishment.

Other Works

[Str]oszek, 1977, starring [Brun]o S. and Eva Mattes	Rescue Dawn, 2006, starring Christian Bale, Steve Zahn, and Jeremy Davies
[Wo]yzeck, 1979, starring [Klau]s Kinski	

[F]itzcarraldo, 1982, starring Klaus Kinski and [Jos]e Lewgoy

[Klau]s Kinski is at his visionary and eccentric best [as a]n opera-loving rubber baron in this colonial [dram]a about ambition and aspiration. An incred[ible] feat of filmmaking and engineering, *Fitzcar[rald]o* required the enormous cast of extras to [mo]ve a 320-ton steamboat across a mountain in [a re]mote area of the Peruvian jungle. The [con]troversy surrounding the production of [the f]ilm is the topic [of L]es Blank's 1982 [docu]mentary, *[Burd]en of Dreams.*

Wim Wenders

1945, Düsseldorf

■ Influenced by French New Wave ■ Films often feature fragmented and disrupted story lines ■ Collaborates with musicians ■ Uses long takes and pressionistic cinematography ■ Films often feature characters in moral dist■ ■ German ■ Drama ■ Directed 28 films

Born in Düsseldorf in 1945, Wim Wenders began as ar student and film critic before becoming part of the N German Cinema movement. His first film, *Summer in City* (1970), was dedicated to the British pop band Kinks, and indicated a close affinity for music that wo permeate his career. In the 1970s, Wenders becam founding member of the production company Filmve der Autoren, and directed *The American Friend*, which apulted him into the spotlight as one of the most taler new directors of the era. At the end of the 1970s, he Germany for the United States, where he was picked by Francis Ford Coppola's (p. 314) American Zoetr studio. Wenders's films often blend long takes and cc plex antiheroes with open-ended narratives and fr mented story lines. His most successful film to date is surreal *Wings of Desire*, which won the Palme d'Or in 19

■ **Wings of Desire**, 1987, starring Bruno Ganz and Solveig Dommartin

Wings of Desire is an Expressionist fantasy that follows an angel's (Ganz) journey through Berlin where he observes humanity. An epic drama full of longing and empathy, it is Wenders's most critically acclaimed film, and features dramatic black-and-white cinematography and a celestial soundtrack.

Politics and Blockbusters 1975–1989

■ **The American Friend**, 1977, starring Dennis Hopper and Bruno Ganz

Drawing inspiration from film noir, *The American Friend* is a crime thriller that follows the story of an American dealer of forged art (Hopper) attempting to convince a terminally ill man (Ganz) to take part in an assassination plot. A clever drama about fate and morality, the film became a cult sensation and was nominated for the Palme d'Or at the Cannes FIlm Festival.

aris, Texas, 1984, starring y Dean Stanton, Nastassja ki, and Hunter Carson

, *Texas* focuses on the story avis Henderson (Stanton), oriented man retracing his s and revisiting his past. uorously shot in the hern deserts of the ed States, *Paris, Texas* is a nant drama that shows ver control of exposition character. lm res

a spectacular performance by Harry Dean Stanton, won the Palme d'Or, and has a meandering soundtrack by Ry Cooder.

Other Works

The Million Dollar Hotel, 2000, starring Jeremy Davies and Milla Jovovich

Peter Weir

1944, Sydney

- Directed films over many different genres ■ Depicted Australian life ■ Cre
unusual and surreal worlds and uses long tracking shots ■ Successful Hol
wood director ■ Favors unresolved endings
- Australian ■ Drama, Adventure ■ Directed 15 films

1944 Born in Australia

1965 Studies art and law at the University of Sydney

1969 Joins production company Film Australia

1974 First feature-length film, *The Cars That Ate Paris*

1981 Directs *Gallipoli*

1985 First Hollywood film, *Witness*; nominated for Best Director

1998 Directs *The Truman Show*

2003 *Master and Commander: The Far Side of the World* is released

When Australian cinema exploded in the 1970s, P
Weir was thrust into the spotlight because of his I
Picnic at Hanging Rock and *The Last Wave* (1977). Borr
raised in Sydney, Weir studied art and law before tur
to television in the mid-1960s. His first feature-length
was the underground classic, *The Cars That Ate I*
(1974) and he followed with 1975's *Picnic at Hanging I*
Weir's films are often praised for their keen observat
unusual scenery, and multifaceted characters. At the
of his films often lies a philosophical dilemma that is
fully revealed through well-crafted cinematography
story. In 2003, Weir earned 10 Academy Award non
tions for the big-budget swashbuckling drama, *M*
and Commander: The Far Side of the World.

■ **Picnic at Hanging Roc**
1975, starring Rachel Robe
Vivean Gray, Helen Morse,
Child, and Tony Llewellyn-

A haunting mystery that d
with the disappearance of
girls in remote Australia, *P*
at Hanging Rock was so co
vincingly realized that it st
an urban legend. Based or
novel of the same name, th
film features an evocative
soundtrack and clever ma
lation of time and plot. It v
international success and
launched Weir's career, ge
ating worldwide interest i
contemporary Australian
cinema.

...allipoli, 1981, starring Mel
...on, Mark Lee, and Bill Kerr

...*poli* centers on the story
...ank Dunne (Gibson)—an
...tious and restless young
... sent to Turkey during
...d War I. An iconic coming-
...ge drama, the film vividly
...nstructs the world of young
...ralian men and their grue-
...e life on the battlefield.
...ded into three movements,
... sober meditation on
...ralian history that became
...dmark film for its consider-
... of friendship and lost
...h.

Other Works

...ness, 1985, starring Harrison
...d

...d Poets Society, 1989,
...ring Robin Williams

...e Truman Show, 1998, star-
...Jim Carrey and Laura Linney

■ **Green Card**, 1990, starring
Gérard Depardieu and Andie
MacDowell

When a French man (Depardieu)
and an American woman (Mac-
Dowell) embark on a cross-cultural marriage of convenience,
they get more than just the
paperwork. A lighthearted and
clever romantic comedy, *Green
Card* deals with themes of love,
bureaucracy, and marriage.
Featuring fond on-screen chem-
istry and likable characters, it
received an Academy Award
nomination for Best Screenplay.

Peter Weir

Krzysztof Kieślowski

1941, Warsaw–1996, Warsaw

■ Iconic figure of European cinema ■ Member of Cinema of Moral Anxiety Poland ■ Often directed serialized films ■ Interested in social politics and ideals of the French Revolution ■ Used symbolic imagery and color ■ Polish ■ Drama ■ Directed 10 films

1941 Born in Poland
1957 Attends Theater Technicians College
1964–68 Studies at Lodz Film School
1975 First feature-length film, *Personnel*
1979 *Camera Buff* wins grand prize at Moscow Film Festival
1988 Creates *Dekalog* for TV
1993–94 *Three Colors* Trilogy
1996 Dies in Warsaw

One of Europe's most revered directors, Krzys. Kieślowski's films are ambitious and lyrical exploration relationships and interconnectedness. Born in Pol during World War II, Kieślowski attended Lodz Film Sch In the late 1970s, along with Roman Polanski and And Wajda, he became a key figure in Poland's Cinema of M Anxiety—a realist movement that focused on socia sues—producing clever political satires including *Cam Buff* (1979). His major successes include the 1988 *Deka* an epic TV series inspired by the Ten Commandments, the *Three Colors* trilogy. Kieślowski's films are praised their expres cinematograp symboli and co plex m themes

■ **Three Colors: White**, 1994, starring Zbigniew Zamachowski and Julie Delpy

The second in the *Three Colors* trilogy, *White* is comparatively light in tone. A well-written and subtle examination of ambition and equality, the film was celebrated upon its release as a masterpiece of contemporary European cinema.

Other Works

A Short Film About Killing, 1988, starring Miroslaw Baka, Krzysztof Globisz, and Jan Tesarz

Dekalog, (TV), 1989–90, starring Miroslaw Baka, Henryk Baranowski, and Artur Barcis

The Double Life of Veronique, 1991, starring Irène Jacob

◀ **No End**, 1985, starring Grazyna Szapolowska and Maria Pakulnis

Dark and poignant, *No End* centers on Ulla, a translator coming to terms with her husband's death. Well crafted and expressively shot, it examines political freedom and morality in Poland.

Three Colors: Red, 1994, starring Irène Jacob and Jean-Louis Trintignant

and follows the relationship between a model and a reclusive judge whose lives become entwined through a chance accident. Kieślowski expertly dissects themes of difference and friendship, exploring the idea of brotherhood and interconnectedness. Featuring many recurring images and symbolic use of color, the film was Kieślowski's

last. Upon its release *Red* was widely praised by critics and received three Academy Award nominations, including Best Director.

Krzysztof Kieślowski

Independent Films

■ Produced outside major Hollywood studios ■ Often challenge the conventions of filmmaking ■ Experiment with cinematic techniques ■ Often made
on a limited budget ■ Director has artistic control ■ Influenced the development of contemporary cinema

■ *left:* **Little Shop of Horrors**, by Frank Oz, 1986, starring Rick Moranis

1940 Orson Welles gets full control over *Citizen Kane*

1959 Cassavetes's *Shadows* uses improvised dialogue and lay actors

1978 First Sundance Film Festival

1979 Establishment of Miramax Films

1990s Increased availability of production software

1999 *The Blair Witch Project* grosses 11,000 times its original budget

Produced outside major Hollywood studios, independe
films are often forward-thinking works that challenge t
conventions of filmmaking, tackle controversial subje
matter, and experiment with cinematic and narrati
techniques. From *Citizen Kane* (1941) and *Shadows* (19.
to *Pink Flamingos* (1972) and *Sex, Lies and Videota*
(1989), the independent film genre has been a vibra
and avant-garde movement that has had a major impa
on modern cinema. The increased availability of produ
tion software invigorated the independent genre in t
1990s, with successful films such as *The Blair Witch Proje*
(1999) and *George Washington* (2000).

■ **Miloš Forman: One Flew
Over the Cuckoo's Nest**, 19
starring Jack Nicholson and
Louise Fletcher

A classic of independent
cinema, *One Flew Ov
the Cuckoo's Nest* w
five major Acade
Awards includi
Best Director
Featuring ca
tivating perfo
mances, icon
characters, a
innovative
cinematog-
raphy, the film
focuses on th
difficulties of
inside a ment
institution.

■ **Sam Mendes: American Beauty**, 1999, starring Kevin Spacey and Mena Suvari

A compelling comedy/drama, *American Beauty*'s subversive treatment of sex, paternity, and pop culture influenced scores of directors and became a cult classic. Examining the suburban life of a dysfunctional family, the film is a study of loneliness and conformity. It won an Oscar for Best Picture and a Grammy for its influential and plaintive soundtrack.

Harmony Korine: Gummo, 1997, starring Jacob Reynolds, Nick Sutton, and Chloë Sevigny

A cult classic, *Gummo* is a portrait of small-town life in rural Xenia, Ohio. Featuring a host of disturbing and terrifying characters played by nonactors, the film is notable for its hyperrealistic aesthetic and controversial themes including drug abuse, sexuality, euthanasia, depression, class, and suicide. Korine, who also wrote the screenplay, employed a story line that is nonchronological and composed of short sketches that are filled with disturbing surreal imagery set to heavy metal music.

Other Works

Shadows, by John Cassavetes, 1959, starring Ben Carruthers

Heavy, by James Mangold, 1995, starring Pruitt Taylor Vince

Little Miss Sunshine, by Jonathan Dayton and Valerie Faris, 2006, starring Abigail Breslin

John Waters

1946, Baltimore

■ Often uses controversial themes ■ Encourages improvisation ■ Renown[ed] for radical sets and costumes ■ Master of shock-exploitation films ■ Influenc[ed] directors such as David Lynch and Todd Solondz
■ American ■ Comedy, Exploitation ■ Directed 12 films

- **1946** Born in Baltimore
- **1964–66** Briefly attends University of Baltimore and New York University
- **1964** First screening of *Hag in a Black Leather Jacket*
- **1966** Directs *Roman Candles*
- **1969** First feature-length film, *Mondo Trasho*
- **1972** First film of his "Trash Trilogy," *Pink Flamingos*
- **1988** Directs first mainstream film, *Hairspray*
- **1988** His collaborator, Divine, dies in Los Angeles at age 42
- **1994** Directs *Serial Mom*
- **2007** Hosts the TV program *'Til Death Do Us Part*

Other Works

Polyester, 1981, starring Divine

Cry-Baby, 1990, starring Johnny Depp

Serial Mom, 1994, starring Kathleen Turner and Sam Waterston

A Dirty Shame, 2004, starring Tracey Ullman and Johnny Knoxville

A master of humor and imagination, John Waters is one [of] cinema's most inventive and challenging directors. [His] films are renowned for their hyper-retro aesthetics a[nd] transgressive themes such as incest, cannibalism, and ab[or]tion. Born in Baltimore, Waters bri[efly] studied at Baltimore University a[nd] NYU. In 1968, he directed *Eat Y[our] Makeup*, starring his childh[ood] friend and longtime partn[er] Divine. Their partnersh[ip] lasted for two deca[des] and their last collabo[ra]tion was 1988's *H[air]spray*, which marke[d a] transition from und[er]ground cult-shockers [to] more mainstream films s[uch] as *Cry-Baby* and *Serial Mom*.

■ **Pink Flamingos**, 1972, starring Divine

A film about a very dysfunctional family, *Pink Flamingos* is a hedon[ic] shock comedy led by the charis[]matic Divine. Featuring mixe[d] film stock, an avant-garde aesthetic and a largely improvised script, it is a[] dangerously twisted and hilarious gross-out film that dis[]turbingly questions morality and values.

Politics and Blockbusters 1975–1989.

■ Hairspray, 1988, starring Ricki Lake, Divine, and Sonny Bono

Hairspray follows Tracy Turnblad (Lake), the schoolgirl outsider chasing fame on a TV dance program. The first Waters film not to receive an X rating, the film marked a dramatic departure from his earlier underground style and gained a broad cult following.

Terry Gilliam

1940, Minneapolis

■ Master of black comedy ■ Member of Monty Python comedy troupe ■ Us
highly imaginative imagery and avant-garde aesthetics ■ Films are often poli
ical or with social commentary ■ Uses animation and special effects
■ American-British ■ Comedy, Fantasy ■ Directed 10 films

1940 Born in Minnesota

1958 Studies physics, fine arts, and politics

1963 Works as an illustrator for *Help!* magazine

1967 Moves to London

1977 First solo feature, *Jabberwocky*

1991 *The Fisher King* is nominated for five Academy Awards

2006 Renounces his US citizenship

From his early career with Monty Python through to I
science-fiction hit *Twelve Monkeys*, Terry Gilliam has be
praised for his creation of unconventional worlds th
push the boundaries of imagination as well as cinema
graphic realization. Born in Minnesota, Gilliam studi
physics, art, and politics before composing illustratic
for Harvey Kurtzman's magazine *Help!* In 1967 he left I
the United Kingdom, where he worked on several mac
zines and television shows. While there he met Micha
Palin, Eric Idle, and Terry Jones and joined their
comedy show, *Monty Python's Flying Circus*. Monty Pyth
quickly developed a cult following a
the aesthetic of his illustrations becar
wildly popular. As in his illustratio
Gilliam's films often depict biza
worlds where chaos and humor reic
His feature films, including *Brazil*, *T
Fisher King* (1991), and *Twelve Monke
are praised for their ability to combi
avant-garde imagery and clever plot

■ **Monty Python and the Holy Grail**, 1975,
starring Graham Chapman, John Cleese, Terry
Gilliam, Eric Idle, Terry Jones, and Michael Palir

Co-directed with Terry Jones, *Monty Python an
the Holy Grail* is a raucous romp through the
Middle Ages and is heralded as one of the
greatest comedies of all time. The first Monty
Python film to use completely new material, it
a witty historical parody that blends Gilliam's
distinctive animations and fanciful narratives
with patented Python humor.

Politics and Blockbusters 1975–1989

■ **Brazil**, 1985, starring Jonathan Pryce, Robert De Niro, Katherine Helmond, and Kim Greist

Brazil is a surreal adventure that illustrates Gilliam's remarkable imagination and dark sense of humor. Centering on government employee Sam Lowry (Pryce), *Brazil* features an extravagant, dystopian set and a host of distinctive characters. Gilliam's most articulate and celebrated film, it blends an avant-garde aesthetic with a story about fear, control, and conformity.

The Adventures of Baron ~~M~~unchausen, 1988, starring ~~Joh~~n Neville

~~De~~spite the fact that it almost ~~do~~ubled its original budget of ~~$~~3.5 million and created skept~~ic~~ism around Gilliam's fiscal ~~rel~~iability, *The Adventures of* ~~Ba~~*ron Munchausen* earned a ~~cu~~lt following. Following ~~th~~e adventures of the ~~my~~thological storyteller ~~Ba~~ron Munchausen, this ~~bi~~g-budget fantasy fea~~tu~~res an immense ~~en~~semble cast, fantas~~tic~~al imagery, and a ~~wh~~imsical narra~~tiv~~e. Due to

issues with the film's production company, *The Adventures of Baron Munchausen* received a limited release in the United States, but despite this it still managed to receive acclaim for its imagination, originality, and humor.

Other Works

Twelve Monkeys, 1995 , starring Bruce Willis, Madeleine Stowe, and Brad Pitt

Fear and Loathing in Las Vegas, 1998, starring Johnny Depp

Terry Gilliam

David Lynch

1946, Missoula

■ Highly influential figure of art-house cinema ■ Manipulates time and narrative ■ Uses expressionistic cinematography ■ Films are often set in suburbia, use surreal colors, and feature unhinged and idiosyncratic characters ■ American ■ Horror, Thriller, Avant-garde ■ Directed 12 films

■ **1946** Born in Montana

1966 Attends art school in Philadelphia

1966 First short film, *Six Men Getting Sick*

1970 Wins a $5,000 grant from the American Film Institute

1970 Makes the 30-minute film, *The Grandmother*

1971 Studies at the AFI Conservatory in Los Angeles

1990 TV series, *Twin Peaks*

2002 Serves as a jury member at the Cannes Film Festival

Born in Montana, David Lynch attended art schools Boston and Philadelphia where he made his first short film, *Six Men Getting Sick* (1966). Throughout the 197C Lynch continued making experimental films befo finding success with the midnight classic, *Eraserhead*. 1980, Lynch received critical acclaim with the poignar and controversial *The Elephant Man*, but his real succe was 1986's *Blue Velvet*—a thriller that reveals the frigh ening underbelly of American suburbia. In the 1990 Lynch capitalized on his film success with the cult 1 series *Twin Peaks*, while in 2001 he won an Oscar for Be Director for his awkward mystery *Mulholland Dr.* Lynch films are characterized by an eerie atmosphere, unse tling characters, and avant-garde imagery.

Other Works

Wild at Heart, 1990, starring Nicolas Cage and Laura Dern

Lost Highway, 1997, starring Bill Pullman, Patricia Arquette, and Balthazar Getty

The Straight Story, 1999, starring Richard Farnsworth and Sissy Spacek

Inland Empire, 2006, starring Laura Dern, Jeremy Irons, and Justin Theroux

■ **Mulholland Dr.**, 2001, starring Naomi Watts and Laura Harring

A glamorous and cynical murder mystery, *Mulholland Dr.*

follows the delusions of an aspiring actress. Lynch lets the audience play detective, manipulating reality and narra-

tive structures. Shot in a shadowy palette, it was name Best Picture by the New York Film Critics Circle.

Eraserhead, 1977, starring Jack Nance

Jack Nance plays an unlikely father with a mutant child and erratic girlfriend. Set in an industrial wasteland that is disturbingly similar to a post-apocalyptic world, *Eraserhead* is a surreal parable of fatherhood and fear that challenges conventional plot and narrative. A cult classic, the film was praised for its unique use of symbolism and animation.

he Elephant Man, 1980, ring Anthony Hopkins, John t, and Anne Bancroft

htmarish and affecting, *The hant Man* traces the story of verely disfigured man iso-d by society. Shot in black white, it blends a unique hetic with a relatively con-tional script and received ely positive reviews.

lue Velvet, 1986, starring MacLachlan, Isabella Ross-i, and Dennis Hopper

en nice-guy Jeffrey Beaumont overs a severed ear in his evolent suburb, he sets out to find the culprit and stumbles upon a volatile group of organized criminals. A disorienting suburban mystery, *Blue Velvet*'s irregular storytelling devices and unhinged characters made the film a cult hit.

New Directions

Peter Greenaway

1942, Newport

- Highly successful art-house film director ■ Uses symbolic imagery ■ Influen[ced] by painter Johannes Vermeer ■ Uses an iconic visual language ■ Focuses [on] allegory and imagery over plot and narrative ■ Uses montage techniques ■ British ■ Avant-garde ■ Directed 12 films

New Directions

■ **1942** Born in the UK

1962 Studies painting at Walthamstow College of Art, in London

1965 Directs and edits at the Central Office of Information

1980 First feature-length film, *The Falls*

1991 Makes *Prospero's Books*

2007 Directs *Nightwatching*, and is awarded the Commander of the Order of the British Empire

Peter Greenaway's films are painterly, expressionis[t] works that utilize imagery and allegory. Born in [the] UK, Greenaway worked as a painter before joining [the] Central Office of Information as a film director and edi[tor] in 1965. In 1980, Greenaway produced his first feat[ure] film, *The Falls*, and followed with *The Draughtsman's C[on]tract* and *A Zed & Two Noughts* (1985), which both receiv[ed] critical acclaim for their striking visual imagery and pl[ay]fully constructed plots. In 1989, Greenaway produced [his] most successful film, *The Cook, the Thief, His Wife, & [Her] Lover*—a controversial and provocative parody of gre[ed] and consumption.

Politics and Blockbusters 1975–1989

rowning by Numbers, **, starring Joan Plowright, t Stevenson, and Richardso

Playfully provocative, *Drowning by Numbers* follows three generations of women who drown their husbands. Using repetition, structure, and symmetry as well as games and folklore, this is a spirited and expressive tale of murder and desire that features languid and fluid cinematography. The numerals 1 to 100 appear in order throughout the film, adding a unique and lively subplot to the on-screen action. The film also features an ambient soundtrack by Michael Nyman.

Other Works

e Belly of an Architect, 37, starring Brian Dennehy, oe Webb, and Lambert son

e Cook, the Thief, His , & Her Lover, 1989, ng Michael Gambon and n Mirren

of Greenaway's most ssible films, *The Cook, the , His Wife, & Her Lover* is a cal portrait of gluttony in ern society. A lyrical drama, Im focuses on Georgina, a rated and unfaithful wife red by her ruthless and iable husband, Albert.

■ **The Draughtsman's Contract**, 1982, starring Anthony Higgins, Janet Suzman, and Anne-Louise Lambert

Set in 1694, *The Draughtsman's Contract* follows the story of a young artist commissioned to produce a series of portraits for a wealthy woman. The film is a mysterious drama full of clever plot twists and intellectual statements on art.

Steven Spielberg

1946, Cincinnati

- Father of the blockbuster ■ Directed some of the highest-grossing films o
all time ■ Uses groundbreaking special effects ■ Directs films of many differe
genres ■ Films often deal with difficult subject matter
- American ■ Science Fiction, Action, Drama ■ Directed 30 films

1946 Born in Ohio

1964 Works at Universal Studios

1965 Enters California State University

1969 Directs pilot for TV series, *Night Gallery*

1971 Directs telemovie, *Duel*

1974 First major directorial project, *The Sugarland Express*

1984 Establishes Amblin Entertainment

1994 Establishes DreamWorks Studios

One of Hollywood's most influential filmmakers, Stev
Spielberg became interested in the industry at an ea
age, making home movies as a child and directing his f
independent film while he was still in high school. Af
working as an unpaid intern at Universal Studios, Sp
berg received a contract in 1969 to make a TV pilot f
turing Joan Crawford. His breakthrough came with
1975 horror film, *Jaws*, which was heralded for its cle
script, amazing special effects, and wide audience app
Spielberg quickly capitalized on his rising success v
Close Encounters of the Third Kind, *ET: The Extra-Terrestr*
and the *Indiana Jones* trilogy, confirming himself as H
lywood's most bankable director. In 1993, Spielberg

■ **Jaws**, 1975, starring Roy Scheider, Robert Shaw, and Richard Dreyfuss

Backed by heavy advertising, *Jaws* set a new benchmark for horror films and sparked mayhem on beaches throughout the world. An immense critical success, it is regarded as a pioneer of the blockbuster genre.

ET: The Extra-Terrestrial, 1982,
...rring Henry Thomas, Dee Wallace, Robert
...cNaughton, and Drew Barrymore

...uplifting and feel-good drama, *ET: The Extra-*
...restrial tapped into the emerging science fic-
...n market and caused a major flurry at the box
...ce. A big-budget family film that follows the
...ndship between a young outcast and a disori-
...ed alien, it featured groundbreaking special
...ects. The film was rereleased in 1985 and 2002,
...h additional scenes and updated special
...ects, and remains a popular rental. Imagina-
... and innovative, it won a plethora of awards
...d earned Spielberg a UN peace medal.

Jurassic Park, 1993, starring Sam Neill, Laura
...n, Jeff Goldblum, and Richard Attenborough

...en an aging scientist uses cloning to create a
...historic fun park, the results do not turn out
...ctly as planned. An impressive set, clever
...ting, and dramatic use of CGI made *Jurassic*
...k an enormous success, seducing audiences
...h its frightening study of scientific develop-
...nts and morality.

Steven Spielberg

had yet another high profile success with *Jurassic Park*, and a year later he established DreamWorks Studios. Due to clever marketing, cutting-edge techniques, and diverse subject matter, Spielberg's films have grossed extraordinarily well at the box office and in the rental market, and he has produced over 100 films. Spielberg's films often encompass themes of isolation, technology, and power, while his heroes and heroines are usually archetypally everyday people caught up in exceptional circumstances. His visual language is often characterized by slow-moving, low-angle tracking shots and dimly-lit open spaces, but his greatest success is his ability to make films that appeal to a wide audience yet remain powerful and lasting.

Other Works

Close Encounters of the Third Kind, 1977, starring Richard Dreyfuss and Franço Truffaut

The Color Purple, 1985, starring Whoopi Goldberg, Danny Glover, and Oprah Winfrey

Saving Private Ryan, 1998, starring Tom Hanks, Edward Burns, and Matt Damon

Munich, 2005, starring Eric Bana, Daniel Craig, and Ciará Hinds

■ **Catch Me If You Can**, 2002, starring Leonardo DiCaprio, Tom Hanks, Christopher Walken, Amy Adams, and Martin Sheen

Filmed in just 56 days at various locations around the United States and Canada, *Catch Me If You Can* is a fast-paced cat-and-mouse film that follows a young swindler and a determined FBI agent. Set in the 1960s, it is a stylish crime film that features a star-studded cast, sharp dialogue, and clever plot twi It was nominated for two Academy Awards and was w received by audiences and critics.

■ **Schindler's List**, 1993, starring Liam Neeson and Ben Kingsley

Based on a true story, *Schindler's List* tells the story of Oskar Schindler (Neeson), an aspiring German businessman who uses Jewish workers during the Nazi occupation of Poland to start a successful factory. As the Nazi agenda becomes clearer, Schindler attempts to save his workers from the concentration camps. Shot mostly on location in Poland and using handheld cameras to capture much of the footage, *Schindler's List* won Academy Awards for Best Picture, Best Director, and Best Score.

Blockbusters

Steven Spielberg

George Lucas

1944, Modesto

■ Father of the blockbuster ■ Uses groundbreaking special effects ■ Worke
with Steven Spielberg and Francis Ford Coppola ■ Films feature imaginative
characters and action sequences ■ Established many production companies
■ American ■ Science Fiction ■ Directed 6 films

Alongside Steven Spielberg (p. 354), George Lucas
largely considered the father of the blockbuster. Bo
in 1944, Lucas led a relatively suburban life in Californ
where he developed a passion for cars and racing.
1962, he began studying at the Cinema School of t
University of Southern California, where he shot seve
independent films. In the late 1960s, Lucas was asso
ated with Hollywood's "Brat Pack," and after worki
alongside Francis Ford Coppola (p. 314) on *The Ra
People* (1969), the two establishe
the independent production compan
Zoetrope. In 1973, Lucas wrote a
directed the nostalgic *American Graff*
before embarking on the scienc
fiction classic, *Star Wars*. The film's hi
intensity action, rousing soundtra
and stirring special effects—some
the most advanced of the day—ca
pulted Lucas into stardom, launchec
pop-culture revolution, and signal
the beginning of the blockbuster.

■ **American Graffiti,** 1973, starring Richard
Dreyfuss, Paul Le Mat, Ron Howard, and Candy
Clark

American Graffiti is a coming-of-age drama tha
is energetically shot in a candy-colored palette
The film traces one eventful night in the lives c
a group of teenage friends in 1962. A highly
charged teen film, it is a nostalgic and poignan
recollection of youth in an era of romance,
racing, and rock and roll.

Star Wars, 1977, starring
~~~k Hamill, Harrison Ford,
~~rie Fisher, and Peter Cushing

~Wars follows the story of the
~~el Alliance, a group of guer-
~fighters attempting to stop
~evil Galactic Empire. When
~r leader is captured she sends
~mportant message that is

**~tar Wars: Episode II—
~ack of the Clones**, 2002,
~ring Ewan McGregor
~Natalie Portman

~Wars's detailed and
~evable universe and
~ting-edge special
~cts inspired a fran-
~e of sequels, tele-
~on series, books,
~comics.

intercepted by Luke Skywalker.
A classic tale of good vs. evil, it
found a new generation of filmgoers and started the era of
blockbusters, thrusting Lucas
into the spotlight and changing
film forever. Upon its reissueing,
the title was changed to *Star
Wars: Episode IV—A New Hope*.

Other Works

Star Wars: Episode I—The Phantom Menace, 1999, starring Liam
Neeson and Ewan McGregor

Star Wars: Episode III—Revenge
of the Sith, 2005, starring Ewan
McGregor and Hayden
Christensen

Blockbusters,
Rentals, and Ratings

The 1970s and '80s were characterized by huge changes in the film industry. New marketing strategies, wider cinema releases, and spectacular developments in special effects pulled audiences into the cinemas to see blockbusters. At the same time, the video rental market was growing as the price of VCRs fell. Fueled by the popularity of the family genre, rented films became high-grossing hits that gave them an alternative and lucrative life outside the cinema complex. In 1990, America's ratings system responded to pressure from directors such as Philip Kaufman to adopt the new category of NC-17—which allowed non-pornographic films that featured adult themes or violence more access to the market than their previously restrictive X rating.

■ **Beverly Hills Cop** (1984) was a substantially influential film. Under Martin Brest's direction, it spawned two sequels and was nominated for an Academy Award.

■ **Ivan Reitman's Ghostbusters** (1984) was the most successful comedy of the 1980s. A groundbreaking mix of science fiction, action, and special effects, it follows unlikely heroes battling a spate of paranormal activity in New York. This blockbuster was also a well-marketed rental.

Blockbuster Inc. opened its first store in Texas in 1985.

Capitalizing on the emerging rental market, the company became a high-profile video store. The affordability of VCRs and the even cheaper production of DVDs in the 1990s opened up a new market.

🔫 **Richard Donner's Lethal Weapon** (1987) stars Mel Gibson and Danny Glover in a blockbuster buddy-cop film. The film features iconic performances, explosive action, and well-choreographed fight sequences that captured the attention of audiences around the world. *Lethal Weapon*'s popularity spawned three sequels and influenced films such as *Bad Boys* (1995) and *Rush Hour* (1998).

Blockbusters, Rentals, and Ratings

Roger Zemeckis

1952, Chicago

- Iconic Hollywood director ■ Influenced by Disney, he pioneered new anim-
tion techniques that blend live action and animation ■ Worked with Steven
Spielberg ■ Directed many blockbusters ■ Uses groundbreaking special effec
■ American ■ Comedy, Drama ■ Directed 16 films

Blockbusters

1952 Born in Chicago

1970s Attends film school

1979 Works with Steven Spielberg on *1941*

1984 Directs first major success, *Romancing the Stone*

1985 *Back to the Future*

1988 Pioneers new anima-tion techniques in *Who Framed Roger Rabbit*

1994 Wins Academy Award for Best Director for *Forrest Gump*

2000 Tom Hanks is nomi-nated for Academy Award for *Cast Away*

2007 Uses pioneering motion capture tech-niques in *Beowulf*

Although Robert Zemeckis's notoriety comes largely fro
his pioneering methods of animation, his film credenti
cover everything from comedy to adventure, drama, a
romance. Born in Chicago, Zemeckis was introduced
special effects while studying filmmaking. Influenced
the work of Walt Disney (p.130), Zemeckis came to t
attention of Steven Spielberg (p. 354) after producing se
eral quality student films. Spielberg became Zemecki
mentor and, in 1979, they worked together on the fi
1941. Although *1941* flopped at the box office, Zemecki
breakthrough came with the 1984 adventure fil
Romancing the Stone. Subsequent films such as *Back*
the Future, *Death Becomes Her*, and *Forrest Gump* ensur
Zemeckis's Hollywood success, earning him an Acader
Award for Best Director in 1994. His most recent work co
tinues to pioneer new methods of filmmaking.

■ **Romancing the Stone**, 1984, starring Michael Douglas and Kathleen Turner

Despite critics believing that *Romancing the Stone* would fail miserably, the film was a surprise adven-ture hit that became one of the highest grossing films of 1984. Cleverly written and featuring high-intensity action, it launched Zemeckis's career and enabled him to make *Back to the Future*.

■ **Who Framed Roger Rabbit**, 1988, starring
Bob Hoskins and Christopher Lloyd

Although it made a substantial profit at the box
office, *Who Framed Roger Rabbit* was one of the
most expensive films ever made at the time,
costing over $70 million to produce. The film
blends live action with animation—a pioneering
technique that generated intense audience
interest. The "Toons" were added in the postproduction phase, using largely hand-drawn and
analog effects, because computer-aided design
was still in its infancy.

Other Works	
Death Becomes Her, 1992, starring Meryl Streep and Bruce Willis	Cast Away, 2000, starring Tom Hanks
Forrest Gump, 1994, starring Tom Hanks	The Polar Express, 2004, starring Tom Hanks

ack to the Future, 1985,
ring Michael J. Fox and
stopher Lloyd

en Marty McFly (Fox)
his friend the Doc
yd) travel back in
e, they put the
re, and their own
tence in jeop-
. *Back to the
re* is a quirky
film with
ovative
ial
cts.

Roger Zemeckis

Tim Burton

1958, Los Angeles

■ Uses groundbreaking animation techniques ■ Master of the gothic fanta
genre ■ Uses dark and expressionistic cinematography ■ His films often
feature isolated or ostracized characters ■ Made films of various genres
■ American ■ Fantasy, Animation ■ Directed 13 films

1958 Born in California

1975 Studies animation

1978 Works as an apprentice animator for Walt Disney Studios

1982 Makes his first stop-motion film, *Vincent*

1982 First live-action film, *Frankenweenie*

1984 *Vincent* wins the Audience Award at Ottawa Animation Festival

1999 Directs *Sleepy Hollow*

2005 Directs *Charlie and the Chocolate Factory*

2005 *Corpse Bride* receives an Academy Award nomination

Tim Burton was fascinated by the escapist world
cinema from a young age. His first foray into filmmak
came in 1978, when he joined Walt Disney Studios as
apprentice animator, where he quickly gained notori
for his quirky, dark characters. In 1985, Burton was co
missioned as a director to work on his first hit, *Pee-w
Big Adventure*, and in the late 1980s and early '90s,
capitalized on its success with a string of cult clas.
including *Beetlejuice* (1988), *Batman*, and *Edward S
sorhands*. Widely praised as one of Hollywood's m
visionary and original filmmakers, Burton's films are of
characterized by a gothic, Neo-Expressionist style t
features childhood images spliced into adult themes.
often works with the same actors on several fil
pushing their acting to the limit.

▌Edward Scissorhands,
1990, starring Johnny Depp, Winona Ryder, and Dianne Wiest

Edward Scissorhands is a gothic drama that follows an unlikely relationship between a curiously deformed man and a suburban housewife. This *Frankenstein*-inspired fantasy deals with isolation and love. Shot in suburban Florida, the film combines stylistic elements from the 1950s and '60s.

orpse Bride, 2005,
ed by Johnny Depp,
ena Bonham Carter, and
y Watson

ose Bride is a stop-
tion-animation film
takes us on a journey
ugh the worlds of the
g and the dead. Similar in style to *The Nightmare*
re Christmas (1993), *Corpse Bride* was shot using
cameras and was the first film to feature puppets
se facial expressions could be manipulated
ugh the "gear and paddle" technique.

atman, 1989, starring Michael Keaton, Jack
holson, and Kim Basinger

of the biggest blockbusters of the early 1990s,
man was an ambitious and impressive film that
k nearly 10 years to produce. Based on the im-
nsely successful DC comic and TV show of the
e name, *Batman* features innovative special ef-
s, high-intensity action, and iconic characters.
ton created an eerie and dark Gotham setting for
film, which was cleverly shot without the use of
nputer-aided design; the sets were created using
ssive painted backdrops that mixed clashing archi-
ural styles and aesthetics to create a dystopian
. The film won an Oscar for the art direction
sets. Though there were several sequels,
first remains the most popular and the
atest box-office success.

Other Works

Ed Wood, 1994, starring Johnny Depp, Martin Landau, and Sarah Jessica Parker

Mars Attacks!, 1996, starring Jack Nicholson, Glenn Close, and Annette Bening-

Sweeney Todd: The Demon Barber of Fleet Street, 2007, starring Johnny Depp and Helena Bonham Carter

Tim Burton

James Cameron

1954, Kapuskasing

- Directed the highest-grossing film of all time ■ Uses spectacular special effects ■ Masterfully blends science fiction and action ■ Films often contain apocalyptic themes ■ Worked as a set designer and screenwriter
- Canadian ■ Action, Thriller, Science Fiction ■ Directed 8 films

1954 Born in Canada

1980 Works on Roger Corman's *Battle Beyond the Stars*

1981 Directs his first film, *Piranha II: The Spawning*

1991 Directs *Terminator 2*

1997 *Titanic* earns 11 Academy Awards and is a box-office hit

2005 Directs TV documentary *Aliens of the Deep*

James Cameron's films are spectacular, high-budget blockbusters that use dramatic zooming effects, computer-generated graphics (CGI), and smart editing. Cameron began his career as a screenwriter and set designer and worked at Roger Corman's film company before directing his first film, *Piranha II: The Spawning* in 1981. He followed with *The Terminator*, a dark science fiction film that was heralded by critics and launched a successful franchise. Cameron followed with a string of high-budget, action/science fiction crossovers, including *Aliens* and *The Abyss*. Despite his commercial success with these films, it was 1997's *Titanic* that filmgoers and critics responded to with greatest enthusiasm. The film's groundbreaking CGI and the stellar performances of Leonardo DiCaprio and Kate Winslet won 11 Oscars, and grossed a staggering $1 billion—making it the most financially successful film of all time.

■ **The Terminator**, 1984, starring Arnold Schwarzenegger, Michael Biehn, and Linda Hamilton

Sarah Connor (Hamilton) is the target of an immortal cyborg, (Schwarzenegger), sent from the future to ensure she never gives birth to her revolutionary son. A human is sent to protect her and the result is a terrifying game of hide and seek. Immensely successful, *The Terminator* is a dark and apocalyptic film that is cleverly paced and well shot, evoking tension, fear, and suspense.

Aliens, 1986, starring
ourney Weaver and Michael
nn

ing over from Ridley Scott,
neron's sequel to 1979's
n is a horrific and stomach-
ning battle against an awe-
piring enemy. Weaver gives
areer-best performance as
courageous and fearless
n Ripley, the only survivor of
spaceship *Nostromo*. *Aliens*
s praised by audiences and
cs for its terrifying and
vorldly imagery, suspense,
ferocious climax.

Blockbusters

Other Works

he Abyss, 1989, starring Ed
arris

erminator 2: Judgment Day,
991, starring Arnold
chwarzenegger, Linda
amilton, and Edward Furlong

ue Lies, 1994, starring Arnold
chwarzenegger and Jamie
ee Curtis

■ **Titanic**, 1997, starring
Leonardo DiCaprio and Kate
Winslet

Among filmgoers and critics,
Titanic proved to be the
defining epic of the decade.
Featuring sizzling performances
by DiCaprio and Winslet, the
film is set on the ill-fated
maiden voyage of the ocean
liner. Made on a staggering
$200 million budget,
Titanic

was filmed on real liners with an
enormous constructed set that
allowed the ship to tilt during
filming. Above the set, a crane
platform was used for lighting
and dramatic camera work.
Cameron's winning combination of CGI and casting made
$1.8 billion at the box office,
making it the highest-earning
film ever.

John Hughes

1950, Lansing

■ Prolific screenwriter ■ Uses popular music soundtracks ■ Worked with "B•
Pack" actors ■ Uses unconventional narrative techniques ■ Dubbed the
philosopher of adolescence ■ References pop culture
■ American ■ Teen, Comedy ■ Directed 8 films

■ **1950** Born in Michigan

1979 Works as an editor at *National Lampoon* magazine

1982 First published screenplay *National Lampoon's Class Reunion*

1984 First major success, *Sixteen Candles*

1987 Makes *Planes, Trains & Automobiles*

2002 Writes screenplay for *Maid In Manhattan*

A reclusive filmmaker who has stayed out of the spotlig
since 1994, John Hughes is renowned for his ability
create realistic and entertaining teen films, earning h
the title "philosopher of adolescence." Hughes was bo
in Michigan and attended Glenbrook North High Scho
a place he would later return to shoot his two most su
cessful films, *Ferris Bueller's Day Off* and *The Breakfast Cl•*
Hughes debuted in comedy, writing jokes for celebriti•
A prolific screenwriter, his first script, *National Lampoo•*
Class Reunion (1982), was part of the humor magazin•
franchise and, despite the film's failure, it earned Hugh

considerable acclaim as a come
writer. However, his biggest succe
came with his ingeniously cast te•
films of the 1980s, which epitomize•
generation and set benchmarks for t•
teen-movie genre. Hughes's films oft•
break with convention by the use•
stills, acknowledgment of the audien•
and suspended or elongated timelin•

■ **Pretty In Pink** (as screenwriter), 1986, starr•
Molly Ringwald and Andrew McCarthy

Pretty In Pink is one of a group of films written b•
Hughes and starring Molly Ringwald. Although
the film was directed by Howard Deutsch,
Hughes's story bears all his trademarks: outside•
characters, frustration with social hierarchy, an•
references to pop culture. A prolific and acclaim•
screenwriter, Hughes has written over 34 scree•
plays, including *Home Alone* (1990), *101 Dalma-*
tians (1996), and *Maid In Manhattan* (2002).

■ **The Breakfast Club**, 1985, starring Molly Ringwald, Emilio Estevez, Paul Gleason, and Anthony Michael Hall

The Breakfast Club takes audiences back to school for a day of detention with a cross section of classroom archetypes. A neatly packaged coming-of-age drama featuring sharp dialogue and a popular soundtrack, *The Breakfast Club* set a benchmark for high school movies and inspired a wave of outsider teen films.

erris Bueller's Day Off, 6, starring Matthew Brod-k, Alan Ruck, Mia Sara, and rey Jones

is Bueller's Day Off centers he escapist world of Ferris *'ler* (Broderick)—a charis-ic 16-year-old who is ured by his idiosyncratic cipal (Jones). An upbeat comedy, it uses unconven-al storytelling devices such reaking the fourth wall. turing an eclectic sound-k, quirky characters, and ally clever dialogue, *Ferris 'ler's Day Off* is one of the t revered teen comedies I time.

Other Works

eird Science, 1985, starring thony Michael Hall, Kelly Brock, and Ilan Mitchell-ith

nes, Trains & Automobiles, 37, starring Steve Martin and n Candy

cle Buck, 1989, starring John ndy and Macaulay Culkin

John Hughes

Ridley Scott

1937, South Shields

■ Directed influential science-fiction films that employ dramatic special effe■
■ Launched the cyberpunk movement ■ Reinvigorated the sword-and-san■
epic ■ Films have won nine Academy Awards
■ British ■ Science Fiction, Thriller ■ Directed 18 films

1937 Born in the UK

1954–58 Studies at West Hartlepool College of Art

1962 Receives degree in graphic design from Royal College of Art, London

1963 Works at the BBC

1965 First short film, *Boy and Bicycle*

1977 First feature film, *The Duellists*

1982 Directs *Blade Runner*

2000 *Gladiator* wins five Academy Awards

Born in the UK, Ridley Scott began working in televisi■ after graduating from London's Royal College of Art. ■ joined the BBC in the mid-1960s, where he worked o■ number of television series including *The Informer*. In ■ late 1970s, Scott turned his attention to feature fil■ directing the phenomenally successful *Alien*. Three ye■ later, he again found success with the science-ficti■ classic *Blade Runner*, which was praised for its grou■ breaking visual effects, dystopian aesthetics, and N■ Noir sensibilities. Scott swapped his heroes for heroi■ in the 1991 road movie *Thelma & Louise*, while ■ 2000 he returned to form with the Oscar-winni■ blockbuster *Gladiator*.

■ **Thelma & Louise**, 1991, starring Geena Davis and Su■ Sarandon

When two women decide to■ take a weekend road trip to escape their troubled home lives, things do not go exact■ as planned. *Thelma & Louise* one of contemporary cinem■ most iconic road movies, featuring an Academy Award–winning screenplay.

Other Works

Alien, 1979, starring Sigourne■ Weaver and Tom Skerritt

American Gangster, 2007, starring Denzel Washington and Russell Crowe

■ Blade Runner, 1982, starring Harrison Ford, Rutger Hauer, and Daryl Hannah

Based on Philip K. Dick's novel *Do Androids Dream of Electric Sheep?*, *Blade Runner* is a Neo-Noir adventure that launched the cyberpunk movement and influenced films such as *The Matrix* (1999). Set in 2019, the film tells the story of an ex-cop hired to "retire" a group of dangerous droids. Featuring a retro-futuristic aesthetic, dark ambience, and dramatic special effects, it performed poorly at the box office but gained a cult following due to a wide VHS release.

■ Gladiator, 2000, starring Russell Crowe and Joaquin Phoenix

Winner of five Academy Awards including Best Picture, *Gladiator* is an epic film that launched a spate of sword-and-sandal dramas including *Troy* (2004), *Alexander* (2004), and *300* (2006). Featuring dramatic battles, spectacular sets, and rousing performances, *Gladiator* recouped its $103,000,000 budget in just two weeks.

David Cronenberg

1943, Toronto

- Directs controversial and explicit films ■ Prominent figure of independent film genre ■ Films often feature themes of violence, biology, and disease
- Used groundbreaking special effects ■ Master of gross-out films
- Canadian ■ Horror, Science Fiction, Drama ■ Directed 19 films

David Cronenberg's films cover many genres, from science fiction and horror to drama and thriller. His films often mix genres with an originality that has changed the traditional understanding of film genres. Born in Canada, Cronenberg directed his first feature film, *Shivers*, in 1975. In 1986, Cronenberg released his biggest hit with *The Fly*, while in the 1990s he directed provocative films such as *Naked Lunch* and *Crash*. His films often include recurrent themes of sex, disease, and science gone awry. A principal figure of underground cinema, Cronenberg has been called the master of gross-out films because of the graphic display of violence or just plain disgusting subject matter. He has also achieved mainstream success with his more recent films, *A History of Violence* (2005) and *Eastern Promises*.

■ **The Fly**, 1986, starring Jeff Goldblum and Geena Davis

The Fly follows the story of Seth Brundle (Goldblum), a revolutionary scientist whose metamorphic experiments take horrific and unexpected turns, turning him into a half-man, half-fly creature. A genre-busting film that set new standards for both horror and science fiction, *The Fly* combines state-of-the-art special effects with an unpredictable plot and clever casting. The film won an Oscar for the makeup, which took nearly five hours to apply in order to turn Goldblum into the fly-man. As with many of Cronenberg's early films, *The Fly* deals with technology in a horrific manner.

■ **Eastern Promises**, 2007, starring Viggo Mortensen, Naomi Watts, and Vincent Cassel

Similar in style to *A History of Violence* (2005), *Eastern Promises* is a dark and poignant film that focuses on the interactions between an British nurse (Watts) and a group of organized criminals. The film was praised for its realistic depiction of the Russian mafia in London and was a departure from Cronenberg's earlier style.

Other Works

Videodrome, 1983, starring James Woods and Deborah Harry

Naked Lunch, 1991, starring Peter Weller

Crash, 1996, starring James Spader

Spider, 2002, starring Ralph Fiennes and Miranda Richardson

Film in Canada

hivers, 1975, starring Paul Hampton, ʁara Steele, and Lynn Lowry

 chaotic science fiction/horror cross-over caused
ʁrecedented controversy upon its release
ʁause of its many foul scenes and sub-
ʁ. The gory story of a murderous
ʁntist whose experiments with
ʁsitic implants—which turn
ʁle into zombies with height-
ʁd violent and sexual
ʁes—has infected an
ʁe apartment block of
ʁle, *Shivers* is the
ʁic gross-out film. Its
ʁoitation film–style
ʁe Cronenberg
ʁous.

David Cronenberg

Action and Adventure

■ Often feature car chases, explosions, and battles ■ Focus on escapism and entertainment ■ Emphasize heroes who triumph against adversity ■ Feature special effects ■ Usually targeted at male audiences ■ Often associated with other genres such as westerns and crime

■ *left*: **Casino Royale**, by Martin Campbell, 2006, starring Daniel Craig

● **1903** First dramatic action sequences in *The Great Train Robbery*

1962 *Dr. No* features action hero James Bond

1968 First modern car chase sequence in *Bullit*

1973 Bruce Lee stars in his first Hollywood-produced film, *Enter the Dragon*

1982 Sylvester Stallone stars as Rambo in *First Blood*

1988 *Die Hard* blends comedy and suspense

2000 *Charlie's Angels*, a women's action movie

2006 *Mission: Impossible III* grosses $397.9 million

Featuring impressive stunts, dramatic car chases, a explosive action sequences, action and adventure fil typically focus on a central hero who triumphs agai adversity or beats the bad guys. With its roots in the we erns of the 1920s and '30s, the action and adventu genre was popularized by the James Bond films of t 1960s, which inspired a spate of stylish action/crime fil like *Bullit* and *The French Connection* (1971). Revitaliz by the rise of the blockbuster and an increase in f budgets, action and adventure films such as *Under Sie Terminator II: Judgment Day* (1991), and the *Indiana Jo* trilogy dominated cinema during the 1980s and '9 Often incorporating spectacular special effects, acti and adventure films typically have big budgets, w audience appeal, and perform well at the box office.

■ **Irvin Kershner: Robocop 2**, 1990, starring Peter Weller, Nancy Allen, and Daniel O'Herlihy

Exploring ideas of authority and control, *Robocop* is a futuristic action series that features groundbreaking special effects and a level of gore previously unseen outside the horror genre. Originally rated X, *Robocop* was an influential film that generated two sequels and was widely discussed by film critics.

Politics and Blockbusters 1975–1989

■ **John McTiernan: Die Hard**, 1988, starring Bruce Willis and Alan Rickman

A huge box-office hit, *Die Hard* is one of the most successful action films of all time. Grossing over $80 million at the box office, it set a new standard of suspense and innovation and influenced films such as *Under Siege* and *Speed*. Featuring one of cinema's most charismatic antiheroes, it follows the story of a troubled detective thrust into the midst of a terrorist plot.

Steven Spielberg: Indiana Jones and the Temple of Doom, 1984, starring Harrison Ford and Kate Capshaw

The second part of the *Indiana Jones* trilogy, this is one of the highest-grossing films of its time. *Indiana Jones and the Temple of Doom* is an iconic action adventure that features impressive chase sequences, groundbreaking visual effects, and a memorable performance by Harrison Ford as Indiana Jones. In *Raiders of the Lost Ark* (1981), which starts the story in China a year earlier, over 7,000 snakes were used throughout the making of the film. A successful combination of special effects, clever humor, fast-paced action, and an unlikely hero, *Indiana Jones and the Temple of Doom* helped its franchise dominate the box office throughout the 1980s.

Other Works

Bullit, by Peter Yates, 1968, starring Steve McQueen

Under Siege, by Andrew Davis, 1992, starring Steven Seagal and Tommy Lee Jones

Speed, by Jan de Bont, 1994, starring Keanu Reeves and Sandra Bullock

The Bourne Identity, by Doug Liman, 2002, starring Matt Damon

John G. Avildsen

1935, Oak Park

- Used innovative shot techniques ∎ Films often center on a male underdog
- Is an accomplished film editor ∎ Began in advertising ∎ Films often feature contact sports ∎ Films popular in rental market
- American ∎ Action, Drama ∎ Directed 12 films

1935 Born in Illinois
1959 Works as an advertising manager
1965 Works as production manager on Arthur Penn's *Mickey One*
1967 Directs short film *Light-Sound-Diffuse*
1969 Directorial debut, *Turn On to Love*
1973 Jack Lemmon earns an Oscar for his role in *Save the Tiger*
1976 Wins Best Director for *Rocky*
1992 Directs *The Power of One*

The son of a tool manufacturer, John G. Avildsen started o as an assistant director for low-budget films and advertis ments. His breakthrough came in 1970, when he directe the hard-hitting and timely *Joe*, which cashed in on th New Hollywood movement and political unrest of the e In 1976, he won an Academy Award for Best Director wi his underdog classic, *Rocky*. In the 1980s, Avildsen took more mainstream approach and found success in the ren market with *The Karate Kid* and *Lean on Me*. Avildsen ofte acts as both director and editor on his films, which typ cally feature an unlikely male hero who triumphs again adversity, and has helped to launch th careers of several famous actors.

Rocky, 1976, starring
[Sylv]ester Stallone and Talia
[Shir]e

[Sylv]ester Stallone lends tremen-
[dou]s energy and pathos to the
[cha]racter of Rocky Balboa—the
[har]dened underdog fighting
[for r]espect and glory in this
[clas]sic tale of trial and triumph.
[On]e of the first films to use
[Ste]adicam shooting, *Rocky* won
[thr]ee Oscars and spawned five
[seq]uels.

■ **The Karate Kid**, 1984, starring Ralph Macchio, Pat Morita,
and Elisabeth Shue

A sleeper hit that wooed audiences well in the late 1980s,
The Karate Kid is a clever martial
arts film that focuses on themes
of perseverance and success.
Like *Rocky*, *The Karate Kid*'s success led to several sequels and
was the inspiration for a franchise of action figures and
video games.

John G. Avildsen

Oliver Stone

1946, New York

■ Often directs controversial and provocative films ■ Directs feature and documentary films ■ Combines various film formats ■ Wrote many highly successful screenplays ■ Films often feature sweeping aerial shots
■ American ■ Action, Political ■ Directed 21 films

1946 Born in New York

1967 Enlists in the US army and serves in Vietnam

1974 Directorial debut, *Seizure*

1978 Writes screenplay for *Midnight Express*

1983 Writes screenplay for *Scarface*

1986 Receives an Academy Award for *Platoon*

1989 Receives Academy Award for *Born on the Fourth of July*

1991 Directs *The Doors*

2006 *World Trade Center* is released

Frequently inspired by real-life events, Oliver Stone's da portraits of American life have often courted controver Stone left university in 1967 to enlist in the Vietnam W completing his degree at NYU for film upon his return. would go on to make three films that deal explicitly w his experiences in Vietnam—*Platoon*, *Born on the Fou of July*, and *Heaven and Earth* (1993). Stone's films oft combine various film formats such as black-and-whi animation, and handheld footage to create a dizzying a frenzied atmosphere. In the 1990s, Stone capitalized the counterculture movement with *Natural Born Kill* and *The Doors* (1991), while in the 2000s he challeng public opinion with the made-for-TV film *America Und cover: Persona Non Grata* (2004) and directed the b budget *Alexander*.

■ **Born on the Fourth of July**, 1989, starring Tom Cruise, Kyra Sedgwick, and Raymond J. Barry

Tom Cruise gives an emotional and spirited performance as the paraplegic veteran in this controversial examination of the Vietnam War and Nixon-era politics. Based on the real-life memoirs of Ron Kovic, *Born on the Fourth of July* is a frightening account of disillusion-ment, depression, and post-traumatic stress disorder that fea-tures a dramatic soundtrack, sweeping cine-matography, and emotive flashbacks.

■ **Natural Born Killers**, 1994, starring Woody Harrelson and Juliette Lewis

In spite of its R rating, *Natural Born Killers* found its niche with the young MTV generation of filmgoers in the same year as Tarantino's *Pulp Fiction*. Graphically violent and hedonistically antiestablishment, it is a satirical Bonnie-and-Clyde adventure that features psychedelic camera work, dizzying cuts, handheld shots, and clever animations.

Other Works

JFK, 1991, starring Kevin Costner

Any Given Sunday, 1999, starring Al Pacino and Cameron Diaz

Alexander, 2004, starring Colin Farrell and Angelina Jolie

Platoon, 1986, starring Charlie Sheen and Willem Dafoe

Platoon is a big-budget examination of youth, brutality, and the enemy within. Following a cast of almost 30 characters, it was praised by critics and became popular with America's youth. Portraying a controversial image of the Armed Forces, *Platoon* uses quick cuts and sweeping aerial shots to take us inside the dynamic battle zone.

Oliver Stone

Jonathan Demme

1944, New York

■ His films appeal to a wide audience ■ Blends cinematic elements and genres ■ Won an Academy Award for Best Director ■ Films often contain controversial subject matter ■ Directed a number of music documentaries ■ American ■ Thriller ■ Directed 22 films

■ **1944** Born Robert Jonathan Demme in New York

1965–69 Works as a writer and film reviewer

1971 Joins Roger Corman's studio

1974 Directs his first feature film, *Caged Heat*

1980 First critical success, *Melvin and Howard* is released

1993 *Philadelphia* earns Tom Hanks an Oscar

2000 Serves on the Jury at Cannes Film Festival

2004 Directs *The Manchurian Candidate*

Jonathan Demme began his career as a film review and TV director before joining Roger Corman's studio a publicist. In 1980, he had his first success with *Melv and Howard*, which was praised for its unusual cinmatography and playful narrative. He followed with a eclectic mix of films—from the offbeat comedy *Marrie to the Mob* through to the poignant and timely *Philade phia* (1993). Alongside his feature films, Demme ha also directed a number of music documentarie including *Stop Making Sense* (1984) about the Talkin Heads and *Neil Young: Heart Of Gold* (2006). Demme fluency with genres and talent for comedy has earne him a reputation as both a creative and financially su cessful director.

■ **Something Wild**, 1986, starring Jeff Daniels and Melanie Griffith

A playful mixture of screwball comedy, film noir, and road movie, *Something Wild* is a light-hearted pastiche of genres and elements that follows an odd couple on a troublesome adventure. Straight-laced

businessman Charles (Daniels is abducted by Lulu (Griffith), wild, free-spirited woman, and they embark on the journey o a lifetime.

Other Works

Swing Shift, 1984, starring Goldie Hawn and Kurt Russell

Swimming to Cambodia, 1987 starring Spalding Gray

Married to the Mob, 1988, starring Alec Baldwin and Michelle Pfeiffer

Jimmy Carter Man from Plains, 2007

The Manchurian Candidate, 2004, starring Denzel Washington, Meryl Streep, Liev Schreiber, and Bruno Ganz

The Manchurian Candidate is a fast-paced thriller with a twisting plot centered around a group of soldiers who may or may not have been brainwashed. Based on Richard Condon's 1959 novel of the same name, the film updated the story for contemporary audiences.

The Silence of the Lambs, 1991, starring Jodie Foster and Anthony Hopkins

The film features Oscar-winning performances by Anthony Hopkins and Jodie Foster as a sophisticated criminal, Dr. Hannibal Lecter, and a hard-edged FBI rookie, Clarice Starling. When the two are reluctantly brought together in the hunt for a serial killer, a psychological thriller unfolds. Demme used extreme close-ups, a shadowy palette, and fast editing to make *The Silence of the Lambs* a complex thriller that keeps audiences on the edge of their seats through clever pacing and controlled plot revelation. The film won five Oscars, including Best Director and Best Picture, and a host of other prizes and nominations.

Romance

■ Focus on love, passion, and desire ■ Often lighthearted, especially the subgenre of romantic comedies ■ Targeted at female audiences ■ Usually use a formulaic structure ■ Reflect changing social attitudes ■ Frequently feature satisfying resolutions or happy endings

■ *left:* **The Princess Bride**, by Rob Reiner, 1987, starring Cary Elwes and Mandy Patinkin

■ **1896** First filmed instance of a couple kissing, *The Kiss*

1920s Rudolph Valentino becomes a romantic icon

1927 Greta Garbo and John Gilbert are the iconic on-screen couple

1934 Influential screwball romantic comedy, *It Happened One Night*

1977 *Annie Hall* wins four Academy Awards

1998 The R-rated *There's Something About Mary* grosses over $176 million at the box office

Often characterized by a lighthearted and poignant to romance films focus on themes of love, desire, and em tion. Since the grandiose epics of the 1920s, audienc have delighted in tales of love overcoming all obstacl In the 1930s and '40s, romantic films began to add mc comedic elements and the screwball comedy subger emerged. In the 1970s, Woody Allen (p. 326) added a ce bral aspect, reinvigorating the genre with hits such *Annie Hall* (1977). The rental market in the late 1980s h a major impact on the genre's popularity, producing h such as *Sleepless in Seattle* (1993), while 1998's *Ther Something About Mary* marked a new phase of roman comedies that melded gro outs with romantic them

■ **Garry Marshall: Pretty Woman,** 1990, starring Richard Gere and Julia Roberts
A modern variation on th Cinderella story, *Pretty Woman* is a classic romantic comedy featuring sizzlin on-screen chem istry. When a wealthy client (Gere) falls in love with an escort (Roberts), sh goes from ra to riches.

■ **Jerry Zucker: Ghost**, 1990, starring Patrick Swayze, Demi Moore, and Whoopi Goldberg

When Sam (Swayze) is murdered, his love for girlfriend Molly (Moore) does not die with him. He returns as a ghost on a mission to save his love. Romance, fantasy, drama, and revenge—*Ghost*'s $500 million success was due, in part, to its ability to merge so many genres into one. A poignant drama about loss and redemption, *Ghost* is a modern tale of love and morality that features iconic love scenes and a popular soundtrack.

Other Works	
When Harry Met Sally..., by Rob Reiner, 1989, starring Billy Crystal and Meg Ryan	Bridget Jones's Diary, by Sharon Maguire, 2001, starring Renée Zellweger

■ **Bobby and Peter Farrelly: There's Something About Mary**, 1998, starring Ben Stiller, Cameron Diaz, and Matt Dillon

A unique combination of gross-out film and romantic comedy, *There's Something About Mary* inspired an avalanche of imitations. Quirky characters and raucous antics, it is a goofball film that impressed young audiences despite its R rating.

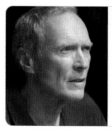

Clint Eastwood

1930, San Francisco

■ Directs and stars in most of his films ■ Founded his own production company ■ Films often feature complex antiheroes and underdogs ■ Influenced by Sergio Leone ■ Films often center around themes of justice and redemption ■ American ■ Western, Thriller, Action, Drama ■ Directed 27 films

● **1930** Born in California

1955 Stars in *Tarantula*

1964 Works with Sergio Leone on *A Fistful of Dollars*

1970 Founds production company, Malpaso

1971 Directorial debut, *Play Misty for Me*

1976 Directs and stars in *The Outlaw Josey Wales*

1988 Directs Charlie Parker biopic, *Bird*

1992 Receives an Oscar for *Unforgiven*

1996 Receives AFI Life Achievement Award

2004 Oscar for Best Director: *Million Dollar Baby*

An instantly recognizable actor, Clint Eastwood ■ directed over 27 films since he began filmmaking 40 ye■ ago. In 1970, he founded his own production compa■ Malpaso, and made his first feature, *Play Misty for I*■ Heavily influenced by his work with Sergio Leo■ (p. 264), Eastwood's early films are predominantly ge■ pieces while his later films, including 2004's *Million Do*■ *Baby* and the dramatic war film *Letters from Iwo Jir*■ strayed from his usual fare with spectacular results. Ea■ wood's films often feature complex antiheroes a■ themes of redemption, justice, and atonement. For ■ directing efforts, Eastwood has been the recipient ■ numerous Academy Award nominations, and contin■ to make films that expand and reinvent traditional Hol■ wood plots, genres, and devices.

■ **Unforgiven**, 1992, starrin■ Clint Eastwood, Morgan Freeman, and Gene Hackma■

Unforgiven is an intimate stud■ of loyalty and justice in front■ America. Centering on a reformed killer mourning the ■ death of his young wife, the f■ is an atypical western that ex■ plodes stereotypes and blurs ■ line between heroes and villa■ Evocatively shot and featurin■ carefully constructed sets an■ breakout performance by Freeman, *Unforgiven* is a pict■ esque and unexpected varia■ on a classic Hollywood plot.

Politics and Blockbusters 1975–1989

■ **The Bridges of Madison County**, 1995, starring Clint Eastwood, Meryl Streep, Annie Corley, and Victor Slezak

Coproduced by Eastwood's production company, Malpaso, *The Bridges of Madison County* is the story of a fleeting love affair between a housewife and a mysterious photographer. Told in retrospect through the woman's diary, *The Bridges of Madison County* is a sensitive and complex romance that deals with themes of loneliness and infidelity.

Million Dollar Baby, 2004, ring Clint Eastwood and ry Swank

ry Swank gives an affecting formance as Maggie gerald, the ambitious and un-ly protégé of veteran boxing ch Frank Dunn (Eastwood). A sic underdog drama, the film trouble finding financial king due to its controversial ject matter. Nevertheless, r several years in production, *ion Dollar Baby* was finally ased to much critical acclaim climbed over Scorsese's *tor* to win Best Picture at the 4 Academy Awards.

Other Works

ue Crime, 1999, starring int Eastwood and James oods

ystic River, 2003, arring Sean Penn and m Robbins

etters from Iwo Jima, 2006, arring Ken Watanabe and azunari Ninomiya

Jim Jarmusch

1953, Akron

- Films often feature multiple narratives ■ Influenced by John Cassavetes
- Collaborates with musicians, artists, and celebrities ■ Films often shot in
black-and-white or stylized color ■ Favors vignettes and anthology
■ American ■ Comedy ■ Directed 10 films

1953 Born in Ohio

1975 Graduates from Columbia University with a degree in English

1975 Discovers the archives of the Cinémathèque Française, Paris

1979 Returns to America and studies film at New York University

1980 First film, *Permanent Vacation*

1984 Wins Camera d'Or at the Cannes Film Festival for *Stranger Than Paradise*

1989 Directs *Mystery Train*

2005 Wins Grand Prize at Cannes for *Broken Flowers*

Jim Jarmusch has been at the forefront of independe cinema since the release of his first successful featu *Stranger Than Paradise*. Jarmusch first became fascinat with film while exploring the archives of the Cinén thèque Française in Paris. On his return to America, enrolled at New York University's film school, whe he met directors Nicholas Ray (p. 162) and Wim Wend (p. 338). Jarmusch produced several successful featu during the 1980s, including the beat-inspired *Down Law* and the quirky anthology, *Mystery Train* (1989) a *Night on Earth* (1991). Jarmusch's talent lies in epitomizi generations and revealing stories in unusual ways. films are often characterized by fractured narratives, m tiple story lines, and expansive, black-and-white cir matography. He works with the same actors time a time again, casting them in drastically different roles.

■ **Stranger Than Paradise** 1984, starring John Lurie an Eszter Balint

When hipster Willie's (Lurie) Hungarian cousin Eva (Balint travels to New York to visit h he is less than pleased about the interruptions to his fashi able lifestyle. Beautifully cap tured in black and white, *Stranger Than Paradise* follow the pair's adventures togeth and by featuring likable char ters and heartfelt observatio examines what it means to b family and an individual.

■ Dead Man, 1995, starring Johnny Depp and Gary Farmer

A meandering post-western, *Dead Man* traces the fall and redemption of a man on his final journey across the United States. Featuring a unique portrayal of Native American relationships, it is a literate film with a haunting score by Neil Young.

Other Works

Down by Law, 1986, starring Tom Waits, John Lurie, and Roberto Benigni

Broken Flowers, 2005, starring Bill Murray, Jeffrey Wright, and Sharon Stone

Coffee and Cigarettes, 03, starring Roberto Benigni, ve Buscemi, Iggy Pop, Tom its, Cate Blanchett, and Bill rray

Consisting of 11 short stories, *Coffee and Cigarettes* is an investigation into addiction, ritual, and chance. Shot in black and white and featuring an en-

semble cast of Hollywood hipsters and musicians, it is a humorous compilation of new material and short films shot throughout the 1980s and '90s.

Jim Jarmusch

Spike Lee

1957, Atlanta

■ Writer, actor, and director ■ Founded 40 Acres & A Mule production compan■
■ Launched the careers of many actors ■ Attacks social stereotypes and preju■
dices ■ Films often feature breathless monologues and disorienting camera wo■
■ American ■ Political Drama ■ Directed 18 films

■ **1957** Born Shelton Lee in Georgia
1977 Attends Morehouse College, Atlanta
1977 First student film, *Last Hustle In Brooklyn*
1980 Graduates from NYU film school
1983 *Joe's Bed-Stuy Barbershop: We Cut Heads* wins student prize
1986 First feature film, *She's Gotta Have It*
1997 Directs *4 Little Girls*
2002 Receives BAFTA Special Achievement Award

Perhaps the most famous African-American filmmaker ■
all time, Spike Lee has consistently produced prickly a■
thought-provoking films that focus on sexual, racial, a■
political issues. Born in Atlanta, Lee made his first film, *L*■
Hustle in Brooklyn (1977), when he was just 20 years old. ■
mainstream breakthrough came with the biopic *Malco*■
X, which influenced a generation of filmmakers and grea■
fueled Denzel Washington's career. Lee uses film to cas■
spotlight on contemporary issues. In 2002, he direct■
25th Hour—the first film to tackle the terrorist attacks ■
September 11, 2001—while in 2006 he released *When t*■
Levees Broke: A Requiem in Four Acts, which dealt with Ne■
Orleans in the wake of Hurricane Katrina.

■ **Jungle Feve**r, 1991, starring Wesley Snipes, Annabella Sciorra, and Halle Berry

Jungle Fever is a complex film about freedom, sex, and prejudice. Set in New York, it looks at the social repercussions for an entire cast of characters when a relationship between a married African-American architect (Snipes) and his Italian-American secretary (Sciorra) stirs racial tensions.

Politics and Blockbusters 1975–1989

Other Works	
Do the Right Thing, 1989, starring Danny Aiello, Ossie Davis, and John Turturro	**Summer of Sam**, 1999, starring John Leguizamo and Mira Sorvino

■ **Malcolm X**, 1992, starring Denzel Washington and Angela Bassett

Malcolm X is Spike Lee's most popular film. Powerful and controversial, it deals with the issues of racism, religion, violence, and prejudice in the postwar United States. An impassioned and well-observed biopic, *Malcolm X* details the life of the self-made leader of the Black Nationalist movement, and was the first American nondocumentary to be shot on location at Mecca. The film uses real footage and speeches. Washington was nominated for an Oscar for his portrayal of the civil rights activist-turned-devout Muslim.

Inside Man, 2006, starring
nzel Washington, Clive
ven, Jodie Foster, Christopher
mmer, and Willem Dafoe

aturing an immense ensem-
e cast, *Inside Man* is a clever
me drama that centers on
emes of conspiracy, corrup-
n, and multiculturalism.
ot in just under two months,
e film follows the events of
ramatic bank heist that
comes a tense hostage
uation. Washington plays
easoned police officer who
s to stop the bank robbers.
alculated and well-scripted
n, *Inside Man* features grip-
g action scenes and clever
t twists.

Spike Lee

A World of Cinema 1990–Today

"This here's the future. Videotape tells the truth."

Paul Thomas Anderson: Boogie Nights, 1997, USA, starring Mark Wahlberg and Heather Graham
Quote: Philip Baker Hall as Floyd Gondolli in *Boogie Nights*

Innovative Hollywood Entertainers

Mixing digital technology and cinema history, these directors create thrilling films that dazzle audiences with visual onslaughts

Darren Aronofsky
Joel & Ethan Coen p. 408
Alfonso Cuarón p. 428

1990   1992   1994   1996   19

David Fincher p. 420
Paul Greengrass p. 424
Spike Jonze
Baz Luhrmann
Christopher Nolan
Robert Rodriguez
Zack Snyder
Quentin Tarantino p. 416
Guillermo del Toro

Independents in America

Though some of these directors have made mainstream films, their allegiance lies with independent art cinema, often making elegant drama

Paul Thomas Anderson p. 406
Wes Anderson
Jane Campion p. 404
Vincent Gallo
Harmony Korine
Ang Lee p. 444
Richard Linklater
John Cameron Mitchell
Gus Van Sant p. 398
Steven Soderbergh p. 412

p.427

392

990–Today

Contemporary European Masters

With greater creative freedom, European directors tend to make visually ingenious and thought-provoking films

393

p. 443

| 00 | 2002 | 2004 | 2006 | 2008 |

Global Cinema

Filmmakers from Latin America, Asia, the Middle East, and Africa offer new perspectives on urban and rural lives

p. 463

A World of Cinema

New Methods of Storytelling for a Globalized World

The 1990s saw a resurgence of film noir. In *Basic Instinct* and David Lynch's *Lost Highway* (1997), what was once sexual subtext came fully to the fore. Films by Quentin Tarantino and the Coen brothers mastered the cinematic homage, creating original and often violent patchworks of film history. The "VCR generation" of filmmakers, raised on an unlimited library of films, produced bigger and bolder directors like Paul Thomas Anderson, Todd Haynes, and Baz Luhrmann. Luhrmann's adaptation of *Romeo + Juliet* updates the story, filming it in a modern city filled with billboards emblazoned with Shakespearean slogans. As Hollywood struggles for audiences increasingly distracted by the Internet and video games, blockbusters need to make bigger splashes, and studios choose safe bets in the form of sequels to hits such as *Shrek* (2001) or *X-Men* (2000).

■ **Paul Verhoeven**
Basic Instinct,
1992, starring
Sharon Stone and
Michael Douglas

■ **Baz Luhrmann**
Romeo + Juliet,
1996, starring Leonardo DiCaprio and
Claire Danes

A World of Cinema 1990–Today

◀ Andrew
Stanton and Lee
Unkrich: Finding
Nemo, 2003

Sam Raimi:
Spider-Man, 2002,
starring Tobey
Maguire and
Kirsten Dunst

Flashier Blockbusters

Some of the talented directors that take on the bigger-budget challenge to create kinetic, engrossingly entertaining works have broken box-office records while earning critical acclaim. Sam Raimi, the cult director behind *The Evil Dead* (1981), made three *Spider-Man* films to date, and brought to life a superhero who can both defeat supervillains and make a political statement about power and responsibility.

Non-American directors such as Paul Greengrass, Alfonso Cuarón, and Peter Jackson bring a similarly smart approach to their action films, using digital technology to create a new realism.

The Asian Invasion

Director Ang Lee is emblematic of a globalized new breed of directors. Lee is equally at home filming in English as in his native tongue, and confidently makes films rooted in different cultures. After *Crouching Tiger, Hidden Dragon*'s 2000 box-office success, Lee seemed just as comfortable filming the equally acclaimed low-key *Brokeback Mountain* (2005). His Malaysia-born Taiwanese countryman Tsai Ming-Liang is not as chameleonic as Lee, instead creating enigmatic, slow-paced portraits of urban lawlessness. His delirious *The Wayward Cloud* is about a pornography production suffering a drought. The sensual films of Wong Kar-Wai have also revitalized filmmaking worldwide.

■ **Tsai Ming-Liang: The Wayward Cloud**, 2005, starring Lee Kang-Sheng and Chen Shiang-Chyi

■ **Fernando Mereilles and Kátia Lund: City of God**, 2002, starring Alexandre Rodrigues and Seu Jorge

Globalized Perspectives

In Latin America, Brazil's Walter Salles and Fernando Mereilles have found strong ways to express the frantic energy of their megalopolis while Europe's latest burst of talent comes from the unlikely Romania—a country with less than 80 cinemas. Like the Palme d'Or–winning abortion drama *4 Months, 3 Weeks and 2 Days* (2007) by Christian Mungiu, films such as Cristi Puiu's *The Death of Mr. Lazarescu* (2005) and Corneliu Poromboiu's *12:08 East of Bucharest* unflinchingly yet artfully capture life since the Iron Curtain fell in 1989. Poromboiu's film is set in a TV studio where several undistinguished guests are asked where they were when Romanian dictator Ceauşescu was overthrown. Its quotidian style is deceptively simple, featuring long takes, documentary editing, and plain lighting, providing—like the best global cinema—a strong counterpoint to Hollywood's visual excess, and championing the ordinary people in danger of being overlooked.

Gus Van Sant

1952, Louisville

■ Returned to independent, experimental cinema after becoming disillusioned with Hollywood ■ Known for his dreamy cinematography and offbeat narrative ■ Champions male beauty ■ Inspired by Stanley Kubrick and John Cassavetes ■ American ■ Drama, Comedy, Shorts, Horror ■ Directed 12 films

■ **1952** Born in Kentucky
1970 Enrolls in the Rhode Island School of Design
1985 First film, *Mala Noche*, is a critical success
1992 Directs the Red Hot Chili Peppers' *Under The Bridge* video
1993 Dedicates *Even Cowgirls Get the Blues* to actor River Phoenix
1995 Nicole Kidman acts in his *To Die For*
1997 *Good Will Hunting* makes $220 million worldwide
2003 Returns to independent filmmaking with *Elephant*; wins two awards at Cannes

Van Sant's early work was dedicated to subcultural portraits with a twist and *My Own Private Idaho* (1991) was his first experimental film. Inspired by Shakespeare's *Henry* and Orson Welles's (p. 126) adaptation *Chimes at Midnight* (1965), Van Sant set his story among Portland's young male prostitutes. The unlikely success turned its stars, River Phoenix and Keanu Reeves, into pinups, and Van Sant into an in-demand director. Though *Good Will Hunting* was a box-office success, Van Sant became disillusioned with Hollywood's conventions. His later films feature longer takes, less narrative, and are tributes to idols such as Béla Tarr and Alan Clarke. From *Gerry*, a hypnotizing film about two friends who get lost in the desert, to *Last Days,* which examines Kurt Cobain's final hours, and *Paranoid Park*'s depiction of an adolescent struggling with guilt, Van Sant has proved his versatility and skill.

■ **Good Will Hunting**, 1997, starring Matt Damon and Ben Affleck

Though Van Sant had already directed music videos and commercials, this film would be his first mainstream feature. Little trace remains of his earlier obsession with lowlifes and outsiders; only an attractive patina of grit remains in the luminous shots of Boston. The young lead actors won the film an Oscar for the screenplay and became major film stars in the process.

Drugstore Cowboy, 1989, starring Kelly Lynch and Matt Dillon

His first film about drug addiction to address the pleasure people take in drugs, the road movie offers an uncompromising, nonjudgmental view of a dysfunctional family of junkies. Van Sant films their misadventures in robbing Portland pharmacies in a daring blend of styles and techniques, creating a bold and poignant work. One of the film's highlights is the fragile cameo of Beat poet, and legendary junkie, William Burroughs.

■ **Elephant**, 2003, starring John Robinson

Inspired by Alan Clarke's experimental TV film of the same name about the IRA killings in Northern Ireland, Van Sant chose similar long takes for his vision of a Columbine-type school shooting. The overlapping sequences, a nod to Béla Tarr's seven-hour farm film *Sátántangó* (1994), create an eerie effect deeply at odds with Hollywood's familiar cause-and-effect stories.

Other Works
Gerry, 2002, starring Casey Affleck
Last Days, 2005, starring Michael Pitt
Paranoid Park, 2007, starring Gabe Nevins

Gus Van Sant

Queer Cinema

■ Originally a label for a few directors such as Todd Haynes, Gregg Araki, Lizz
Borden, and Derek Jarman ■ Now includes films that honestly address lesbia
gay, bisexual, and transgender issues ■ Can also include films with "camp"
sensibilities, in which clichés are heightened but played straight
■ *left:* **Boys Don't Cry**, by Kimberly Peirce, 1999, starring Hilary Swank

■ **1938** The word "gay" first
used in *Bringing Up Baby*

1950 Jean Genet directs
the prison fantasy *A Song
of Love*

1976 Derek Jarman's
debut feature *Sebastiane*

1991 Bruce LaBruce's first
film, the explicit *No Skin Off
My Ass*

1992 A new wave of gay-
themed films is dubbed
New Queer Cinema

1994 Director Derek
Jarman dies of AIDS

2006 *Shortbus*, John
Cameron Mitchell's ex-
plicit tribute to sexuality
premiers at Cannes

Though New Queer Cinema was originally conceived a
label for a specific set of American directors (Todd Hayne
Poison, 1991, Gregg Araki's *The Doom Generation*, 1995, a
Tom Kalin's *Swoon*, 1992) touring the world's film festiva
these filmmakers have since expanded their narrati
range to include heterosexual subjects. Gay issues ha
also been successfully and imaginatively addressed
directors who do not share their protagonists' sexual ori
tation, and audiences worldwide have become mo
accepting in their reception of these films. The success th
acclaimed and commercially appealing directors such
Ang Lee (p. 444) and Peter Jackson have had in this rega
is significant. Homosexual characters have been prese
in film for a long time, but are often relegated to minor, f
roles. Queer Cinema strives to portray characters in
honest and equal manner.

■ **John Cameron Mitchell:
Hedwig and the Angry Inc**
2001, starring John Cameron
Mitchell and Michael Pitt

Hedwig was a young East
Berliner, but the price he pai
to be a US soldier's liberated
bride left him with a botched
sex change, and the titular
"angry inch." This vibrant roc
musical stages its performances in chain restaurants
and suburban lunchrooms.
Mitchell's debut film, it is
based on his off-Broadway
stage musical.

■ **Stephan Elliott: The Adventures of Priscilla, Queen of the Desert**, 1994, starring Terence Stamp and Guy Pearce

This cult Australian drag-queen-road movie features a wild young man, a dignified aging man, and another struggling with fatherhood trying to make it across the outback. The campy soundtrack bursts with ABBA songs—as does its contemporary Australian film *Muriel's Wedding*—in a hilarious and poignant tale.

◀ **Peter Jackson: Heavenly Creatures**, 1994, starring Melanie Lynskey and Kate Winslet

Jackson surprised critics with this subtle and imaginative tale of a dangerous love affair between two young girls (Lynskey and Winslet). Its combination of realism and fantasy was a dramatic shift away from his earlier style.

Other Works
Orlando, by Sally Potter, 1992, starring Tilda Swinton
The Adventures of Sebastian Cole, by Tod Williams, 1998, starring Adrian Grenier
Mysterious Skin, by Gregg Araki, 2004, starring Joseph Gordon-Levitt and Brady Corbet

Sofia Coppola

1971, New York

- Director, actor, and fashion designer ■ Part of a true Hollywood family tre[e]
- Characteristically uses contemporary soundtracks to underscore her impr[e]ssionistic narratives ■ Her female protagonists are vulnerable yet strong
- American ■ Drama, Historical Biopic ■ Directed 3 films

1971 Born to director Francis Ford and Eleanor Neil

1972 First appears on screen in *The Godfather*

1989 Writes her father's segment of *New York Stories* anthology film

1990 Replaces Winona Ryder in *The Godfather: Part III*

1997 Stars in husband Spike Jonze's video for The Chemical Brothers' *Elektrobank*

2003 First American woman nominated for a Best Director Oscar

The daughter of Francis Ford Coppola (p. 314), and cou[sin] to actors Jason Schwartzman and Nicolas Cage, Sofia C[op]pola did not have the most auspicious start in the f[ilm] industry. After being widely derided for her performanc[e in] her father's third *Godfather* film, she sought to engage [her] talents on the other side of the camera, soon establish[ing] a unique style characterized by impressionistic storytel[ling] and vibrant colors. She underscores this recogniza[ble] ethereal style by soundtracks of contemporary pop, m[ost] memorably by the French electronica act Air. Her fem[ale] protagonists are singular creatures: strangely untainte[d by] experience, yet weary of the world. Coppola is the o[nly] female director to receive three Oscar nominations— Best Director, Picture, and Original Screenplay.

■ **The Virgin Suicides**, 1999, starring Kirsten Dunst and Josh Hartnett

Basing her screenplay on the novel by Jeffrey Eugenides, Coppola replicated the book's

1970s anemic suburbia with an eerie accuracy. Like the novelist, she managed to turn a story about a series of suicides within the same family into a meditation on nostalgia and

memory. Her debut as a director, the film shows a neighborhood's gawky teen[age] boys' lustful worship of the mysterious Lisbon sisters in [an] almost palpable manner.

A World of Cinema 1990–Today

Lost In Translation, 2003, starring Bill Murray and Scarlett Johansson

The director came into her own with this critically acclaimed, Oscar-nominated story of a not-quite-love affair in Tokyo between a photographer's young wife and a jaded actor. Without exoticizing Japanese culture, Coppola instead focused on her protagonists' estrangement and solitude in the face of a deeply foreign city. As in all her work, the film's contemporary pop soundtrack creates a hazy, impressionistic mood that is enhanced by luminous cinematography. Murray underplayed his character brilliantly, his deadpan performance evidence of his character's deep emotional disconnect.

■ **Marie Antoinette**, 2006, starring Kirsten Dunst and Jason Schwartzman

Coppola reunited with her star Dunst for this innovative biopic of history's most tragically misguided royal. The director took a daring step in enriching the film with an anachronistic but effective soundtrack that includes period pieces as well as music by Air and New Order. The costuming also pays tribute to that era: one shot reveals a pair of Converse shoes.

Sofia Coppola

Jane Campion

1954, Wellington

■ Her strong female protagonists challenge conventions ■ Frankly depicts desire and sexuality ■ Her films' moods often strongly correspond with her imagery and color schemes
■ New Zealand ■ Drama, Historical, Comedy ■ Directed 7 films

■ **1954** Born in New Zealand

1975 Studies anthropology

1979 Studies painting at the Sydney College of the Arts

1982 Directs his first short, *Peel*, which wins an award at Cannes in 1986

1984 Makes two shorts, *After Hours* and *A Girl's Own Story*

1986 First feature, *Two Friends*, for TV

1993 The second woman nominated for a Best Director Oscar after Lina Wertmüller

2006 Makes the anthology film *8* with, among others, Mira Nair, Wim Wenders, and Gus Van Sant

With an Oscar, Silver Lion, and two Palmes d'Or, Campi is the world's most critically successful female direct Though most of her films revolve around women, th are not feminist manifestos but instead present fem characters and their choices with all their flaws and faul After a series of smart shorts, Campion made t acclaimed feature *Sweetie*, about two troubled te sisters. The director returned to the theme of awkwa adolescence for her second film, *An Angel at My Table Holy Smoke* Kate Winslet plays a young woman forced undergo "deprogramming" at the hands of the gr Harvey Keitel, after becoming involved in a cult. U mately, Campion has Winslet convert Keitel, not just s ually, but mentally as well. Still, Campion's films are r simply about the joys of sexual liberation, also showi the dangers of falling into an abusive relationship bas on lust, as in the shocking *In the Cut*.

A World of Cinema 1990–Today

■ **An Angel at My Table**, 1990, starring Kerry Fox

Based on the autobiographic writings of New Zealand's Jan Frame, this was originally screened as a TV miniseries. T shy and depressed writer was misdiagnosed with schizo-phrenia and spent a large par her life in mental institutions. The three actresses playing th frizzy red-haired Frame are pr sented with a visual simplicity centered on close-ups and medium shots.

The Piano, 1993, starring
lly Hunter and Anna Paquin

tern Scottish widow and her
ughter arrive in lush but
erwhelming New Zealand to
rry a man (Sam Neill) the
man has never met. Ada
unter) has not spoken since
e was six. She communicates
ough sign language, her
ughter (Paquin) acting as
erpreter, but also through
sic (written for the film by
ter Greenaway's composer

Michael Nyman). They are
dropped on a deserted beach
with their piano, but her husband and his Maori workers
decline to carry the heavy
instrument through the jungle.
A neighboring man (Harvey
Keitel) hears Ada play on the
beach and buys the piano from
her husband. Privately, he
offers to trade it back to her in
exchange for sexual
favors, and Ada
starts

her erotic awakening. A huge
crossover success, the film
made over $40 million
in the US and
won three
Oscars.

■ The Portrait of a Lady, 1996, starring Nicole Kidman and John Malkovich

Campion daringly opens her
adaptation of Henry James's
19th-century novel with a montage of contemporary teen girls
discussing their first kiss. When
we cut to the repressed visage of
Isabel Archer (Kidman) the audience realizes the inroads made
in women's liberation. Though

financially independent Isabel
fends off most of her suitors,
she is soon trapped by the mali-
ciously plotting Malkovich. By
opening up James's ending,
Campion counters his assertion
that women when granted independence will fail due to their
weaker nature. The delicious ensemble cast also includes Barbara
Hershey, Viggo Mortensen, Christian Bale, and Mary-Louise Parker.

Jane Campion

Paul Thomas Anderson

1970, Studio City

■ Camera always in motion inspired by Max Ophüls and Jean Renoir ■ Large ensemble casts and long takes reminiscent of Robert Altman ■ Philip Baker Hall, John C. Reilly, and Melora Walters appear in three of his films ■ American ■ Drama, Comedy, Historical, Music Videos ■ Directed 5 films

■ **1970** Born in California

1988 Makes *The Dirk Diggler Story*, a short that inspired *Boogie Nights*

1990 Production assistant on TV show *The Quiz Kids Challenge*

1993 His short *Cigarettes & Coffee* screens to great acclaim at Sundance

2000 Directs Fiona Apple's music videos, *Paper Bag* and *Limp*

2006 Standby director on Robert Altman's *A Prairie Home Companion*

2007 *There Will Be Blood* is nominated for Best Screenplay Oscar, wins Silver Bear

After his well-received debut film, *Hard Eight,* Paul Thomas Anderson's second film, *Boogie Nights*, took the film world by storm. The filmmaker's love of cinema shows in the film tributes to classic sequences in Martin Scorsese's (p. 32) *Goodfellas* or Mikhail Kalatozov's *I Am Cuba*. His second film *Magnolia*, juggles an ensemble cast in the manner of Robert Altman (p. 328). *There Will Be Blood* (2007) Anderson's most mature work. Lacking his previous comedic flair, it offers a grim vision of the destructive force of unconstrained capitalism and organized religion on the American landscape. Daniel Day-Lewis's Oscar-winning performance is influenced by the booming voice of director John Huston (p. 138), and shares its desolate Marfa, Texas, setting with the Coen brothers' (p. 408) *No Country for Old Men* (2007).

■ **Boogie Nights**, 1997, starring Mark Wahlberg and Heather Graham

Spanning two decades of the history of the Californian pornography industry, Anderson's ensemble drama is surprisingly poignant. Though his tone is often comedic, the director portrays his adult film studio as a dysfunctional family. Julianne Moore's character is a failing mother figure to Mark Wahlberg's Dirk Diggler. The film also stars Burt Reynolds, John C. Reilly, Luis Guzman, and William H. Macy.

Magnolia, 1999, starring
~~~m~~ Cruise, Melora Walters,
~~~d~~ Julianne Moore

~~is~~ audacious ensemble drama
~~con~~sists of nine intersecting
~~sto~~ries coincidentally con-
~~ne~~cting characters over the
~~co~~urse of a single, dramatic day
~~in~~ Los Angeles. Capped with an
~~ou~~trageous raining-frog
~~se~~quence, the film has a sound-
~~tra~~ck by singer Aimee Mann. The
~~wi~~nning cast is rounded out by
~~Ph~~ilip Seymour Hoffman, John C.
~~Rei~~lly, and William H. Macy.

Other Works

~~H~~ard Eight, 1996, starring Philip
~~B~~aker Hall

~~T~~here Will Be Blood, 2007,
~~s~~tarring Daniel Day-Lewis

■ **Punch Drunk Love**, 2002,
starring Adam Sandler and
Emily Watson

Though Sandler was at that time
the highest-paid actor in Hollywood, he took a chance on a

dramatic role in this low-key
comedy about a small business
owner and a mysterious woman.
Shot on a smaller scale than his
other films, it features his typically fluid cinematography.

Paul Thomas Anderson

Joel and Ethan Coen

1955 (Joel) and 1958 (Ethan), Minneapolis

■ Inspired by Preston Sturges and Frank Capra ■ Frequently feature less intelligent protagonists ■ Often use ironic voice-overs ■ Graphic bursts of violence often played for laughs ■ Edit their films under the alias Roderick Jaynes ■ American ■ Comedy, Drama, Literary Adaptation ■ Directed 12 films

■ **1955** Joel is born
1958 Ethan is born
1981 Joel is assistant editor on Sam Raimi's *The Evil Dead*
1984 The brothers make their first film, the film noir *Blood Simple*
1991 *Barton Fink* wins them the Palme d'Or and Best Director award at Cannes
1996 *Fargo* wins an Oscar for Best Original Screenplay
2007 Win three Oscars for *No Country for Old Men*.

With their deadpan dialogue and eye for grotesque roles, Joel and Ethan Coen brothers have made a career out of bumbling characters getting in over their heads. They share writing, directing, producing, and editing duties on all their films. Their comedic style hails from the screwball comedies of Preston Sturges (p. 114) and Frank Capra (p. 118), though the Coens usually add a darker violent subtext to their stories. Their films are always set in a specific and significant landscape or setting. The Coen brothers have a unique style that is indicative of contemporary independent American storytelling, outside the Hollywood system.

Other Works

Blood Simple, 1984, starring Frances McDormand

Raising Arizona, 1987, starring Nicolas Cage

Miller's Crossing, 1990, starring Gabriel Byrne

Barton Fink, 1991, starring John Turturro

The Man Who Wasn't There, 2001, starring Billy Bob Thornton

■ **No Country for Old Men**, 2007, starring Josh Brolin and Javier Bardem

An aging cop (Tommy Lee Jones) trails a brutal killer (Bardem).

Lacking much of the dry wit and stylistic pizzazz that characterizes their other work, this film stands out for its restraint. Matching novelist Cormac McCarthy's terse prose, the reserved cinematography lets the desolate scenery speak for itself. Perennial Coen collaborator Carter Burwell's eerie score is also minimalistic.

The Big Lebowski, 1998, ★arring Jeff Bridges and John ●odman

●is crazy tale of a man in search ●his rug has attracted a cult fan ■se that drink Lebowski's cock- ●l of choice (a White Russian), ●ow much of the ●otable dialogue ●heart, or dress ●like John ●rturro's ●wler, ●sus.

■ **Fargo**, 1996, starring Frances McDormand and William H. Macy

The first Coen film to be a true commercial hit, this story of a faked kidnap- ping gone hor- ribly wrong is set in the snowy fields of the directors' native Min- nesota. A radiantly pregnant police officer

played by Frances McDormand (Joel Coen's wife) investigates a series of murders that lead her to a nervous car salesperson, Jerry Lundegaard (Macy). Through a complex, and bloody series of twists in the plot, but without much actual investi- gating, the police officer learns that Jerry hired two violent goons to kidnap his wife for ransom so he could pay back his gambling debts. With the actors delivering their lines with an exaggerated, slow Midwestern accent, the Coens have been accused of portraying the char- acters as laughable simpletons.

Cult Films

■ Films that gain a large following among a generation and often go on to be stylistically influential ■ Box-office flops that later win attention through repeat midnight screenings ■ Avid fan bases ■ Sometimes screened interactively, inviting sing-alongs or dressing up with props

■ *left*: **Blues Brothers**, by John Landis, 1980, starring John Belushi and Dan Aykroyd

1958 The "worst director ever," Ed Wood Jr., films *Plan 9 From Outer Space*

1970 New York's Elgin Theater starts popular midnight screenings of Kenneth Anger's *Invocation of My Demon Brother*

1981 Danny Peary popularizes the term in his book *Cult Movies*

1994 Tim Burton films *Ed Wood*, starring Johnny Depp and Martin Landau

2004 David Lynch's cult hit *Eraserhead* is selected to the National Film Registry in the US Library of Congress

Most cult films come in two distinct varieties: The first a films that are "so bad they're good" and the other cons of films that are uncommercial, too complex, and to artistic to make it in a regular release. Though there we midnight screenings of exploitation films from the 193 onward, it was not until a theater in Chelsea, New Yor started midnight screenings of strange and rare films, th one could first speak of films earning a true cult followin Films developed fan bases fueled by a kindred outca spirit. In many cases fans interact with films by singin along, dressing up, or delivering ironic commentari during the screening. DVDs have enabled cult films build fan bases more quickly, often prompting studio rereleases or sequels.

■ **Jim Sharman: The Rocky Horror Picture Show**, 1975, starring Tim Curry and Susan Sarandon

One stormy night a nervous couple takes refuge in a castle where the annual Transylvanian Convention is being held. Based on a British stage musical, the film became the most successful and longest-running midnight movie. Interactive screenings were held with fan participation—shouting at the screen, dressing in character, and sing-alongs—while other screenings have a cast perform the film in front of the screen.

A World of Cinema 1990–Today

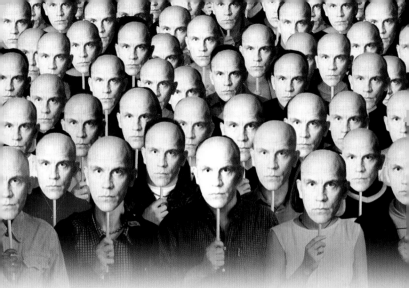

Spike Jonze: Being John Malkovich, 1999, starring John Cusack and Catherine Keener

Charlie Kaufman (who also wrote *Adaptation*, 2002, and *Synecdoche, New York*, 2008) wrote the script to this self-reflexive film about a frustrated puppeteer who is forced to find a job as an office worker. While working in his half-sized office—located between floors seven and eight on floor seven and a half—he discovers a mystical portal into the head of actor John Malkovich (played by himself). The office workers begin to abuse the portal by charging admission into the actor's brain. Nominated for three Oscars, *Being John Malkovich* is full of quirks and, like John Malkovich himself, has developed a cult following. As the story progresses, it delves deeper and deeper into weirdness.

Richard Kelly: Donnie Darko, 2001, starring Jake Gyllenhaal and Patrick Swayze

Drew Barrymore produced this spectacular tale of fate and redemption about a troubled teen who gets strange messages from the near future. The story blurs the lines between schizophrenia and the paranormal as a grotesque rabbit takes over Donnie Darko's life. After flopping at the box office, the film played midnight screenings for more than two years before being theatrically revived in a 20-minute-longer director's cut in 2004.

Other Works

Freaks, by Tod Browning, 1932, starring Wallace Ford

Valley of the Dolls, by Mark Robson, 1967, starring Patty Duke

Heathers, by Michael Lehmann, 1989, starring Winona Ryder

Steven Soderbergh

1963, Atlanta

■ Alternates commercial studio films with smaller, experimental ones ■ Often shoots and edits films he writes and directed under aliases ■ Known for his lively editing and innovative use of chronology
■ American ■ Drama, Comedy, Action, Crime ■ Directed 17 films

1963 Born in Georgia

1976 Starts making films

1986 After an unsuccessful attempt at screenwriting in Hollywood, makes music documentary *Yes: 9012 Live*

1989 Is the youngest winner to date to win the Palme d'Or at Cannes for *Sex, Lies, and Videotape*

1995 Remakes Robert Siodmak's *Criss Cross* (1949) as *The Underneath*

2000 Is nominated for two Best Director Oscars for *Erin Brockovich* and *Traffic*; the latter won

2001 Founds Section Eight Productions with George Clooney

2005 Releases *Bubble* to theaters and DVD within the same week

Other Works

Gray's Anatomy, 1996, starring Spalding Gray

Schizopolis, 1996, starring Steven Soderbergh

The Limey, 1999, starring Terence Stamp

Solaris, 2002, starring George Clooney

The Good German, 2006, starring Cate Blanchett and Tobey Maguire

Steven Soderbergh's debut *Sex, Lies, and Videotape* pave the way for a wave of independent films now associate with the Sundance festival and Harvey Weinstein's pr duction company Miramax. In the late 1980s, the rise of th video market created a demand for films that the studic alone could not satisfy. This great demand enabled di tributors and independent producers to have films mac on their own. These new "indies" range from Jim Ja musch's (p. 386) low-budget films to the raw work of Joh Cassavetes (p. 292) in their aesthetic and commercial se sibility. Soderbergh's stunningly varied oeuvre ranges fro the frivolously star-studded (*Ocean's Eleven*) to the hila ously experimental (*Schizopolis*); from haunting crime film (*The Limey*) to a small-town drama cast with only nonacto (*Bubble*, 2005). His passion for film shows in his playful u of editing and references to other films. Together with act George Clooney, Soderbergh also produces politica edgy films like *Michael Clayton* (2007).

■ **Sex, Lies, and Videotape,** 1989, starring Andie MacDow and James Spader

The first American independe film to resonate commercially this was bought and thereafte aggressively marketed by Harvey Weinstein, who helpec turn this low-budget film into an international success and create a market for inde-pendent film. The usually vil-lainous Spader is cast as the filmmaking protagonist.

Ocean's Eleven, 2001, [st]arring George Clooney and [Br]ad Pitt

[Sp]awning two sequels (*Ocean's [T]welve*, 2004, and *Ocean's [Th]irteen*, 2007), this ensemble [he]ist film remakes the 1960 ["R]at Pack" film in name only.

A playful action film, *Ocean's Eleven* is most successful simply showcasing its star-studded cast's cool. Influenced by the French New Wave, the series is self-reflective—in *Ocean's Twelve* Julia Roberts plays her own look-alike.

Out of Sight, 1998, starring [Je]nnifer Lopez and George [Cl]ooney

[Fo]r Soderbergh's return to [stu]dio filmmaking, Scott Frank [ad]apted Elmore Leonard's sexy [cri]me novel about a bank robber [(Cl]ooney) who breaks out of jail

and kidnaps a US Marshal (Lopez). The film follows the fight between duty and passion. Clooney and Lopez's vibrant love scenes are sharply edited and nonchronologically presented. The film was nominated for two Oscars.

■ **Erin Brockovich**, 2000, starring Julia Roberts

Based on the true story of a dramatic environmental lawsuit, this is Steven Soderbergh's most straightforward film. Julia Roberts's performance earned her an Oscar.

Steven Soderbergh

New Stardom

No longer limited by studios' publicity departments, today's stars tend to be more vocal in their political opinions—seemingly always aware that the size of their political platform depends on their films' commercial and critical success. They also have to cope with more vicious media exposure at the hands of anonymous bloggers and harsh paparazzi. Today's most successful stars can negotiate these twin publicity minefields by either remaining resolutely private (like Johnny Depp) or by using their publicity to draw attention to political causes.

■ **Johnny Depp** emerged as a young star in the 1980s. After gaining pinup status on TV's *21 Jump Street*, Depp began to cultivate a uniquely offbeat career in film that peaked commercially with his role in *Edward Scissorhands* (1990) and was further perfected with his Keith Richards-inspired role in the *Pirates of the Caribbean* trilogy. His roles are usually outsiders and eccentrics, much like himself. In 1999, he moved to France, where he lives with French actor Vanessa Paradis.

■ **Scarlett Johansson** emerg from her career as a child star in the 1990s and developed into a voluptuous young acto She has worked in a variety of genres with directors such as the Coen brothers, Woody Allen, Brian DePalma, and Christopher Nolan, and, like many contemporary actors, crusades for her beliefs, inclu ding campaigning for the Democratic Party. Sofia Copp la's *Lost In Translation* saw her most memorable role to date.

Leonardo DiCaprio had
 fight for serious roles
 er his work in *Titanic*
 997). Having worked with
orsese twice, he recently
oduced and narrated the
ological documentary
e 11th Hour (2007).

George Clooney began
s career as a doctor on
's *ER*. He swore off com-
ercial filmmaking after
e campy *Batman & Robin*
997), and has successfully
versified into writing,
oducing, and directing.

▶ **Brad Pitt and Angelina
Jolie** represent the power
couple. After exhausting
mediatized breakups with
Gwyneth Paltrow and Jen-
nifer Aniston, Pitt
started a quickly
growing multicul-
tural family with
his *Mr. and Mrs.
Smith* (2005)
costar Jolie, who
has changed her
previously dark
persona into that
of a humanitarian
superwoman.

Quentin Tarantino

1963, Knoxville

■ Inspired by exploitation films and B-movies ■ The violence in his films is often over-the-top ■ Dialogue often deals with popular culture ■ Sound tracks consist of pop songs and other films' scores
■ American ■ Crime, Drama, Action ■ Directed 5 films

1963 Born in Tennessee

1979 Drops out of high school to act

1985 Meets *Pulp Fiction* co-writer Roger Avary working at Manhattan Beach Video Archives in California

1988 Appears as an Elvis impersonator in an episode of *The Golden Girls*

1993 Tony Scott directs Tarantino's script *True Romance*

1994 *Natural Born Killers*'s script adapted and directed by Oliver Stone

2007 Acts in Takashi Miike's *Sukiyaki Western Django*

Other Works

Pulp Fiction, see p. 418

Four Rooms, 1995, segment: *The Man from Hollywood*, starring Tim Roth

Jackie Brown, 1997, starring Pam Grier and Robert Forster

CSI: Crime Scene Investigation (TV), 2005, two episodes: *Grave Danger*

Though he is accused of having abased independen[t] cinema by creating a fashion for hyperviolent Neo-Noi[r] whose scripts are filled with ramblings about popular cu[l]ture, Tarantino's work uses B-movies and exploitatio[n] films to create a wildly popular new style. The violence [of] his films is stylized, made into choreographies of limb[s,] weapons, and blood that are distinct from their paralle[ls] in contemporary action films. Tarantino's creative[ly] restructured chronologies also differ from the perhap[s] more simplistic films he references. The casting of old[er] actors whose heydays have passed also has a specif[ic] effect. Pam Grier's strong female protagonist in *Jack[ie] Brown* builds on blaxploitation films like her own *Fo[xy] Brown* (1974), thus charging the film with both her an[d] the genre's past. Tarantino's soundtracks work in th[e] same way; by adding a piece from an old Ennio Morrico[ne] score, he creates a reference that enriches the film.

■ **Kill Bill: Vol. 1 & 2**, 2003/4, starring Uma Thurman

After a bride (Thurman) is widowed and left for dead at the altar, she recovers and sets off to take revenge on the people behind the massacre. *Kill Bill* is a stylish and bloody homage to spaghetti westerns, samurai films, and e[x]ploitation cinem[a,] released in tw[o] volumes.

Reservoir Dogs, 1992, starring Steve Buscemi and [To]m Roth

[An] ensemble heist drama with a [tw]ist, *Reservoir Dogs* never shows the robbery itself. Tarantino's debut has all the hallmarks of his later work: pop-culture-referencing dialogue, sudden bursts of graphic violence, and strong casting that takes actors' past roles into account. The soundtrack features an ironic use of Stealers Wheel's "Stuck in the Middle with You."

Death Proof, 2007, starring [Zo]ë Bell and Kurt Russell

[Th]e film's first part sees a psy-[ch]opathic stunt driver follow [an]d kill a group of young [w]omen in Texas. The second [ha]lf confronts him with a team [of] young stuntwomen who fight [ba]ck. Released in the US with [Ro]bert Rodriguez's *Planet Terror* [un]der the banner title *Grind-[ho]use*, the film's look and story [pa]y tribute to the exploitation [m]ovies that used to play in [do]uble bills at rundown cinemas [cal]led grind houses.

Quentin Tarantino

Pulp Fiction

■ by Quentin Tarantino, USA, 1994, Crime Drama

An international sensation on its release, this postmodern crime drama was the first "independent" film to gross over $100 million. Tarantino's typically nonchronological film is composed of three overlapping storylines: Bruce Willis's boxer who dares not throw a fight; John Travolta's aging thug charged with the care of his boss's misbehaving girlfriend, played by Uma Thurman; and Samuel L. Jackson, Travolta's partner in crime, who undergoes a religious epiphany. The rich screenplay, with its many pop culture references and scenes of brutal violence, won the only Oscar of the film's seven nominations.

■ **Pulp Fiction**, 1994, starring John Travolta and Samuel L. Jackson

Travolta and Uma Thurman's dance duet was not primarily inspired by Travolta's role in *Saturday Night Fever* (1977); instead Tarantino wanted to pay tribute to the impromptu dance sequence in Godard's *Bande à Part* (*Band of Outsider* 1964), the film after which he named his production company, A Band Apart.

Pulp Fiction

David Fincher

1962, Denver

■ Characterized by low-key lighting and low-focus photography ■ Plots revolve around fighting apathy and lethargy in consumer culture ■ Use of digital technology to create "impossible" shots and enhance set design ■ American ■ Thriller, Music Video ■ Directed 6 films

1962 Born in Colorado and raised in Marin County, California

1983 Begins filming commercials and music videos; is the assistant cameraman for *Star Wars: Episode VI—Return of the Jedi*

1984 Directs his first music video, for Rick Springfield

1986 Co-founds the video-production company Propaganda Films

1994 Wins a Grammy for the Rolling Stones's "Love is Strong" music video

2002 Appears in Steven Soderbergh's *Full Frontal*

Other Works

Express Yourself and **Oh Father** (music videos), 1989, for Madonna

Alien³, 1992, starring Sigourney Weaver

Who Is It? (music video), 1993, for Michael Jackson

The Game, 1997, starring Michael Douglas and Sean Penn

Zodiac, 2007, starring Jake Gyllenhaal and Robert Downey Jr.

After working in special effects for George Lucas's (p. 358 Industrial Light & Magic, David Fincher won acclaim wit a gruesome cancer awareness ad featuring a bab smoking in the womb. He first made a name for himself i music videos, directing iconic works for Billy Idol ("Crad of Love"), Madonna ("Vogue"), and George Micha ("Freedom '90"). These videos show Fincher's influentia style, characteristically shot in dark, saturated tones, usin low-key lighting in order to create a high contrast betwee light and dark that accentuates certain aspects of a scen or shrouds the image in mystery. The use of low-focu wide-angle photography leaves most of his images out focus, and he has been known to experiment with sublim inal one-frame images flashing on screen. Fincher ha combined this style with a meticulous attention to deta a passion he shares with his most memorable character

Fight Club, 1999, starring Edward Norton and Brad Pitt

adapting Chuck Palahniuk's angry novel about anti-consumerist terrorism and thwarted machismo, Fincher used the book's raw energy and added unprecedented aspects—having Pitt's character literally shake the edges of the frame, point out the "cigarette burns" marking seams between film reels, and appear in spliced-in single frames, only subliminally visible.

Se7en, 1995, starring Morgan Freeman and Brad Pitt

Fincher's obsession with detail shows in Se7en's elaborate setpieces. The story of two detectives (Freeman and Pitt) on the trail of a serial killer whose crimes mirror the seven deadly sins, the film's low-key lighting and wide-angle, low-focus photography underscore the dark mood. A relentlessly bleak and gruesome thriller, this film paved the way for his more elegant, yet equally chilling real-life crime thriller Zodiac.

■ **Panic Room**, 2002, starring Jodie Foster and Kristen Stewart

Nicole Kidman was originally cast for the film, but was injured during rehearsals and Jodie Foster replaced her. Fincher used digital technology to shoot the suspenseful, seemingly impossible tracking shots that move through the house.

David Fincher

Documentaries

■ Popular subjects are wildlife, rock music, history, and politics ■ Lighter technology enabled different styles that rely less on voice-over and more on observation ■ Originally claiming to be objective, today the genre often presents specifically subjective views

■ *left:* **March of the Penguins**, by Luc Jacquet, 2005

Existing somewhere between journalism and fiction documentaries have historically changed along with cinematic technology. Early documentaries, such as Robert J. Flaherty's (p. 82) ethnographic reconstruction *Nanook of the North* (1922), were silent. Later documentaries mainly used voice-over narration, and the calm authoritative voice helped to validate the genre by giving it an objective and detached air. In the 1960s, the Direct Cinema filmmakers found a new way to be objective—by following their subjects with less obtrusive lightweight cameras and microphones. Their technique was later picked up by the recent wave of Reality TV, which also attempts to present a "fly-on-the-wall" vision of celebrity life. There has been a recent craze of documentarians abandoning attempts at seeming objective, in favor of presenting their subjective views through filmed diaries, re-creations or obvious manipulations of scenes, or by appearing in their films front and center, like Michael Moore.

■ **D. A. Pennebaker: Dont Look Back**, 1967, starring Bob Dylan and Joan Baez

Rooted in Direct Cinema, also called Cinéma Vérité, Pennebaker's films usually eschew narration, instead using "fly-on-the-wall" scenes that are captured on handheld cameras. *Dont Look Back* documents Dylan's chaotic 1965 tour of the UK.

A World of Cinema 1990–Today

■ Walter Ruttmann: Berlin: Symphony of a Great City, 1927

Portraying a day in the life of the modern metropolis, this silent avant-garde documentary does not have a traditional plot or narration, but presents a powerful visual collage that in and of itself can be understood as a sequencing or narrative on life in Berlin. Ruttman's film pays homage to Soviet montages by superimposing the different layers of Berlin on top of one another, creating a snapshot of the city that encapsulates its life and motion.

Other Works

High School, by Frederick Wiseman, 1968

Woodstock, by Michael Wadleigh, 1970

Grey Gardens, by the Maysles Bros. et. al, 1975

Brass Unbound, by Johan van der Keuken, 1993

Tarnation, by Jonathan Caouette, 2003

■ Michael Moore: Bowling for Columbine, 2002

aking the Colorado school shooting as the starting point for a tudy of American gun culture and its ensuing violence, *Bowling or Columbine* was Moore's introduction to a larger audience. *ahrenheit 9/11* (2004) and *Sicko* (2007) later perfected is subjective and effective political showmanhip. Because of his own presence in his lms and his often humorous collage tyle, his documentaries are alled self-reflexive and re often criticized as ropagandistic and actually unreliable.

Paul Greengrass

1955, Cheam

■ Focuses on recent events and political issues informed by his background in documentary journalism ■ Immersive, tense style typified by handheld camera work and hectic editing ■ His raw fight scenes have a realistic, strong energy ■ British ■ Documentary, Drama, Action ■ Directed 8 films

1955 Born in the UK

1980 Finishes college, and visits Northern Ireland while working on *World in Action*

1985 Co-writes the book *Spycatcher*, the banned autobiography of a senior MI5 officer

1988 *Spycatcher* is finally allowed to be sold in the UK

1989 Directs his first feature, *Resurrected*, about a missing soldier in the Falklands War

2004 Co-writes *Omagh*, a TV film about the 1998 bombing in Ireland

2007 *The Bourne Ultimatum* is released

Trained in investigative journalism for ITV's *World in Action* program, where he worked for 10 years, Greengrass brings a documentary sensibility to his raw and often politically charged films. After an unsuccessful attempt at filming a more traditional drama in 1998, *The Theory of Flight*, he found success with his shocking films that were made for television. Many of his works effectively reconstructed traumatic recent events, such as *The Murder of Stephen Lawrence*, which chronicles the murder of a black teenager whose murderers were arrested, but never convicted due to institutional racism. This focus on real-life issues, handheld camera work, rapid editing, and anti-stereotypical characterization creates a style that has proved fruitful in two installments of the Bourne saga. His most recent project, *Green Zone* (2009), is based on a book by war chronicler Rajiv Chandrasekaran that deals with life in Baghdad's Green Zone.

■ **The Bourne Supremacy**, 2004, starring Matt Damon and Joan Allen

Damon's amnesia fuels his quest for his identity, leading him to a government agency that intended to turn him into a human weapon. The Bourne trilogy began with director Doug Liman, but Greengrass's energetic and hectic handheld shots and rough fight scenes in the sequels now characterize the story.

A World of Cinema 1990–Today

United 93, 2006, starring Khalid Abdalla

United 93 is a reenactment of the events leading up to the Pennsylvania crash on September 11, 2001. The documentary approach avoids senti- mentality by casting some of the original people for scenes on the ground—in particular FAA manager Ben Sliney—and by not giving characters stereotypical backgrounds.

Bloody Sunday, 2002, starring James Nesbitt

Made for TV, this re-creation of the bloody outcome of a 1972 pro-IRA march in Northern Ireland won the Berlin Film Festival's Golden Bear and was subsequently released in cinemas worldwide. Greengrass's style, with its erratic camera work and wild editing, came of age in this film. The subject is typical of his work—a complex, morally am- biguous study of violence and politics.

Other Works

The Theory of Flight, 1998, starring Kenneth Branagh and Helena Bonham Carter

The Murder of Stephen Lawrence (TV), 1999, starring Marianne Jean-Baptiste and Hugh Quarshie

The Lord of the Rings Trilogy

■ by Peter Jackson, New Zealand, 2001–2003, Fantasy

After making several comic low-budget horror films, director Peter Jackson's *Heavenly Creatures* (1994) enabled him to make *The Lord of the Rings*. Budgeted at $280 million dollars, it is a literary adaptation that combines magical worlds with precise realism, set against a stunning backdrop and aided by some of the most advanced special effects of the time. Principal photography on all three films lasted nearly a year, shooting at 150 locations, sometimes by several different units at the same time, with Jackson monitoring all via satellite feeds. Both the films' cutting-edge special effects, such as the character Gollum, an entirely digital creature whose movements and expressions were captured from the face and body of Andy Serkis through motion-capture technology, and sweeping landscape scenes made them a hit.

Elijah Wood plays Frodo, an earnest hobbit who becomes the unlikely leader of a group that includes Viggo Mortensen as a mysterious wanderer, Orlando Bloom as a haughty elf, Sean Astin as Frodo's adoring friend Sam, and Sir Ian McKellen as the sage wizard Gandalf. As the heroes are split apart during the course of the story, all are forced to overcome themselves in order to defy the ultimate evil, Sauron. The films were nominated for 13 Oscars and won four.

The Lord of the Rings Trilogy

Alfonso Cuarón

1961, Mexico City

■ Equally at home in children's movies and edgy art films ■ Heads New Mexican Cinema with Guillermo del Toro, Alejandro González Iñárritu, and Guillermo Arriaga ■ Interested in political issues of globalization ■ Mexican ■ Drama, Comedy, Fantasy ■ Directed 7 films

■ **1961** Born in Mexico

1973 Receives his first camera as a birthday gift

1983 Makes two shorts, *Vengeance Is Mine* and *Who's He Anyway*

1988 Directs six episodes of the Mexican science-fiction TV show *Hora Marcada*

1991 Debut film, *Sólo Con Tu Pareja*

1993 Sydney Pollack asks him to direct two episodes of *Fallen Angels*

2006 Participates in the omnibus film *Paris, Je T'Aime*

2007 Co-writes his son Jonás's short Naomi Klein documentary *The Shock Doctrine*

After seeing Cuarón's stylish and sexy comedy *Sólo Con Tu Pareja*, director Sydney Pollack (p. 278) gave him his first chance—working on a TV show in the United States. His first English-language film, *A Little Princess*, earned critical acclaim and Cuarón's frequent collaborator Emmanuel Lubezki's sumptuous cinematography was widely celebrated. After a disappointing experience directing the Charles Dickens adaptation *Great Expectations* for 20th Century Fox, Cuarón returned to Mexico to make *Y Tu Mamá También*. The road movie's candid depiction of teen sexuality and its subtle political undercurrent won him many accolades and soon Warner Bros. executives offered Cuarón the chance to direct a *Harry Potter* film. For two years, the director would work on a film that was to receive the best critical reception of the Potter series to date. Cuarón used his newfound commercial leverage to make the politically charged science-fiction/action film *Children of Men*.

■ **Children of Men**, 2006, starring Clive Owen and Julianne Moore

The stunning, seemingly single-take action sequences in this adaptation of P. D. James's dystopic novel about global infertility were actually a combination of painstaking choreography, advanced camera technology, and a little computer-generated imagery. The scenes deliver a visceral intensity through their raw sense of realistic immersion

■ Harry Potter and the Prisoner of Azkaban, 2004, starring Daniel Radcliffe and Alan Rickman

Cuarón was a daring choice for the third film based on J. K. Rowling's wildly successful series of books. The studio's gamble not only paid off in box-office receipts, but critics recognized a darker tone in the film that paralleled underlying themes in the book, and Cuarón was credited with helping the *Harry Potter* films to mature, keeping pace with the young wizard protagonists struggling into adolescence on-screen.

Other Works

Sólo Con Tu Pareja, 1991, starring Daniel Giménez Cacho

A Little Princess, 1995, starring Liesel Matthews

Great Expectations, 1998, starring Ethan Hawke and Gwyneth Paltrow

■ Y Tu Mamá También, 2001, starring Gael García Bernal and Diego Luna

One of the most celebrated New Mexican Cinema films, *Y Tu Mamá También* is the story of two teenagers who convince a sexy older woman to join them on a road trip . Their romantic triangle develops unexpected conse-quences. At key points on their road trip, Cuarón adds small narrative digressions offering topical political commentary.

Alfonso Cuarón

Alejandro González Iñárritu

1963, Mexico City

■ Often juggles story lines that take place in different social classes, or even continents ■ Films are often concerned with globalization ■ Influenced by Quentin Tarantino, Lars von Trier, and Wong Kar-Wai
■ Mexican ■ Drama ■ Directed 4 films

1963 Born in Mexico

1984 Becomes a radio DJ at Mexico's WFM

1989 Composes the score for Hernando Name's *Garra de Tigre*

1991 Begins directing advertisements after setting up his own production company, Zeta Films

1995 Directs his first short, *Detrás del Dinero*

2000 His debut film, *Amores Perros*, wins two awards at Cannes

2002 Works on the Mexico segment of *11'09"01— September 11*

2006 Becomes the first Mexican to be nominated for a Best Director Oscar

Lauded by critics for his stylistic verve and narrative skill Iñárritu takes a deeply serious approach to filmmaking. O his Mexican contemporaries—Alfonso Cuarón (p. 428 Guillermo del Toro, and Guillermo Arriaga—he is the mo: committed to portraying the negative effects of globaliza tion and modern man's failure to communicate despit advances in communication technologies. His interde pendent characters are only linked through their action their class or cultural differences prevent them from co: necting as humans. A directors' director, he has clearl learned from the best; his saturated imagery is reminiscer of Wong Kar-Wai (p. 442) and his rigorous cinematograph and cultural pessimism resemble Lars von Trier's (p. 456 Though his deft juggling of story lines owes something t Quentin Tarantino's (p. 416) *Pulp Fiction* (1994), one ca also recognize the influence of other great directors wh have portrayed Mexican underworlds: Luis Buñuel (p. 228 Arturo Ripstein, and Alejandro Jodorowsky.

■ **21 Grams**, 2003, starring Naomi Watts and Benicio Del Toro

Three couples' lives are forever altered by a freak car accident. The director (and his co-writer Guillermo Arriaga) reveal the story in nonchronological piece building a narrative tension tha heightens the film's ultimate, heartbreaking revelation of the crash's details. Iñárritu named h stunningly edited film after the alleged weight of the soul.

A World of Cinema 1990–Today

■ **Babel**, 2006, starring Brad Pitt and Rinko Kikuchi

Spanning five continents and filmed in as many languages, this ensemble drama shows links in a globalized web of coincidence and culture clash. It also stars Cate Blanchett and Gael García Bernal.

Other Works	
El Timbre, 1996, starring Damián Alcázar	**Mexico** (segment in *11'09"01 — September 11*), 2002
Powder Keg (short), 2001, starring Clive Owen and Stellan Skarsgård	**Anna** (segment in *To Each His Cinema*), 2007, starring Luisa Williams

Amores Perros, 2000, starring Gael García ▸rnal and Emilio Echevarría

▸ in his second film, *21 Grams*, Iñárritu connects ▸e three narrative strands of his debut with a ▸r crash. With cinematographer Rodrigo ▸ieto, he used different color schemes ▸r each of the Mexico City–set stories. ▸ough reminiscent of Tarantino's ▸sjointed, violent *Pulp Fiction*, ▸árritu's style is more rooted in ▸elodrama and Social ▸alism.

Pedro Almodóvar

1949, Calzada de Calatrava

■ Self-taught but influenced by Douglas Sirk, Rainer Werner Fassbinder, and Federico Fellini ■ Photography and sets are painted in primary hues
■ Foregrounds female solidarity and empowerment
■ Spanish ■ Melodrama, Comedy ■ Directed 17 films

■ **1949** Born in a small town in Spain

1968 Moves to Madrid

1972 Starts making short films

1978 Makes his first 8 mm feature, *Folle... Folle... Fólleme Tim!*

1980 Directs his first film on 35 mm, *Pepi, Luci, Bom and Other Girls on the Heap*

1987 Starts production company El Deseo with his brother Agustín and wins a Teddy at the Berlin Film Festival for *Law of Desire*

1990 A legal battle around the US release of *Tie Me Up! Tie Me Down!* results in the new NC-17 rating

2002 *Talk to Her* wins an Oscar for Best Original Screenplay

After moving to Madrid at the end of the 1960s, Almodóvar spent the dictatorship of Franco making money by selling secondhand wares at flea markets and working at the national telephone company. In his free time he was a major figure in the bustling Madrid art and gay scene, working on satirical cartoons and journalism, participating in experimental theater, and even performing in a glam-rock duo. Almodóvar's work is imbued with colorful camp sensibility—an ironic heightening of old-fashioned conventions that is intended to subvert those very conventions. Almodóvar's typically vibrant, primary hues and hysterical plots are even more shocking and daring than Douglas Sirk's 1950s wide-screen melodramas. Like Sirk, Almodóvar favors female protagonists usually played by his muses Carmen Maura, Victoria Abril, and Penélope Cruz, granting them an independence and dramatic strength that creates characters of rare emotional force.

■ **All About My Mother**, 1999 starring Cecilia Roth and Marisa Paredes

Almodóvar's first film to perfectly balance his gift for heartbreaking melodrama and his more outrageous impulses, the film is a< story of grief in the Barcelona transsexual scene. The script, though rife with coincidence and parody, portrays its characters honestly. Penélope Cruz shines in her small part as a nun with a deadly secret.

Women on the Verge of a Nervous Breakdown, 1988, starring Carmen Maura and Antonio Banderas

Scripted like an out-of-control screwball comedy, the director combines outrageous plots involving adultery and terrorism, yet preserves his female protagonists' integrity and dignity within the logic of his candy-colored soap-opera universe. In one scene, Almodóvar pays tribute to the radical colors and feminist sensibility of director Nicholas Ray by showing Carmen Maura dub a scene from *Johnny Guitar* (1954) in Spanish.

Volver, 2006, starring Penélope Cruz and Carmen Maura

After a series of big-budget Hollywood roles, Cruz returned to Spain for this restrained comedy about life, death, and celebration of women's solidarity. When Raimunda's (Cruz) daughter kills her abusive alcoholic boyfriend in self-defense, Raimunda's deceased mother (Maura) is forced to return from the afterlife to help her and the other women in their family regain control over their lives.

Other Works

Live Flesh, 1997, starring Javier Bardem

Talk To Her, 2002, starring Javier Cámara

Bad Education, 2004, starring Gael García Bernal

Pedro Almodóvar

Animation

■ Techniques include stop-motion, hand-drawn, Claymation, rotoscoping, 2-D and 3-D digital animation, or combinations ■ Mostly aimed at children, but some animators also address adult themes ■ A global phenomenon with prominent styles hailing from the United States, Japan, and Czech Republic
■ *left:* **Ratatouille**, by Brad Bird and Jan Pinkava, 2007

■ **1906** The first animation is created by J. Stuart Blackton

1921 Walter Ruttmann makes the first abstract animation, *Opus 1*

1928 Mickey Mouse comes to life in *Steamboat Willie*

1937 Marlene Dietrich attends the premiere of *Snow White and the Seven Dwarfs*

1945 Salvador Dalí collaborates with Disney on *Destino*, finished in 2003

1986 Pixar animation studios is founded

1988 The success of *Akira* leads to a worldwide surge of interest in Japanese anime

2007 *Beowulf* uses motion-captured acting

Other Works

Akira, by Katsuhiro Ōtomo, 1988

The Nightmare Before Christmas, by Henry Selick, 1993

The Fall, (short) by Aurel Klimt,1999

Shrek, by Andrew Adamson and Vicky Jenson, 2001

The Incredibles, by Brad Bird, 2004

A World of Cinema 1990–Today

Since the early years of the 20th century, American animators have made short animations by transferring a series of sequential drawings on film and projecting them to suggest movement. Apart from Walt Disney (p. 130), other innovators of the technique include Winsor McCay (*Little Nemo*, 1911), Max Fleischer (*Betty Boop*, 1930), and Tex Avery (*Looney Tunes* series, begun in 1935). Considered purely entertainment in the United States, animation first took on more adult themes behind the Iron Curtain. Czech animators like Jiří Trnka and later Jan Švankmajer pioneered animated adult, political themes in their Surrealist stop-motion works, which combine puppets with real-life backgrounds and props. Though an established practice since 1907 in Japan, anime gained a larger fan base with the growing popularity of manga comic books since the 1970s. Here too, subjects range from dramatic to futuristic, violent to erotic. Contemporary animation has been largely shaped by the use of computers to aid in their creation.

■ **Nick Park and Bob Baker: Wallace and Gromit—A Close Shave**, 1996

While washing windows, Wallace falls in love with a shop owner. Meanwhile, his intrepid but mute dog Gromit is arrested for the murder of a sheep and a zany series of events ensues. Executed in plasticine, *Wallace and Gromit—A Close Shave* was filmed using stop-motion animation.

■ John Lasseter: Toy Story, 1995

This first entirely computer-generated feature animation was produced by Disney and Steve Jobs's Pixar Studios, a company born from George Lucas's Industrial Light and Magic effects studio. It tells the story of what happens when a child is not watching their toys—they come alive. A boy's favorite toy, cowboy Woody (voiced by Tom Hanks), flares in jealousy when he is replaced by the shiny new astronaut Buzz Lightyear (voiced by Tim Allen). Their competition for the boy's attentions parallels the waning popularity of westerns in the 1950s and the growing success of the science fiction genre. TV's *Buffy*-creator Joss Whedon contributed to the hilarious script.

■ Marjane Satrapi and Vincent Paronnaud: Persepolis, 2007

Animated in luscious black and white, *Persepolis* is the touching story of an outspoken girl coming of age in Iran, but who is exiled to Austria. The political message led to controversy upon the film's release.

▲ Robert Zemeckis: Beowulf, 2007

Based on the epic poem dating back as far as the 8th century, this animated IMAX 3-D feature was made using motion-capture technology similar to that used in bringing *The Lord of the Rings*'s Gollum to life. The animators used actors such as Angelina Jolie to capture movements, even their facial expressions, and transform them into all-digital counterparts. Revolutionary for its use of computer-generated actors, *Beowulf* blurs the line between animation and nonanimated films, reality and the magic of cinema.

Animation

Hayao Miyazaki

1941, Tokyo

■ Often features optimistic young girls as heroes ■ Does not use much computer-generated imagery, preferring hand-drawn animation instead ■ His childlike, often illogical narratives have mystical undertones
■ Japanese ■ Animated Children's Drama, Fantasy ■ Directed 12 films

1941 Born in Japan

1963 Graduates with a degree in political science and economics, and starts work as an animator

1965 Marries fellow animator Akemi Ota

1969 Publishes his first manga comic, *Puss in Boots*

1978 Directs his first TV series, *Future Boy Conan*

1979 Makes his first feature, *The Castle of Cagliostro*

1985 Cofounds Studio Ghibli

2006 His son Goro directs his first film, *Tales From Earthsea*

The dreamlike, associative quality of Miyazaki's films is a direct consequence of his creative process; he never works from a script, always confident that the story will come as he starts sketching the storyboards. His flowing style was inspired by animators Paul Grimault, Yuri Norstein, and Lev Atamanov. Ever since 1984's *Nausicäa of the Valley of the Wind*, his optimistic girl protagonists seem rooted in Astrid Lindgren's Pippi Longstocking archetype. Apart from the 1930s-set air-pirates film *Porco Rosso*, all his work is aimed at children, even if its scenes of violence might scare off more squeamish Western parents. Miyazaki and his Studio Ghibli gained international recognition when Miramax released *Princess Mononoke* in the United States, and *Spirited Away* won a Golden Bear as well as an Oscar.

■ **Spirited Away**, 2001

This answer to *Alice in Wonderland* sees a spoiled young girl disappear into a mysterious world populated by witches and spirits. Although his films are aimed at children, Miyazaki's characters are not morally simplistic, and his plots do not end with evil's destruction, but with reconciliation.

Other Works

Nausicäa of the Valley of the Wind, 1984

Castle in the Sky, 1986

My Neighbor Totoro, 1988

Kiki's Delivery Service, 1989

Porco Rosso, 1992

Princess Mononoke, 1997

This environmental parable is set during a crucial time in Japanese history—the onset of the Iron Age when gunpowder and industrialization were wreaking havoc on the country and its people. As the complex story progresses, ancient forest deities join the fray and the two young heroes are forced to choose sides in a mystical battle between tradition and modernity.

Howl's Moving Castle, 2004

Less futuristic or dystopian than contemporaries Katsuhiro Otomo (*Akira*, 1988) or Mamoru Oshii (*Ghost in the Shell*, 1995), Miyazaki is committed to the internal realism of his fantasy worlds, adding small details even to the edges of his frames. This magical film was based on the book by Diana Wynne Jones, and was the director's first literary adaptation.

Hayao Miyazaki

Digital Technology and Big Budgets

After the success of Steven Spielberg (p. 354) and George Lucas's (p. 358) 1980s films, producers like Jerry Bruckheimer (Tony Scott: *Top Gun*, 1986) and director Michael Bay (*Armageddon*, 1998; *Transformers*, 2007) ushered in the era of the summer blockbusters that celebrated masculine consumerism and violence. With studios scrambling for the biggest stars and explosions, budgets ballooned. Studios stumbled when budgets started to exceed $150 million and digital technology was used to create even flashier effects. Films like Kevin Reynolds's *Waterworld* (1995, above) or Chris Weitz's *The Golden Compass* (2007) were called flops when they did not immediately recoup the huge investments in production and promotion.

Technology can be used to sew together shots from different cameras, like those positioned around Keanu Reeves in *The Matrix* (1999, below right). Director Zack Snyder went even further in *300* (2006, right), using CGI to create the entire set.

The development of motion capture technology allows all-digital characters to look more lifelike. Sensors that capture movement are placed on actors' bodies and translate reality into a 3-D digital image, infusing them with the spontaneity of live performance. The failure of Douglas Corrigan's *The Polar Express* (2004) was blamed on the characters' lifeless eyes, a problem remedied in Peter Jackson's *King Kong* (2005) through the use of "electro oculography." Actor Andy Serkis (Gollum in *The Lord of the Rings*, 2001, pictured) was fitted with three sensors around his eyes to create King Kong's every blink.

Zhang Yimou

1950, Xi'an

- A Chinese Fifth Generation director along with Chen Kaige and Tian Zhuang zhuang ■ Taoism plays a major role in his stories ■ Trained as a cinematographer ■ Imagery characterized by bold colors and perfect symmetrical framing ■ Chinese ■ Drama, Historical, Martial Arts ■ Directed 14 films

New Asian Masters

- **1950** Born in the Shaanxi province of China
- **1978** Petitions the government to enroll in film school
- **1982** Graduates from Beijing Film Academy
- **1984** Shoots Chen Kaige's seminal *Yellow Earth*
- **1986** Stars in Wu Tian-Ming's *Old Well*
- **1988** Wins the Golden Bear at Berlin for his directorial debut, *Red Sorghum*
- **1991** *Raise the Red Lantern* nominated for an Oscar
- **2006** Produces composer Tan Dun's opera *The First Emperor* in New York
- **2008** Commissioned for the opening and closing ceremonies of the Beijing Olympics

When the Beijing Film Academy reopened its doors i 1978 after 12 years of forced closure by Chairman Mao Cultural Revolution, its first class, graduating in 198. would be known as the Fifth Generation. Tian Zhuang zhuang (*The Blue Kite*, 1993) and Chen Kaige (*Farewell M Concubine*, 1993) graduated as directors and Zhang Yimo as a cinematographer. Zhang would shoot four films, in cluding Chen's *Yellow Earth* (1984) before making his ow debut, *Red Sorghum* (1987). His work is visually characte ized by its bold colors and composed, symmetric framing. Ideologically, his work can be interpreted a Taoist in the sense that it is not morally black and white

Zhang's international success paved the way fo Sixth Generation directors such as Jia Zhang K (*The World*, 2004), Wang Xioashuai (*Froze* 1996), Lou Ye (*Suhzou River*, 2000), and Zhan Yuan (*East Palace, West Palace*, 1996).

■ **Raise the Red Lantern**, 1991, starring Gong Li

The Fifth Generation filmmakers turned away from traditional Chinese Neo-Realism, choosing politically challenging new paths. The negative reaction to the Tiananmen Square protest forced directors to take a new, indirect approach. Zhang's Tech nicolor masterpiece about a fourth wife's struggles to fit in can be read as an allegory of Communist authoritarianism.

■ **Hero**, 2002, starring Jet Li and Zhang Ziyi

The first in his series of three martial arts epics (*House of Flying Daggers* and *Curse of the Golden Flower*), *Hero*'s elegant battle scenes were completely new terrain for Zhang. Its *Rashômon*-like narrative is composed of different characters' perspectives. The Asian all-star cast reunited Maggie Cheung with *In the Mood for Love*'s Tony Leung and their cinematographer Christopher Doyle.

■ **To Live**, 1994, starring Gong Li and Ge You

The sixth film of the eight Zhang would make with his muse and lover Gong Li, *To Live* follows a resilient family's troubled existence through the 1940s to the 1960s' Cultural Revolution. The film's stark realism and political message caused it to be banned in China.

Wong Kar-Wai

1958, Shanghai

■ Often collaborates with cinematographer Christopher Doyle, using an expressive color palette and sped-up and slowed-down imagery ■ Works without scripts ■ Eccentric use of Western pop songs and operatic soundtracks ■ Chinese ■ Drama, Martial Arts ■ Directed 9 films

1958 Born in China

1963 Emigrates to Hong Kong

1980 Enrolls in a screen-writing program after studying graphic design

1982 His first feature script is filmed

1987 Writes the script for Patrick Tam's *Final Victory*

1988 Directorial debut, *As Tears Go By*

1994 Releases *Ashes of Time*

1997 Wins Best Director at Cannes for *Happy Together*

2006 Presides over the Cannes jury

2007 Presents *Ashes of Time* redux in Berlin

More acclaimed than first-wave Hong Kong directors like John Woo (*The Killer*, 1989), Tsui Hark (*Once Upon a Time in China*, 1991), or Johnny To (*Election*, 2005), who make more commercially palatable work, Wong's films have consistently been ranked very high on all-time best films lists. His themes are mostly romantic, dealing with love affairs long past or attractions left unanswered. Set in bustling cities, his films often move between countries, a metaphor for the displacement of the Hong Kong identity since its British colonial days and the 1997 handover to China. Stylistically, his work with cinematographer Christopher Doyle—who also worked with Gus Van Sant (p. 398), Pen-Ek Ratanaruang, and Phillip Noyce—is characterized by bold hues, color grading, and daring film-speed manipulation, creating a whirl of visual energy.

Since Wong never works from a finished script, he can discover his stories as he is filming. This loose approach can sometimes lead to production delays, such as on *In the Mood for Love*, which took two years to film and was barely finished when it screened at Cannes.

■ **2046**, 2004, starring Tony Leung

Leung returns to Hong Kong in this evocative sequel to *In The Mood for Love*. While he is sequestered in hotel room 2047 writing a science-fiction novel, the room next to his hosts a series of women (Carina Lau, Faye Wong, Zhang Ziyi, and Gong Li) who are also still wrapped up in the loss of past love affairs. Christopher Doyle did the camera work.

■ **In the Mood for Love**, 2000, starring Tony Leung and Maggie Cheung

In the cultural whirlpool of 1960s Hong Kong, a man and a woman rent neighboring apartments. When they both learn their partners are cheating on them, they embark on a very tentative affair. Shot in rich, expressionistic hues, the film builds its tragically romantic tension through the use of slow motion and repetition. Cheung wears a different figure-hugging cheongsam in every shot. The cryptic ending is set in Angkor Wat, Cambodia.

Other Works
Fallen Angels, 1995, starring Leon Lai
Happy Together, 1997, starring Tony Leung
My Blueberry Nights, 2007, starring Norah Jones

■ **Chungking Express**, 1994, starring Faye Wong and Takeshi Kaneshiro

Two Hong Kong cops wander the streets pining for the women they love. The women have their own agendas, one smuggling people, the other breaking and entering. Establishing Wong's singular style, this energetic, two-part romantic comedy was inspired by Jean-Luc Godard's improvisational approach. Western pop songs, or Chinese covers of them, feature heavily on the soundtrack, often repeatedly. The film's original third act was later released as *Fallen Angels*.

Ang Lee

1954, Pingtun

■ Deft at depicting familial intimacy ■ Renowned for his calm and restrained images ■ Mastery of a variety of genres ■ Makes films in English and Chinese ■ Producer James Schamus often writes or co-writes his films ■ Taiwanese-American ■ Drama, Action ■ Directed 10 films

1954 Born in Taiwan

1975 Graduates from art school in Taiwan

1983 Assists Spike Lee on his thesis film

1984 Earns his MFA from New York University

1992 First feature, *Pushing Hands*, in the US

1993 Golden Bear in Berlin for *The Wedding Banquet*

1995 *Sense and Sensibility* nominated for seven Oscars, wins one

1999 His Civil War drama *Ride with the Devil* flopped

2000 *Crouching Tiger, Hidden Dragon* wins four Oscars out of 10 nominations

2005 Best Director Oscar for *Brokeback Mountain*

■ **Eat Drink Man Woman**, 1994, starring Sihung Lung

When a master chef is forced to retire, he learns his three daughters might have outgrown his kitchen, and his advice. Lee's first film shot in Taiwan, this story features a wistful nostalgia for cultural traditions, but also makes a case for intergenerational tolerance. It was remade in 2001 by María Ripoll as *Tortilla Soup*.

Hailing from Taiwan, Ang Lee is the most commercially and internationally successful director of his more artistic contemporaries like Edward Yang (*Yi Yi: A One and a Two*, 2000), Hou Hsiao-Hsien (*Flowers of Shanghai*, 1998), and Tsai Ming-Liang (*Goodbye, Dragon Inn*, 2003). Where his first three comedic dramas, starting with 1992's *Pushing Hands*, explicitly deal with Taiwanese and Chinese issues, his later work touches on all kinds of subjects and genres from Jane Austen's ironic romance *Sense and Sensibility*, to the Civil War epic *Ride with the Devil*, and even the superhero drama *Hulk*. Though he is renowned for his composed images, his real strength is dramatic narrative. His films, always written or co-written by Focus Features producer James Schamus (except in the Oscar-winning cases of Emma Thompson's *Sense and Sensibility* and Larry McMurtry and Diana Ossana's *Brokeback Mountain*), have a great eye for intimate family detail.

■ **Crouching Tiger, Hidden Dragon**, 2000, starring Chow Yun Fat and Michelle Yeoh

Lee's first martial arts epic adds a poetic spirituality to the genre, while retaining its narrative expression. Even the gravity-taunting action sequences, by *Matrix* choreographer Yuen Woo-Ping, float with the grace of a Fred Astaire musical.

Other Works

The Wedding Banquet, 1993, starring Winston Chao

Sense And Sensibility, 1995, starring Kate Winslet

The Ice Storm, 1997, starring Elijah Wood

Hulk, 2003, starring Eric Bana

■ **Brokeback Mountain**, 2005, starring Jake Gyllenhaal and Heath Ledger

This elegiac tale of an impossible love between two manly cowboys was adapted from Annie Proulx's novella. Though its reception was controversial, the film itself is understated and the acting restrained. Set in the 1960s and 70s, the story follows the men from their first, charged encounter as they camp out on a mountaintop, through their later, yearly "fishing trips," and the affair's tragic end. Lee uses the raw and remote Wyoming landscape as a metaphor for the men's primal passions.

Bollywood and Beyond

■ A history as old and rich as Hollywood's ■ Bollywood films features lavish musical sequences overdubbed by famous singers ■ Not confined to Hollywood's genre boundaries ■ Longer running times, up to four hours ■ Melodramatic performances ■ Reminiscent of the American films by Vincente Minnelli
■ *left*: **Mother India**, by Mehboob Khan, 1957, starring Nargis

1896 The Lumière brothers screen silent shorts in Mumbai

1913 *Raja Harishchandra*, the first silent Indian film

1931 First sound film, *Alam Ara*, is a huge hit

1957 *Mother India* nominated for an Oscar

1996 Deepa Mehta's *Fire* causes great controversy

2006 *Krrish*, the first Indian superhero film

2007 Navdeep Singh remakes Roman Polanski's *Chinatown*

A portmanteau of Bombay and Hollywood, 'Bollywood' has uncomfortably come to denote the entire Indian film industry, responsible for about 1,000 films a year and entertaining nearly 14 million viewers a day. With its history as rich and long as Western cinema's, and counting eight different languages, it would be reductive to state that the following characteristics apply to all Indian films. Still, what sets Bollywood apart are its three-to-four-hour running times, exuberant musical numbers, and melodramatic performances. Genre boundaries are not as rigid as in Hollywood, with comedic and dramatic moments appearing throughout crime, historical, or even horror films. The plentiful musical performances are always dubbed, with original performers like Lata Mangeshkar, Asha Boshle, and Geeta Dutt often earning top billing in movie advertisements.

■ **Sanjay Leela Bhansali: Devdas**, 2002, starring Madhuri Dixit and Shahrukh Khan

After his return from a long stay in the UK, Devdas's true love is married off to a stiff aristocrat and he looks for comfort in the arms of an adoring prostitute. The third, and first color, adaptation of a 1917 novella, this musical melodrama was the most expensive film ever made in India at 500 million rupees.

■ **Ashutosh Gowariker: Lagaan**, 2001, starring Aamir Khan and Gracy Singh

The third Hindi film to be nominated for a Foreign Language Oscar, this 1893-set story revolves around a tense cricket match between cruel British officers and a

■ **Deepa Mehta: Water**, 2005, starring Sarala and Seema Biswas

Not traditional Bollywood in any sense, each of the films in Mehta's *Elements* trilogy (*Fire*, *Earth*, and *Water*) caused considerable controversy in India over their frank discussion of sociocultural and political issues and, in the case of *Water*, the oppressive treatment of widows under Hindu law .

first-time team of poor villagers. They play over their exorbitantly raised land tax, or *lagaan*. If its plot mechanics are familiar from the Hollywood underdog sports dramas, the film's drought-stricken landscape and political subtext add poignancy.

Other Works

The Tramp, by Raj Kapoor, 1951, starring Nargis and Prithviraj Kapoor

Sholay, by Ramesh Sippy, 1975, starring Dharmendra and Amitabh Bachchan

Mira Nair

1957, Bhubaneshwar

■ Vivid colors reminiscent of Bollywood films ■ Often features strong female characters and comedy ■ Often focuses on second-generation immigrants ■ Politically engaged in stimulating independent Indian and African cinema ■ Indian ■ Drama, Comedy, Documentary ■ Directed 9 films

■ **1957** Born in the province of Orissa

1976 Studies sociology at Harvard

1979 Graduates in film; first short documentary, *Jama Masjid Street Journal*

1985 Documentary about Bombay strippers, *India Cabaret*

1988 Directs her first feature, *Salaam Bombay!*

2002 Heads the jury at the Berlin Film Festival

2003 Uma Thurman wins a Golden Globe for her role in *Hysterical Blindness*

After stumbling into documentary filmmaking during a summer course in photography at Harvard, Nair worked with legendary directors Richard Leacock and D. A. Pennebaker. Though she made several short and feature films on specifically Indian issues, her success as a filmmaker came with her first fiction film. Co-written by Sooni Taraporevala, with whom Nair would work three more times, *Salaam Bombay!*'s elements of "cinéma verité" gave its narrative a documentary-like feel of urgency that was hailed around the world. Her later work is inspired by the rich palette of Bollywood, but it also does not shy away from political commentary on race, gender, and class. Her fiercely independent female characters take center stage in gently comic dramas.

■ **Salaam Bombay!**, 1988, starring Shafiq Syed

Nominated for an Best Foreign Language Film Oscar, this realistic, but hopeful film was shot on Mumbai's streets, cast with almost 24 actual street children.

▶ **Vanity Fair**, 2004, starring Reese Witherspoon and Eileen Atkins

Based on the novel by William Thackeray, also born in India, this satirical tale revolves around 19th-century social climber Becky Sharp.

A World of Cinema 1990–Today

Monsoon Wedding, 2001, starring Vasundhara Das and Naseeruddin Shah

Shot in just 30 days, Nair conceived this ensemble drama about an arranged Delhi marriage with her Columbia University teaching assistant, Sabrina Dhawan. Unlike in Bollywood films, the song and dance here is logically integrated in the narrative. When it won the Golden Lion in Venice, Nair became the first woman to receive the award and the second Indian (after Satyajit Ray's *Aparajito* in 1957).

■ **The Namesake**, 2006, starring Kal Penn and Zuleikha Robinson

Adapted from the Pulitzer Prize–winning novel by Jhumpa Lahiri, this film deftly tells the multigenerational story of the Gangulis, immigrants from Calcutta to New York. As in *Mississippi Masala*, Nair focuses on the cross-cultural difficulties a second-generation immigrant experiences, feeling neither Indian, nor American. The Gangulis' struggling son, Gogol, played by *Harold & Kumar Go to White Castle*'s comic star Penn, takes that role here.

Mira Nair

New African Cinema

■ Native African film production only started after the colonial era in the late 1950s ■ Very heterogeneous film culture ■ Some directors continue ancient oral storytelling, or *griot*, traditions on film ■ Nigeria has quickly become the world's third largest producer of films

■ *left:* **Moolaadé**, by Ousmane Sembène, 2004, starring Fatoumata Coulibaly

1954 Egyptian director Youssef Chahine first casts Omar Sharif in *The Blazing Sun*

1965 Senegalese director Ousmane Sembène directs the first native African film, *Black Girl*

1969 The FESPACO African Film Festival is founded in Burkina Faso

1973 Djibril Diop Mambéty releases the Senegalese comedy *Touki Bouki*

1982 Gaston Taboré directs one of the first Burkinabé films, *God's Gift*

2007 Ousmane Sembène dies at age 84

Though Egypt's film industry was active in the 1930s, film production in the rest of the continent only became possible in the postcolonial era. Senegal was at the forefront with pioneers Djibril Diop Mambéty and Ousmane Sembène (*Xala*, 1975), whose debut predates that of African-American filmmakers by three years. Burkina Faso's Idrissa Ouedraogo (*Yaaba*, 1989) and Dani Kouyaté (*Këita! Voice of the Griot*, 1994) continue ancient *griot*—oral storytelling—traditions. In 1992, Cameroon's Jean-Pierre Bekolo made the first urban African film, *Quartier Mozart*. Over the last 15 years, Nigeria has become the site of the world's fastest growing film industry. Enabled by cheaper digital technologies, "Nollywood" directors like Izu Ojukwu and Chico Ejiro contribute to an industry that produces more than 200 straight-to-DVD films a month, ranging in theme from horror to romantic comedies.

■ **Youssef Chahine: Destiny**, 1997, starring Nour El-Cherif

Forty years after *Cairo Station*, Egyptian director Chahine filmed the life of exiled 12th-century philosopher Averroes. With musical scenes filmed in Lebanon and Syria, the film conveys a message against intolerance.

Other Works

Hyenas, by Djibril Diop Mambéty, 1992, starring Ami Diakhate

The Silences of the Palace, by Moufida Tlatli, 1994, starring Amel Hedhili

U-Carmen, by Mark Dornford-May, 2005, starring Pauline Malefane

Bamako, by Abderrahmane Sissako, 2006, starring Aïssa Maïga

■ **Mahamat-Saleh Haroun: Dry Season**, 2006, starring Ali Bacha Barkai and Youssouf Djaoro

After a government amnesty sets Chad's civil war criminals free, a mourning grandfather sends his grandson to the city to murder the man who killed his son. Before the boy can approach him, the childless murderer, now an exemplary, kind citizen, offers him a job. Soon the men are working alongside each other in his bakery, their violent pasts smoldering just below the surface. Sparsely narrated by the boy, this solemn and austere film makes a powerful point about reconciliation in a country torn apart during 30 years of war.

■ **Gavin Hood: Tsotsi**, 2005, starring Presley Chweneyagae and Terry Pheto

A hardened young thug kills a woman and steals her car, but when he finds it holds a baby, he cannot bring himself to kill it. With the forced help of a neighboring woman, the thug starts on his rocky, and slightly sentimental path to redemption. One of the most famous African films, *Tsotsi* won an Academy Award for Best Foreign Film.

New African Cinema

Abbas Kiarostami

1940, Tehran

■ Documentary style with long takes of daily life often set in rural areas of Iran
■ Threat of censorship deflects all suggestions of his films' political messages back to the audience ■ Part of the Iranian New Wave
■ Iranian ■ Drama ■ Directed 14 films

Kiarostami is the best-known director of the Iranian New Wave, which started during the 1970s and counts among its filmmakers Majid Majidi, Mohsen Makhmalbaf, and his daughter Samira Makhmalbaf. Similar to the Italian Neo-Realists in its episodic storytelling and focus on Social Realism, the style is poetic and has a painterly sensibility. Though never overtly political, an impossibility in Iran, Kiarostami's work, focusing on human resilience, is often set in or near contested areas such as Afghanistan and Kurdistan; his films are certainly understood politically in the West. Critics suggest that his poetic and often self-reflexive style is a response to censorship. *Ten*, which was improvised and shot in a Tehran cab with a mainly female cast, creatively offers women's voices a chance to be heard outside Iran.

The Wind Will Carry Us, 1999, starring Behzad Dorani

Under the pretense of being on a telecommunications project, a group of engineers travels from Tehran to a tiny Kurdish mountain hamlet to chronicle their mourning traditions. As they wait for the town's centenarian to pass away, life continues around them, enabling the viewers to witness daily life for Iran's Kurdish minority. The impatient protagonist, who at one point flips a turtle upside-down to be spared its slow trek, is ultimately lectured by an old doctor on the value in observing nature, defining death as what happens when "you close your eyes on the beauty of the world." Kiarostami's focus on the dialectic between life and death is set against the foreground of the beauty in the mundane. As in much of his work, many characters remain offscreen. *The Wind Will Carry Us*'s imagery references some of Iran's most famous poetry.

Taste of Cherry, 1997, starring Homayoun Ershadi

A man decides he wants to end his life, and drives into the countryside to find someone who will bury him. When he finds a candidate, he takes the man for a ride. Hypnotically shot from a distance, one sees his car wind through the dusty hills, and hears the conversation. A succession of men—a soldier, a laborer, and a seminarist who are all in their own way familiar with death—decline. Finally a taxidermist agrees. After the man lies down in a ditch and closes his eyes, Kiarostami audaciously cuts to fuzzy footage of the film's crew shooting in the hills. The supposedly dead man smokes a cigarette while the crew records background sound. The title refers to the idea that the smallest pleasures can bring back one's lust for life.

Other Works

Close-Up, 1990, starring Mohsen Makhmalbaf

Life, and Nothing More, 1991, starring Farhad Kheradmand and Buba Bayour

Through the Olive Trees, 1994, starring Mohamad Ali Keshavarz

Ten, 2002, starring Mania Akbari

Tickets, 2005, starring Carlo Delle Piane, Valeria Bruni Tedeschi, and Silvana De Santis

Abbas Kiarostami

Dogme 95

■ Founded by Thomas Vinterberg and Lars von Trier ■ Shot on location with handheld cameras with sound and image produced at the same time ■ Director credits, added props or music, artificial lighting, and genre films were not allowed ■ Dogme's style put the actor at the center
■ *left:* **Mifune**, by Søren Kragh-Jacobsen, 1999, starring Iben Hjejle

■ **1995** Dogme 95 founded at the "Le Cinéma Vers Son Deuxième Siècle" conference in Paris
1998 *The Celebration* is the first certified Dogme film
1999 Actor/director Jean-Marc Barr makes first non-Danish Dogme film, *Lovers*
1999 Thomas Vinterberg directs Blur's *No Distance Left to Run* video
2002 After 31 films, certification is deemed no longer necessary and the Dogme movement effectively breaks up

Inspired by the possibilities of digital cameras and incensed by formulaic filmmaking, Thomas Vinterberg and Lars von Trier (p. 456) drafted the Dogme 95 manifesto, containing a list of stylistic rules that forced directors to scale down and rethink what had become a bulky enterprise. The ten rules for Dogme certification concern production as well as script: "The sound must never be produced apart from the images or vice versa," and "the film takes place here and now." Shooting with handheld cameras on location, using only existing materials became a purifying opportunity. Through its rigorous regulation and challenging obstacles, the Dogme movement aimed to recapture the innocence lost since cinema's early days.

■ **Lars von Trier: The Idiots,** 1998, starring Bodil Jørgensen and Jens Albinus

The second film to be Dogme certified, this was the most controversial, mostly due to a graphic sex scene. The second entry in von Trier's *Golden Heart* trilogy, it tells the uncomfortable story of a commune of people who protest the bourgeois culture of comfort by pretending to be mentally disabled. In a way, the Dogme filmmakers can be compared to von Trier's "idiots" in that they also try to recapture a certain kind of innocence through a release from manners and conventions.

Other Works

Italian for Beginners, by Lone Scherfig, 2000, starring Anders Berthelsen and Anette Støvelbæk

The King Is Alive, by Kristian Levring, 2000, starring Miles Anderson

Open Hearts, by Susanne Bier, 2002, starring Mads Mikkelsen

■ **Harmony Korine: Julien Donkey-Boy**, 1999, starring Chloë Sevigny and Ewen Bremner

After the oddball *Gummo*, Korine made the sixth, and first US, Dogme film. Often using up to 30 cameras, he shot in and around his grandmother's house. Korine cast his idol, director Werner Herzog to play schizophrenic Julien's father.

■ **Thomas Vinterberg: The Celebration**, 1998, starring Ulrich Thomsen

The first and most successful Dogme work, Vinterberg's debut film seethes with anger. As a large family prepares to celebrate Helge's (Henning Moritzen) six-tieth birthday, the son (Thomsen) calmly reveals the incestual abuse he and his deceased twin sister endured at Helge's hands. Rife with dark comedy, the film's energy comes from an ever-moving camera, and is proof of Dogme's refreshing effect.

Lars von Trier

1956, Copenhagen

■ Cofounded the ascetic Dogme 95 movement that promoted handheld camerawork ■ Enjoys setting up challenging obstacles for himself, like making a film without a set or shooting a musical sequence with 100 cameras
■ Danish ■ Drama, Comedy, Musical ■ Directed 11 films

Lars Trier added the "von" to his name when he graduated from film school in 1982. Made up of complex shots, double exposures, and back projections, his earliest films are characterized by their technical proficiency. His self-possessed tone changed after he was approached to create and direct a TV show. Using the techniques he had seen on American TV shows, von Trier moved away from rigidly storyboarded shots into the blurry world of handheld camera, thrusting actors into the foreground. Inspired by TV's natural restrictions, he co-drafted the Dogme 95 manifesto, but soon set off on his own again, making films as limited in their self-imposed restrictions as they are challenging—and infuriating—to his audiences. His deeply political films about the United States, *Dogville* and *Manderlay*, were both shot on a soundstage without sets, like a rehearsal for a stage production.

■ **Dancer in the Dark**, 2000, starring Björk, Catherine Deneuve, and David Morse

A World of Cinema 1990–Today

With original music by Björk, the film tells the convoluted story of Selma (Björk), an immigrant factory worker who, in trying to save her son from the genetic disorder that is destroying her sight day by day, is forced to kill a man.

■ Breaking the Waves, 1996, starring Emily Watson and Stellan Skarsgård

Living in a tiny Protestant community on the Isle of Skye in the early 1970s, Bess (Watson) is something of an idiot savant, a childlike woman who, when she earnestly converses with God, provides both sides of the conversation. After her new husband leaves to work on an oil rig, she fervently prays for his return, only to have him come back paralyzed. She sets off on a sacrificial journey that will take her life, but might save her husband's. Shot on dizzying handheld video and then captured off a monitor on Cinemascope by master cinematographer Robby Müller, the film shares stylistic features with Dogme, but is ultimately a dark parable from von Trier's imagination.

■ Dogville, 2003, starring Nicole Kidman

When a woman on the run finds refuge in a remote village, the villagers slowly start to take advantage of her. With dry narration by John Hurt and shot on HD-video, the film is without a set; the action of a door opening is represented by its sound and the actor stepping over a chalk line.

Other Works	
Epidemic, 1987, starring Lars von Trier	**The Kingdom II** (TV), 1997, starring Ernst-Hugo Järegård
Europa, 1991, starring Jean-Marc Barr and Barbara Sukowa	**Manderlay**, 2005, starring Bryce Dallas Howard

Lars von Trier

Emir Kusturica

1954, Sarajevo

■ His comic, chaotic style is inspired by gypsy culture and the films of Federico Fellini ■ Gypsy music, sometimes by his own band, charges his work with raucous energy ■ One of six directors to win two Palmes d'Or
■ Serbian ■ Drama, Comedy, Documentary ■ Directed 9 films

Contemporary European Masters

- **1954** Born in Yugoslavia
- **1978** Graduates from the Academy of Performing Arts in Prague
- **1981** Golden Lion at Venice for his debut *Do You Remember Dolly Bell?*
- **1985** *When Father Was Away on Business* wins the Palme d'Or at Cannes
- **1986** Starts playing bass in The No Smoking Orchestra
- **1995** Wins his second Palme d'Or for *Underground*
- **2007** Premieres an opera based his *Time of the Gypsies* at the Paris National Opera
- **2008** Releases his documentary about soccer player Diego Maradona, *Maradona*

Extremely popular in his new home, France, but controversial in his native country, the former Yugoslavia, Emir Kusturica divides audiences with his hectic, chaotic style and sometimes heavy-handed political statements. His surreal comedies are reminiscent of Federico Fellini's (p. 204) ensemble sequences, featuring large-scale set-pieces made up of ramshackle structures, screaming animals, and energetic brass bands. After shooting his optimistic romance *Life Is a Miracle* in western Serbia, he decided to build a town there using abandoned buildings he had bought and brought over, since he had lost his own during the war. Küstendorf now boasts a film festival, which kicked off with a symbolic funeral for *Die Hard* (1988).

■ **Arizona Dream**, 1993, starring Johnny Depp and Faye Dunaway

Though a financial flop, this absurdist comedy about a New York fish labeler (Depp) reeled back to Arizona for his uncle's wedding, has earned a cult following.

The dreamlike tale sees Depp torn between an older woman whose only dream is to fly and her daughter, who plays an accordion for turtles. Kusturica's only US-set film is bookended by the tale of an arctic halibut, which features Jerry Lewis and Depp speaking in a mock-Inuit language.

Other Works

Time of the Gypsies, 1988, starring Davor Dujmovic

Life Is a Miracle, 2004, starring Slavko Stimac and Natasa Solak

Promise Me This, 2007, starring Uros Milovanovic and Marija Petronijevic

■ Underground, 1995, starring Miki Manojlovic and Lazar Ristovski

When a gun runner is forced underground with a group of refugees to escape the Nazis, the friend who guards the only exit declines to pass on news of the conflict's end. As the man emerges after 40 years, he is very confused about being in the middle of yet another war and to learn that Yugoslavia no longer exists. Critics have claimed that this often surreally hilarious parable tackles the complexity of war and Communism in the Balkans with too broad of strokes.

■ Black Cat, White Cat, 1998, starring Bajram Severdzan and Florijan Ajdini

After *Underground*'s political controversies, Kusturica directed this small but riotous comedy that would prove his greatest commercial success in Europe. Set on the banks of the Danube, we follow a band of gypsy musicians along two story lines: one dealing with a misguided heist, the other with a mismatched wedding. Like Fellini's films, Kusturica's blend of slapstick and drama can best be enjoyed as a celebration of life.

Emir Kusturica

Tom Tykwer

1965, Wuppertal

■ Explores coincidence's role in connecting people, or severing those connections ■ Co-composes his own soundtracks ■ Uses a variety of cinematic techniques ■ Sometimes said to value style over substance
■ German ■ Drama, Action, Literary Adaptation ■ Directed 9 films

A self-taught filmmaker, Tykwer has always styled his work with panache. Since his first short, *Because*, his films have revolved around fate's random powers. In *Because*, a couple's fight causes the death of a passerby; in *Heaven*, his most mature work, fate plays a central role in a terrorist's guilt over her attack's collateral damage. Still, Tykwer's narratives are not grimly fatalistic, instead suggesting metaphysical forces that can sometimes enforce a happier ending, as in *Run Lola Run*'s multiple possibilities, or *The Princess and the Warrior*'s final tribute to the healing power of the heart. In bringing these stories to the screen, Tykwer uses a wide array of cinematic techniques: slow motion, elaborate crane shots, and even animation. Though these stylistic interventions have served his narratives without overpowering them completely, they have become more focused over the years.

■ **The Princess and the Warrior**, 2000, starring Benno Fürmann and Franka Potente

Potente plays a lonely nurse whose life is spectacularly saved by a fleeing bank robber. Convinced they belong together, she tracks the reluctant thief down and hides him in her institution to let destiny have its way. Like *Run Lola Run*, this metaphysical romance also deals with coincidence's role in connecting people. Tykwer shot this stylish film in his native Wuppertal.

200

80

60

■ **Run Lola Run**, 1998, starring Franka Potente and Moritz Bleibtreu

Lola (Potente) has 20 minutes to find a bag of money her boyfriend lost, and get it back to him before he robs a bank.

After her first try fails, Tykwer gives us two more possible outcomes as Lola repeats her run through Berlin, but takes a different route. The director blends his fast-paced film with animation and black and white,

creating the closest thing cinema has seen to a video game. In a technique also used in Jean-Pierre Jeunet's *Amélie*, Tykwer sometimes offers minor characters' future life stories in a few flash-frames.

Other Works
Deadly Maria, 1993, starring Nina Petri
Winter Sleepers, 1997, starring Ulrich Mattes
Heaven, 2002, starring Cate Blanchett and Giovanni Ribisi
The International, 2008, starring Clive Owen and Naomi Watts

■ **Perfume: The Story of a Murderer**, 2006, starring Ben Whishaw and Dustin Hoffman

This adaptation of Patrick Süskind's novel was Tykwer's largest production yet. Its tale of a serial killer with a passion for

preserving smells features lush landscapes and stunning set design, using a wandering camera with a haunting soundtrack.

Tom Tykwer

Jean-Pierre Jeunet

1953, Roanne

■ Films feature a distinct, visually cluttered style informed by his darker work with Marc Caro ■ Became disillusioned with Hollywood after making his entry in the *Alien* series ■ Inspired by Marcel Carné's films from the 1930s and '40s ■ French ■ Drama, Comedy, Literary Adaptation ■ Directed 6 films

■ **1953** Born in France

1978 Creates his first animated short with Marc Caro, *The Escape*

1989 Directs the award-winning short *Foutaises*

1991 Caro and Jeunet make their debut feature, *Delicatessen*

2001 Jeunet's solo feature debut *Amélie* is nominated for a Best Original Screenplay Oscar

2008 Caro releases his solo debut film *Dante 01*

Other Works

The City of Lost Children (with Marc Caro), 1995, starring Ron Perlman and Judith Vittett

Alien: Resurrection, 1997, starring Sigourney Weaver and Winona Ryder

■ **A Very Long Engagement**, 2004, starring Audrey Tautou and Gaspard Ulliel

A tuba-playing woman foolhardily searches for her fiancé, who is said to have died in WWI's trenches. Though Jeunet vividly portrays the war's brutal violence, he also expands on the tale with poetic digressions starring Marion Cotillard and Jodie Foster.

After making a series of animations and shorts with Marc Caro, Jean-Pierre Jeunet first found success with their collaborative debut feature, *Delicatessen*. Its quirky style and dark comedy created a cult appeal that enabled the duo to make *The City of Lost Children*, a eerie fairytale for children of all ages. Hollywood took notice and Jeunet was hired for *Alien: Resurrection*. Though a box-office success, the experience working with a studio left him frustrated. Like his German counterpart Tom Tykwer (p. 460), or his American precursor Terry Gilliam (p. 348), Jeunet delights in cinema's power to depict anything imaginable, from beating hearts to suicidal goldfish in *Amélie*. His iconic hero mirrors his own Magical Realist–skill, turning the lives of those around her into dreams come true. More inspired by Marcel Carné's (p. 148) prewar Poetic Realism than the aesthetics of the French New Wave, Jeunet's films are a celebration of imaginative creation.

A World of Cinema 1990–Today

■ **Amélie**, 2001, starring Audrey Tautou and Mathieu Kassovitz

Born in an imaginary, romanticized version of Paris, Amélie (Tautou) is the ingenious child of "a neurotic and an iceberg." Now that she is a waiter, she revels in sneakily intervening in other people's lives, but her prankish nature makes it hard for her to directly express her feelings for the man she loves. Instead she prepares a scavenger hunt through a fabulous Montmartre. Her story and its images are cluttered with details and narrative digressions, meandering past subplots that are all resolved at the film's end. Brighter than his Caro-collaborations, this was Jeunet's breakthrough into the mainstream, collecting five Oscar nominations.

■ **Delicatessen** (with Marc Caro), 1991, starring Dominique Pinon and Karin Viard

In a postapocalyptic world where food is rationed, one enterprising butcher hires handymen, fattens them up, and serves them to his neighbors. Decorated with great detail—a tendency Jeunet credits to co-director Caro—this macabre comedy is peopled with deviant characters. Stylistically reminiscent of Terry Gilliam's anarchism, Jeunet and Caro produced an increasingly hectic film brimming with comic and gruesome setpieces. As with all of his films, each shot has a unique twist, a strategy that turns his images into visual puzzles.

Jean-Pierre Jeunet

François Ozon

1967, Paris

■ Favors spare, theatrical staging ■ Often features female or gay protagonists with a fluid sexuality ■ Films often explicitly refer to other works ■ Inspired by Rainer Werner Fassbinder, Luis Buñuel, and Douglas Sirk ■ French ■ Drama, Comedy, Historical, Musical, Thriller ■ Directed 28 films

Contemporary European Masters

■ **1967** Born in France

1988 Casts his family in his first short, *Photo de Famille*

1993 Graduates from film school in Paris

1998 His feature debut, *Sitcom*, is selected for the Critic's Week competition at Cannes

2000 *Water Drops on Burning Rocks* wins a Teddy

2004 *5x2* is nominated for a Golden Lion

2007 Directs his first English-language film, *Angel*

Other Works

Sitcom, 1998, starring Marina de Van

Water Drops on Burning Rocks, 2000, starring Malik Zidi and Anna Levine

5x2, 2004, starring Valeria Bruni Tedeschi and Stéphane Freiss

■ **Under the Sand**, 2000, starring Charlotte Rampling and Bruno Cremer

Ozon's first "straight" drama—in both senses of the word—unsentimentally deals with one woman's grief. When her husband of

After directing nearly a dozen shorts—a format the filmmaker still works in—François Ozon's debut film, *Sitcom*, was a racy, pansexual parody of the TV genre. His next films, also featuring stories of sexually confused characters, won him acclaim at festivals around the world. Mainstream renown would follow for his films with Charlotte Rampling, and since then Ozon has been France's most prolific filmmaker. In 2007 he made *Angel*, an innovative visual remix of Douglas Sirk's *All That Heaven Allows* and Rainer Werner Fassbinder's (p. 334) tribute to that film, *Ali: Fear Eats the Soul*. Ozon's homage to his two favorite directors shows his commitment to Sirk's subversive "women's pictures," as well as Fassbinder's stylization and staginess.

25 years suddenly disappears from their beach holiday, she cannot accept his passing and starts to see him everywhere. With Rampling's precise performance and its strong score, Ozon's film nods to Hitchcock, but maintains a fine balance between drama and dream.

■ **8 Women**, 2002, starring Isabelle Huppert

A mix of Vincente Minnelli's musicals and Agatha Christie's whodunits, this film stars French screen legends, suspected of murdering the man of the house. Ozon grants each woman a 1950s-style musical number. Based on a play, the film is consciously stagy, with stuffed animals populating the garden. Ozon also uses his cast to pay tribute to French cinema by drawing stylistic similarities.

■ **Swimming Pool**, 2003, starring Charlotte Rampling and Ludivine Sagnier

Ozon's second collaboration with Charlotte Rampling, whose career was revitalized by their work together on *Under the Sand*, casts her as Sarah, a British mystery writer who, while on a retreat in France, is tempted by a young girl and gets involved in a murder mystery of her own. Ozon helped write the script to *Swimming Pool*, catering to the talents of Rampling: She sprang to fame in films by Woody Allen and Luchino Visconti, and gives a fearless, sexy performance.

François Ozon

Mike Leigh

1943, Broughton

■ Improvises his screenplays with his cast, developing their characters from the ground up, blending drama and comedy ■ His Social Realist style is rooted in British Free Cinema ■ Never worked in Hollywood
■ British ■ Drama, Comedy, Historical ■ Directed 10 films

A typically restrained genre, Social Realism is rooted in British Free Cinema's documentary style and its focus on the lives of ordinary people. Mike Leigh's work adds an unscripted, comic tension to the genre. Still, both his plays and films can be seen as a continuation of the Free Cinema project, as can the films of his contemporaries Stephen Frears (*The Queen*, 2006), Ken Loach (*Ladybird Ladybird*, 1994), and Alan Clarke (*Elephant*, 1989). Like these Social Realist directors, Leigh has inspired the raw films of the next generation of British filmmakers, such as Antonia Bird (*Priest*, 1994), Lynne Ramsay (*Morvern Callar*, 2002), and Shane Meadows (*This Is England*, 2006).

■ **Secrets & Lies**, 1996, starring Brenda Blethyn and Marianne Jean-Baptiste

Leigh's unique creative process, which never involves a script, starts with his chosen actors acting out his story idea, and developing a dialogue. As the actors build their characters from the start, they are always rooted in reality, never heightened for dramatic or comic effect. Thus, his straightforwardly filmed stories aspire to the socio-political awareness of documentaries with emotional truth. After the light domestic comedy *Life is Sweet* (1991) and the grim *Naked*, about a bitter misogynist's adventures in London's underbelly, Leigh set his sights on an adoption comedy with a twist. *Secrets & Lies* deals with a white London family that suffers from unspoken resentments. When one day a black woman appears, claiming to be a daughter once given up for adoption, the family's forgotten secrets are revealed.

◀ **Vera Drake**, 2004, starring Imelda Staunton and Philip Davis

After the boisterous musical comedy of his Gilbert and Sullivan biopic, *Topsy-Turvy*, Leigh's second foray into period storytelling was a much more restrained affair. Set in the 1950s, it centers on a kind backstreet abortionist and her struggles with the law. Using his typically three-dimensional characters, Leigh captures the grim reality of the postwar social fabric. Though he has treated the topics of pregnancy and adoption in his more domestic dramas, this film more specifically explores the controversial topic of abortion in the light of the era just before it was legalized in the UK.

Other Works

Naked, 1993, starring David Thewlis

Topsy-Turvy, 1999, starring Jim Broadbent

All or Nothing, 2002, starring Timothy Spall

Happy-Go-Lucky, 2008, starring Sally Hawkins and Alexis Zegerman

Mike Leigh

Nanni Moretti

1953, Brunico

■ Actor, director, producer, and theater owner ■ Moretti always acts in his own films, some of which portray his own life ■ Expresses his frustration with the politics of Silvio Berlusconi, but also Italian leftists
■ Italian ■ Drama, Comedy, Mockumentary ■ Directed 16 films

1953 Born in Italy
1973 Makes his first short, *Paté de Bourgeois*
1976 Directs his first film, *I Am Self Sufficient*
1978 *Ecce Bombo* gains a large cult following in Italy
1981 *Sweet Dreams* wins Grand Jury Prize in Venice
1996 Appears in Raoul Ruiz's *Three Lives and Only One Death*
2001 *The Son's Room* wins the Palme d'Or
2006 His satirical portrait of Silvio Berlusconi, *The Caiman*, creates controversy in Italy

Nanni Moretti starred in his own first four features as Michele Apicella, a thinly veiled alter ego who shared the director's middle-class background and Communist sympathies. His second film, *Ecce Bombo* (1978), proved a box-office success—his greatest until *The Son's Room* in 2001. Moretti became a moral compass for Italy's youth, disillusioned with politics and corruption, but also frustrated with the political actions of the Italian left. Over the years, his protagonists have started to resemble himself more and more, finally reenacting his own life for *Caro Diario*'s account of his experience of a mistaken cancer diagnosis. He owns the only independent movie theater in Rome, where he champions directors like François Ozon (p. 464) and Abbas Kiarostami (p. 452).

■ **Caro Diario**, 1993, starring Nanni Moretti

After winning Best Director at Cannes, this was Moretti's first film to be distributed abroad. Its third part is a comic reconstruction of his own cancer scare.

Other Works

Bianca, 1984, starring Nanni Moretti and Laura Morante

The Mass Is Ended, 1985, starring Nanni Moretti

Red Wood Pigeon, 1989, starring Nanni Moretti

The Caiman, 2006, starring Silvio Orlando

■ **The Son's Room**, 2001, starring Nanni Moretti

Lacking the lively structure of his previous films, this muted study of grief is precisely paced. Moretti's first straight drama, it is also his first not set in Rome. Moretti plays a therapist father who works from home, a home he shares with a contented, normal family. When he cancels a jog with his son for an emergency session with a patient with lung cancer, and his son dies in a diving accident, the therapist blames himself and starts to imagine what could have been. His wife and daughter also become isolated in their grief, and it takes a letter from the son's acquaintance to slowly bring the family together again. The unsentimental film's final scene shows the surviving family members on a beach at dawn, spatially separated, but emotionally close again, at peace.

Contemporary European Masters

■ **Aprile**, 1998, starring Nanni Moretti

As much as Moretti's character tries to make a political film, his real life, and his almost-forgotten ambition to make a Vincente Minnelli–style musical about a Trotskyite baker, keep derailing his plans. This sequel to *Caro Diario* stars Moretti and his wife, and documents the birth of their son, Pietro. More so than his previous films, which packaged their political message in allegories, this openly deals with the director's disillusionment with Italy's government.

Nanni Moretti

Index

The Academy Award, or Oscar, is awarded annually by the Academy of Motion Picture Arts and Sciences for films of the previous year. The previous year is the date cited for awards.

471

First published in Great Britain in
2008 by the Herbert Press
an imprint of A&C Black Publishers
38 Soho Square
London W1D 3HB
www.acblack.com

ISBN: 978 1408 106 242

A CIP record for this book is available from the British Library

480

Printed and bound in China
10 9 8 7 6 5 4 3 2 1

Staff at Peter Delius Verlag

Authors: Daniel Borden (pp. 86–149, 254–255, 262–263), Florian Duijsens (pp. 150–219, 390–469),
Thomas Gilbert (pp. 220–253, 256–261, 264–265, 268–289, 292–299), Adele Smith (pp. 266–267,
290–291, 300–389)
Contributing Author: Fran Johnson (pp. 10–41, 42–85)

Editor-in-chief: Silke Körber
Editor: Elizabeth Corso
Image Research and Assistant: Natalie Lewis
Design: Burga Fillery
Layout Assistants: Angela Aumann, Andreas Bachmann, and Christine Engler

The publishers would like to express their gratitude to akg-images Berlin/Paris/London, Corbis,
Getty Images, and Leni Riefenstahl Produktion for the permission of image reproduction in this
book. For detailed picture and credit information, please visit our Web site
www.TheKnowledgePage.com.